An Introduction to
Econometrics

D.W. Verry.

1969.

An Introduction to Econometrics

A. A. WALTERS

PROFESSOR OF ECONOMETRICS AND SOCIAL STATISTICS
UNIVERSITY OF BIRMINGHAM

MACMILLAN

Published by
MACMILLAN AND CO LTD
Little Essex Street London WC2
and also at Bombay Calcutta and Madras
Macmillan South Africa (Publishers) Pty Ltd Johannesburg
The Macmillan Company of Australia Pty Ltd Melbourne
The Macmillan Company of Canada Ltd Toronto

Printed in Great Britain by
ROBERT MACLEHOSE AND CO LTD
The University Press Glasgow

To Audrey

Contents

Preface   9

Part I   *METHODOLOGY, PROBABILITY AND SAMPLING*
1   The Methodology of Econometrics   13
2   Probability   22
3   Statistical Inference   32

Part II   *REGRESSION AND CORRELATION*
4   Relations between Variables   81
5   Multiple Regression   120
6   Sampling – Correlation and Regression   145

Part III   *ECONOMETRIC MODELS*
7   Identification   163
8   Equation Systems   177

Part IV   *APPLICATIONS*
9   Consumer Expenditure   207
10 Econometric Studies of Production   269
11 Linear Programming – an Economic and Accounting
    Interpretation   341

Select Bibliography   370
Index   375

Preface

This book is meant to serve as an introduction to statistics and econometrics for the student who wishes to acquire some working knowledge of the subject as an aid in applied economics. It is not intended for the student who wishes to become a mathematical statistician, or an econometric theorist; nor will it serve the purpose of those who want an introduction to 'economic statistics' (such as index number techniques and practices, etc.). The text is primarily directed to those non-specialists who will use *simple* econometric techniques in undertaking econometric research.

I hope that this book will convey the ideas and principles that lie behind the quantitative analysis of economic phenomena. The close and intimate connection that exists, or should exist, between the economic theory on the one hand and the organisation and evaluation of statistical material is one of the themes of this book. (The reader must note, however, that there is no attempt made here to teach efficient computational methods; the student will find many excellent texts that describe modern computational methods.)

It is assumed that students reading this book will begin with some knowledge of the concepts of mean and standard deviation, and with some experience with representing frequency distributions. In the first three parts of this text the student can manage without a knowledge of calculus – and even in Part IV most of the chapters can be assimilated without recourse to calculus. But the student should be adept at using summation and subscript notations, and should be at least conversant with the elements of school algebra.

This book grew out of a series of lectures I have given since the mid-1950s at the University of Birmingham to second-year non-specialist students. I suspect that the original idea of a course of this kind was due largely to my colleagues W. M. Gorman and John Wise. Teaching at Birmingham during the 1950s was a most enjoyable social process, but at this stage I find it quite impossible to identify who was primarily responsible for the pedagogic ideas that gradually emerged. As the book took shape in typescript, several colleagues read and commented on parts of the text, including T. W. Hutchinson, Zmira Prais, Gordon Fisher, Noel Kavanagh and Esra Bennathan. My deepest debt is, however, to Peter Fisk of the University of Edinburgh. He saved me from making many errors in the partly finished text.

The manuscript notes have been used extensively on many short courses for 'mature' students – notably at the Graduate Centre for Management Studies in Birmingham and at the International Bank for Reconstruction and Development in Washington, D.C. I am particularly grateful to Mr H. G. van der Tak of the Bank for helping me improve the text at several critical points. But of course I must claim the responsibility for obscurities and errors that remain in the text.

It is inevitable that a book that attempts to present modern ideas in statistics and econometrics should involve a large element of personal interpretation. Although I have often indicated the state of debate on several controversial topics, I have tried to avoid fence-sitting. One must make up one's mind. (The critical reader will note that I have often set up imaginary Aunt Sallies – such as the rather bigoted 'classical statistician' in Chapter 3. But these serve some pedagogic purpose.)

The one abiding hope of any writer of textbooks is that he will not give the student too much to unlearn at a later stage of his studies. Stimulating a student's imagination inevitably runs the risk that he will go off down the wrong trail. And too many warning words may result in either paralysis of purpose or deafness. I do not know whether I have struck the right balance in this book; the reader only can judge that.

Birmingham   A. A. WALTERS
October 1967

Part One

Methodology, Probability and Sampling

In Part I of this book the main purpose is to introduce the student to the statistical approach to economics. The econometrician must be concerned with measuring the 'constants' or parameters of economic theory and with predicting the values of economic variables. In order to estimate the parameters of economic theory, and in order to test the hypotheses, we must turn the conventional models of economic theory into *statistical* models. In Chapter 2 we set out the basic notions on probability, and in Chapter 3 the concepts of statistical inference are discussed. The purpose is not to supply a course in statistical methods – this has been achieved adequately in many other books. The primary aim is to give some appreciation and interpretation of the many, and to some extent competing, concepts of statistical inference which are currently expounded and used. We hope to give a critical interpretation of ideas rather than rules and techniques of computation and testing.

1 The Methodology of Econometrics

'Economics', says Alfred Marshall, 'is a study of mankind in the ordinary business of life; it examines that part of individual and social action which is most closely connected with the attainment and with the use of the material requisites of wellbeing.'† It is concerned with the study of man's behaviour in society and so it is classed as one of the social sciences. Indeed most social scientists would concede that economics is the most advanced of all disciplines which study man's behaviour in society. Compared with other social scientists, one of the main advantages enjoyed by the economist is that he deals with phenomena which are normally measurable. He can easily measure the weight of coal consumed by households; but the sociologist, for example, finds it almost impossible to quantify the concept of social class.

The quantitative approach to the subject matter of economics enables the economist to bring into play many of the formal operations of mathematics in exploring the consequences of his ideas about human behaviour. For example, we suppose that each businessman organises his productive arrangements so that he minimises the cost of producing any given output. With measurable inputs, outputs and prices, this problem is simply solved by applying the mathematics of constrained maxima. The formal structure of the economic problem – the satisfying of needs with scarce resources – is most conveniently worked out in terms of mathematics. But *a priori* reasoning on the basis of these simple assumptions creates only the empty framework of economics. So constructed, the theory of economics merely elaborates the consequences of the assumptions; we do not get any more out of a theory than we put in. The principles of economics provide us with a method of ordering and arranging our knowledge – a sort of grand system of filing.

Consider, for example, the traditional theory of demand. We suppose that the individual has a certain pattern of preferences so that he can and does choose consistently between different bundles of goods. Much of the formal theory is concerned with developing the postulates for

† *Principles of Economics*, 8th ed. (1920), p. 1.

consistent choices. From this basis we examine the effect of changes in relative prices and income on the bundle of goods bought. For most commodities the theory predicts that, *ceteris paribus*, if the price of that good is reduced the quantity sold will increase. The demand curve slopes downwards from left to right.

This theory is, of course, an enormous simplification of reality. Such important elements as advertising, fashion, quality, expectations, etc. have been ignored. This is, after all, the purpose of theory – to distil from a complicated reality those important elements that explain a large part of the observed phenomena. In demand theory we concentrate on prices and income in the hope that this handful of variables will be useful for explaining variations in quantities purchased. Of course there are many alternative 'theories' of demand. For example, it can be argued that the quantity bought depends primarily on tastes; changes in quantities then are the result of changes in tastes which, it might be argued, are functions of time. Thus the quantity bought depends simply on the year. Clearly these alternative theories are not equally efficient.

How, then, do we distinguish good theory from bad? There are, of course, many criteria. A theory that is simple and cheap to employ in practice is better than one that is complicated and expensive. A theory that can be communicated and understood by a large number of people is, *ceteris paribus*, better than one which can be appreciated only by a small number of the initiated. A theory that tells us a great deal about a situation is better than one that indicates only general directions. For example, a theory which says that if export prices are reduced by 10 per cent our exports will rise by more than 10 per cent is more useful than one that predicts merely that exports will rise. But the crucial characteristic of good theory is that it corresponds to the facts. The theory should be 'realistic'. One of the most useful features of a quantitative formulation is that theories can be sorted out on the basis of more or less clearly defined criteria; it is easier to reject false or bad theories when the criteria are described in terms of measurements of quantities than when the criteria are qualitative in character.

The theories of economics tell us what data should be collected in order to test and discriminate between them. But there still remains the question of how the theories are to be tested. One view is that we should test the assumptions of the theory.† In the theory of production, for

† Lionel Robbins, *An Essay on the Nature and Significance of Economic Science*, 2nd ed. (1935).

example, we assume that the businessman maximises his profits. There have been many enquiries concerned with testing the validity of the assumption of profit maximisation. These economists believe that, in testing the assumptions of a theory, they are testing the whole theory. If the assumptions of the theory are discredited then, they would argue, the theory is discredited and we cannot rely on any of its conclusions. This approach deserves a label – so we shall call it 'assumption' method, and those who practise it we shall call the 'assumptionists'.

The view of the assumptionists is challenged by those who argue that the theories of economics should be judged according to the accuracy of their predictions; correspondence between the assumptions and the facts is not necessary for a theory to be useful. The validity of a theory is determined solely by the efficiency of the model in predicting events. The 'predictionists' – as one might christen them – argue by analogy with the physical and biological sciences. Here the success of a scientific theory is always judged by the correspondence between the predictions of a theory and the experimental outcome. Results, and results only, matter in science; the assumptions can be forgotten. The theory of gravity, for example, predicts that bodies accelerate at a rate of 32 ft (per second)^2. In deriving this theory we assume that the body falls through a perfect vacuum. But physicists tell us that there is no such thing; indeed, no one can *create* a perfect vacuum; it is physically impossible. This does not mean that the theory is no good. On the contrary, we know that this simple theory is useful in a very wide variety of atmospheric conditions, both experimental and practical. For many purposes the predictions of the theory are near enough to the actual values; indeed, the theory gives more correct predictions than any alternative theory of a similar (or smaller) degree of complexity. In constructing the theory of production we assume that businessmen maximise their profits. We then develop hypotheses about the behaviour of businessmen in response, for example, to reductions in the prices of their inputs; the theory predicts that output will be expanded. Now the 'predictionists' argue that we should not judge the efficiency of the theory by enquiring whether businessmen in fact do or do not maximise their profits. This is almost as irrelevant as judging the law of gravity by requiring a perfect vacuum. The theory of production must be judged solely on the relative frequency of the actual cases where the predictions of an increase in output is not discredited. As in the biological and physical sciences, our confidence in a theory increases with the number of tests which do not reject the hypothesis. Prediction tests also serve to delimit the area of applicability of theory. Just as we know that the use of the simple gravity law alone is no good for feathers, so we are beginning to suspect that the law of demand does not apply to female clothes! The theoretical predictions in both cases appear to be discredited by the evidence.

Between these two apparently polar views on the methodology of economics and econometrics one must choose the 'predictionists'. These are the methods of experimental science which have generated the immense advances in our knowledge of the physical universe over the last century. One may reasonably hope that the approach provides a similar stimulus in the social sciences. But with the study of man there is one important snag: the opportunity for experimentation is very limited. We have to be satisfied with what men actually do in the situations in the real world; we cannot exclude those 'other effects' which are normally controlled in a laboratory experiment (or allowed to have an equal effect on all items in a well-designed experiment). Somehow we must try to eliminate from our data the extraneous effects which would be excluded from an experiment. As will be shown later, much of econometrics is concerned with the special difficulties created by the lack of experimental data. (These arguments, however, cut both ways. Theory which has been tested in laboratory conditions may be quite useless when applied in the outside world.) For the time being, however, we can see that there need be no distinction *in principle* between the methodology of econometrics and the biological or physical sciences. The difference really lies in the interpretation of the results. The experiments of the physical sciences usually provide clear and unequivocal evidence of the validity of a theory; with econometics, however, there seems to be more room for different interpretations of any given set of results. Partly this reflects merely the youth of econometrics, but to a large extent it is due to the lack of experimental data and the movement of uncontrolled variables. Probably more important than this distinction is the fact that the social scientist can only examine a *limited* number of situations; the number of useful independent enquiries he can pursue is restricted. The physical scientist, however, can perform any number of experiments (if he has the money!)

If we grant that the analogy between the physical sciences and econometrics is close enough to enable us to adopt the scientific method, we must now examine what we mean by 'predictions' and 'assumptions'. It is obvious that each of these terms is used in a particular way in a given context. The assumptions of one theory tend to be the predictions of another. For example, in the theory of production, we assume that, *inter alia*, there are certain technical restraints on production, and then we predict what will be the behaviour of costs as output expands. In the theory of aggregate economic models of stabilisation policy, we usually assume, *inter alia*, that the cost curve of the firm has a specific form and then we predict what will be the effect of different policies.† The cost curve is a prediction in one theory and an assumption in the other. Our viewpoint differs according to the use we want to make of our theory. In the first case, we may use the theory to predict the empirical behaviour of the costs of a firm or an industry. In the second case, we may use the model for predicting the effect of stabilisation policies. If the cost curves are discredited, it does not mean that the stabilisation theory is no good; on the contrary, the stabilisation theory might well be better than any alternative theory in spite of the discrediting of one of the assumptions.

The important point about these examples is, however, the *use* to which we put the theory. The hypothesis of a U-shaped long-run cost curve may be required for predicting the effect on an industry's costs of an increase in output in order to judge the effects of an increase in demand caused by a reduction in an excise tax. For this particular purpose, certain degrees of accuracy may be required; these should depend in turn on the various costs of making wrong decisions on the basis of false hypotheses. For example, the costs of reducing taxes when there are real diseconomies of scale in the industry are large (if there are alternative taxed industries with economies of scale); we should thus be anxious to guard against rejecting as false the hypothesis of decreasing returns when it is, in fact, true. Indeed, we can argue that for each specific use of a theory we require a different kind and degree of accuracy. But to carry out separate studies of the cost curve for each use to which we want to put our theory seems (and usually is) a most

† In econometrics we often include in our predictions some of the 'physical' constants of the system (the analogues of the velocity of light or the coefficient of gravitation). One such constant is the long-run average propensity to consume – see Chapter 9.

inefficient employment of resources. In fact, we normally hope that the same results will be suitable for a wide class of uses. Putting it roughly, the wider the class of applications, the more valuable are the results. This is indeed the hope of most econometric investigations.

We can now go back and pick up one of the threads of the previous argument. We left the assumptions of the theory untested and seemingly irrelevant to the real business of using the results. But surely the assumptions *are* a matter of some concern; we do in fact distinguish between good and bad assumption. In fact we often try to sort out theories in a preliminary way by *a priori* reasoning about their assumptions. No one would bother to construct a theory of investment of the firm which, for example, is based on the postulate that businessmen maximise the growth rate of the value of their sales irrespective of cost and profit. We know that this would be a bad assumption partly because it would lead to results that are discredited by casual observation. But the most important reason is that the 'normal' assumption – that he maximises his profits – has been used for a wide variety of other purposes for predicting business behaviour. And the assumption has produced predictions which have been undeniably useful. One's hunch is, then, that the assumption will also be useful for exploring investment behaviour. An assumption which was useful for one branch of the theory of the firm may easily prove to be useful for other facets of the behaviour of the firm. This is indeed what we usually mean by a unified or integrated or consistent theory of the firm. We can then easily explain the interactions of the various phenomena, such as the output, employment and investment plans. But the range of applicability of assumptions is only one of the criteria. They must also be simple. Experience shows that it is difficult to construct a theory with useful predictions unless the assumptions are drastically simple. We could, of course, so elaborate the postulates that many of the criteria which businessmen say are important (such as fair wages, fair treatment for supplying firms, growth of market share, etc.) are incorporated in the assumptions. But it would be found that the theory would become so general that it quickly degenerates to mere description. The predictions of such a theory would tend to be that 'anything may happen' This is, of course, useless. The art of theorising consists in distilling the essence of behaviour into a simple premise and then proceeding to predictions that are capable of being discredited. The more precise the predictions the more useful they are – and the greater the chance of being discredited.

There is one important use of the term 'assumption' in econometric literature that departs from the use we have adopted so far. Frequently we are forced to use empirical measures of variables that correspond but are not identical to the theoretical magnitudes. Thus we sometimes use consumer expenditure, which includes durable consumer goods, as a measure of the theoretical magnitude 'consumption', which includes only the *services* of durable goods. It is frequently said or implied that 'we shall assume that consumption is measured by consumer expenditure'. This assumption is nothing to do with the theory. It is merely concerned with statistical approximations. If this assumption is not 'near enough correct' any tests based on the measurement of consumer expenditure may be irrelevant for judging the validity of the theory. Clearly this 'measurement assumption' is one that should be tested directly. We cannot ignore these assumptions, since they are part and parcel of our predictions. In other words we must always be self-conscious and critical of our statistical approximations.

Unfortunately, we cannot easily apply the predictionist criteria with all economic theory. Some of the predictions of economics are concerned with rather vague concepts. Welfare economics, for example, is often concerned with the final prediction that 'if we follow certain policies, the community will be better off'. This is a 'non-operational' concept; we cannot measure whether the community is better off. We can, however, estimate whether Jones has enjoyed an increase in income, while Smith has suffered a decline in income. It is clearly desirable then to attempt to translate the proposition that the 'community is better off' into statements about the incomes of Smith and Jones. This is, however, a most difficult task. Economic theory has not got much further than saying that an unequivocal improvement occurs when Smith (or Jones) has a larger income while the income of Jones (or Smith) is no less than it was before. With 50 million Joneses, this is an impossible criterion! Almost no policy prescription could pass this test. But economists, in writing about taxation, growth and public expenditure, of course *do* make recommendations about policy; they often suggest that certain policies will be better for the community than others. Clearly these normative statements made by economists are a mixture of a forecast of the probable outcome of policies and a judgement about the desirability of the outcomes. But judgements about desirability are intensely personal views and vary from individual to individual. Obviously, we cannot test the reliability of normative statements since there is no commonly accepted standard of judging the evidence to enable us to refute the allegations. It is, therefore, impossible to apply the predictionist approach to the normative statements of economics. Indeed, it is convenient to divide economics into *normative* economics and *positive* economics. *Normative* economics is concerned with value judgements, concepts of good and moral obligation. *Positive* economics, on the other hand, consists of propositions which are primarily matters of fact rather than of moral judgements. If we are considering a payroll tax, for example, the positive question would be to forecast the effect on wages and profits, capital formation and employment; the normative question would be whether these effects are desirable.

Naturally, almost all the empirical work in econometrics is directly concerned with *positive* economics. Research has been concentrated on the great relations of economics: the demand curve, the consumption function, the production and cost functions, the velocity of circulation (of money) and the accelerator. These problems have been investigated largely because they provide important evidence for making decisions about economic policy.

Econometrics and economics, as we have described them above, look like exceedingly utilitarian disciplines. We suggested that we should formulate and investigate hypotheses which are most useful for government and business in making decisions. This gives a useful guide, but it is no more than that. It should not, for example, preclude some speculative enquiries which have no foreseeable useful application. One can rarely look around corners in scientific development. In the sphere of physics, for example, it was widely thought in the thirties that atomic physics and astrophysics had no practical use. (Perhaps if we had known their uses in the thirties, the development of physics would have been a little different.) Similarly, one should not condemn work in the theory of games because it has few practical economic applications. The real gain from speculations in this field is the *insight* we gain into other problems. Insight is a very personal characteristic that cannot be satisfactorily explained and never usefully measured. But one feels that it is of great importance and should never be ignored.

We can summarise the main tasks of the econometrician. First he must take the theory of economics and provide some measures of the magnitudes of parameters. He must not be content with the theoretical proposition that the demand for exports is elastic; he must collect data to measure that elasticity, to find whether it is 1·0 or 10. Secondly, he should then use his empirical parameters to predict events. Then the predictions of the model should be compared with the actual outcome. This will weed out the inefficient or bad theories from the good.

2 Probability

The methods of statistics have direct relevance for econometric studies. The two main problems of econometrics – estimating the parameters of economic models and testing the predictions of theory – have counterparts in the theory of statistics. But the methods of statistics were developed primarily to deal with experimental situations in the biological and physical sciences. They are not ideally adapted to the problems of econometrics where the opportunity for experimentation is very limited.† Nevertheless the basic ideas of statistics are important for understanding much of applied econometrics. Consequently we shall discuss the basic ideas of probability in this chapter. It is, however, in no sense a substitute for a proper course in statistical theory. What we are attempting to do is to set a sufficient foundation to enable the reader to appreciate the main ideas of econometrics to be introduced later.

The concept of probability is in everyday use from football pools forecasts to actuarial calculations for insurance. The common idea is that the probability of an event represents the odds on the particular event occurring. Now these odds must be determined in some way. Probably the most common approach is the 'relative frequency' definition. Thus we say the probability of a 'head' in a single toss of a coin is best determined by spinning the coin a large number of times and observing the number of heads. The probability is then given by the proportion of heads. This then tells us the probability of a head appearing on any toss. There are many difficulties with this definition. There is no rule to say when we should stop the number of tosses and count the proportion of heads; if we have a number which is 'large' we can always increase it by another trial to give a different value for the probability.‡ We of course take refuge in the empirical fact that the

---

† There are, however, many opportunities for using survey techniques in econometrics that are apparently not exploited.

‡ Formally, the series is not mathematically convergent. The ratio of the number of heads divided by the number of tosses, for different varieties of tosses, cannot be shown to approach a certain value as the number of tosses increases.

variation of the proportion tends to be within narrow limits as the number of tosses increases, so that these variations in the number of trials make little difference. A far more serious difficulty with the relative frequency definition is that it can only be applied to events which are reproducible, such as coin tossing, or to happenings for which there is a large volume of quantitative evidence, such as deaths. We cannot apply this concept to events such as the probability of a hydrogen bomb being dropped in the world during the year 1975; catastrophes of this kind are not repeatable and we have no quantitative evidence to which we can refer. There is of course *some* kind of evidence – the past pattern of behaviour of statesmen, the past technology of weapons development, etc. But it is not the simple demonstrable frequency of the coin-tossing example. Evaluations of this mass of evidence differs from one person to another and there is no general agreement on the odds of a hydrogen bomb attack. With the penny, however, most people would be willing to agree on the odds.

Much of the application of the theory of statistics is built on relative frequency idea of probability and it is this concept which we shall have in mind for the remainder of this chapter.† We require certain basic laws of probability. The first is the simple law of additive probabilities. Let us denote a particular event occurring, such as a die showing a number one as E_1, and a second event, such as another die showing a number two, as E_2. We describe the probability of E_1 as $P(E_1)$, the probability of E_2 as $P(E_2)$ (or occasionally by the mnemonic prob (E_2)). Finally we denote the probability of a one on the first die and a two on the second as $P(E_1, E_2)$. Now the possible outcomes of tossing the two dice are

(i) E_1 occurs but not E_2
(ii) E_2 occurs but not E_1
(iii) E_1 and E_2 occur together
(iv) Neither E_1 nor E_2 occur.

The most convenient way of illustrating these outcomes is to draw a diagram. The boxes describe all 36 possible outcomes.

† Modern probability theory is, however, built on a much broader base. A probability is a non-negative set function satisfying a few simple axioms. But in applications we usually require the concept of equiprobable events – and so the relative frequency is a natural approach.

1st die

2nd die		1	2	3	4	5	6
	1	E_1					
	2	E_1, E_2	E_2	E_2	E_2	E_2	E_2
	3	E_1					
	4	E_1					
	5	E_1					
	6	E_1					

The squares with only E_1 in them describe the cases where E_1 *only* occurs (i.e. (i) above). Similarly described are the cases where E_2 *only* occurs (i.e. (ii) above). The single case in which both E_1 *and* E_2 occur is shown by E_1, E_2 (i.e. (iii) above). The appearance of this outcome means that the events are *not mutually exclusive*. Both E_1 and E_2 occur together. And finally the blank boxes show that in this case neither E_1 nor E_2 occur (i.e. (iv) above).

To find the probability that E_1 or E_2 or E_1, E_2 occurs we can see that it is given by

$$P(E_1) + P(E_2) - P(E_1, E_2). \tag{2.1}$$

The first two terms include the six boxes in the first column and the six boxes in the second row. But in adding these we include one box twice; and so this probability, $P(E_1, E_2)$, must be deducted to get the probability of the event either E_1 or E_2 or E_1, E_2.

So far in this example we have simply counted events (i.e. boxes) and have not formulated numerical probabilities. Obviously one is tempted to suppose that the dice are fair or unbiased. By this we mean that the probability of any face appearing is the same. With six faces the chances of any given face appearing is then 1 in 6 or $\frac{1}{6}$. If the two dice do not interfere with one another when thrown, each of the 36 outcomes is equiprobable, i.e. with probability of $\frac{1}{36}$. Thus the probability of E_1 is represented by the six boxes of $\frac{1}{36}$ probability. The probability of (E_1, E_2) is represented by the single box of probability $\frac{1}{36}$. (Thus the events are not mutually exclusive.) So we have

$$P\begin{Bmatrix} E_1 \text{ or } E_2 \\ \text{or } E_1, E_2 \end{Bmatrix} = P(E_1) + P(E_2) - P(E_1, E_2) \qquad (2.2)$$

$$= \left(6 \times \frac{1}{36}\right) + \left(6 \times \frac{1}{36}\right) - \frac{1}{36}$$

$$= \frac{11}{36}.$$

In this example the ordering of the dice is critical; we always distinguish the result on the first die from that on the second. Suppose, however, that we do not mind *which* die shows the one or two. Then we can easily elaborate our example to ignore the order by describing the event E_1 as the first die giving either a one or two, i.e. the first two columns. The event E_2 is the second die giving either a one or two, i.e. the first two rows. The probability of at least a one *or* at least a two appearing in the two throws is then

$$P(E_1) + P(E_2) - P(E_1, E_2)$$

$$= \left(12 \times \frac{1}{36}\right) + \left(12 \times \frac{1}{36}\right) - \left(4 \times \frac{1}{36}\right)$$

$$= \frac{5}{9}.$$

This theorem naturally extends to three, four or n dice. For three dice we have a new definition $P(E_1, E_2, E_3)$ which is the probability of the occurrence of the events E_1 *and* E_2 *and* E_3. We can then show

$$\left. \begin{aligned} &\text{probability of } E_1 \text{ or } E_2 \text{ or } E_3 \text{ or any combination} \\ &= P(E_1) + P(E_2) + P(E_3) - P(E_1, E_2) \\ &\quad - P(E_2, E_3) - P(E_1, E_3) + P(E_1, E_2, E_3). \end{aligned} \right\} \qquad (2.3)$$

Let us now examine the terms $P(E_1, E_2)$ and $P(E_1, E_2, E_3)$. If the events are 'mutually exclusive', that is to say if the events E_1 and E_2 cannot occur together, then $P(E_1, E_2) = 0$ and the formula (2.1) above is much simplified to

$$P(E_1 \text{ or } E_2) = P(E_1) + P(E_2). \qquad (2.4)$$

(The reader might well wonder how the occurrence of a one or two on the first die prevents the second die from showing a one or two? But we shall later see an example with playing-cards where this interpretation is 'natural'.) We have already used this formula in finding the probabilities in the dice example. To illustrate again suppose that we want to find the probability that in a single throw of dice we get a score of either one or two. Since these two scores cannot occur together we have

$$\text{probability of score of 1 or 2} = \frac{1}{6} + \frac{1}{6} = \frac{1}{3}.$$

In the two-dice example above we used another important theorem of probability to find the numerical value of $P(E_1, E_2)$. Provided that the two dice do not interfere with one another the occurrence of the event E_1 on the first die will not affect the occurrence of E_2 on the second die. Thus we get the result

$$P(E_1, E_2) = P(E_1)P(E_2) \tag{2.5}$$

or generally $P(E_1, E_2, ..., E_n) = P(E_1)P(E_2), ..., P(E_n)$. The simplicity of this result is due to the restriction that the dice 'do not interfere with one another'. Each is thrown independently of the other. The probability of the first die giving a one is in no way influenced by the fact that the second die scores a two. When the tosses are independent in this way they are called 'Bernoulli trials'. Probably the most common examples of Bernoulli trials are the tosses of a coin. It seems likely on *a priori* arguments that the probability of a head at a throw of a coin is not influenced by the outcomes of previous tosses. Even though we have got 20 heads in a row, the probability of a head on the next toss will be still $\frac{1}{2}$. The coin, so to speak, has no memory.

To illuminate this crucial feature of Bernoulli trials, consider an example which is *not* Bernoullian, i.e. where the result at any trial does depend on the outcome of the previous trials. Given a pack of 52 cards the probability of drawing a red card on the first draw is $\frac{26}{52}$ or $\frac{1}{2}$. Now suppose that the first card is not replaced and we then take a second card from the pack. The probability of the second card being red is not $\frac{1}{2}$. We have to distinguish two cases. If the first card was black the probability is then $\frac{26}{51}$. If the first card were red the probability would be $\frac{25}{51}$. The probabilities depend on the whole history of the outcomes. We normally call the chance of a second red card being drawn, *given* that a certain colour appeared on the first drawing, the *conditional* probability of a red. Generally we define $P(E|A)$ as the probability of the outcome E *given* that A has occurred or does occur. Thus if A is the event 'first card red' and E is the event 'second card red', then

$$P(E|A) = \frac{25}{51}.$$

The throw of two dice gives us another interesting example of conditional probability. Let us suppose that we want to find the probability of the event E_1, E_2 (i.e. a 1 on the first die and a 2 on the second) *given that* the first die does not score more than 3. The obvious way to deal with this is to cut down our boxes in the diagram by eliminating the last three columns. Because the probability of the first die giving one, two or three is $\frac{1}{2}$, the conditional probability of E_1, E_2, given the first die's outcome is three or less, is thus twice the unconditional probability:

$$P(E_1, E_2 \mid \text{1st die is three or less}) = \frac{P(E_1, E_2)}{P(\text{1st die is three or less})} \quad (2.6)$$

$$= \frac{1}{36} \Big/ \frac{1}{2} = \frac{1}{18}.$$

And this can easily be verified by counting the squares. This formulation is generally valid and we can write conditional probabilities as

$$P(E|A) = \frac{P(E, A)}{P(A)}$$

or $\qquad\qquad P(E, A) = P(E|A)P(A).$ $\qquad\qquad$ (2.7)

This is often a convenient way of calculating joint probabilities.

If is, of course, possible to generalise this approach. If $P(E|A, B)$ is the conditional probability of E given that both A and B occur, then we can clearly write

$$P(E, A, B) = P(E|A, B,) \cdot P(A, B). \qquad (2.8)$$

(This simply follows from the fact that the joint event A, B has replaced the single event A.) Now we can rewrite $P(A, B) = P(A|B) \cdot P(B)$ so that

$$P(E, A, B) = P(E|A, B) \cdot P(A|B) \cdot P(B), \qquad (2.9)$$

and by an obvious development of the argument

$$P(A, B, C, ..., \mathcal{Z}) = P(A|B, C, D, ...) \cdot P(B|C, D, ...) \cdot P(C|D, E, ...)$$
$$... P(\mathcal{Y}|\mathcal{Z}) \cdot P(\mathcal{Z}). \quad (2.10)$$

We can string the conditional probabilities together to find the probability of the joint event $(A, B, C, ..., \mathcal{Z})$. It is also worth noting that we can change the order of 'elimination':

$$P(A, B, C) = P(A|B, C) \cdot P(B|C) \cdot P(C) \qquad (2.11)$$

$$= P(C|A, B) \cdot P(A|B) \cdot P(B)$$

and there are, of course, other combinations.

It is now simple to define a Bernoulli process. The characteristic feature of these processes is that 'history is forgotten'. At each trial the probability of the outcome is in no way influenced by the outcome of other trials. Thus we may write

$$P(A|B) = P(A) \qquad (2.12)$$

because it does not matter whether B occurs or not, for it in no way affects the probability of A. Thus we have

$$P(A, B) = P(A|B) \cdot P(B) = P(A) \cdot P(B). \qquad (2.13)$$

and obviously this may be generalised, since

$$P(A|B, C, ...) = P(A) \qquad (2.14)$$

if the process is Bernoulli. So that one may write

$$P(A, B, C, ..., \mathcal{Z}) = P(A) \cdot P(B) \cdot P(C) ... P(\mathcal{Z}). \qquad (2.15)$$

This shows the great simplification involved in a Bernoulli process.

A simple example of coin-tossing will illustrate. Suppose that a coin follows a Bernoulli law so that the probability of a head is in no way influenced by the number of times it has come down heads in the past. If it were tossed three times, then we can find the probability of getting 'head-tail-head' *in that particular order* as

$$P(H, T, H) = P(H) \cdot P(T) \cdot P(H) \qquad (2.16)$$

using H for head and T for tail. Now consider the probability of getting 'head-head-tail' in that particular order, then we note that is

$$P(H, H, T) = P(H) \cdot P(H) \cdot P(T) \qquad (2.17)$$

which is numerically the same as the HTH ordering. Thus it does not matter which order the heads and the tails arrive – the probability of a certain number of heads (and the remainder tails) is the same. (This example is continued in the exercises.)

Bernoulli theory is often used to characterise a process. Coin or die tossing are often thought to be analogues of many chance processes that occur in actual situations. But no process can be invoked on *a priori* grounds (the precision of the engineering of the coin, for example) as Bernoullian. Whether or not it 'forgets' its history depends on the performance of the process in fact. It so happens that many processes in real life do behave approximately as Bernoullian and so it is sensible to use this theoretical process to describe events and outcomes.

This completes our very incomplete and brief introduction to probability theory. Later in this book, in Chapter 3, we shall consider more complicated and conceptually more difficult ideas of probability and a related concept, the likelihood. In this chapter the idea of probability has been developed in terms of *repeatable* trials and of notional experiments. It is, of course, a very limited concept and cannot be used for events and trials that are of the 'once-and-for-all' variety. But it is sufficient as a basis for much of the standard orthodox theory of sampling – and we turn to this in the next chapter.

Questions for Discussion

1. The following quotation is taken from a prominent economic weekly paper in April 1967

    'After two years of drought [in India] it is surely almost inconceivable that another year of drought will follow. Thus it is almost certain that the agricultural sector will achieve a very large increase in output.'

    Examine this statement critically. Discuss the implications of basing economic policy on this theory. Consider the correct formulation of the probability of 3 droughts in a row.

2. (Bernoulli processes and the binomial distribution)

    A die is tossed three times. Find the probability that it comes down on side 1 on three occasions. [Ans: $(\frac{1}{6})^3$]

    Find the probability that the first toss gives a 1 and the other two give other figures. [Ans: $(\frac{1}{6}) (\frac{5}{6})^2$]

Find the probability that (i) the second toss gives a 1 and the first and third another figure, and (ii) the first two tosses give other figures but the third gives a 1. [Ans: $(\frac{5}{6})$ $(\frac{1}{6})$ $(\frac{5}{6})$ and $(\frac{5}{6})$ $(\frac{5}{6})$ $(\frac{1}{6})$]

Hence the probability of one 1 and two not-1s. [Ans: $3(\frac{1}{6})$ $(\frac{5}{6})^2$]

Show that if p is the probability of a success, the probability of r successes and $3 - r$ failures *in a particular order* is

$$p^r(1-p)^{3-r}, \quad \text{where } r = 0, 1, 2, 3.$$

3. (Continuation of 2)

With a Bernoulli process in which the probability of success is p, we know that with one toss the outcomes are (using S to describe success and F to describe failure)

Outcome	F	S
Probability	$(1-p)$	p

With two tosses:

Outcome	FF	FS	SF	SS
Probability	$(1-p)^2$	$(1-p)p$	$p(1-p)$	p^2

If we *ignore the order* of successes and failures and merely count the *numbers* of successes we obtain for two tosses:

Outcome (no. of successes)	0	1	2
Probability	$(1-p)^2$	$2p(1-p)$	p^2

With three tosses we obtain

Outcome	FFF	FFS FSF SFF	SSF SFS FSS	SSS
Probability	$(1-p)^3$	$p(1-p)^2$ each	$p^2(1-p)$ each	p^3

So ignoring the order:

Number of successes	0	1	2	3
Probability	$(1-p)^3$	$3p(1-p)^2$	$3p^2(1-p)$	p^3

Consider the extension to four tosses. [See W. Feller, *An Introduction to Probability Theory and its Applications* (1966).]

4. (Continuation of 3)

If a fair coin is tossed four times find the probability that (i) exactly two heads appear; (ii) *at least* two heads appear.

5. (Continuation of 2)

If it is known that at least one head will appear, find the probability that more than one head will appear in four tosses of the fair coin.

6. There are two urns, one (no. 1) containing 4 black and 1 white balls and one (no. 2) containing 3 black and 4 white balls. We toss a die and if the

die comes down on the 1 or 2 side we choose a ball from no. 1 urn, but if the die falls on sides 3, 4, 5 or 6 we choose a ball from no. 2 urn.

(i) Find the probability that the ball is black.

(ii) Assuming that the ball that is drawn is returned before the next drawing, suppose that 2 balls are drawn; find the probability that (a) two are black; (b) two are white.

7. (Continuation of 6)

Suppose that two balls are drawn from no. 1 urn and that the first ball is *not returned* before the second is drawn.

(i) Find the probability that both balls are black.

(ii) Find the same probability for no. 2 urn.

(iii) Find the probability that, when the urns are selected by the die-casting rule, both balls are black.

8. Of 100 males sampled it was found that 29 bought a car during the previous year, 85 bought at least one suit, and 20 bought a television set. Calculate:

(i) the *minimum* number who bought both a car and at least one suit;

(ii) the *minimum* number who bought both a television and a car;

(iii) the *minimum* number who bought neither car nor television nor suit.

9. (Continuation of 8)

Supposing that you know that

(i) 27 of those who bought a car also bought a suit;

(ii) 15 of those who bought a television also bought a suit;

(iii) 14 of those who bought a television also bought a car.

Find an estimate of the probability that a male selected at random will have bought (a) either a television set or a car; (b) either a suit or a car.

10. (Continuation of 9 and 10)

Find the minimum and maximum number that bought car *and* television *and* suit.

[Hint: use the formula (multiplying by 100)

$$P(A \text{ or } B \text{ or } C)$$
$$= P(A) + P(B) + P(C) - P(AB) - P(BC) - P(AC) + P(ABC).]$$

Note that $P(ABC)$ is always no greater than $P(AB)$ or $P(BC)$ or $P(AC)$.

[Ans: maximum 14, minimum – nil]

11. If the government allocates contracts to three firms at random with a constant probability of $\frac{1}{3}$ for each firm, and if each firm has a 0·9 chance of making a profit if it gets a contract, find the probability that a particular firm will make a profit if there are 9 contracts awarded.

3 Statistical Inference

Significance

The main applications of probability concepts are in sampling. The problem is to distil as much information as we can from a sample of the observations of the process in which we are interested. Consider, for example, the problem of finding the average income (the arithmetic mean income) of 'families' in the United Kingdom. Questions of definition immediately arise – terms such as 'United Kingdom', 'family' and 'income' must all be precisely specified. When this is done, we have some 18 million or so families with their associated incomes in the United Kingdom – this is called the 'population'.

Let us suppose that, for reasons of expense, we can sample only 100 of these families. How should they be drawn from the population? The sample should in some sense be representative of all possible samples of size 100 from the population. One simple way to achieve this is to give each family an *equal* chance of being included in the sample. We must then design a method of selection such that each family has the same probability of being selected. In choosing the first family in our sample we know that the probability of any given family being selected (if we suppose there are exactly 18,000,000 families) is 1/18,000,000. On choosing the second family, however, we see that the probability has fallen to 1/17,999,999; just like our pack of 52 cards the probability changes with each drawing, since we do not give the first family a chance of being chosen *again*. With 18,000,000 families, and a sample of 100, however, the differences in the probabilities do not matter and we can take 1/17,999,999 as near enough to 1/18,000,000. In other words, we can suppose that each family is chosen *independently*; like Bernoulli trials, the previous choices do not effectively influence the current choice.

The incomes of the 100 families are measured and we can then find the average income of the 100 families in the sample. The question is how to use the information in the sample to shed light on the values in the population.

The traditional approach to this problem is known as *testing a hypothesis*. We suppose that there exists some hypothesis about the population which we wish critically to examine. The hypothesis may be derived as a theoretical proposition or from other empirical evidence; for example, one may put up the hypothesis that the average income this year is the same as last year's figure, which was calculated from data collected by the Inland Revenue. Let us suppose that the hypothetical value for our population is £1,000 p.a. Now we want to assess whether the results from our sample are somehow 'consistent' with this hypothesis. If, for example, we found that the average income in our sample of 100 was £2,000 p.a., common sense would suggest that the hypothesis is not true; for we know that the variation of income is not so large as to give a value as high as this. If, on the other hand, the sample value was £1,001 p.a. our confidence in the hypothesis would be considerably increased. The question we ask is then, 'Could we have reasonably expected the particular sample average which we have in fact obtained to have been selected from a population which has an average income of £1,000 p.a.?' And clearly the interpretation of what is reasonable depends on the probability of the outcome. A result which (if the hypothesis £1,000 p.a. were true) is highly improbable (e.g. £2,000 p.a.) suggests that the hypothesis is false or discredited.

To examine the way in which these probabilities can be assessed, we can *imagine* carrying out an experiment. Suppose that we have a population with an average income of the hypothetical value, i.e. £1,000 p.a. Now we take a sample of a 100 observations from this population. Suppose that we continued sampling from this population by taking a second sample of 100, a third sample 100, and so on. For each sample we measure the average income, so we might tabulate the results:

	Average Income (£ p.a.)
1st sample	1,064
2nd sample	922
3rd sample	1,021
4th sample	1,014
etc.	etc.

We can imagine that enough of these samples have been taken to enable us to draw a detailed histogram of the *sample average incomes* listed above. And we can then draw in the frequency curve by smoothing out the discontinuities in the histogram. This curve is called the *sampling distribution* of the sample average income. We can now interpret and use this distribution.

Clearly the first important point is that the experiment was performed on the *assumption that the hypothesis is true*. This histogram and frequency curve tell us the number of outcomes in which the averages of samples lie in a given interval. Thus we can find the number of samples (of 100 observations each) for which the same averages are *less* than a given value. If this number of samples is divided by the total number of samples then we have the probability of *a* sample average, chosen at random, being less than the given value. For example, suppose that we had drawn 1,000,000 samples of 100 observations each and we find that 25,000 of the samples have average values less than £800 p.a. Samples with an average of less than £800 only arise in one out of forty cases. Then we are justified in saying that the probability of a sample average being less than £800 p.a. is 25,000/1,000,000 or 0·025, *provided that the hypothesis is true*. These calculations then give us a measure of the chances of getting extremely low values when the hypothesis is correct.

We can now put this sampling distribution to work. Let us now approach another population similar in all respects except, possibly, in average income (perhaps roughly the same population a few years later) and ask whether our hypothesis is now discredited. We take a random sample of 100 families and measure their income. *If the hypothesis is true* the average income of *this* sample should be a random drawing from the sampling distribution of the sample averages. We know that if our sample has an average income of £800, the probability of a value as low as (or lower than) this being obtained from a population with an average income of £1,000 p.a. is only 0·025, i.e. one chance in 40. By most people's ideas one chance in forty denotes an unlikely event. We might then decide that if the average income of this sample fell at or below £800 p.a. we should say that the hypothesis is discredited. We should 'reject' the hypothesis. In one out of forty cases we should, of course, be wrong in making statements of this kind – since there is a 0·025 chance that values as low as this, or lower, will occur when the population average is £1,000. But we might be quite willing to accept this small chance of being wrong.

The basic idea is thus to find the sampling distribution of the sample averages, under the assumption that the hypothesis is true; we then set the proportion of chances in which we are willing to be wrong (e.g. 0·025) and this gives the borderline (£800) between rejecting the hypothesis and accepting it. Our actual sample value then decides the issue. But the reader will recall that this sampling distribution was built up from a conceptual experiment. Obviously we cannot do such an experiment for all conceivable samples – there are in fact an infinity of such samples. Fortunately we can instead find the sampling distribution by theoretical reasoning (and there is ample evidence that this theory is correct). In the case of the sample average the sampling distribution is a remarkably simple special form called the normal distribution. This is a symmetrical distribution which is fully determined if we know the mean and standard deviation. The normal distribution is illustrated in the following Figure

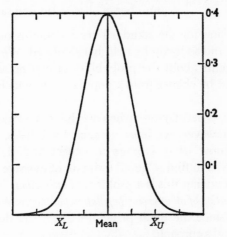

FIG. 3.1. Normal Sampling Distribution of Mean

The area under the curve can be described in terms of distance measured in standard deviations from the mean. If we measure two standard deviations below the mean to give a value X_L in the Figure, the area (frequency) in the tail is approximately $2\frac{1}{2}$ per cent of the total. Similarly two standard deviations in excess of the mean gives a value X_U which cuts off an upper tail of $2\frac{1}{2}$ per cent.

Thus if the standard deviation of the normal sampling distribution is known we can find any limits such as X_U, X_L, etc. The standard deviation of the sampling distribution of the average is usually called the *standard error* of the mean. And the value of the standard error is derived from the standard deviation of the population.

If standard deviation of family income in the population $= \sigma$

and number of families in the sample $= n$,

then

standard error of the average income of sample $= \sigma/\sqrt{n}$.

Provided that the sample is large (as a rough rule over 50 observations) we can use the standard deviation of income in the sample as an approximation to the standard deviation of income in the population. So that approximately

$$\text{standard error} = \frac{\text{standard deviation from sample}}{\sqrt{\text{number of observations in sample}}} \qquad (3.1)$$

This new expression for the standard error contains only information from the sample and so it can be readily calculated. We can then make the usual statements about the probability of getting sample averages as low (or as high) by chance from a population in which the hypothesis is true.

This approach is satisfactory when we have a working hypothesis. In some cases, however, we have no such hypothesis. Frequently we simply do not know what average to expect and the object of the statistical enquiry is to find a 'good' estimate of average income. In the jargon of the statistician this is a problem of *estimation* – or to give it the full title: *the estimation of an unknown population parameter*. We shall consider this very briefly since the main principles are easily derived from the 'hypothesis-testing' approach.

The first question is naturally 'What is the single value that may be derived from the sample which is a "best" estimate of the population average?' What function of sample values will, when applied to the observations in our sample, give the 'best' estimate of the population average? Obviously the answer to this question turns on what we mean by 'best'. Two features of estimators are normally thought to be desirable qualities. First, the quality of *consistency*; the best estimator should clearly be one such that if we take larger and larger samples, the estimator gives values which 'tend towards' the true value. We do not want to use estimators which, when the size of sample is increased, lead us away from the true value. A second condition, the quality of *efficiency*, is that the standard error should be as small as possible for a given size of sample. Obviously if we used only a randomly chosen half of our sample (i.e. 50 observations) to calculate a mean the standard error would be larger than if we used all 100 observations.

Now it might seem intuitively likely that the best estimate of the population mean is, in fact, the mean of the 100 observations in our sample. This is the estimator most frequently used. It is consistent for almost all populations.† Since it is also easily calculated the sample mean is frequently used as an estimate of the population mean. The second question we must ask is: 'how far can we trust this estimate?' The approach adopted is to construct a range around the sample mean. This range is called the *confidence interval*. We can then make statements about the probabilities of the confidence interval enclosing the average of the population. Analogous to the argument above, we construct an interval about the sample mean:

$$\text{sample mean} + (2 \times \text{standard error}),$$
$$\text{sample mean} - (2 \times \text{standard error}).$$

In repeated samples from the distribution the confidence interval will, in 95 out of a 100 cases, cover the population mean. Only in 1 in 20 cases will the confidence interval miss the population mean. The reader will carefully note that it is the position of the confidence interval which changes from sample to sample – not the population mean, which is, of course, fixed.

The sampling theory discussed above is applicable only for large samples (50 observations or more). In econometrics one frequently has to be content with samples of 20 or even less. Fortunately methods are available for dealing with small samples. Let us take first the example of sampling to test (or to estimate) the mean of a population. When a large sample is available we said that it was possible to take the standard deviation of the sample as a good approximation to the standard deviation of the population. With a small sample this approximation is not good enough.

---

† An exception is the Cauchy distribution. It is, however, not efficient for many populations.

Small Samples

One main comfort of having a large sample is derived from the fact that we may assume that the estimate of the standard deviation from the sample is very close to the true standard deviation. With large samples we do not need to worry about the fact that the standard deviation of the sample is only an *estimate* of the true standard deviation; the estimate is always near enough to the true value to make our tests and estimates useful.

With small samples, however, this is not the case. We must take into account that the standard deviation of the sample is only an estimate and may differ considerably from the true value. The variation from one sample to another of the standard deviation of the sample must be considered – just as we examined the various sample means which we obtained from a very large number of samples of a given size.

One very important difference between large sampling and small sampling is that the theory for small samples only applies when the population is *normally distributed*. Almost all the statements and conclusions of small-sample theory are strictly true only for populations that are normally distributed with respect to the variables in which we are interested. If, for example, we are sampling the income of families, then, for our small sample statements to be strictly true, the distribution of income in the population must be normal. As one might expect, however, the statements are 'nearly' or 'approximately' correct if the population is nearly normal, so the theory can be applied with some confidence to populations that are near-normal. But the strict statements of small-sample theory apply only to normal distributions, and we shall continue to assume normality for the remainder of this chapter.

One result of sampling means is that the average value of the sampling distribution is equal to the hypothetical (true) mean. The distribution of sample means clusters around the true value with simple random sampling. This seems an 'obvious' or 'natural' property of estimators. But, strangely enough it does not apply to the variance. If we take repeated samples of a given size from a population, calculate the variance of each sample and then plot the results in the usual histogram, we find that the mean of this distribution will be *lower* than the true value. The variance of the sample tends, on the average, to *underestimate* the true variance of the population. The estimate is biased downwards. It is instructive to consider intuitively why this occurs. Let us suppose that we obtain the values x_1 and x_2 in a random sample of two observations from the distribution described. Now we can calculate the variance of the sample as

$$\frac{(x_1 - \bar{x})^2 + (x_2 - \bar{x})^2}{2}$$

or

$$\frac{1}{2}\left[\left(x_1 - \frac{x_1 + x_2}{2}\right)^2 + \left(x_2 - \frac{x_1 + x_2}{2}\right)^2\right] \tag{3.2}$$

Now the value of $\bar{x}$ is obtained *from the sample*. And it is well known that the sum of squares of deviations *from the mean* will give a lower value than the sum of squares of deviations from any other value. The sensible approach seems to be, therefore, to calculate

$$\frac{1}{2}[(x_1 - \xi)^2 + (x_2 - \xi)^2] \tag{3.3}$$

and use this as a measure of the variance. This will not have the downward bias associated with the former measure. Unfortunately, we often do not know the value of ξ and so this course is rarely open to one. But we can write

$$\sum (x_i - \bar{x})^2 = \sum \{(x_i - \xi) - (\bar{x} - \xi)\}^2$$
$$= \sum (x_i - \xi)^2 - 2 \sum (x_i - \xi)(x - \xi) + \sum (\bar{x} - \xi)^2.$$

But $\qquad \sum (\bar{x} - \xi)^2 = n(\bar{x} - \xi)^2$

and $\qquad \sum (x_i - \xi)(\bar{x} - \xi) = n(\bar{x} - \xi)^2,$

so $\qquad \sum (x_i - \bar{x})^2 = \sum (x_i - \xi)^2 - n(\bar{x} - \xi)^2.$

The second term on the right-hand side is (n times) the square of the difference between the sample mean and the true mean. Let us again imagine taking a very large number of samples of a given size and recording the average of the results in the above equation. We would get (on dividing throughout by n)

$$\begin{matrix} \text{average} \\ \text{sample} \\ \text{variance} \end{matrix} = \begin{matrix} \text{variance} \\ \text{of population} \end{matrix} - \begin{pmatrix} \text{standard error} \\ \text{of sample mean} \end{pmatrix}^2 \tag{3.5}$$

Let us write $E(s^2)$ for the average sample variance and σ^2 for the average population variance.

Then
$$E(s^2) = \sigma^2 - \frac{\sigma^2}{n} \qquad (3.6)$$

$$E(s^2) = \sigma^2 \left(1 - \frac{1}{n} \right).$$

This proves our conjecture that the ordinary measure of the sample variance will on the average give too low a value. It also gives an obvious formula for adjustment. Consider the new measure s'^2:

$$s'^2 = \frac{n}{n-1} \, s^2, \qquad (3.7)$$

then clearly this will correct the underestimation since the average overall samples of s'^2 is now σ^2. So s'^2 is a more satisfactory estimator than s^2. And

$$s'^2 = \frac{n}{n-1} \cdot \frac{\sum (x_i - \bar{x})^2}{n}$$

$$s'^2 = \frac{\sum (x_i - \bar{x})^2}{n-1}. \qquad (3.8)$$

The estimate of the population variance is obtained by finding the sum of the squares of deviations from the sample mean and then *dividing by* $(n-1)$ instead of the usual n. This has the effect of bringing the estimated variance, *on the average*, nearer to the true variance. The qualification 'on the average' is important; in any particular sample it may well be that the variance of that sample (obtained by dividing by n) *exceeds* the true variance. The vagaries of sampling makes this occurrence not a particularly rare event. In those cases, then, the adjustment of dividing by $(n-1)$ instead of n will actually make that particular estimate worse; it will deviate even more from the true value. But we know that although this will occur in some cases, *on the average* the adjustment will make the estimate better, so it is clearly worth while.

An accepted terminology for this adjustment process is available. Instead of dividing the sum of squares by n the number of observations, we divide instead by the *number of degrees of freedom* $(n-1)$. The concept of degrees of freedom replaces the number of observations as the critical denominator in the variance estimator. To interpret the degrees of freedom, examine the case of two observations x_1 and x_2. We find the sum of squares of deviations from the *mean*. The first deviation is $(x_1 - \bar{x})$. But if we knew this deviation we would know also the value of $(x_2 - \bar{x})$. Since $\bar{x} = (x_1 + x_2)/2$ knowledge of $\bar{x}$ and x_1 is sufficient to calculate x_2. Thus we conclude that there is only *one degree of freedom* in this estimate of the variance. This is one less than the number of observations. And obviously this rule for calculating the degrees of freedom of this estimate of the variance is quite general. If we have n observations then knowledge of the values $x_1 - \bar{x}$, $x_2 - \bar{x}$, ..., $x_{n-1} - \bar{x}$ is clearly sufficient to find the nth deviation. So the number of degrees of freedom is $(n-1)$.

Note, however, that if we had *known* the value of ξ and we had calculated the estimate of variance from the sum of squares $\sum\limits_{i}^{n} (x_i - \xi)^2$ the degrees of freedom is n not $(n-1)$. A knowledge of the deviations $x_1 - \xi$, $x_2 - \xi$, ..., $x_{n-1} - \xi$, is *not* sufficient to determine the value of $x_n - \xi$. For it is clear that ξ is not equal to $\sum\limits_{i=1}^{n} x_i$. Thus each of the observations contributes independently to the sum of squares and the number of degrees of freedom is then n, and not $(n-1)$.

We can employ this new estimate of the variance for small samples to derive a test of the mean. The standard error is $\sigma/\sqrt{n}$ and an *estimate* of the standard error is given by inserting the estimate s'^2 instead of σ^2, i.e.

$$\text{estimate of standard error of mean} = \frac{s'}{\sqrt{n}}$$

or

$$= \sqrt{\frac{\sum (x - \bar{x})^2}{n-1}} \Big/ \sqrt{n} \qquad (3.9)$$

Now we compare the deviation between the mean $\bar{x}$ and the hypothetical value (ξ) with the standard error of the mean. The most useful statistic is defined as t, the ratio of a sample value to the estimate of the standard error, i.e. t – deviation of mean from hypothetical value/ estimate of the standard error of the mean for the case of the mean.

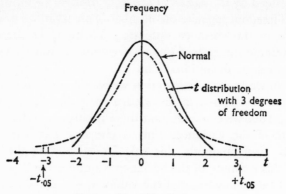

FIG. 3.2. The t Distribution

This gives

$$t = \frac{\bar{x} - \xi}{s'/\sqrt{n}}$$

$$= (\bar{x} - \xi) \Bigg/ \left[\sqrt{\frac{\sum(x_i - \bar{x})^2}{n - 1}} \right] \Bigg/ \sqrt{n}. \qquad (3.10)$$

If the deviation $|\bar{x} - \xi|$ is large relative to the standard error $s'/\sqrt{n}$ the hypothesis is discredited.† On the other hand, if the difference $|\bar{x} - \xi|$ is small compared with the standard error the sample provides no evidence that more doubt be cast on the validity of the hypothesis. Indeed if the sample were *large* and $|\bar{x} - \xi|$ exceeded two standard errors we should 'reject' the hypothesis at the 5 per cent level. This means simply that if the value of $|t|$ exceeds 2, we reject the hypothesis. But these statements are true only for *large* samples, where, for a given large n, the denominator does not vary very much. In small samples the additional variation in the denominator must be taken into account. This means that the variation in t will be the larger, *ceteris paribus*, the smaller the size of sample, or more accurately the smaller the number of degrees of freedom.

The shape of the distribution of t is similar to that of the normal distribution, but it is not exactly the same. It is rather flatter than the normal distribution, and the variance increases as the number of degrees of freedom decreases. But for large samples the distribution of t approximates to the normal – and this is, of course, the assumption

† The notation $|\bar{x} - \bar{\xi}|$ means that we take the absolute value by converting all negative values of $(\bar{x} - \bar{\xi})$ into positive ones.

which was made in large sample-theory. The mean value of the sampling distribution of t is zero. This is simply another version of the result which we observed for large samples that, as we take repeated samples of a given size from a population, the average of these sample means is the value of the hypothetical or true mean. Another useful property of the sampling distribution of t is that it is symmetrical. If we 'fold' the distribution around the mean value we find that the right-hand side has exactly the same pattern as the left-hand side; the one is a mirror image of the other. This means that the chances of a value of t being greater than say 2·5 are exactly the same as the chances of it being less than 2·5.

As with large-sample theory, one can divide the value of t into ranges. Suppose the hypothesis is true; then if we took many many samples of size (say 4) from this population, the value of t would have the distribution shown in the Figure. Two values of t called $\pm t_{.05}$ may be determined which cuts off two tails which each contain $2\frac{1}{2}$ per cent of the total distribution. As we take a sample of 4 from this population, we shall stand a 95 per cent chance of obtaining a value of t in the range $0 \pm t_{.05}$. Granted the hypothesis is true, there is a 5 per cent chance of getting a value of t outside this range. Thus if we say 'the hypothesis is rejected' when t exceeds $t_{.05}$ or is smaller than $-t_{.05}$ we shall be rejecting a *true* hypothesis in only 1 out of 20 cases. These are exactly analogous to the statements made with large-sample theory.

Since the t distribution varies according to the number of degrees of freedom it is obviously convenient to have key values tabulated. Included in any set of standard tables one may find $t_{.05}$ tabulated for various numbers of degrees of freedom. As the degrees of freedom increase, the value of $t_{.05}$ declines; thus we find that for 3 degrees of freedom $t_{.05} = 3\cdot108$ whereas as the number of degrees of freedom increases to infinity $t_{.05}$ goes down to 1·976, or approximately 2.

The t test is easily extended to include testing the differences between two sample means. Suppose that we draw two samples one of size n_1 and one of size n_2 *independently* from the *same* population and calculate the mean of the first sample $\bar{x}_1$ and the mean of the second sample $\bar{x}_2$. The question is: how does the value $\bar{x}_1 - \bar{x}_2$ behave as we take repeatedly pairs of samples of size n_1 and n_2 from this population? In other words, we need to know the characteristics of the *sampling distribution* of the value $\bar{x}_1 - \bar{x}_2$.

The mean of the value $\bar{x}_1 - \bar{x}_2$ over many many samples is, of course, zero. This is readily expected since we know that the mean of the sampling distribution of $\bar{x}_1$ and $\bar{x}_2$ will also be ξ. The standard error of the difference $\bar{x}_1 - \bar{x}_2$ is more complicated. The solution is to add the two variances of the separate sampling distributions (i.e. the squares of the standard errors) to get the variance of sampling distribution of the difference. Thus we obtain

$$\text{variance of sampling dist. of } (\bar{x}_1 - \bar{x}_2) = \frac{\sigma^2}{n_1} + \frac{\sigma^2}{n_2} \tag{3.11}$$

or

$$[\text{standard error of } (\bar{x}_1 - \bar{x}_2)]^2 = \sigma^2 \left[\frac{1}{n_1} + \frac{1}{n_2} \right], \tag{3.12}$$

where σ^2 is the true variance of the population. Now we do not normally know the value of σ^2 so we have to provide an estimate from our samples. A suitable estimate is obtained by taking the total sum of squares of deviations from the means of the two samples divided by the degrees of freedom in that total. This is

$$s_0'^2 = \text{estimate of } \sigma^2 = \frac{\sum_{i=1}^{n_1} (x_{1i} - \bar{x}_1)^2 + \sum_{i=1}^{n_2} (x_{2i} - \bar{x}_2)^2}{n_1 + n_2 - 2}, \tag{3.13}$$

or in words:

$$s_0'^2 = \frac{\left(\begin{array}{l}\text{sum of squares of deviations} \\ \text{of the } n_1 \text{ observations from} \\ \text{the mean } \bar{x}_1\end{array}\right) + \left(\begin{array}{l}\text{sum of squares of deviations} \\ \text{of the } n_2 \text{ observations from} \\ \text{the mean } \bar{x}_2\end{array}\right)}{\text{degrees of freedom}}.$$

We calculate the sum of squares (of each sample separately as though we were simply estimating the variance) then pool the two sums of squares and divide by the degrees of freedom of the total. The degrees of freedom is *two* less than the total number of observations. Since the two values $\bar{x}_1$ and $\bar{x}_2$ are fixed from the samples, two degrees of freedom are lost. So the number of degrees of freedom is then $n_1 + n_2 - 2$.

The t statistic is defined as the ratio of a deviation of sample value from hypothetical value to the estimate of the standard error of that deviation. Thus in the case of a difference between two means we have

$$t = \frac{\bar{x}_1 - \bar{x}_2}{\text{estimate of standard error}} \, ,$$

i.e.

$$t = (\bar{x}_1 - \bar{x}_2) \Big/ s_0' \sqrt{\left(\frac{1}{n_1} + \frac{1}{n_2}\right)} \, . \qquad (3.14)$$

This t is defined for $n_1 + n_2 - 2$ degrees of freedom.

In effect for small samples the t statistic expands the concept of the simple standard error of large-sample theory. So far we have discussed only tests of hypothesis – but the t statistic is naturally carried over to the problem of *estimation and confidence intervals*. Since t is defined as

$$t = \frac{\text{deviation of sample value from hypothesis}}{\text{estimate of standard error}}$$

we can easily write it as

$$\text{deviation} = t \, (\text{estimate of standard error}).$$

Thus, in the simple case of testing a mean,

$$\xi = \bar{x} \pm t \, (\text{estimate of standard error}). \qquad (3.15)$$

If we select a given t, say $t_{.05}$, which cuts off the two $2\frac{1}{2}$ per cent tails, we can state that the range $\bar{x} \pm t_{.05}(\text{estimate of standard error})$ will, in 95 per cent of the cases, cover the true value ξ. This is again analogous to the statement in large sample theory except that we now substitute $t_{.05}$ instead of $1 \cdot 96$ (or approximately 2) in the formulation.

Example

In a sample of 4 small equal-sized local areas chosen at random in Great Britain, the unemployment rate is found to be

Town
A $2 \cdot 5$ per cent
B $3 \cdot 0$ per cent
C $3 \cdot 5$ per cent
D $4 \cdot 0$ per cent

The hypothesis is suggested that the true unemployment rate is only $2 \cdot 0$ per cent. Test this hypothesis.

The mean unemployment rate is

$$\bar{x} = \tfrac{1}{4}[2\cdot5 + 3\cdot0 + 3\cdot5 + 4\cdot0] = 3\cdot25.$$

The variance may be found by calculating

$$\sum(x - \bar{x})^2 = \sum(x^2 - 2\bar{x}x + \bar{x}^2).$$

Since $\bar{x} = (1/n)(\sum x)$ $\qquad = \sum x^2 - (1/n)(\sum x)^2$

So that $\qquad\qquad \sum x^2 = 7\cdot25 + 9\cdot00 + 11\cdot25 + 16\cdot00$

$$= 43\cdot50$$

$$\sum(x - \bar{x})^2 = 43\cdot5 - \tfrac{1}{4}(13)^2$$

$$= 43\cdot5 - 42\cdot25$$

$$\sum(x - \bar{x})^2 = 1\cdot25.$$

Now we make an estimate of the variance:

$$\text{estimated variance} = 1\cdot25/3 = 0\cdot417$$

$$\text{Estimate of the standard error} = \sqrt{\frac{\text{estimated variance}}{\text{number of observations}}}$$

$$= \frac{\sqrt{0\cdot417}}{4} = 0\cdot323.$$

The 'experimental' t is measured as

$$\frac{\text{deviation of sample average from hypothesis}}{\text{estimate of the standard error}}.$$

$$\text{Experimental } t = \frac{3\cdot25 - 2\cdot00}{0\cdot323} = 3\cdot9.$$

Now let us settle on a 'significance level' of 0·05 or 5 per cent, and let us also suppose that the test is a 'two-tailed' one, i.e. we might expect that the evidence from the towns would be as likely to reveal values lower than 2·0 per cent as they are to produce high values on the average.

With 3 *degrees of freedom* we find that theoretical $t_{.05} = 3\cdot182$.

Thus the hypothesis that these data were obtained from a population with an average unemployment rate of 2·0 per cent is discredited. There is only a 1 in 20 chance that we should obtain a sample with an average value as low as this from a population with a mean of 2·0 per cent.

One further test, known as the F or *variance ratio test*, is important in econometrics. Frequently one is faced with the problem of deciding whether a variable is systematically influenced by another variable or classification – an example is consumer expenditure with income (or social class). Does consumer expenditure vary with income or according to social classification? If we had only *two* social classes then the problem would be solved by the *t* test. We should simply test that the two samples are from the same population, and that can be done by using the *t* test discussed above. But suppose there were three or more social classes. The obvious approach is to do a comparison of all possible *pairs* of social classes. But as the number of classes increases, the number of possible tests increases enormously.† A more general method is obviously required.

Consider a situation where we have k classes and we have m persons in each class $km = n$. If there are real differences between the classes then these should be revealed by comparing the averages of each class. Substantial variation between the averages would suggest that class matters – it is not something to be ignored. One critical statistic is clearly the variance of these class averages – but how are we to interpret whether a particular variance of class averages is 'large' or 'too large to have arisen from chance'? If there were no effects due to class then the estimate of the variance obtained from these class averages would be a good estimator of the variance of the population. If we suppose that the class effects *were* zero in the population, then the variance of the class averages multiplied by the number of classes will deviate only by chance from the true variance of the population. Clearly we require an independent estimate of the variance of the population so as to provide a standard by which to judge the size of the variance of the means of classes. Now one clearly cannot use the ordinary variance of all n persons since this includes the variation due to the k class means – i.e. it is not independent of the estimate of variance between classes. The standard is provided by the variation *around* the mean of each class – the 'within class' variance. The total sum of squares is divided as follows:

$$\begin{array}{c} \text{total sums} \\ \text{of squares} \end{array} = \begin{array}{c} \text{sum of squares} \\ \text{around class} \\ \text{means} \end{array} + \begin{array}{c} \text{sum of squares} \\ \text{between class} \\ \text{means} \end{array}$$

† With k classes there are $\dfrac{k(k-1)}{2}$ possible pairs.

Thus if we label x_{ij} as the ith observation in the jth class, we have for the total sum of squares $\sum\limits_{ij}^{km} (x_{ij} - \bar{x})^2$ where the sum is taken over all the $n = km$ observations. Thus, where $\bar{x}_j$ is the average of the jth class we have†

$$\sum_{ij}^{km} (x_{ij} - \bar{x})^2 = \sum_j^k \sum_i^m (x_{ij} - \bar{x}_j)^2 + m \sum_j^k (\bar{x}_j - \bar{x})^2 \qquad (3.16)$$

i.e.   total = within class + between class.

From this we form two independent estimates of the variance by dividing the sums of squares by an appropriate number of degrees of freedom. In the total there are $(n-1)$ (or $km-1$) degrees of freedom. For the 'between classes' there are obviously $(k-1)$ degrees of freedom since there are k class means. So we find the estimate of the variance by dividing the sums of squares between classes by $k-1$. The remainder of the degrees of freedom are used up within classes, i.e. the degrees of freedom within classes are $n - 1 - (k - 1)$, i.e. $n - k$. So we have another

† One curious feature deserves mention here. We have talked about comparing the variance between the class averages with the variance within the classes. Now if one takes the sum of squares between class averages, i.e.

$$\sum_{j=1}^k (\bar{x}_i - \bar{x})^2 \quad (j = 1, 2, ..., k), \qquad (3.17)$$

one only has k observations in this sum, i.e. there are as many observations as there are classes. But every observed class mean $\bar{x}_j$ represents m observations in that class. Thus if all observations in that class were concentrated at the mean of the class the contribution of the class to the total sum of squares would be

$$m(\bar{x}_j - \bar{x})^2. \qquad (3.18)$$

Summing, then, over the k classes we have

$$m \sum_{j=1}^k (\bar{x}_j - \bar{x})^2 \qquad (3.19)$$

since there are m observations in each class. This is, then, that part of the total sum of squares which is due to variations in class averages. Variations within the classes is found by taking the sum of squares in a particular class (say the jth), i.e.

$$\sum_{i=1}^m (x_{ij} - \bar{x}_j)^2, \qquad (3.20)$$

This represents the sum of the squares of deviations from the mean of the jth class of the m observations in that class. We then sum these over the k classes, i.e.

$$\sum_{j=1}^k \sum_{i=1}^m (x_{ij} - \bar{x}_j)^2. \qquad (3.21)$$

estimate of the variance where we divide the sum of squares within classes by $(n-k)$. We now form the ratio

$$F = \frac{\text{estimate of variances between classes,}}{\text{estimate of variance within classes}}$$

or in algebra:

$$F = \frac{m \sum_j (\bar{x}_j - \bar{x})^2/(k-1)}{\sum_j \sum_i (x_{ij} - \bar{x}_j)^2/(n-k)} \qquad F \geqslant 0. \qquad (3.22)$$

Now suppose we have a population where class does not matter; and let us take one sample after another from this population. For each sample we can calculate the value F, and so one can imagine the sampling frequency distribution of F being formed. One can discover the chances of getting a value of F in excess of any particular value; thus one can measure the probability that, from a population where class does not matter, we can get a value of F as high or higher than a given value.† As before, one can determine a value $F_{.05}$ such that in only 5 per cent of the samples from this population will one obtain sample values of F in excess of $F_{.05}$.

This value of $F_{.05}$, therefore, provides a suitable standard by which one may judge the size of a value of F obtained from a particular sample. If the sample F exceeds the value of $F_{.05}$ then we may reject the hypothesis that class does not matter. In making this statement we run a 1 in 20 chance of discrediting a hypothesis which is in fact true.

The F test provides quite a general statistic for testing the size of variances. The critical condition is that in the ratio the two estimates must be independent. If, for example, we compared the between-class variance with the *total* variance, the test would clearly be invalid since the denominator would be influenced by the extent of the between-class variation in the numerator. In the denominator there must appear an independent estimate of the variance within classes – an estimate of the *residual variance*.‡

The distribution of the F statistic varies according to the number of degrees of freedom. There are, however, *two* sets of degrees of freedom to be taken into account, one associated with the numerator and one

† Naturally we are interested only in Fs which exceed a value of unity.
‡ One interesting interpretation is when we have only *two* classes. Then $F = t^2$ and the link between the two tests is clearly seen.

with the denominator. Thus the value of $F_{.05}$ varies according to the *two* sets of degrees of freedom, and suitable tables enable one readily to obtain $F_{.05}$ for the two specified degrees of freedom.

In all small-sample theory there are more restrictive assumptions than apply with large samples. With a large number of observations one does not need to specify the character of the distribution of the population. This does not apply with small samples. Indeed the t and F distributions are developed on the assumption that the *population* is *normally distributed*. But more than this, we also assume that in the F distribution the variance within each class is the same. As we go from one class to another we test to see whether or not the means change; but we must retain the assumption that the variance *within* each class is the same. The possibility we test is that the means of the classes differ while the variance within each class does not vary. (This is the assumption that has the long name of *homoskedastic*, i.e. same variance.)

Although these assumptions seem fiercely restrictive at first sight, this does not mean that the tests can be used only in the very limited number of cases when in econometrics we find ourselves blessed with a normal distribution. Firstly it has been shown by simulation studies that small departures from normalcy do no great harm and the tests are still near enough. Secondly there are obvious transformations which will convert a non-normal distribution into one near to normalcy. One common one is to take the logarithm of the variable – and then one may find that the logarithm is normally distributed. For example, in the cases of family income distributions, the distribution of firms by size, and many other economic and sociological variables, the logarithm of the income, or firm size is distributed approximately normally. While these considerations do expand considerably the applicability of small-sample theory, one must use considerable caution in interpreting these statistics in econometric applications.

Likelihood, Bayes Theorem and Decision Theory

So far in this chapter we have considered the orthodox approach to statistical inference. The main emphasis was on the test of significance of a specific hypothesis; we put up an Aunt Sally and then tried to knock it down with experimental evidence. Our confidence in the hypothesis increases according to the number of times we try to discredit it and fail in the attempt. This method of using experimental and observational evidence has been, and in many respects is still, the dominant approach in scientific work.

But in recent years the classic approach of hypothesis testing has come under considerable fire from two more or less distinct groups. The first group are those who believe that the language of hypothesis testing is too restrictive. It requires us to make an all-or-nothing decision on the basis of the evidence – either to reject or accept the hypothesis, and to accept or reject an alternative hypothesis. But in practice we never carry through such black-or-white decisions; when a hypothesis is rejected we usually regard it as having been 'discredited'. It is out-in-the-cold but not beyond-the-pale. Unfortunately the language of hypothesis testing gives us no way to describe how 'cold' or 'hot' a hypothesis is relative to its rivals. We obviously need a language of this kind – and, as we shall see, the concept of 'likelihood' provides a suitable way of attaching 'odds' of one hypothesis against another. The likelihood approach is a development of the method of estimating an unknown population parameter. It shows that, as a general proposition, it is much more efficient to *estimate*, using the language of likelihood, rather than to test hypotheses. It involves no new concepts of probability; the chances that appear in this approach are simply the probabilities of getting specified evidence given the hypothesis is true.

The second group of critics, however, do depart quite radically from the orthodox concepts of probability. So far we have argued that one cannot attach a probability to a hypothesis; for a hypothesis is either true or it isn't. A hypothesis is a statement about the state of nature and cannot be interpreted as being true 'on the average x per cent times in a long series of trials'. But, although it is clear that a hypothesis is either true or false, the *degree of our belief* in the hypothesis does vary according to our hunches and according to the evidence that has been collected. Indeed it might be argued that we begin every experiment with a number of hypotheses in mind; and to each hypothesis we ascribe a certain degree of belief – or a *prior probability* – before the evidence is collected and analysed. Then the question we ask is: 'how are our prior probabilities changed by the evidence which we have collected and analysed?' This is the approach of *Bayes Theorem* and Bayesian methods.†

Some statisticians, broadly classified in the second group and largely located in the United States, would go even further than this. They argue that the only reason for conducting experiments and collecting data is to enable us to improve the process of *decision-making*. We are interested in the truth or falsehood only in so far as it enables us to take better decisions. Consequently our experiments should be designed so that they give rise to the evidence that most improves the decision-making. Of course this raises a host of problems about what we mean by the 'best outcome' – how do we evaluate losses and gains, and so on. This general approach to the problem is normally known as *decision theory*, and we shall describe the basic approach in the last part of this section. In a sense, decision theory argues that the job of statistician and econometrician should not end with making statements about the plausibility of the values of parameters – but that he should be concerned with the consequences of the decisions which are influenced by the data he collects and analyses; so, in turn, the data to be collected and the analysis to be performed should be influenced by the likely amendments to the decision-making and the gains so obtained.

One cannot pretend that these methods discussed in this section present a new 'cook-book' with a recipe nicely classified for each type of data and for all forms of problem. It is obvious that there is no broad consensus among statisticians; each will have his own ideas about the appropriate methods to use in each set of circumstances. If one were to risk a generalisation, however, I would say that most statisticians would much rather use estimation procedures than the approach of hypothesis testing. And it is the reason for this preference that we go on to examine.

LIKELIHOOD

It may be a good idea to stand back at this stage and discuss critically some of the logical foundations of hypothesis testing as it appears in

† It is, incidentally, true that Bayes theorem can be used with any concept of probability – it is not merely restricted to use with prior probabilities. But most uses are within the context of prior probabilities, and we shall interpret the uses of Bayes theorem within this framework in the remainder of this chapter. (The informed reader will note that we have not used the related concept of fiducial probability.)

standard elementary accounts of the technique. This is an important task since in recent years the normal 'elementary' approach to hypothesis testing has been found to have serious deficiencies. Indeed modern statisticians tend to lean much more towards estimation rather than testing, and towards decision-making rather than making statements about acceptability. Some of these problems will be discussed in the following pages. Here we shall examine critically the logic of hypothesis testing, and how these criticisms might be met. The reader is, however, warned that this is a very inferior substitute for a course in statistical inference; but something is better than nothing.

When we set up a hypothesis – such as the one about income examined above – it is often stated in 'black-and-white' terms, such as the hypothesis that 'average income is £1,000 per annum'. Now if we accept that hypothesis as stated, it implies that average income is *exactly* £1,000 per annum – not a fraction of a penny more, and certainly not a mite of a penny less. This is a very 'sharp' hypothesis indeed – and it is typical of formal statements that are in fact made.

Now let us consider the sampling process and the attempt to reject this hypothesis. With a suitably large sample – say 100 observations – we find the mean and make statements about rejecting the hypothesis. There will be, one supposes, occasions on which the hypothesis is not rejected – provided that such a hypothetical value is not too far from the true value. But now suppose that we take a very large sample indeed – imagine that our sample number approaches infinity. Now it is obvious that with such a sample we get a sample average which will be very close indeed to the true value in the population.† This would not matter if the hypothetical value were *exactly the same* as the true value. But they can never be exactly the same. They are measures of a continuous variable and can only be 'approximately' the same.

But a very large sample will discover this difference – however small – between the hypothetical and the true value. Indeed it is always possible to reject any 'sharp' hypothesis if one chooses a sufficiently large sample. This is an important conclusion because it implies that the probability of rejecting a hypothesis is not independent

† Note that we are thinking of sampling '*with* replacement' here. In principle this statement should be made in terms of the probability of a given divergence between sample value and true value being made as small as we like by a suitably large size of sample.

of the size of sample. A larger sample will give rise to a higher probability of rejecting the hypothesis.

It is instructive to examine the reason for this sort of result. It arises largely because there are two sorts of error. First there is the *sampling* error – which we can make smaller and smaller by having a larger sample; second there is a *specification* error due to the deviation between the hypothesis and the true value. Even though the specification error is trivially small, we can see that it will be relatively the most important element with samples of a large enough size to make the sampling error even smaller.

But, of course, common sense revolts against such a rigid interpretation of a hypothesis. For 'practical purposes' it may not matter whether the true value is between £998 and £1,002. A few shillings either way will make little difference. And this is surely the intuitive response which most of us would give if confronted by such a situation.

The logic of this perfectly sensible reaction must be examined in terms of the consequences of *using* this hypothesis in practice. It may not matter at all, or very little, if the income is just a few shillings less than £1,000 for *the purposes which we have in mind*. The accuracy of the statement depends on the uses to which it is put; we shall return to this aspect in considering decision theory.

But the main importance of this discussion is to point out the necessity for considering *alternative* hypothesis. Obviously if we are prepared to reject the hypothesis that income is £1,000, we are implicity saying that income could therefore be at some other level. When we test a hypothesis we must automatically consider the alternative hypotheses that might be true.

Now it is intuitively obvious that if the alternative hypotheses are very close to the hypothesis with which we are primarily concerned, it will be very difficult to distinguish one from the other – as we discovered above. Very large samples are required in order to discriminate between them. But fortunately it may not matter very much – as we saw when we considered the incomes between £998 and £1,002 – the alternatives may then be just as good. As a formal approach the hypothesis may be stated as 'income is between £998 and £1,002' and, with a few rather obvious amendments, we can proceed as before. But now let us suppose there is an alternative hypothesis that is a 'long way' from the £1,000 – let us suppose that the alternative is £2,000 per annum.† Consider now the choice between these two hypotheses.

In the usual way we consider the consequences of repeated samples of a fixed size taken from these populations. We record the sample averages in the form of the sampling distribution I (in Figure 3.3) when the hypothesis I (income averages £1,000) is true. When hypothesis II is true (income averages £2,000), the sampling distribution of the averages will take the form of II (in Figure 3.3). We have assumed that the standard deviations of the two income distributors are the same, and that the same number is taken in all samples; thus the sampling distributions have the same variance and standard deviation. They differ only in location along the (sample average) income axis.

Now it is obviously silly to proceed mechanically to test the hypothesis that average income is £1,000 (i.e. hypothesis I) by rejecting it if the sample value falls outside the range £1,000 ± 2 (standard error). For this means rejecting I when the sample average falls *below L* (below which lie $2\frac{1}{2}$ per cent of the distribution of I); but rejecting I means accepting II, which is much *higher* than I. This would lead to the ludicrous result that a low sample average would lead to accepting the high-valued hypothesis!‡ Clearly much the same conclusion will be reached with regard to the very high sample values with respect to hypothesis II. Obviously if we get a high sample average – such as *H* – we choose II and reject I.

The 'hard' cases occur in the middle region – where there is a significant overlap of the probability distributions.§ Consider a sample average of *C* (in Figure 3.3). Now the probability of obtaining this sample value, *given that hypothesis I is true*, is measured by the ordinate *BC*.‖ Or, to put it in the notation of probability theory,

$$P(C|\text{I}) = \text{the probability } CB \text{ on the graph.}$$

Now if, on the other hand, *hypothesis II were true*, we see that the probability of a sample average of *C* would be *CA*, i.e.

$$P(C|\text{II}) = \text{the probability } CA \text{ on graph.}$$

† What is meant here by a 'long way' of course depends on the variance of income, as well as on the use to which the results are to be put.

‡ Of course no 'classical' statistician would ever suggest using such an approach; but the student must be warned off such mechanical applications of 'tests of significance'.

§ Note that there is always *some* overlap at all levels of sample income. It is possible to ignore the overlap over a large fraction of the total scale – since the amount is so small.

‖ Strictly one should talk about the probability of a sample value falling in an *infinitesimal range* about the value *C*, then the probability is measured by the rectangle of infinitesimal width and of height *BC*.

We can compare these two probabilities in the form of a ratio, which we call the *likelihood ratio*. This gives us the 'odds' on the two hypotheses:

$$\text{likelihood ratio of I as opposed to II} = \frac{P(C|\text{I})}{P(C|\text{II})} = \frac{CB}{CA}.$$

These are the odds on I against II. Symmetrically we find the odds on II as against I are CA/CB.; this is therefore the likelihood ratio of II as opposed to I.

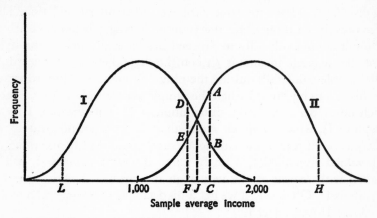

Fig. 3.3. Sampling Distribution of Means with Two Alternative Hypotheses

Intuitively this comparison of the odds gives us a way of choosing between competing hypotheses. If the sample is taken, we simply calculate the sample average and then inspect the odds. We then choose the hypothesis which is favoured by the odds and reject the alternative hypothesis. Thus if the sample average is C we reject I in favour of II. If, however, the sample average is F we reject II in favour of I. If we obtain a sample average of J, then we merely dither between the two.† (We may toss a fair coin to decide the issue.)

This discussion does, however, emphasise the limitations of the language and procedure of hypothesis testing of the accept-or-reject

† In all this discussion we are not talking about the 'probability of a hypothesis'. By its nature, a hypothesis is either true or it is false; we cannot sensibly talk about the probability of a hypothesis unless we use Bayesian concepts of *prior* and *a posteriori* probability. The statements in the text must be interpreted strictly: they tell us the probability of the sample value *given* a hypothesis is true, i.e. $P(C|\text{I})$. We do not use the Bayesian concept of $P(\text{I}|C)$; see below.

type. The formal process is to try to discredit, and if it is not rejected it is accepted (albeit as a 'tentative' or working hypothesis). But surely one may not find it possible to decide in such a black-and-white or yea-or-nay way. One may wish to indicate the hypothesis I is much the better bet (L in the figure), a slightly better bet (F in the figure) or 'even money' (J in the figure). Instead of coming down wholly against one hypothesis and in favour of another, one may wish to indicate more subtly the likelihoods of sample values from the various hypotheses. And we can see that such graduations of confidence can easily be made from the nature of the sampling process.

In other words, one of the great disadvantages of the 'accept-reject' approach is that we are forced to express the result in two extreme ways. All our eggs go into one basket. There is no room for intermediate grades – such as 'I lean towards this hypothesis a lot, – and much more than the alternative', or 'I find it impossible to choose between them' (in the region of J). In practice we often want to express these subtleties and it seems inefficient not to have a statistical 'language' in which they can be communicated. It is obvious that the concept of the likelihood ratio provides such a language.

Of course the language of likelihood is more complex and difficult than the 'yea-or-nay' of standard significance tests. And this makes it more difficult to express ideas to the 'outsider' or the statesman or the common man. But this approach is more faithful to the facts; and, in any case, even with the standard significance test the statistician is often constrained to add qualifying statements to the accept-or-reject results.†

It is easy to see how the likelihood approach can be naturally adapted to the problem of estimating an unknown population parameter. Consider, for example, the situation illustrated in Figure 3.3, but imagine that there is an enormous number of admissible hypotheses of average income, instead of merely two as we have in the Figure. Suppose that *any* average income of the population is possible. Now let us select a particular sample, and ask what is our best estimator of the population average. It is intuitively clear that we should choose that value that gives the highest likelihood. We should select the estimate of the population value that has the best 'odds'.

---

† Thus we often read that a result is 'very significant', 'only just', and so on.

In the simple case we have considered – the estimate of the mean – it is easy to see that the maximum likelihood estimator is in fact the sample mean itself. If, for example, we found that the sample average was £2,000 per annum, then we must select as the most likely population value £2,000 per annum, for it is clear that the likelihood is highest with distribution II. The likelihood ratio is greater than unity when we compare II with any other population value. (It must be observed that such simple results do not always occur with maximum likelihood estimators; sometimes they are difficult to develop, and in many cases the estimate differs from the analogous sample statistic.)

Probably the most imaginative use of likelihood concepts is that we can sensibly talk about the 'odds' of nearby values, or indeed quite distant values. For example, as we look at values of the population parameter in the region of the maximum likelihood estimate, we may well find that the likelihood goes down very little. The odds of values in the region of the estimate that maximises likelihood may be only a fraction less that the estimate itself. Thus it may not matter much if we choose any value in that region. On the other hand one may find that in one direction, perhaps, the odds slump sharply. Thus the parameter is not likely to be located in that region of low likelihood.

This completes our survey of some of the problems of hypothesis testing and estimation. The reader must not imagine, however, that there is any 'correct' or 'right' approach for each problem. We have warned against the mechanical application of hypothesis testing, but such warnings should be applied to any statistical technique. The tools of statistics, like those of economics, must be used with a sense of relevance, discretion and smell.

BAYES THEOREM†

One of the most interesting aspects of the concept of conditional probability is that many students of probability theory believe that we can turn it around and examine the *plausibility* of underlying hypotheses. In the conditional probability formula we examine the chances of an

----

† The methods discussed in this part are sometimes called 'Bayesian methods'. They were originally devised by Thomas Bayes in 1764.

event E occurring given that A is true. Now let us regard A as a hypothesis then the probability $P(E|A)$ tells us the chances of E occurring if the hypothesis A is true. In the formula

$$P(E|A) = P(E, A)/P(A) \qquad (3.24)$$

there appears the term $P(A)$, which we should normally interpret as the probability that A is true. But clearly the hypothesis A is either true or not true; it is part of the 'state of nature'. For example, suppose that the hypothesis is that 'the coin is unbiased'. Let us call the event E the occurrence of 2 heads when the coin is tossed twice. One can easily interpret now the probability $P(E|A)$ in the ordinary frequency sense; applying Bernoulli's rule we know that the probability is $\frac{1}{4}$. In a large number of experiments with this coin we should expect that about one-quarter would give rise to 2 heads. But now consider $P(A)$. This tells us the 'probability' that the coin is unbiased – but we clearly cannot interpret this as a 'probability' in the sense that we can examine a large number of identical coins experimentally to determine whether 'unbiasedness' results. The coin is either unbiased or it is not; there is no way in which we can interpret this statement in an ordinary probability sense.

But although we cannot attach a frequency interpretation to $P(A)$ we do in practice think of the 'chances' of the coin being unbiased. We might reasonably examine how our ideas of the 'chances' of a coin being unbiased are affected by the outcome of a particular experiment. We start the experiment with an *a priori* probability $P(A)$ that the coin is unbiased. This represents our prior knowledge of the state of the coin. Such knowledge may be based on our 'previous experience' with coins from the particular source from which we obtained it; but we may have observed that coins of a certain vintage have a tendency to be biased. On the other hand an *a priori* probability may be based on nothing more substantial than a simple hunch, a vague suspicion or an irrational prejudice.

One might reasonably ask – suppose one has neither hunch, suspicions or prejudice, how then can one proceed to attach a value to $P(A)$? Of course, the simplest answer is to decide that Bayesian methods are not applicable. Without some prior probabilities we cannot construct a Bayesian solution. An alternative course is to invoke the 'principle of insufficient reason'? This simply means that we attribute to each of the alternative hypotheses an *equal* prior probability. Thus in our simple case the coin can either be unbiased or biased, thus the $P(A) = \frac{1}{2}$ and the $P(\text{not } A) = \frac{1}{2}$. The main weaknesses of this 'principle' can easily be listed: there is no 'natural' classification of hypotheses. We might equally have added 'very biased' and 'a little biased' to the hypothesis A of unbiased. This would then have resulted in $P(A) = \frac{1}{3}$. Obviously by suitable definition of the nature of a hypothesis one can make these prior probabilities take on almost any value. In using this principle it is often easy to arrive at absurdities.

But let us suppose that these difficulties with formulating prior probabilities do not arise and that we can attach a value to the probability of unbiasedness $\{P(A)\}$ before we carry out the experiment. Now the question which we ask is: how should we revise our estimate of the chance of unbiasedness $\{P(A)\}$ in the light of the evidence derived from an experiment? Obviously we need an operation of the following kind

$$P\left[A \middle| \begin{array}{l} \text{experimental} \\ \text{evidence} \end{array} \right] \leftarrow \begin{array}{l} \text{revise in the} \\ \text{light of} \\ \text{experimental} \\ \text{evidence} \end{array} \left[P(A) \right]. \qquad (3.25)$$

The left-hand side shows the probability of A after taking into account the revisions suggested by the outcome of the experiment. To simplify let us suppose that there are simply *two* hypotheses, A the coin is unbiased and B ('not A') that the coin is biased. Let us also suppose that the evidence from the experiment is denoted by E; a typical example may be that in 100 throws of a coin, 30 heads appear. From this evidence E we seek to revise the prior probability $P(A)$ to find the posterior probability $P(A|E)$.

Clearly we can write

$$P(A|E) = P(A, E)/P(E). \qquad (3.26)$$

The denominator may be written

$$P(E) = P(E, A) + P(E, B)$$

$$= P(E|A)P(A) + P(E|B)P(B) \qquad (3.27)$$

since there are only two hypotheses, A and B.

And also the numerator

$$P(A, E) = P(E|A)P(A). \tag{3.28}$$

So that we can substitute these two results into (3·26) above to get

$$P(A|E) = \frac{P(E|A)}{P(E|A)P(A) + P(E|B)P(B)} \cdot P(A). \tag{3.29}$$

This is *Bayes Theorem*.

We see then that the experimental evidence E forces us to revise our original probability of the coin being unbiased $P(A)$ by multiplying $P(A)$ by the ratio

$$\frac{P(E|A)}{P(E|A)P(A) + P(E|B)P(B)} \cdot \tag{3.30}$$

In words this is the chance of the experimental outcome occurring *if* A is true divided by the unconditional probability of the experimental outcome whatever the true state of the coin, i.e.

$$\frac{\text{probability of } E \text{ if } A \text{ is correct}}{\text{probability of } E} \cdot \tag{3.31}$$

This may be called the *plausibility ratio*.†

It may be observed that the denominator of the plausibility ratio $P(E)$ is expressed as the sum of two conditional probabilities – where the condition is the truth of the hypothesis A or B – multiplied by the prior probabilities of the hypotheses. This very round about way of expressing $P(E)$ does serve to bring out its dependence on the prior probabilities of the hypotheses.

A short example will illustrate the application of Bayes Theorem. Let A be, as before, that the coin is unbiased. Let B be the *only* alternative hypothesis and suppose that the coin is then biased and that the probability of a head is $\frac{1}{4}$. All other possibilities are excluded. Suppose we have the prior probabilities

$$P(A) = \tfrac{5}{6}$$
$$P(B) = \tfrac{1}{6},$$

i.e. we are much more confident in it being unbiased.

† One can see that the plausibility ratio is the same as $L/\{1 + P(A)[L - 1]\}$, when L is the likelihood ratio of A against B.

Carry out the experiment by tossing the coin twice and suppose that we observe the number of heads. Suppose that we obtain two tails, then we apply Bayes Theorem:

$$P\left(A \middle| \begin{array}{c} \text{two} \\ \text{tails} \end{array}\right) = \left\{ P\left(\begin{array}{c} \text{two} \\ \text{tails} \end{array} \middle| A\right) \middle/ \left[P\left(\begin{array}{c} \text{two} \\ \text{tails} \end{array} \middle| A\right) P(A) + P\left(\begin{array}{c} \text{two} \\ \text{tails} \end{array} \middle| B\right) P(B) \right] \right\} P(A)$$

$$= \left\{ \left(\frac{1}{2}\right)^2 \middle/ \left[\left(\frac{1}{2}\right)^2 \left(\frac{5}{6}\right) + \left(\frac{3}{4}\right)^2 \left(\frac{1}{6}\right) \right] \right\} \left(\frac{5}{6}\right)$$

$$= \frac{20}{29}.$$

As a consequence of an experiment, therefore, we have revised our prior probability that the coin was unbiased $\frac{5}{6}$ down to $\frac{20}{29}$. The fact that we got two tails out of two tosses has inclined us towards believing that the coin is more likely to have a tail-bias. $P(B)$ is then revised from $\frac{1}{6}$ to $\frac{9}{29}$.

There are many difficulties involved in using Bayesian methods – and the reader may have seen intuitively some of these drawbacks in the exercise discussed above. There is, for example, no allowance for the size of sample that is for the importance of the experimental evidence. We would have much more confidence in the revision of $P(A)$ and $P(B)$ if the experiment consisted of one hundred tosses instead of two. Indeed we may regard the quantity of evidence from a mere two tosses as too small to affect at all our prior probabilities. The strength of our prior knowledge may not be upset at all by a mere two tosses.

This is not the place to expand on the various difficulties of Bayesian methods. Debate between probabilists, statisticians and philosophers still goes on and there is much disagreement on quite basic issues. It seems likely, however, that Bayesian methods must play an increasing role in economics and econometrics.

DECISION THEORY

It is often claimed that the ultimate purpose of any investigation is to enable us to make better decisions. From a judgement of the state of the world we evaluate the consequences of each potential course of action. We then decide to pursue one of these courses of action according to our view of the attractiveness of the consequences. For example, suppose we are concerned with finding the optimum tax to impose on confectionery and that we know that the elasticity of supply is infinite; then the question turns on the elasticity of demand. With the traditional approach we would either estimate the elasticity of demand or examine certain hypotheses about the elasticity. Let us suppose, for simplicity, that the elasticity of demand is *either* unity *or* 0·5. We might then set up our experiment to discover which hypothesis has the highest likelihood – using either Bayesian methods or the traditional methods of hypothesis testing. At this stage the statisticians job *per se* is completed and the decision-maker takes over.

With decision theory, however, the statistical problem is extended to consider the costs of making various decisions if certain hypotheses hold. Again let us simplify and assume that there are only two possible courses of action – to tax at 10 per cent or not to tax at all. Then we can characterise the four outcomes by the following costs:

| | Elasticity | |
	1	0·5
Tax	£10 m.	0
No tax	0	£5 m.

Now if the main purpose of the tax is to raise revenue, it is clear that taxing confectionery when the elasticity is unity involves expense and no tax revenue – so we have supposed that the cost is £10 million which has been entered in the appropriate box of the table of outcomes. If, on the other hand, we impose a tax and the elasticity is only 0·5, we have taxed 'correctly' and we reckon the cost at zero. Similarly, if we do not tax when we should not, the cost can be taken as zero. If we miss an opportunity for taxing, i.e. no tax when the elasticity is 0·5, we incur a cost of £5 million.

Now let us suppose that we have *already carried out the survey* and found that the chance of unit elasticity is 0·2 and the likelihood of 0·5 elasticity is 0·8. Then we can find the expected costs of adopting the tax as

$$[(£10 \text{ m. }) \times 0 \cdot 2] + [(£0 \text{ m.}) \times 0 \cdot 8] = £2 \text{ m.}$$

This is simply the sum of the outcome multiplied by the likelihood of that outcome. Similarly, the expected costs of not adopting the tax is

$$[(£0 \text{ m.}) \times 0 \cdot 2] + [(£5 \text{ m.}) \times 0 \cdot 8] = £4 \text{ m.}$$

So we have

Strategy	Expected costs
Tax	£2 m.
No tax	£4 m.

and it is clearly the best strategy to tax confectionery.

This result is, however, critically dependent on the criteria we have adopted – that is, the minimising of expected costs. There is nothing sacrosanct about this aim; and it is natural to consider alternative approaches. One such is to find the strategy which results in as low a value as possible for the *maximum* loss. In short the strategy is concerned with minimising the maximum loss – or even shorter 'minimax'.

In our table we see that, if we tax, the maximum possible loss is £10 million. If we do not tax, the maximum possible loss is £5 million. Clearly the maximum loss is minimised if we then choose not to tax confectionery – and we are ensured that the maximum loss is £5 million. This is a different solution from that developed for the 'expected loss' criterion. The minimax strategy represents a 'safety-first' attitude to decision-making. In this strategy the numerical value of the likelihoods, provided they exceed zero, do not play a part – whereas in the 'expected loss' case they play a critical role.

There are, of course, many other criteria for decision-making. But there is no obvious rule for choosing between the criteria available. Each must be chosen according to the 'utility function' of the decision-maker. An ultra-cautious individual may choose 'minimax', a less cautious man the 'expected loss' criterion. If it is possible to describe each situation by means of a utility function we can generalise the choice criterion to one of maximising expected utility (or minimising expected disutility). This will then enable us to take account of the fact that a large loss, for example, has enormous disutility, while a small loss has proportionately less disutility. For example, we may assume that the disutility function is simply the *square* of the loss so that we have the disutility table in 'utils':

	Elasticity	
	1	0
Tax	100	0
No tax	0	25

Units: utils.

And now calculating expected disutility

for tax $(100 \times 0.2) + (\ 0 \times 0.8) = 20$ utils;

for no tax $(0 \times 0.2) + (25 \times 0.8) = 20$ utils.

There is a tie! It does not matter whether we choose to tax confectionery or not – they have equal disutility. If the disutility function had been the *cube* of the loss, then we should have been better off *not* introducing a tax. For the rest of this discussion we shall adopt only one of the various criteria discussed above – we shall use the simple 'expected loss' formulation.

Up to now we have supposed that the experiment (the survey) had already taken place and that we were concerned with taking a decision on the basis of its results about the likelihoods. But frequently we find ourselves in the situation where *whether to do a survey or not is actually part of the decision-making procedure.* In other words we start our decision-making process *before* the sample; we ask whether it is worthwhile sampling or not. This is a question in addition to those about choosing an action strategy, i.e. whether to tax or not.

Obviously the question of whether to sample or not will depend on two things: first the cost of the sample itself and secondly our ideas about how the sample result is likely to affect our views about the likelihoods of the elasticities. To develop the latter point suppose that *if the elasticity is actually unity* there is a very high chance (say 0·9) that the experiment will produce the correct result (elasticity = 1·0), and only a low chance (0·1) that the experiment will produce the wrong result, i.e. falsely allege that the elasticity is 0·5.

Now let us suppose that, as before, we can, before we decide whether or not to sample, ascribe probabilities to the hypotheses elasticity = 1, and 0·5, and let us suppose that these are respectively 0·3 and 0·7. These figures measure our degree of belief in the validity of the hypothesis before the sample is carried out. (They correspond to the values of 0·8 and 0·2 which we assumed in the previous example, when we assumed that we had already sampled and incorporated the results in these two likelihoods.) We can now calculate the chances of *both* the elasticity being unity *and* the experiment producing evidence showing that it is unity (and we use the mnemonic 'prob' for probability):

$$\text{prob}\begin{bmatrix}\text{elasticity} = 1 \\ \text{sample indicates unity}\end{bmatrix}$$

$$= \text{prob}\begin{bmatrix}\text{sample} \\ \text{indicates unity}\end{bmatrix}\begin{vmatrix}\text{elasticity} \\ = 1\end{vmatrix} \cdot \text{prob}[\text{elasticity} = 1] \quad (3.32)$$

by the ordinary laws of conditional probability.
Numerically

$$\text{prob}\left[\text{elasticity} = 1, \frac{\text{sample}}{\text{indicates unity}}\right] = 0.9 \times 0.3$$

$$= 0.27.$$

Similarly

$$\text{prob}\left[\text{elasticity} = 1, \frac{\text{sample}}{\text{indicates } 0.5}\right] = 0.1 \times 0.3$$

$$= 0.03$$

– this shows the likelihood that *both* the elasticity is unity *and* the sample evidence indicated that it is (wrongly) 0.5.

We have dealt with the case when the elasticity is unity; now we examine the case when the elasticity is 0.5. Suppose now that in fact the elasticity were 0.5. Then let us assume that the likelihood of the sample survey pointing to the correct result (i.e. elasticity = 0.5) is 0.6, and the likelihood of it indicating the wrong result (unity) is 0.4. One can then construct the chances of the outcomes:

$$\text{prob}\left[\text{elasticity} = 0.5, \frac{\text{sample indicates}}{\text{elasticity} = 0.5}\right]$$

$$= \text{prob}\left[\frac{\text{sample indicates}}{\text{elasticity} = 0.5}\middle|\text{elasticity} = 0.5\right] \cdot \text{prob}\left[\text{elasticity} = 0.5\right]$$

$$= 0.6 \times 0.7 = 0.42. \quad (3.33)$$

Similarly

$$\text{prob}\left[\text{elasticity}=0.5, \begin{array}{l}\text{sample indicates}\\\text{elasticity}=1\end{array}\right]$$

$$=\text{prob}\left[\begin{array}{l}\text{sample indicates}\\\text{elasticity}=1\end{array}\middle|\text{elasticity}=0.5\right] . \text{prob}\left[\text{elasticity}=0.5\right]$$

$$=0.4 \times 0.7 = 0.28. \tag{3.34}$$

These chances give us a measure of how the sample is likely to influence our views of the elasticity. We can portray them in a table which gives us the chances of outcomes when it is *assumed that we have decided to sample*.

Table 3.1
Joint Chance of Sample Outcome and Actual Elasticity

		Actual elasticity:		*Sum* Prior probability of sample outcomes
		0·5	1·0	
Sample indicates elasticity to be	0·5	0·42	0·03	0·45
	1·0	0·28	0·27	0·55
Sum	Prior probability of actual elasticity	0·70	0·30	1·00

Notice that the sum of the joint chances over the sample outcomes gives us the prior probabilities of the elasticities, 0·7 and 0·3. The sum horizontally gives the prior probabilities of the sample outcomes.

Now we can specify the decisions open to us and the costs associated with each eventuality. Let us assume that the survey costs £2 million. The costs of the various outcomes can be tabulated as follows:

Costs in £m.

Strategy	Elasticity	
	0·5	1·0
Sample and tax	2	12
Sample and no tax	7	2
No sample and tax	0	10
No sample and no tax	5	0

We have simply incorporated the cost of the sample in this Table. Thus when we sample and tax and the elasticity is actually unity we incur the total cost of £12 million, of which £2 million was spent on the sample.

We might set out the process of decision-making in the form of a 'tree'. We begin on the left with the problem whether or not to sample – and there are two branches, the upper one representing no sample and the bottom one representing the decision to sample. The bottom branch is then split into two according to the results of the sample – the upper one indicating the sample outcome favourable to the elasticity being 0·5, and the lower one favourable to the elasticity being 1·0. To each of these outcomes of the sample we can attach the prior probabilities (given that the sample has been carried out) indicated in the last column of Table 3.1 – 0·45 for the elasticity = 0·5, and 0·55 for the elasticity = 1·0. We then continue our tree with the *action* branch – to tax or not to tax. The two sample branches, as well as the upper 'do not-sample' branch, are each split into two, so that we have six possible positions at the end of the action stage. Note that there are no probabilities attached to the action stage – we choose one course or another, just as we choose whether or not to sample. The last stage is the actual *realisation* of the elasticity, i.e. whether it is 0·5 or 1·0. The costs of each of the outcomes, as described in the table above, is now attached to each of the final branch-ends. (Note that we have assumed that the outcome of the sample makes no difference to the branch-end costs.)

The problem is now tackled in reverse. We start at the branch-ends and work backwards to the root of the tree. Consider, for example, the topmost action branch – (do not sample)→(tax). Now we know that two possibilities arise – the elasticity may be 0·5 with prior probability

0·7 and the elasticity may be 1·0 with prior probability 0·3. So we can find the expected costs as

$$(£0 \text{ m.}) \times 0·7 + (£10 \text{ m.}) \times 0·3 = £3 \text{ m.}$$

Now consider the 'no tax' strategy, the second action branch, and we calculate expected costs as

$$(£5 \text{ m.}) \times 0·7 + (£0 \text{ m.}) \times 0·3 = £3·5 \text{ m.}$$

We insert these values on the diagram at the appropriate junctions and encircle them. Clearly this calculation makes the no-tax strategy (when we have already decided *not* to sample) redundant – the expected costs of taxing are £0·5 *less*. Thus, effectively, the expected costs of not sampling – and then following the best policy of taxing – are £3 million, so enter that value, duly encircled at the junction at the beginning of the action branch.

More difficulties are involved with the sampling branches. Again let us start at the top branch-end – the process of: (sample) – (outcome favourable to elasticity = 0·5 – (tax) – (elasticity = 0·5). Working backwards from the branch-ends we see that the final process is the probabilistic realisation that the elasticity is either 0·5 (1st branch) or 1·0 (2nd branch), each of which has associated costs £2 million and £12 million. These probabilities are conditional upon the fact that we (i) chose to sample; (ii) observed an outcome of the sample favourable to elasticity = 0·5; (iii) chose to tax. On (ii) looking back to Table 3.1 we can see that the prior probability of the sample indicating an elasticity of 0·5 is given as 0·45. (And if we get a sample which indicates this elasticity we would choose to tax.) So we can write

$$\text{prob} \left[\text{elasticity} = 0·5 \,\middle|\, \begin{array}{l} \text{(i) sample} \\ \text{(ii) outcome of sample} \\ \quad \text{favourable to } 0·5 \end{array} \right]$$

$$= \text{prob} \left[\text{elasticity} = 0·5 \,\middle|\, \begin{array}{l} \text{outcome of} \\ \text{sample favourable} \\ \text{to } 0·5 \end{array} \right], \quad (3.35)$$

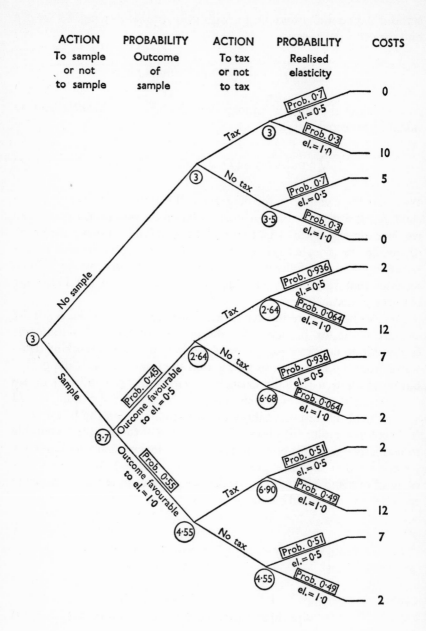

ACTION	PROBABILITY	ACTION	PROBABILITY	COSTS
To sample or not to sample	Outcome of sample	To tax or not to tax	Realised elasticity	

since (i) sampling is already implied in (ii) the particular sample outcome favourable to 0·5. So we can construct:

$$\text{prob}\left[\text{elasticity}=0\cdot5 \left| \begin{array}{l}\text{outcome of}\\ \text{sample favourable}\\ \text{to } 0\cdot5\end{array}\right.\right]$$

$$= \frac{\text{prob}\left[\text{elasticity}=0\cdot5,\begin{array}{l}\text{outcome of}\\ \text{sample favourable}\\ \text{to elasticity}=0\cdot5\end{array}\right]}{\text{prob}\left[\begin{array}{l}\text{outcome of}\\ \text{sample favourable}\\ \text{to elasticity}=0\cdot5\end{array}\right]}, \qquad (3.36)$$

by the ordinary rules of conditional probability. Returning to Table 3.1 we see that this is

$$\text{prob}\left[\text{elasticity}=0\cdot5 \left| \begin{array}{l}\text{outcome of sample}\\ \text{favourable to elasticity}=0\cdot5\end{array}\right.\right] = \frac{0\cdot42}{0\cdot45}$$

$$= 0\cdot936,$$

and

$$\text{prob}\left[\text{elasticity}=1\cdot0 \left| \begin{array}{l}\text{outcome of sample}\\ \text{favourable to elasticity}=0\cdot5\end{array}\right.\right] = \frac{0\cdot03}{0\cdot45}$$

$$= 0\cdot064.$$

One can now calculate the expected costs of the strategy of sampling and taxing if the outcome is favourable to 0·5. We have, as expected, costs

$$(\pounds2 \text{ m.}) \times 0\cdot936 + (\pounds12 \text{ m.}) \times 0\cdot064 = \pounds2\cdot64 \text{ m.}$$

which we enter, duly encircled, at the appropriate junction. Secondly let us examine the no-tax branch of the 'outcome-favourable-to-0·5' case. This, of course, should be the same as the case considered immediately above. Only the decision tax or no tax differs.

Now consider the other main branch of the sample result where the evidence favours an elasticity of 1·0. Taking the 'tax' branch first, we calculate the probability of an elasticity of 0·5 emerging, given that the sample outcome favoured 1·0.

$$\text{prob}\left[\text{elasticity} = 0{\cdot}5 \,\middle|\, \begin{matrix}\text{outcome of sample}\\\text{is favourable to } 1{\cdot}0\end{matrix}\right]$$

$$= \frac{\text{prob}\left[\text{elasticity} = 0{\cdot}5, \begin{matrix}\text{outcome of sample is}\\\text{favourable to } 1{\cdot}0\end{matrix}\right]}{\text{prob}\left[\begin{matrix}\text{outcome of sample is}\\\text{favourable to } 1{\cdot}0\end{matrix}\right]}, \qquad (3.37)$$

which from Table 3.1 is

$$\frac{0{\cdot}28}{0{\cdot}55} = 0{\cdot}51.$$

The probability of the other branch where elasticity is unity is then $1 - 0{\cdot}51 = 0{\cdot}49$. These two probabilities are repeated for the last 'no tax' branches. To find the expected costs at this last stage we repeat the operation – for example, for the last two branches

$$\{(\pounds7 \text{ m.}) \text{ with prob} = 0{\cdot}51)\} + \{(\pounds2 \text{ m.}) \text{ with prob} = 0{\cdot}49\} = 3{\cdot}57 + 0{\cdot}98$$
$$= \pounds4{\cdot}55$$

which we enter in a circle at the junction.

In the action of choosing to tax or not we clearly wish to consider only those which have the lowest cost. Thus if we find ourselves at the point of having sampled and found that the evidence favoured the elasticity of $0{\cdot}5$ we should clearly tax, since the expected cost $\pounds2{\cdot}64$ million would be lower than not taxing. We enter then $\pounds2{\cdot}64$ m. at the junction of sample outcome and tax. Similarly if the sample outcome were favourable to elasticity $= 1{\cdot}0$, then the choice is clearly 'no tax' with an expected cost of $\pounds4{\cdot}55$ million.

Lastly we see whether it is worthwhile sampling. From the sample branch there are two outcomes:

(i) an expected cost of $\pounds2{\cdot}64$ m. with an associated probability of $0{\cdot}45$;

(ii) an expected cost of $\pounds4{\cdot}55$ m. with an associated probability of $0{\cdot}55$.

We then form the expected costs of sampling as

$$(\pounds2{\cdot}64 \text{ m.}) \times 0{\cdot}45 + (\pounds4{\cdot}55 \text{ m.}) \times 0{\cdot}55 = \pounds3{\cdot}7 \text{ m.}$$

Now it is clearly not efficient to sample the population since the expected costs of sampling are £3·7 million whereas, in the no-sample branch the expected costs are only £3 million. The optimum policy, therefore, is *not* to sample, and to introduce the tax. This completes the analysis of the decision-making process.

One of the results of this example is that it is not worth while to sample. We can get a more direct measure of why this is the case. The sample, we assumed, costs us £2 million, and if we sampled the minimum costs, including the sample costs, are £3·7 million, i.e.

Sample costs	£2 m.
Other expected costs	£1·7 m.
Total	£3·7 m.

To be worthwhile the sample would have to cost less than £1·3 million; this would give a total cost less than £3 million – so it would be then preferable to sample before making the decision. As it stands, however, the sample information is worth less than it costs to acquire it.

We must now touch on some of the problems of the decision-theory approach. One which will certainly have occurred to the reader is that of attributing costs to each possible outcome. Often one just cannot formulate what the costs are likely to be. It is, however, a compelling argument that one always in fact behaves *as if* there were costs attributable to every outcome. Surely it is a good discipline to have to formulate them explicitly. In practice one often uses useful short-cuts; one commonly used rule is to use the square of the deviation of the estimate of the unknown parameter from its true value as the 'loss function'. Thus in our example the relative 'loss' would be measured by the square of the estimated elasticity from its true value, e.g.

Loss when elasticity $= 1·0$ and we judge it to be $0·5 = (0·5 - 1·0)^2$

$$= 0·25.$$

When the elasticity is estimated at its correct value, the loss is zero. This loss function is, of course, quite arbitrary, but statisticians have found in practice that this is a useful loss function to use in the absence of any detailed cost specification.

Another major difficulty lies in attaching values to the probabilities which need to be quantified in using decision functions. This involves specifying the prior probabilities of the elasticities assuming certain values, and the more complex task of stating the probabilities of the sample indicating the correct and incorrect elasticities. This is merely a way of evaluating what the sample is going to tell us – but it is not at all easy to put quantities on the probability of the sample results revealing the true facts.

Our example is extremely simple. We have not considered the enormous number of opportunities which occur in practical cases. For example, we might consider many samples of various size, complexity and cost. Formally it is easy to extend the theory to deal with multiple opportunities, but the problems of specifying the probabilities of the outcomes are not simplified! Even so, it is often useful to draw a decision tree, or at least certain of the main branches, to clear one's mind about the decision problem.

Questions for Discussion

1. The average annual household income of the country as a whole is thought to be £1,300 (from Inland Revenue statistics).

   A sample of 44 households in the Jarrow area gave the following data (X = family income) in £s.

   Define

   $$X' = X - 1,000,$$

   $$\Sigma X' = 7,200,$$

   $$\Sigma X'^2 = 16,400,000.$$

   It is known that Jarrow is a depressed area. Discuss whether the average income in Jarrow is *below* the national average. (Note that this is a '*one-tailed*' test.)

2. In a sample of consignments from British Railways and British Road Services in the West Midlands for 1953, it was found that

	B.R.S.	British Railways (excl. minerals)
Total weight	32·0 tons	49·6 tons
No. of consignments	36	100
Sums of squares	310	830

   Source: Walters and Sharp, *A Report on Costs Competition and Rates in U.K. Transport* (mimeo), 1958.

Note: if X_i is weight of ith consignment

total weight $=\sum_i X_i$

and sum of squares $=\sum_i X_i^2$.

Find whether the difference between the average weight of consignment on B.R. and B.R.S. was significant.

3. Suppose that instead of the problem outlined in Question 1, we have *two* alternative hypotheses. Either Jarrow is one of a class of depressed areas with an average income of £1,100 or it belongs to the class of non-depressed areas with an average income of £1,500. Discuss the use of the data to discriminate between the two hypotheses. (Hint: use the likelihood approach.)

4. A concept if considerable importance in modern statistical inference is the 'power' of a test. If we fix the probability of *rejecting a true hypothesis* at 5 per cent – as usual – then we wish also to reduce the probability of *accepting a false hypothesis*. Consider the probability of accepting a false hypothesis in terms of the example in Question 3 above.

5. It was alleged by one investigation that 'the probability of the hypothesis lying in the confidence interval was 0·95'. Comment on this interpretation: does it imply that there is a probability associated with the hypothesis?

6. Contrast the use of Bayesian prior probabilities with the concept of likelihood and likelihood ratios.

7. Indicate *how* you would apply Bayesian methods to the two hypotheses, using the prior probabilities of $\frac{1}{2}$ and $\frac{1}{2}$ for each of the hypotheses in the example of Question 3 above. (Those who can fit a normal distribution to the data may actually calculate the two posterior probabilities as a consequence of the data collected in Question 1.)

8. One of the great advantages alleged for the likelihood approach is that the inference statements are independent of the 'stopping rule'. That is to say, if we toss a coin a specified number of times and observe the number of heads we shall make the same likelihood statements as if we had simply tossed the coin until we had got a specified number of heads, then stopped. This seems intuitively implausible (to many statisticians also!), but the reader should explore the literature and write an account of this property.

See Barnard, Jenkins and Winsten, 'Likelihood inference and time series', *Journal of Royal Statistical Society* (1962), *A, 125*, 321–72.

9. A Bayesian to a non-Bayesian:
   'You fix as many prior conditions as I do – but you just don't admit it.' Comment.

10. My prior probability (or degree of belief) in the hypothesis that the British Government will devalue the pound in 19— is 0·1 against a probability that they will not devalue of 0·9.

   If the government does intend to devalue, the government would most likely (i.e. with probability of 0·8) say every week that it did *not* intend to devalue. On the other hand, if it actually does not intend to devalue, it would say it did not intend to devalue, weekly, with a probability of 0·3. Suppose that the government spokesmen start reiterating that they intend 'to maintain the integrity of the pound'. Find my posterior probability that they will devalue.

11. A population consists of the four numbers 1, 3, 5, 7. Consider all possible samples of two, drawn with replacement, from this population. Find: (i) the mean of the population; (ii) the variance of the population.

   Carry out an experiment by selecting dominoes with the appropriate numbers, put them in a bag, and select two each time. Record the numbers selected in each sample of two. Select 64 such samples and record the means of the samples and the variance of each sample.

   Plot the sampling distribution of the mean. Find the average of your experimental sampling distribution, and compare the distribution and the mean with your expectation.

12. (Continuation) Plot the sampling distribution of the variances of samples where the variance is calculated as

$$\frac{1}{2}\left[\left(X_1 - \frac{X_1 + X_2}{2}\right)^2 + \left(X_2 - \frac{X_1 + X_2}{2}\right)^2\right]$$

and find the mean of this distribution. Plot the sampling distribution of the variances of the samples when the population mean ($\bar{\xi}$) is known, i.e. the variance is

$$\tfrac{1}{2}[(X_1 - \bar{\xi})^2 + (X_2 - \xi)^2].$$

Discuss your results. (Note that small-sampling theory cannot be applied to this population since it is clearly not normally distributed.)

13. From the following data find whether there is any difference between grocery takings per employee in Northern and Southern States

Annual $000 takings per employee

North	South
95	71
103	50
84	45
60	

Describe carefully the assumptions and implications of your argument.

14. (i) Show that the t distribution is merely a special case of the 'F' distribution. (Hint: consider t^2.)

(ii) Suppose that we have three samples and we wish to test the hypothesis that they all come from the same population. Discuss the alternatives of t tests of pairwise comparisons or an F test.

15. Discuss how one would use the t distribution to describe a confidence interval for the estimate of the mean of the annual cost of education at private universities in the United States in 1967. (Note: cost includes tuition, fees, room and board, books, etc.)

University A	$2,820
B	2,740
C	2,310
D	2,100
E	2,000

16. A sample of 8 towns in the United Kingdom shows the following results:

Annual Highway Expenditure per capita (£)
Towns in England and Wales

| 4·1 | 3·5 | 4·9 | 6·0 | 3·1 |

Towns in Scotland

| 2·5 | 2·1 | 3·0 |

(i) Consider the proposition that the average expenditure of towns in Scotland is the same as the average of Great Britain as a whole. Would it be proper to test the average of Scottish towns against the average of the eight towns? Carry out appropriate tests.

(ii) From the definition of towns it is known that there are 120 in England and Wales and 35 in Scotland. How does this information affect your analysis? (A description, not an exact analysis, is all that is required.)

17. The following data represent the number of units of production a day turned out by 4 workmen using 4 different types of machines. Test to see whether the mean productivity is the same for the 4 different machine types.

Workman	Machine type			
	A	B	C	D
1	24	18	27	16
2	26	20	32	23
3	14	16	22	12
4	13	18	26	13

Would you suspect that the workmen differed also in their performance? Discuss how you would test this conjecture. [Hint: one may find the mechanics of this test in any statistical textbook, e.g. M. J. Moroney, *Facts from Figures* (1964)].

(Decision Theory)

18. Let there be a firm that has a policy of either investing to cash in on a suspected 'good' market or not investing for a suspected 'bad' market. The firm can carry out a market survey, that costs money, and has the following pay-off matrix (in £00,000) where we use S for survey $\bar{S}$ for no survey, I for invest and $\bar{I}$ for not invest.

Policy	Market	
	Good	Bad
$S\bar{I}$	1	5
$S I$	8	1
$\bar{S} I$	9	2
$\bar{S}\bar{I}$	2	6

The prior probabilities of a good and bad market are respectively 0·3 and 0·7.

The conditional probabilities of the survey results are

if market is good, then the probability that the survey will indicate that it is good is 0·9

and, probability that survey will indicate it is bad is 0·1;

if market is bad, then the probability that the survey will indicate that it is bad is 0·8

and, probability that survey will indicate it is good are 0·2

Find the optimum decision.

(Note that the pay-off is a *profit* not a cost.)

Part Two

Regression and Correlation

In Part II the main tool of econometrics is introduced and developed. Most of economics is concerned with predictions of the effect of one variable on another. Regression and correlation are the techniques used to analyse the association when the effect is linear. The key chapter in this Part is Chapter 4. This serves as a corner-stone around which most of the remainder of the book is constructed. A mastery of – or at least an intimate acquaintance with – the elementary two-variable regression model is the essential precursor of all work in econometrics. Again, however, the purpose of Chapter 4 is to interpret the concepts of regression and correlation; it is not a course in techniques and calculation. The aim is to see how regression 'works' – and to uncover at least some of the main occasions when it does not 'work'. Chapter 5 merely develops the simple two-variable case into a three-variable and the many-variable case. Chapter 5 involves very few basically new ideas (compared with Chapter 4) but, unfortunately, it includes much algebra. Nevertheless, since much practical work in econometrics involves at least partial or multiple regression a thorough understanding of the main principles is desirable. Chapter 6 discusses the sampling properties of regression and correlation models and it is not absolutely necessary to read it for one to follow the remainder of this book.

4 Relations between Variables

Regression and Theoretical Relationships

Much of scientific knowledge may be formulated as a relationship between two or more measurements. The search for broad regularities in variables is one of the main streams of both physical and social science. The methods by which one discovers and charts these relationships are the main tools of econometrics. This chapter will consider them in some detail.

Consider the age-old problem of neo-classical economics – the shape and slope of the demand curve. The theory of consumer demand is concerned with predicting the reaction of an individual consumer (or family) to a change in the market price. We assume that 'tastes' are constant, that his real income does not change, and that the commodity constitutes such a small fraction of his total budget that variations in the price of the commodity do not make him noticeably better or worse off. Further assumptions require that the consumer behave in a 'consistent' manner, the definition of which varies with the degree of sophistication of the theory. But, elaborations aside, the *law of demand* emerges more or less clearly from the theory that

if the price of a commodity is reduced the quantity bought will increase.

This law, deduced for the individual, is easily carried over into the market. To get the market demand curve we simply add the quantities purchased by individuals at a given price. And since on a reduction of price the law forecasts that each individual will increase the quantity bought, it follows that there will be an expansion of aggregate purchases. The law then applies both to the individual and to the market.

Let us suppose that the commodity is supplied by a monopolist. He fixes his price and observes the reaction of the market to this price. Now it is conceivable that the monopolist wishes to learn about the character of demand because he wishes to choose the price which gives him the largest return. Suppose then that the monopolist carried out *experiments.* He fixes the price at different levels each month and observes the quantity sold at that price. These observations then should trace out the demand curve for the product and should give the downward slope which the theory predicts.

But even in this experimental environment we know that the observations will not *exactly* conform to the theory. 'Tastes' may have changed from one period to another and prices of unsuspected substitutes and complements may vary and incomes may have increased. All these assumptions of the theory may be violated by the experiment. So the observed outcome contains at least two ingredients: the theoretical prediction and the experimental 'errors', including errors of measurement. But no one (in economics at least) pretends that if there were no experimental errors data would always exactly conform to theory. Even in perfect experimental conditions the theory may give only an imperfect prediction of the data. Thus there is also a third ingredient in an experimental result, i.e. the error due to the theory itself being only an approximate description of reality. This error is then in the theory as such but it will appear also in the experimental result.

The errors in an experiment are so important that they always must be treated with great respect. The usefulness of the theory turns largely on the hope that in applications the errors will be small relative to the systematic explanatory power of the theory. Indeed the experimental method must involve a specification not merely of the theory – the systematic relationship between the variables – but also the 'errors'.

Consider the hypothetical example of the monopolist 'discovering' his demand curve. Let us suppose that the theory predicts that the relationship between price and quantity is *linear* with a negative slope.†
We may characterise the *theory* or the theoretical regression line as

$$Y = \alpha + \beta_{yx}X \quad \text{for some specified range of } X, \quad \text{where } \alpha > 0, \beta_{yx} < 0, \quad (4.1)$$

where Y is the quantity purchased, X is the price, and α and β_{yx} are constants. The order of the subscripts of the β_{yx} indicates that Y is the dependent variable and X is the independent variable, i.e. given X, we predict Y. We are going to suppose that the theory specifies that a

† Note that we are making the theory of demand much sharper than usual. In econometrics it is usually necessary or desirable to take much more restricted hypotheses than those implied by pure theory.

linear relation exists, but apart from predicting that the slope is negative, it does not tell us the *numerical* value of the slope or exactly where the line is located. The hypothesis is merely that a negative linear relation exists; it is the job of the experiment (i) to discover whether data do conform to this hypothesis, and (ii), more ambitiously, to estimate the location and slope of the demand line. A geometrical

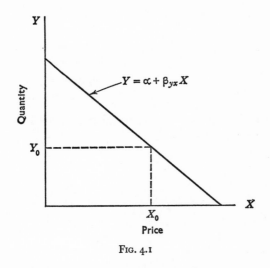

FIG. 4.1

representation of the theory is shown in Figure 4.1. The demand relationship is interpreted as

given price X_0 then the quantity sold will be Y_0.

It is a prediction of the quantity, on the vertical axis, from a knowledge of price, on the horizontal axis. Quantity is the dependent variable which is predicted from a knowledge of the independent variable price. (The reader will observe that we have interchanged the axes from the normal presentation of demand curves in Anglo-Saxon textbooks. No change of substance is here involved and this presentation fits in better with accepted conventions in science and statistics.)

Only in a perfect experiment with a perfect theory would all the observed results lie on the line. In the real world the best we can expect is that the observed prices and quantities will lie close to the line. We might plot the quantities bought on the market as it responds to various prices fixed by the monopolist. Let us suppose that the following quantities are observed:

Month	Price (cents)	Quantity
I	20	1,200,000
2	21	1,000,000
3	22	900,000
4	23	800,000
5	24	600,000
6	22	1,000,000
7	23	900,000
8	24	700,000

These data can be plotted on the usual two-variable graph – the so-called *scatter diagram* – as follows:

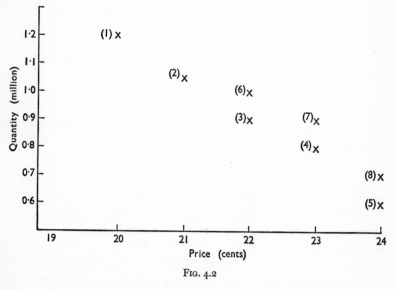

Fig. 4.2

Now these observations do not neatly lie on a line. Errors have crept into the results and the problem is to peer through the veil of error to see if we can discern the underlying linear relationship of the theory, and, if possible, to locate the line.

Looking at our example it is clear that there is some negative relationship between the variables. But it is also certain that the errors in the theory and experiment are not negligible. The observations are not displayed along a line; they are scattered in a cigar-shape oriented in the NW-SE direction. The slimmer the cigar the greater the power of the theory and the smaller the errors. If, however, the cigar is very loosely packed and very fat, errors are important relative to the predictive value of the theory. The situation is illustrated in the following diagrams: (a) shows data which fit closely to the theory, whereas

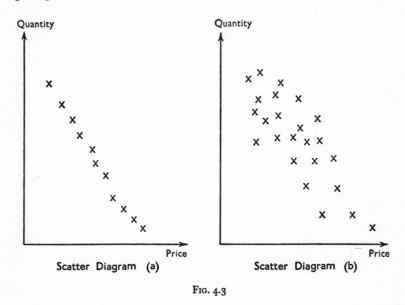

Scatter Diagram (a)   Scatter Diagram (b)

FIG. 4.3

(b) shows the case where the errors are very important and the theory has little predictive power.

To examine the data one must clearly recast the simple linear theory so that it specifically includes the 'errors'. In other words the theory must be recast in a statistical form so that it can properly describe the data. Let us write X_i and Y_i for the price and quantity in the ith month. Now it is clear that we cannot simply substitute X_i and Y_i in equation (4.1) since Y_i is affected by the errors. Let us therefore write ε_i for the 'error' in Y_i, i.e. the 'error' in the model is reflected in the dependent variable during the ith month. Formally we specify

$$Y_i = \alpha + \beta_{yx} X_i + \varepsilon_i. \tag{4.2}$$

The 'error' is simply added in. This is represented diagramatically as follows:

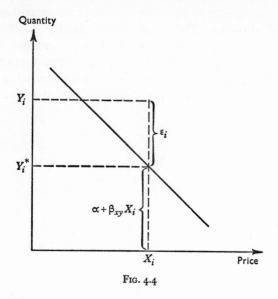

FIG. 4.4

Given the value X_i (price) we observe in month i the quantity (Y_i). This quantity may be decomposed into two elements. First there is the value of Y predicted by the theory; this is simply the quantity of Y which is predicted by the linear relation; we can call this quantity Y_i^*. Thus

$$Y_i^* = \alpha + \beta_{yx} X_i$$

and

$$Y_i = Y_i^* + \varepsilon_i$$

or in words:

$$\frac{\text{observed}}{\text{quantity}} = \frac{\text{predicted}}{\text{quantity}} + \frac{\text{'error'}}{\text{(or disturbance)}}.$$

Such is the pervasive importance of the error that it is usually described by the less pejorative label of 'disturbance'. (We reserve the term 'error' to describe the *observed* disturbance.)

The problem now is to find a suitable specification for the disturbance ε. In econometric applications this is used to represent the effect of influences and factors omitted from the theory. In the demand application it is easy to identify some of the causes of divergences from the model; the weather, wars, scares, and changes in taste are only a few of the important reasons for differences between prediction and fact.

The really important question is: what rules do the distributions of the disturbances obey? The normal procedure is to specify that the disturbances behave like *random variables*. To be specific, the disturbance might be described as a normally distributed variable with a zero mean. On each occasion that the monopolist chooses a price X_i we have, in addition to the systematic linear part, a disturbance drawn from a normally distributed population. It can be imagined, diagramatically, that a normal distribution of the disturbance in the direction of the

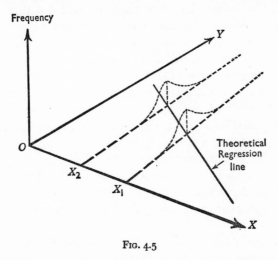

Fig. 4.5

Y axis lies astride the regression line. If we measure the frequency on a third axis, the form of our model can be illustrated as in Figure 4.5.

The formal interpretation of the model is that when the monopolist fixes a price there is only one output which is systematically predicted by the theory, and that is Y^*. But this value is simply the mean of the probability distribution of actual realised Y's for a given price. We can interpret this experimentally. The monopolist fixes a price of 22 cents month after month after month. On each occasion he records the quantity sold. The theory states that the mean quantity sold will be given by the law,

$$\text{mean quantity} = Y^* = \alpha + \beta_{yx}(22).$$

Let us take the *true theoretical* values of α and β_{yx} as 30 and -0.5 respectively. Then

$$Y^* = 20 - 0.5(22) = 9.$$

Thus with a price of 22 cents the mean quantity sold is 9. For any given month, however, the number sold may exceed, or may be less than, this figure due to the disturbance ε_i. The actual sales are found by adding to the mean value a number ε drawn from a normal probability distribution. On each month that 22 cents is charged, the only thing that varies is the drawing from the normal probability distribution. It is as though each month we added to the 9 million a number which we drew at random from a hat into which we had put slips representing the relative frequencies of numbers derived from a normal distribution.

We might pause at this point to enquire why we should represent the 'errors and effects omitted from our model' by a random variable. It seems extraordinarily artificial to treat the errors and omissions as though they were generated by some law of chance. These laws were developed to describe the results of repeatable experiments which anyone could do if he had a penny. Ample evidence failed to discredit penny tossing – but this is clearly not the same thing as experimental price fixing by a particular monopolist. The only answer – and an unsatisfactory one – is that this specification of the disturbance term is the best one usually available. It really comprises no more than giving a name to our ignorance and specifying for it a broad quantitative form.

The specification of the disturbance term is often couched in the form of a normally distributed random variable. But it is not essential, though it is often convenient, that it be normally distributed. We really require only that the ε be distributed according to some specified law of chance. Most important of all the rules of the chance distribution must *not* depend on the value of X. Whatever X is chosen the distribution of the ε's must not be affected. In a probability sense the distribution of the ε's must be *independent* of the X's. This critical assumption will be examined in detail in subsequent chapters, but it may be useful to present a rationalisation at this stage. Suppose, *per contra*, that the distribution of the ε's did in fact depend on the X. For example, suppose that as X increased, the value of ε was more probably positive than negative. Then it is clear that the ε contains a component which is systematically connected with the X chosen. This part of ε can be predicted by a knowledge of X and so is no longer part of our ignorance. Hence the rule that the distribution of the ε's musr be independent of the value of X.

Before we proceed to the analysis, it is convenient to introduce a simplification. Since there are two constants to be measured, β_{yx} and α, it is best to proceed one-at-a-time; and so we first measure β_{yx} and then α. So we are faced with the problem of (temporarily) getting rid of α from the equation. The value of α locates the position of the line – by pushing it up or down the y-axis. It is intuitively sensible to define the position of the line such that it passes through the *arithmetic means* of the *sample* of *observations* of Y and X – and we shall see later how this is to be done in practice. If now we 'move-over' the axes of X and Y such that they go through the means of X and Y, then the two axes and the line will meet at the means. Thus if we take the measures

$$\varepsilon_i' = \varepsilon_i - \bar{\varepsilon}, \quad \text{where} \quad \bar{\varepsilon} = (1/n)\sum_i \varepsilon_i$$

$$x_i = X_i - \bar{X}, \quad \text{where} \quad \bar{X} = (1/n)\sum_i X_i$$

and $$y_i = Y_i - \bar{Y}, \quad \text{where} \quad \bar{Y} = (1/n)\sum_i Y_i,$$

using the letters x_i, y_i and ε_i' to indicate *deviations from means*, the value of the intercept may be taken to be zero – since the line then goes through the (new) origin. Thus we concentrate first on finding the slope β_{yx} in the equation

$$y_i = \beta_{yx}x_i + \varepsilon_i'$$

and only later on do we face the problem of estimating α.

Least Squares

With this specification of our model we can now proceed to find methods of estimating the value of β_{yx} (and later on α) from a sample of observations. It is *assumed* that the variables follow the pattern of the model (but note that for notational simplicity we write ε_i as the *deviation from the sample mean* instead of ε_i')

$$y_i = \beta_{yx}x_i + \varepsilon_i \qquad (4.3)$$

and that our only problem is to get an estimate of the value of β from a sample of observations of x_i (price) and y_i (quantity). Furthermore, we are assuming that x_i and y_i are accurately observed and measured without error. From our sample of x_i and y_i we must adduce what is the best estimate of β_{yx}.

There is a wide variety of methods of fitting a line to data of this kind. The simplest technique is often to draw a line which, in the eye of the beholder, best represents the linear relation underlying the data. Though much maligned, the simple fit-by-eye method is often good enough for many purposes. The main trouble is that it is not objective – there are many beholders and so many lines are possible. Nor is it clear that one exploits to the full extent the underlying properties of the model. Another method is simply to connect the points of the highest and lowest x_i, or perhaps the highest and lowest y_i. This might be quite a sensible procedure but in addition to the fact that it does not explicitly use the structure of the model, it seems on *a priori* grounds to be wasteful to ignore all the observations between the two extremes.

The method which most commends itself to statisticians is 'regression by least squares'. Consider the equation

$$y_i = \beta_{yx} x_i + \varepsilon_i$$

for which we have n independent observations

$$x_1, x_2, ..., x_n$$

and
$$y_1, y_2, ..., y_n,$$

and where the sample means of x, y and ε are zero. Now multiply the equation throughout by x_i, so we have

$$y_i x_i = \beta_{yx} x_i^2 + \varepsilon_i x_i \quad (i = 1, 2, ..., n). \tag{4.4}$$

This gives us then n equations $(i = 1, 2, ..., n)$ of the form (4.4). We now form an aggregate equation by summing equation 4.4 over the n observations, so obtaining

$$\sum_{i=1}^{n} y_i x_i = \beta_{yx} \sum_{i=1}^{n} x_i^2 + \sum_{i=1}^{n} \varepsilon_i x_i. \tag{4.5}$$

The quantity $\sum y_i x_i$ is the *cross-product* of x and y. When divided by the number of observations (n) it is called the *covariance*, i.e. covariance $(x, y) = (1/n) \sum y_i x_i$. The covariance is analogous to the variance; instead of squaring the variable we multiply it by another.

In Equation 4.5 we can calculate the value of the cross-product of x and y on the left-hand side, since we know all the x's and y's. On the right-hand side we can easily calculate the sum of the squares of x_i, i.e. $\sum x_i^2$ (but, of course, we do not know β – we seek an estimate of that). The second term on the right-hand side cannot be computed since we do not know the values of ε_i. But can we deduce anything about the size of this term relative to the other component of the right-hand side $\sum x_i^2$? Clearly $\sum x_i^2$ is a sum of squares and, it will normally be strictly positive.† On the other hand, the cross-product $\sum \varepsilon_i x_i$ will not necessarily be positive. Since we have postulated that the ε_i is distributed independently of the value of x we can regard the x's as fixed weights in the summation; the ε's only vary according to the laws of chance. For any given x_i the mean of the probability distribution of the ε's is zero. Thus the sum $\sum x_i \varepsilon_i$ can be regarded as a weighted sum of random variables which have zero means. Just as with ordinary sampling theory the most probable value of this sum is zero; but in practice one expects that if the experiment is repeated a large number of times, the values will be distributed evenly – sometimes positive, sometimes negative, about a zero mean.

Thus it seems that $\sum \varepsilon_i x_i$ is likely to be small relative to $\sum x_i^2$ and the covariance of ε and x is likely to become smaller and smaller relative to the variance of x as the sample size (n) is increased.

Consider the equation (4.5) in the form

$$\frac{\sum y_i x_i}{\sum x_i^2} = \beta_{yx} + \frac{\sum \varepsilon_i x_i}{\sum x_i^2} \qquad (4.6)$$

by dividing throughout by $\sum x_i^2$. Then the last term is going to be relatively small. This then suggests that one ignores the last term and uses as an estimate of β_{yx}

$$\frac{\sum y_i x_i}{\sum x_i^2} = \hat{\beta}_{yx}, \qquad (4.7)$$

where the hat on the beta denotes that this is an *estimate* from the data. The difference between the estimate and the true value is then

$$\hat{\beta}_{yx} - \beta_{yx} = \frac{\sum_i \varepsilon_i x_i}{\sum_i x_i^2}. \qquad (4.8)$$

† There is an odd uninteresting case when $\sum x_i^2 = 0$, which is when $x_1 = x_2 = \dots = x_n = 0$. (If the monopolist does not change his price then nothing can be adduced about the law of demand!) Normally $\sum x_i^2$ approaches infinity as we increase the number of observations included in the sum.

Now we saw that in sampling a mean, as we increased the size of the sample, the chances of a given deviation between the sample mean and the true mean become smaller and smaller. The sample means tend to cluster closer and closer around the true value. In the same way, as the sample size increases the value of $\sum_i \varepsilon_i x_i / \sum_i x_i^2$ tends to concentrate nearer and nearer to a value of zero. Thus the estimates $\hat{\beta}_{yx}$ group themselves closer and closer to β_{yx} as the sample size grows. Thus it follows that, provided ε is distributed independently of x, the estimate $\hat{\beta}_{yx}$ will be a *consistent* estimator of β_{yx}. Roughly speaking as the sample size increases the estimated value $\hat{\beta}$ tends to get closer and closer to the true value β.

One can also show that this estimator $\hat{\beta}_{yx}$ has other very desirable properties. It is *efficient* in the sense that the variation of the $\hat{\beta}_{yx}$ about the true value is less than for any alternative estimator. It is also *unbiased* in the sense that, for a *given size of sample*, the average value of the sampling distribution of the $\hat{\beta}_{yx}$'s is the true value β_{yx}. Indeed one can show that, if the ε's are normally distributed, the estimator $\hat{\beta}_{yx}$ extracts as much information as possible from the sample about the true value of β_{yx}.

Many other interpretations are possible of the estimator $\hat{\beta}_{yx}$ in this model. Probably the simplest approach is to regard it as a weighted average of the dependent variable y. The weight of y_i is then

$$\frac{x_i}{\sum x_i^2}$$

so that

$$\hat{\beta}_{yx} = \sum_i \left\{ \left(\frac{x_i}{\sum\limits_i x_i^2} \right) \cdot y_i \right\}.$$

Thus $\hat{\beta}_{yx}$ is a *linear* combination of y's with fixed weights.

Another interpretation – probably the most popular – is that it is a 'least-squares' fit to the observations. Consider the ith observation in Figure 4.6 in the theoretical model outlined above; we continue to assume that there is no constant so that the linear relation goes through the origin at $x = 0$, $y = 0$. Suppose that the *theoretical* linear relation or true line

$$y_i^* = \beta_{yx} x_i$$

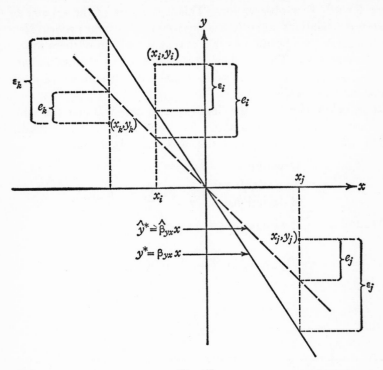

FIG. 4.6

is the solid line in the figure. The distance, in the direction of the y, axis, of point (y_i, x_i) from this true line is ε_i. Now we do not know the slope of the true line. We seek, however, a method of estimating a line like the broken line in the diagram which best fits the points (x_i, y_i), (x_j, y_j), etc. The method of least squares fits that line by finding the slope $\hat{\beta}_{yx}$ which makes the sum of the squares of the observed deviations from the line (in the y direction) as small as possible.

This opaque definition of least squares can be clarified by examining the figure. Imagine that many observations of (x, y) appear in the problem but we have plotted only three (x_i, y_i), (x_j, y_j) and (x_k, y_k) on the diagram. We can rotate the dotted line about a fulcrum at o until a suitable fit is obtained. We rotate it and examine the deviations (in the y direction) of the points from the line. The deviation of (x_i, y_i) from the line is clearly e_i and the deviation of (x_j, y_j) is e_j, etc. Take the squares of the deviations e_i^2, e_j^2, e_k^2 and form the sum $e_i^2 + e_j^2 + e_k^2 +$ the same for all other observations. This is the sum of the squares of the observed deviations *when the line is fixed in a particular position.* Now we simply choose the position so that it makes the sum of these squares as small as possible. This is, then, the 'least-squares regression line of y on x'. [Note that we always say regression of (dependent variable) on (independent variable).]

It is not obvious that the 'least-squares' line will give the same coefficient as that calculated above by much more direct methods. But a little mathematics will prove that it is precisely the same.

$$\text{Deviation} = y_i - \hat{\beta}_{yx} x_i = e_i.$$

$$\text{Sum of squares of deviations} = \sum_{i=1}^{n} e_i^2 = \sum_i (y_i - \hat{\beta}_{xy} x_i)^2.$$

Minimising $\sum_i e_i^2$ with respect to $\hat{\beta}$ gives

$$\frac{\partial}{\partial \hat{\beta}} \left[\sum (y_i - \hat{\beta}_{yx} x_i)^2 \right] = 2 \sum x_i (y_i - \hat{\beta}_{yx} x_i) = 0,$$

i.e. $\quad \sum x_i y_i - \hat{\beta}_{yx} \sum x_i^2 = 0.$

So that

$$\hat{\beta}_{yx} = \frac{\sum x_i y_i}{\sum x_i^2},$$

which is the same as our previous result. The connection between the two approaches needs to be explored a little more. But before doing so it is advisable to give a name to the observed deviation e_i. These are the observed or experimental counterparts to the theoretical disturbance ε_i. The e_i's are normally called the 'residuals'. But sometimes they are given other names: 'error' is frequently used to describe the observed counterparts of the disturbance, and occasionally they are given the full name 'observed deviations from the regression line in the y direction'. We shall use all these terms throughout this book – although we shall normally call them either 'errors' or 'residuals'. The residuals differ from their theoretical counterparts, the disturbances, because the estimated line differs from the theoretical (or true) linear relation.

Why do the two methods give the same result? Clearly it must be because they use the same basic postulate. In minimising the sum of the squares of residuals we obtained the equation

$$\sum_i x_i (y_i - \hat{\beta}_{yx} x_i) = 0,$$

which, since $e_i = y_i - \hat{\beta}_{yx}x_i$, can be written as

$$\sum_i x_i e_i = 0.$$

And from the direct approach we can write

$$y_i = \hat{\beta}_{yx}x_i + e_i$$

$$\sum x_i y_i = \hat{\beta}_{yx}\sum x_i^2 + \sum_i x_i e_i$$

by multiplying both sides by x_i and adding over the number of observations in the sample. But we took the equation

$$\sum x_i y_i = \hat{\beta}_{yx}\sum x_i^2$$

to estimate $\hat{\beta}_{yx}$ – and this implies that $\sum_i x_i e_i$ is zero. In other words we *choose* a line that will make $\sum_i x_i e_i$ zero. And this is also a consequence of minimising the sum of squares of residuals.

Intuitively it seems a sensible thing to do to make $\sum_i x_i e_i = 0$ because the fundamental postulate of our approach was that the *disturbance* was independent of x, i.e. a knowledge of x did not help in predicting what ε would emerge from the hat. By writing $\sum_i x_i e_i = 0$ we have said that, as far as our *sample* is concerned, knowing x_i will give one no information on the value of e_i. In fact we assume that the covariance *in the sample observations* of e and x is zero. And this corresponds to the assumption that the value of the covariance of ε and x tends probabilistically to approach zero as the sample size becomes very very large. In any particular sample the value of $(1/n)\sum_i x_i \varepsilon_i$ will usually differ from zero and so the assumption that $\sum_i x_i e_i = 0$ will give rise to sampling errors and a $\hat{\beta}_{yx}$ different from the true value β_{yx}.

Variance of Residuals and Correlation Coefficient

The residual is obviously of key importance in the regression method. The larger the residual, *ceteris paribus*, the smaller the fraction of the variance of y explained by the regression. The obvious measure of the size of the residual variation is the variance of the residuals

$$\text{residual variance} = \frac{\sum e_i^2}{n}.$$

This is really an *estimate* of the variance of the disturbances. It in fact measures the variation of observations *about* the *estimated* regression line. The variance can be expressed as

$$\frac{\sum e_i^2}{n} = \frac{\sum (y_i - \hat{\beta}_{yx} x_i)^2}{n}$$

$$= \frac{\sum y_i (y_i - \hat{\beta}_{yx} x_i) - \hat{\beta}_{yx} \sum x_i (y_i - \hat{\beta}_{yx} x_i)}{n}.$$

But the last term on the right-hand side is zero since it is simply the covariance of x_i and e_i.

$$\text{residual variance} = \frac{1}{n} \left[\sum y_i^2 - \hat{\beta}_{yx} \sum y_i x_i \right].$$

Substituting for $\hat{\beta}_{yx} = \dfrac{\sum y_i x_i}{\sum x_i^2}$:

$$\frac{\sum e_i^2}{n} = \frac{1}{n} \left[\sum y_i^2 - \left(\frac{\sum y_i x_i}{\sum x_i^2} \right) \sum y_i x_i \right]$$

$$= \frac{1}{n} \left[\sum y^2 - \frac{(\sum yx)^2}{\sum x^2} \right],$$

which might also be put in the rather more useful form

$$\text{residual variance} = \frac{\sum y^2}{n} \left[1 - \frac{(\sum yx)^2}{(\sum x^2)(\sum y^2)} \right]$$

$$= \left(\begin{array}{c} \text{variance of } y \\ \text{in sample} \end{array} \right) \left[1 - \frac{(\sum yx)^2}{(\sum x^2)(\sum y^2)} \right].$$

Now it can be seen that this formula tells us the relationship between the variance of y and the residual variance about the regression line. In fact the total variance of y can be decomposed into two parts (and one must observe that this variance is that of the n sample observations of y, and is *not* the population variance of y; so it should be called s_y^2):

$$\begin{array}{ccc} \text{variance} & = & \text{variance due} \\ \text{of } y & & \text{to regression} \end{array} + \begin{array}{c} \text{residual} \\ \text{variance} \end{array}$$

or:
$$s_y^2 = r^2 + [1 - r^2],$$

where $r^2 = \dfrac{(\sum yx)^2}{(\sum x^2)(\sum y^2)}$.

The value r^2 tells us the fraction of the variance of y which is explained by the regression. The remaining fraction $(1 - r^2)$ of the variance of y is the residual variance about the regression line.† In other words r^2 indicates the 'goodness of fit' of the regression line to the observations. The higher the value of r^2 the closer the observations cluster along the regression line and the smaller the variation of points about the line. It measures the slimness of the cigar which encloses the observations around the regression line.

The value r^2 indicates the power of the theory in using x to predict y. The value r is called the *correlation coefficient*:

$$r = \dfrac{\sum\limits_i x_i y_i}{+ [\sqrt{(\sum x_i^2)(\sum y_i^2)}]} \qquad \text{(where we always take the positive root)}.$$

It is a pure number since the numerator is in terms of units of x multiplied by units of y, and the denominator is in terms of similar units. Another interpretation of r is that it is the slope of the regression line of y on x when we measure x and y in units of their respective standard deviations. This sounds a complicated operation, but in fact all one needs to do is to rearrange the equation $y_i = \hat{\beta}_{yx} x_i + e_i$ so that the y_i is divided by s_y and the x_i divided by s_x, where $s_y^2 = (\sum y^2)/n$ and $s_x^2 = (\sum x^2)/n$ Thus, on inserting the estimate $\hat{\beta}_{yx}$,

$$y_i = \left(\dfrac{\sum x_i y_i}{n s_x^2}\right) x_i + e_i,$$

dividing throughout by s_y,

$$\left(\dfrac{y_i}{s_y}\right) = \left(\dfrac{\sum x_i y_i}{n s_y s_y}\right)\left(\dfrac{x_i}{s_x}\right) + \left(\dfrac{e_i}{s_y}\right)$$

$$\left(\dfrac{y_i}{s_y}\right) = r\left(\dfrac{x_i}{s_x}\right) + \left(\dfrac{e_i}{s_y}\right).$$

† We shall show later that $r^2 \leqslant 1$.

The variables are expressed in units of their standard deviations (sometimes called 'standardised variables'). Thus we may interpret r as the regression of y on x when the variables are divided by their standard deviations.

To display the properties let us examine the case of perfect regression where there is no residual variation, i.e. where the regression is perfect.

$$y_i = \beta_{yx} x_i \quad \text{and} \quad \varepsilon_1 = \varepsilon_2 = \ldots = \varepsilon_n = 0.$$

Substituting in r:

$$r = \frac{\beta_{yx} \sum x^2}{+\sqrt{[\beta_{yx}^2 (\sum x^2)(\sum x^2)]}} = \frac{\beta_{yx}}{|\beta_{yx}|}.$$

Thus if $\beta_{yx} > 0$, $r = +1$; if $\beta_{yx} < 0$, $r = -1$, which are the cases of perfect positive correlation and perfect negative correlation respectively. With $r = +1$ the line is in the NE-SW direction, and when $r = -1$ the line is in the NW-SE direction (the same direction as the demand curve discussed above). Of course all coefficients in practice lie between these two extremes – but the sign continues to indicate the direction of the slope of the cigar enclosing the observations. (And a precise estimate of the slope of the regression y on x is given by $\hat{\beta}_{yx}$.) The value r^2 indicates the tightness of pack of the cigar. When $r^2 = 0$ it suggests that knowledge of x_i is no use at all in (linearly) predicting y_i. The observations are scattered without any obvious *linear* pattern. This may result if they are scattered at random, 'all over the place' – so there is just a blur of observations all over the scatter diagram. On the other hand it may result if there is a well-defined pattern in the observations – but such a pattern cannot neatly be expressed in a single linear relation.

Non-Linearities

In Figure 4.7 the 16 observations fit neatly into 4 groups. If we calculate $\sum x_i y_i$ we find that it is zero – so there is zero correlation. Another example is illustrated in Figure 4.8, which shows that the y and x have a distinct parabolic pattern. Absence of correlation, therefore, does not mean that there is no relationship between the variables; it merely shows that there is no *linear* relation. With both the above examples $r = 0$, $\hat{\beta}_{yx} = 0$, because the cross-product $\sum x_i y_i = 0$. Thus

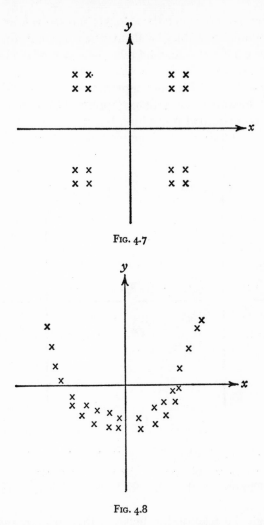

FIG. 4.7

FIG. 4.8

both regression and correlation coefficients suffer from the same defect that they cannot take into account that part of the relationship which is not linear.†

The lesson to be learned from this discussion is that one should *always* plot the data on a scatter diagram to see whether there is a linear or near-linear relation revealed by the scatter. One meets many

† Again the exceptions are in the very odd curve where *x* or *y* does not vary.

non-linear forms in economic data. Partly this stems from the fact that the chief economic variables, such as price and output, cannot take negative values. Thus the demand relation may take the form shown in Figure 4.9 where all observations (P, Q) are never less than zero but $p = (P - \bar{P})$, $q = (Q - \bar{Q})$. We may approximate this by taking a segment such as p_l to p_u and using a linear approximation over that range. This is often quite a good procedure, but it is obviously of little use for forecasting outside this range. A better procedure may be to transform to logarithms.

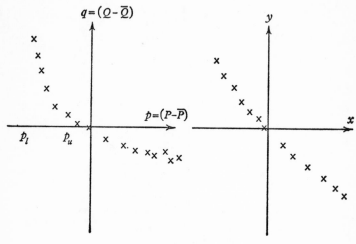

FIG. 4.9

Thus the values $X = \log_e P$ and $Y = \log_e Q$ may be approximately linearly related (and, of course, they can take negative values). We shall see in Chapter 5 that this formulation has a number of other advantages.

Even though the relationship between the variables may appear to be roughly linear, a plot of the observations may reveal unsuspected regularities in the residuals. One quite common result in these series of observations is that cyclicalities or 'ratchet effects' appear. In Figure 4.10 observations are shown numbered in time from 1 to 14. Clearly as x increases y increases and over the whole period the movement is roughly linear. But a plot of the observations reveals clear cyclical loops around the line. This could be checked by plotting the residuals against x_i. There would, of course, be no correlation between e_i and x_i, but the non linear pattern of the residuals could clearly be observed. Another common effect in econometric applications is a 'sawtooth' pattern of observations. An extreme example of a 'sawtooth' is illustrated

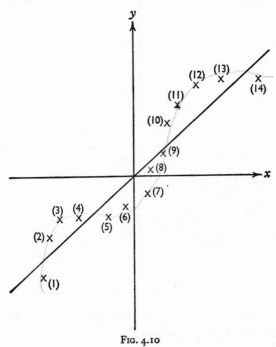

FIG. 4.10

in Figure 4.11. Again the general trend is positively linear, but it is clear that, as x increases from one period to another, y actually *decreases*. When x decreases, however, y *increases*. Although the general trend of the figures is positive – a high y will be associated with a high x, on the average – it is clear that an *increase* in x from one year to another will be associated with a *decrease* in y. The *changes* from one year to another will be *negatively* correlated. Another interesting case is the 'ratchet effect', where, although there is an overall positive relationship between x and y, if x increases from one year to another, the value of y actually *increases* but by a much larger amount than that predicted by the general trends. But if x is lower than the value in the previous year, then y *still increases*, but by a smaller amount than that predicted by the trends. (The reader should draw a figure to illustrate this effect; it is a phenomenon which is thought to be important in several fields of consumer analysis.) Clearly one must then discover a method of analysing separately the effects of increasing x, from year to year, from

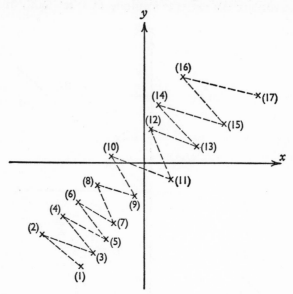

FIG. 4.11. The years are labelled (1), (2), (3) etc.

those of decreasing x. Thus much richer and more complex patterns of behaviour can usually be uncovered.

Estimating α

We shall return to transformations and diagrams periodically throughout the remaining chapters of this book. But we must now return to complete this account of simple regression and correlation. The first point to be cleared up is the estimation of the constant α. We assumed for most of the discussion that the means of the variables were zero. It would be most unusual if that were so, but the excuse for treating this case in some detail is that *any* observed series of X can be transformed to one with a zero mean by moving the axis so that it coincides with the mean of X. Instead of measuring the variable as a distance from zero we measure it as a deviation from the mean of $\overline{X}$. Thus

$$x_i = X_i - \overline{X}.$$

Similarly
$$y_i = \Upsilon_i - \Upsilon.$$

The original equation was measured as:
$$\Upsilon_i = \hat{\beta}_{yx} X_i + \alpha + e_i.$$

And the transformed equation
$$y_i = \hat{\beta}_{yx} x_i + e_i.$$

Substituting:
$$\Upsilon_i - \Upsilon = \hat{\beta}_{yx}(X_i - \bar{X}) + e_i$$
$$\Upsilon_i = \hat{\beta}_{yx} X_i + (\Upsilon - \hat{\beta}_{yx}\bar{X}) + e_i.$$

So that, since the sample mean of e_i is zero:
$$\hat{\alpha} = \Upsilon - \hat{\beta}_{yx}\bar{X}. \qquad (4.10)$$

This equation gives us a natural method of estimating α.

$\hat{\alpha} =$ sample mean of $\Upsilon - \hat{\beta}_{yx}$ (sample mean of X).

Thus the general procedure is to first calculate $\hat{\beta}_{yx}$ from the covariance of x and y and the variance of x, then one can find an estimate $\hat{\alpha}$ from the above formula.

Calculation of Regression

Example. Suppose that we observe four persons over the period of a month, and we record Υ, their savings, and X, their 'unexpected' consumers' expenditure with the following results:

Person	A	B	C	D
Υ	3	1	-2	-3
X	-1	0	1	2

Find the regression of savings on the 'unexpected' consumer expenditure.

Computing Note. It is always more convenient to compute X^2 and $\sum X^2$ rather than $\sum(X - \bar{X})^2$. So we may write
$$\sum(X - \bar{X})^2 = \sum[X^2 - 2\bar{X}X + {}^2\bar{X}]$$
$$= \sum X^2 - 2\bar{X}\sum X + n\bar{X}^2.$$

But $\bar{X} = \frac{1}{n}\sum X$, so

$$\sum(X - \bar{X})^2 = \sum X^2 - \frac{2}{n}(\sum X)^2 + \frac{1}{n}(\sum X)^2$$

$$\sum(X - \bar{X})^2 = \sum X^2 - \frac{1}{n}(\sum X)^2.$$

Similarly we may show that

$$\sum(X - \bar{X})(Y - \bar{Y}) = \sum XY - \frac{1}{n}(\sum X)(\sum Y).$$

Person	Y	X	YX	X^2	Y^2
A	3	-1	-3	1	9
B	1	0	0	0	1
C	-2	1	-2	1	4
D	-3	2	-5	4	9
Sum	-1	2	-10	6	23

$$\sum(X - \bar{X})^2 = \sum X^2 - \frac{1}{n}(\sum X)^2$$

$$= 6 - \tfrac{1}{4}(2^2) = 5$$

$$\sum(Y - \bar{Y})^2 = \sum Y^2 - \frac{1}{n}(\sum Y)^2$$

$$= 23 - \tfrac{1}{4}(-1)^2 = 22\tfrac{3}{4}$$

$$\sum(X - \bar{X})(Y - \bar{Y}) = \sum XY - \frac{1}{n}(\sum X)(\sum Y)$$

$$= -10 - \tfrac{1}{4}(2)(-1) = -9\tfrac{1}{2}$$

$$\hat{\beta}_{yx} = \frac{\sum(x - \bar{x})(y - \bar{y})}{\sum(x - \bar{x})^2}$$

$$\hat{\beta}_{yx} = (-9\tfrac{1}{2})/5$$

$$\hat{\beta}_{yx} = -1\cdot9$$

$$r_{yx} = \frac{\sum(x - \bar{x})(y - \bar{y})}{\sqrt{[\{\sum(x - \bar{x})^2\}\{\sum y - \bar{y})^2\}]}}$$

$$= \frac{-9\frac{1}{2}}{\sqrt{(5 \times 23\frac{1}{2})}}$$

$$r_{yx} = -0\cdot 88.$$

We can fit the regression equation of Y on X:

$$Y - \bar{Y} = \hat{\beta}_{yx}(X - \bar{X}),$$

i.e.

$$Y - (-\tfrac{1}{4}) = -1\cdot 9(X - \tfrac{2}{4})$$

$$Y + \tfrac{1}{4} = -1\cdot 9(X - \tfrac{1}{2})$$

$$Y = -1\cdot 9X + 0\cdot 7.$$

We now show that the variance of Y, calculated as follows:

$$s_y^2 = \tfrac{1}{4}(22\tfrac{3}{4}) = 5\cdot 69$$

can be split into two parts. First we know that $r^2 \operatorname{var}(Y)$ is explained by the regression of Y on X. Thus $(0\cdot 86)^2 \times 100$ per cent of the variance of Y is explained by the linear regression on X – i.e. about 74 per cent of the variance of Y is explained by X. Thus 26 per cent of the variance of Y is due to the residual variation about the regression line of Y on X.

Regression and Causation

The second and very important point to be cleared up is concerned with the causal interpretation of regression which we have so far adopted. An extension of the example of the monopolistic demand curve will again shed some light on this problem. We supposed that our monopolist was a *price setter*; he first fixed the price and then sold as much as the market was willing to take at the price. Thus we found the regression: *given x* (price) what is the best prediction of *y* (quantity)? Now it is obvious that all monopolists do not proceed in this way. Certain monopolists, such as the diamond monopolists in South Africa, fix the *quantity* to be sold on the market and then permit the price to be fixed by auction or some similar market arrangement. They are price *takers* rather than price givers.

It is intuitively obvious that the regression of y on x which served so well for the price giver will not be suitable for the quantity giver – price taker. The question asked by the latter is exactly the same as we discussed above in the case of the price giver except that the roles of quantity (y) and price (x) are now interchanged. The problem is given y (quantity) what is the best predictor of x (price)? Thus we calculate the regression of x on y, i.e.

$x_i = \beta_{xy} y_i + \varepsilon_i'$ (ε_i' is the disturbance in the x-*direction* measured as a deviation from sample mean).

The regression coefficient is shown here as β_{xy}. The subscripts indicate that it is the regression of x on y – the dependent variable preceding the independent variable. Thus we have *two* regressions one for the price giver and one for the price taker.

The interchanging question which we might ask is whether there is any relationship between the two regressions. Let us suppose that the *same* theoretical relationship is measured. Thus we might express this as

$$y_i = \beta_{yx} x_i + \varepsilon_i, \tag{4.11}$$

or as

$$x_i = \beta_{xy} y_i + \varepsilon_i'. \tag{4.12}$$

But Equation 4.11 may be rearranged as

$$x_i = \frac{1}{\beta_{yx}} y_i + \frac{\varepsilon_i}{\beta_{yx}} \quad \text{if } \beta_{yx} \neq 0. \tag{4.13}$$

And comparing it with Equation 4.12 we see that

$$\beta_{xy} = \frac{1}{\beta_{yx}} \quad \text{and} \quad \varepsilon_i' = \frac{\varepsilon_i}{\beta_{yx}}.$$

Now the question arises whether our *estimates* of β_{yx} and β_{xy} will obey such a law. If $\hat{\beta}_{yx} = 1/\hat{\beta}_{xy}$ then there would only be one estimate of the line and it would not matter whether we measured it as a regression of y on x or x on y.

We can easily see that this property does not in general hold. The requirement

$$\hat{\beta}_{yx} \cdot \hat{\beta}_{xy} = 1$$

implies that

$$\left(\frac{\sum yx}{\sum x^2}\right)\left(\frac{\sum yx}{\sum y^2}\right) = 1$$

$$\frac{(\sum yx)^2}{(\sum x^2)(\sum y^2)} = 1,$$

i.e. $r^2 = 1.$

Thus we get the result that only where there is perfect correlation, either positive or negative, do the two regression lines coincide. And one can see intuitively an implication of this result. The lower the r^2 the wider the lines will be apart. On rearranging the above result we can write

$$\hat{\beta}_{yx} = \frac{r^2}{\hat{\beta}_{xy}}.$$

This tells us that if one wishes to predict y given x but measures the 'wrong' regression of x on y, one can obtain the correct slope by multiplying the reciprocal $1/\hat{\beta}_{xy}$ by r^2.† In other words, if one measures the 'wrong' regression x on y the measured slope will be too steep for making predictions of y from x; it must be reduced by the proportion r^2.

It must be recalled that the above results were developed assuming that the theoretical line was the same whether one was a price giver or a price taker. In fact we supposed that the same numerical data would appear whether the monopolist is price setter or not, This is an extreme assumption which was meant to bring out the characteristics of least-squares regression. It is especially difficult to imagine two experiments, one where the prices are fixed and quantity not, and another where quantity is fixed and the price is free, to give the *same* results. An extended discussion of the difference between the outcomes of experiments of this kind would take us far into economic theory and cannot be pursued here.

But the reader may well wonder what value can be attached to an *experimental* interpretation of regression methods. In econometrics experimental data are rare. In demand analysis one usually has to be content with the quantity determined by the weather, productivity,

† The square of the correlation coefficient is the product of the two regression slopes, i.e.

$$\hat{\beta}_{yx}\hat{\beta}_{xy} = r^2.$$

movements of international prices, etc., rather than fixed by some interested research worker. Occasionally one may find circumstances where the price is fixed – such as by the government or some marketing agency – but these situations often have attendant difficulties such as rationing, etc. The real question is, then, can we usefully interpret regressions although the independent variable is not fixed exogenously? Can we continue to interpret the sample as though it is simply one realisation of a process whereby the x's are fixed at the same values from one experiment to another and the y's are observed as the random outcomes (due to the component ε)? To give an answer let us suppose that the independent variable (x) is generated by some random process – such as the weather. The particular set of n observations $x_1, x_2, ..., x_n$ which appear in our data are, therefore, a random sample; another sample would give another set of x's. But we can interpret the regression as a predictor of y for the *particular set* of x's, i.e. $x_1, x_2, ..., x_n$ we have in our sample. In other words, we work out our results *as though* the $x_1, x_2, ..., x_n$ were fixed. This trick enables us to use the same theoretical structure of regression and correlation even though the x's are generated by a random process. The critical condition is that the ε and x are *independent* in the probabilistic sense discussed in Chapter 3. One necessary condition for this to hold is that there be no correlation between x and ε. This is, of course, the old condition which was required in the case of *fixed* $x_1, x_2, ..., x_n$, but it now takes on a different character since the x's are random variables. With this change in interpretation the regression technique is exactly the same as before.

Errors in the Variables

The last point to be dealt with in this chapter concerns the problem of *errors of measurement or observation* in the variables. Up to this stage we have assumed that y and x were measured or observed without error. This disturbance term was incorporated in the equation to take account of deviation between theory and fact. Let us now take the other extreme case and assume that there is no deviation between theory and fact – that the disturbance in the equation is always zero so that

$$y = \beta_{yx} x \qquad (4.14)$$

and

$$x = y / \beta_{yx}.$$

The constant β_{yx} describes the *perfect* linear relationship between the variables x and y. But now suppose we do not actually record x and y. This may be because, although x and y are the true values, we make errors when we attempt to record them. Human errors of measurement may account for deviations between the recorded value and the true value. Thus we may have

$$x_i^* = x_i + \varepsilon_{xi} \tag{4.15}$$

and

$$y_i^* = y_i + \varepsilon_{yi}. \tag{4.16}$$

The starred value x_i^* represents the recorded value, x_i the true value and ε_{xi} the error of measurement of the ith observation. Similar definitions apply to the y variables and ε_{yi} is the error involved in recording the ith observation of y.

An alternative interpretation of this model is that the observer cannot get a perfect measure of x and y. He has to be content with some other measures which are similar to but not exactly the same as the true variable. The measures x_i^* and y_i^* are sometimes called the *empirical correlates* of the true variables x_i and y_i. We then put forward the particular hypothesis that the empirical correlates and the true values are related in the simple way specified by the above equations.

Before one can explore the implications of this model, it is necessary to specify more precisely the behaviour patterns of the errors ε_{yi} and ε_{xi}. Just as we supposed that the disturbance was a chance variable distributed about an average of zero, so the most useful assumption is that these ε's are also random variables with zero means. Similarly, we might suppose that the error in measuring the true variable is in no way influenced by the size of the true variable. This means that the ε_{xi} and x_i are independent in the probabilistic sense; whatever the value of x, one has exactly the same chances of getting a specified value for ε. A necessary condition is that there exists no correlation between the true value and the error of measurement. These assumptions also apply to the y's, so that a necessary condition is that there is zero correlation between the ε_y and the y. Furthermore we must also assume that the ε_y is uncorrelated with x and the ε_x is uncorrelated with the y. Yet one other condition is required: it is necessary that ε_y and ε_x are independent. There is, then, no correlation between the errors in measuring x and the errors in measuring y. Putting all these necessary conditions together in a tabular form:

(i) no correlation between error ε_x and true variable x;

(ii) no correlation between error ε_y and true variable y;

(iii) no correlation between error in $x(\varepsilon_x)$ and error in $y(\varepsilon_y)$;

(iv) no correlation between ε_x and y and between ε_y and x.

To put this model to work one needs to substitute the definitions (4.15), (4.16) of x_i and y_i in Equation 4.14. Thus

$$y_i^* - \varepsilon_{yi} = \beta_{yx}(x_i^* - \varepsilon_{xi}). \tag{4.17}$$

The interesting question is obviously whether the least-squares estimator of β_{yx} still retains the properties of the simpler model which we discussed above. In Equation 4.17 we observe y_i^* and x_i^*, so let us form the least-squares estimate by writing

$$y_i^* = \beta_{yx}(x_i^* - \varepsilon_{xi}) + \varepsilon_{yi}$$

and multiplying both sides by x_i^* and then summing over the $i = 1, \dots, n$ values

$$\sum x_i^* y_i^* = \beta_{yx}\{\sum x_i^{*2} - \sum x_i^* \varepsilon_{xi}\} + \sum x_i^* \varepsilon_{yi}.$$

The least-squares estimate is then obtained by dividing by $\sum x_i^{*2}$:

$$\hat{\beta}_{yx} = \frac{\sum x_i^* y_i^*}{\sum x_i^{*2}} = \beta_{yx}\left\{1 - \frac{\sum x_i^* \varepsilon_{xi}}{\sum x_i^{*2}}\right\} + \frac{\sum x_i^* \varepsilon_{yi}}{\sum x_i^{*2}}. \tag{4.18}$$

Now the last term on the right-hand side is rather similar to the analogous term that appeared in the simpler case with no measurement error. It is, however, a little different, though the result is the same. Substituting in the denominator for $x_i^* = x_i + \varepsilon_{xi}$:

$$\frac{\sum x_i^* \varepsilon_{yi}}{\sum x_i^{*2}} = \frac{\sum x_i \varepsilon_{yi} + \sum \varepsilon_{xi} \varepsilon_{yi}}{\sum x_i^{*2}}. \tag{4.19}$$

In view of the assumptions (iii) and (iv) above it is clear that as the size of sample becomes larger and larger this term will on the average approach zero. This is the same comforting conclusion that we reached in the simple case.

The real difficulty appears with the second term in the curly brackets. If $\hat{\beta}_{yx}$ is to have smaller and smaller chances of differing, by a given small amount, from the true value β_{yx} as we increase the size of sample, we must show that the probability of $\sum x_i^* \varepsilon_{yi}/\sum x_i^{*2}$ deviating from zero, by a given small amount, must become smaller and smaller as the number in the sample grows. Substituting again: in Equation 4.18

$$\frac{\sum x_i^* \varepsilon_{xi}}{\sum x_i^{*2}} = \frac{\sum (x_i + \varepsilon_{xi}) \varepsilon_{xi}}{\sum x_i^{*2}}$$

$$= \frac{\sum x_i \varepsilon_{xi} + \sum \varepsilon_{xi}^2}{\sum x_i^{*2}}. \tag{4.20}$$

By virtue of assumption (i) above there will be a decreasing probability that the first term will deviate from zero by more than a given amount as the size of sample increases. Roughly (and inaccurately) we might say that the first term tends to approach zero as n increases. The second term, however, clearly does not have this property. It is always positive because it is a ratio of sums of squares; or it might be interpreted as the ratio of the variance of the errors of observation to the variance of the observed values x. It measures the relative importance of the errors of measurement in the 'independent' variable, i.e. the *relative error*.

Returning to Equation 4.18, the second term in the curly brackets will always be positive (except if $\varepsilon_{xi} = 0$ for all i). Thus we have

$$\hat{\beta}_{yx} = \beta_{yx} \left\{ 1 - \frac{\text{relative}}{\text{error in } x^*} \right\} + \frac{\text{other terms which tend to cluster}}{\text{closer to zero as } n \text{ increases.}}$$

This implies that our least-squares measure $\hat{\beta}_{yx}$ will *not* be distributed closer and closer to the true value β_{yx} as the size of sample gets larger. In other words, $\hat{\beta}_{yx}$ will not be a *consistent* estimator of β_{yx}. In fact $\hat{\beta}_{yx}$ will tend to 'home onto' a lower value than β_{yx} as n increases. Similarly for any *given* fixed size of sample, the various values of $\hat{\beta}_{yx}$ which one would obtain from repeated samples size n of the process, would have a mean value *less than* β_{yx} (see Chapter 3). This means that the least-squares estimator is *biased downwards*.

It must be emphasised that this does not mean that the calculated $\hat{\beta}_{yx}$ will *always* be less than the true value β_{yx}. All we have shown is that *on the average* the estimated $\hat{\beta}_{yx}$ will be less than the true value. In any particular sample it may be that the terms which are on the average zero will in this particular case chance to have such large positive values so that, by offsetting the second term in the curly brackets in Equation 4.18 above, they may make $\hat{\beta}_{yx}$ exceed β_{yx}. As with all statements about sampling properties, we assert properties about chances or probabilities; the odds-against case may well be the one which appears in a particular experiment.

The unsatisfactory properties of least squares estimators in those cases where there are errors in the variables suggests that other methods should be used which do not suffer from this unfortunate effect of underestimation. One simple procedure which avoids this is to divide the observations into three equal groups, one for high x's one for low

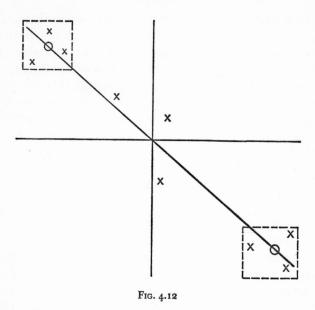

FIG. 4.12

x's and one for the middle x's. To illustrate, consider the 9 observations in the scatter diagram; there the high x's are enclosed in the box with the broken line on the right-hand side, and the low x's in a broken line box on the left-hand side. Now the procedure is to calculate the mean x and y in each of the two boxes. The means of each box is shown by a circle in each of them. The estimate of the slope β_{yx} is obtained simply by drawing the line through the two circles, that is through the means of the high group and the means of the low group. Let us call the resulting estimator $\bar{\beta}_{yx}$. This will give a consistent estimator of β_{yx} provided that the process of dividing the observations into groups is not affected by the errors. If the classification into groups does depend on the errors then the estimator is not consistent. One can easily imagine cases when the error in x_i, ε_{xi}, does not affect the division into groups. One case is when the observations are spaced a long way apart in the x direction and where it is known that the errors cannot exceed half the smallest difference in the x direction between two adjacent observations. Another case is when the classification into groups can be done before the experiment is carried out, then this division is certainly independent of the errors. For example, if one were measuring the relationship between income and expenditure on liquor, one might divide the population into groups according to their job classifications; this grouping may clearly be independent of errors in measuring income. But in practice it may not always be possible to get a prior or independent classification of this kind.

It is useful, therefore to examine other possible approaches. One obvious approach is to take the geometric average of the least-squares regression of y on x and the reciprocal of x on y, i.e.

$$\underline{\beta}_{yx} = \sqrt{\left(\hat{\beta}_{yx} \frac{1}{\hat{\beta}_{xy}} \right)}.$$

If we insert the least-squares formulae in here we obtain

$$\underline{\beta}_{yx} = \sqrt{\frac{\sum y^{*2}}{\sum x^{*2}}},$$

which is simply the ratio of the standard deviation of the observations of x to that of the observations of y. This is a consistent estimate if it is known that the relative variance of the errors in measuring x is equal to the relative variance of the errors in measuring y. This is probably the best one can do in a wide variety of cases.†

It is clear, from this brief survey of the problem of errors of measurement or observation in both variables, that there is no simple solution. No ready-made set of rules is available to estimate coefficients. Indeed one cannot get a 'reliable' estimate without some knowledge of the form and magnitude of the errors of observation. In practice it is probably best to attempt to collect as much extraneous information as possible about the errors, to survey other forms of data that incorporate the phenomenon in which we are interested, and to attempt to reconcile

† On the other hand, if one knows other evidence that the relative variances are not equal and if one knows the *ratio* of the error variances, one can use more complicated methods to estimate β_{yx}.

and integrate the various bodies of information.† In Chapters 9 and 10 we shall discuss practical cases – particularly in estimating the consumption function – where these various approaches are used. As we shall stress throughout much of this book, a sensible analysis of the data depends as much on the economics as on the formal statistical properties.

This completes our survey of regression methods in the simple two-variable case. It is essential to have a thorough grasp of the elements of the two-variable model in order to understand subsequent chapters in this book. Much of econometrics is erected on the foundation of this simple regression model; it serves as a corner-stone for all that is to follow.

Questions for Discussion

1. From O.E.C.D. statistics, index numbers for 1962 (1953 = 100) are as follows:

Country	Production	Exports
Austria	194	247
Belgium	157	203
Canada	130	140
France	195	205
Germany	205	273
Italy	225	377
U.K.	133	131
U.S.A.	128	124

Plot these data on a scatter diagram. Round off the figures to the nearest 10 and calculate the regression of exports on production. Do you think this is an appropriate regression in this case?

2. Write an essay on the trends in productivity (output per man-hour) and output over the period 1950–60. Examine in particular the suggestion that 'other European countries are merely catching up with Britain'.

† For example, it is often possible to make sensible conjectures about the rough magnitudes of errors of measurement in economic statistics. As a particular case, it may be observed that during war-time the price index, as officially computed, much understates the true increase in prices; this effect may be taken into account in estimating the linear relationship.

RATES OF GROWTH

Country	Annual percentage change in manufacturing 1950–60		Gross national product per head as percentage of U.K.		
	Total output	Output per man-hour	1938	1950	1959
Germany	10·0	5·6	82	65	96
Italy	8·9	6·7	48	42	55
Austria	6·8	5·3	—	60	80
France	6·5	5·9	82	83	95
Netherlands	6·1	4·6	80	80	92
Norway	5·5	4·8	87	93	99
U.S.A.	3·7	3·2	129	184	181
U.K.	3·4	2·6	100	100	100
Ireland	2·8	2·1	—	55	60

Source: C. Saunders, 'Comparisons of Productivity Growth in the 1950's', *Journal of the Royal Statistical Society*, vol. 126 (1963), p. 230.

It is argued that output per man-hour changes are largely determined by output changes. Calculate suitable regressions.

Find the fraction of the variance of the growth of output per man-hour that is explained by the growth of output. Plot the data and discuss the residual.

3. ## MONEY AND INCOME, U.K., 1910–18

Year	Quantity of money in December	National income
	£ m.	£ m.
1910	948	2,080
1911	982	2,150
1912	1,020	2,190
1913	1,062	2,300
1914	1,200	2,490
1915	1,330	2,640
1916	1,660	3,120
1917	1,910	3,701
1918	2,300	4,500

Source: N. J. Kavanagh, *Statistics of Money in the U.K., 1877–1962* (Birmingham, 1964).

(i) According to 'quantity theorists' national income is largely determined by the quantity of money. Plot the data in a scatter diagram so that you may examine this hypothesis.

(ii) Round the data to hundred millions and find the regression equation of national income on the quantity of money. Discuss your results.

(iii) Carry out the same regression, using the *logarithms* of the variables.

(iv) Consider the *changes* in the logarithms from one year to the next. Find the regression of changes in the logarithm of national income on the logarithm of the quantity of money.

(v) Compare the coefficients of correlation of the logarithm and the difference in the logarithms.

(vi) Consider the interpretation of the coefficients as 'monetary multipliers.'

(vii) Calculate the velocity of circulation and discuss the stability of the concept.

4. From a family budget study undertaken in Sweden in 1923, the following values relating to consumption of flour $(Y = \log C)$ and income $(X = \log M)$ of 1,192 families (workers and low-grade employees) were obtained:

$$\sum(Y - \bar{Y})^2 = 6.4090 \qquad \sum(X - \bar{X})^2 = 15.6107$$

$$\sum(X - \bar{X})(Y - \bar{Y}) = -9.9681.$$

Estimate the parameter α_1 of the equation $C = \alpha_0 M^{\alpha_1}$, using the above values.

5. $X_1 = \log$ of retail sales per head in Illinois cities in 1954; $X_2 = \log$ of distance to next larger city.

$$\sum(X_1 - \bar{X}_1)(X_1 - X_2) = 1.7291$$

$$\sum(X_2 - \bar{X}_2)^2 = 16.4881$$

$$\sum(X_1 - \bar{X}_1)^2 = 0.5497$$

$$\sum(X_1) = 162.798$$

$$\sum(X_2) = 68.748$$

$$N = 51.$$

Use the data to estimate a and b in the equation $X_1 = a + bX_2 + \varepsilon$.

6. NUMBER OF HORSES AND MULES AND
TRACTORS ON FARMS IN THE UNITED
STATES, AT I JANUARY, FOR YEARS 1939–50

Year	Horses and mules (m.) Y_a	Tractors (m.) Y_b
1930	19·1	0·9
1935	16·7	1·1
1940	14·5	1·5
1945	12·0	2·4
1950	7·5	3·8

Source: M. J. Hagood and D. O. Price, *Statistics for Sociologists* (1952).

(i) Assuming the trend in the above series may be represented by the equation

$$Y = \alpha_0 + \alpha_1 t + \varepsilon, \quad \text{where} \quad t = (\text{year} - 1940),$$

by the end of what decade, according to the equation, will the horse and mule be replaced by tractors?

(ii) Discuss the suitability of the equation for the purpose of predicting values of the two variables.

7. A research worker was interested in racial differences in the south-eastern area of the U.S.A. and the level of living of farm operators. He used the presence of running water in farm dwellings as a partial index of the level of living and used as his measure 'the percent of farms reporting running water in the dwelling'. The other measure used was the colour of farm operators. These two measures were calculated for 31 economic areas in North Carolina, South Carolina and Georgia for the year 1945.

The following values were obtained:

$$\sum(X - \bar{X})^2 = 86,660$$

$$\sum(Y - \bar{Y})^2 = 929 \cdot 828$$

$$\sum(X - \bar{X})(Y - \bar{Y}) = -4626 \cdot 2$$

$$\sum(X) = 1953 \qquad \sum(Y) = 452 \cdot 3$$

$$N = 31,$$

where

X = non-white farms per 100 white farm operators;

Y = per cent of farms reporting running water in dwellings.

The regression coefficients of the equation $\Upsilon = \beta_0 + \beta_{yx}X + \varepsilon$ were estimated by the method of least squares and the corresponding coefficient of correlation was calculated.

(i) Using the above data, calculate the regression coefficients and the coefficient of correlation.

What light do these values throw on the facts about the association between the two variables?

(*To be completed after Chapter 6*)

(ii) Test the hypothesis that there is no linear relationship between the two variables.

(iii) Do you agree with the research worker's view that as the observations of the measures on the 31 economic areas of the southeast may be considered as comprising an entire limited population there is no real sampling situation and therefore there is no need to make a test of significance such as (ii)?

8.   POPULATION OF THE UNITED STATES 1910–50

Year	1910	1920	1930	1940	1950
Population (m.)	92·0	105·7	122·8	131·7	150·7

Source: Bureau of Census, Washington, D.C.

(i) Estimate the population of the United States for 1960 by finding the parameters of the following equations

$$\Upsilon = \alpha + \beta t + \varepsilon,$$

$$\Upsilon = \alpha \beta^t \varepsilon.$$

Compare these estimates with the official estimate of 180·7 millions.

(ii) In what sense are your equations best-fitting equations?

9. Some investigators believe that the productivity of labour is determined primarily by the level of aggregate demand, which is approximately measured by aggregate output. Denoting aggregate labour by L and aggregate output by X, investigate the equations below.

(i) $\Upsilon = \alpha X^\beta$,   where $\Upsilon = X/L$.

Show that this might be expressed as

(ii) $\log L = -\log \alpha + (1 - \beta) \log X$

or as   (iii) $\log X = [1/(1 - \beta)] \log L + [1/(1 - \beta)] \log \alpha$.

Examine the economic and statistical arguments for each formulation. Investigate the case when labour productivity changes are very nearly proportional to the change in output.
Examine these equations in the light of the data in Question 2 above.

10. It is known that the variables in Question 1 have errors of measurement which, however, are also known to be less than $\frac{1}{2}$ per cent. Furthermore, it is known that the *true relationship* between the variables is linear. Find an estimate of this true linear relation. (Hint: note that with an error of $\frac{1}{2}$ per cent maximum the rank order of the countries according to their production index will not be changed by these errors of observation.)

11. (Continuation)
    Consider the problem of finding an estimate of the true linear relationship when the percentage error in the variables may be as large as 5 per cent.

12. It is alleged that the following data support the proposition that none of the countries 'has a general comparative advantage based on payments for labour at a level lower than that which its economy could support.'

VALUE OF OUTPUT AND INCOME PER WORKER
IN MANUFACTURING 1955

Country	Gross domestic product from manufacturing per worker (U.S. $)	Labour income in manufacturing per worker (U.S. $)
Argentina	877	578
Belgium	2,060	1,194
Canada	4,760	3,194
Denmark	2,206	1,497
Germany	1,594	1,068
India	335	247
Japan	633	475
Netherlands	1,731	776
Norway	2,428	1,444
U.K.	1,954	1,315
U.S.A.	6,146	4,351

Source: Faith Williams and Edgar Eaton, 'Payments for Labour and Foreign Trade', *American Economic Review*, XLIX (Sep 1959), no. 4.

Plot these data and discuss the relationship between the output and labour income. Consider the regressions which might be fitted, and examine the problem of 'grouping' the countries.

5 Multiple Regression

Regression Coefficients

We have examined extensively the case when one variable depends upon one other. In practice, however, one rarely has a theory as simple as this. Normally one can only explain the dependent variable in terms of many variables. The quantity demanded for example may depend not merely on the relative price of the good but also the relative prices of substitutes and complements, and the level of personal disposable income. The theory of demand indicates the signs of the coefficients – negative for its own price and for prices of complements and positive for prices of substitutes and personal income. The obvious way of developing a model to test this hypothesis is to extend the simple regression model.

To simplify the problem suppose there are only two independent variables, which we label by subscripts X_1 and X_2. We shall continue to indicate the ith observation by writing an i after the variable identifying subscript. Thus X_{1i} indicates the ith observation of the variable X_1. The random variable ε_i will again be used to indicate the difference between the value predicted by the true regression relationship and the actual value of the ith observation of the dependent variable Y_i. The natural way of writing the theoretical or true regression equation is then

$$Y_i = \beta_0 + \beta_{y1.2}X_{1i} + \beta_{y2.1}X_{2i} + \varepsilon_i, \qquad (5.1)$$

where β_0 is a constant. $\beta_{y1.2}$ is the coefficient which indicates the effect of an increase of one unit in X_1 (with X_2 held fixed) on the value of Y and $\beta_{y2.1}$ indicates the effect of an increase of one unit in X_2 (with X_1 held fixed) on the value of Y. The barrage of subscripts associated with the regression coefficients clearly calls for some explanation. If we regressed Y on X_1 only and did not worry about X_2 we should describe the coefficient as β_{y1} where the '1' subscript indicates that the independent variable is X_1. The new coefficient $\beta_{y1.2}$ indicates that 'the value of X_2

is held constant' by the fact that '2' appears in the subscript after the full stop. Or to express it another way, the coefficient $\beta_{y1.2}$ indicates the effect on Y of a unit increase in X_1 when the effect of variations in X_2 has been eliminated. The full stop in the subscript acts as a reminder that variables which are listed after it have been 'held constant' or 'the effect on Y has been eliminated'. These coefficients are usually called *partial* regression coefficients and we can proceed now to find estimates of them.

The model we propose to use is a simple one where one fixes the independent variables and then examines the value of the dependent variable. Thus the value of X_1 and X_2 are fixed and Y is the dependent variable. The disturbance term ε is assumed to be a random variable which accounts for influences omitted from our model. The theoretical or true equation

$$Y_i = \beta_0 + \beta_{y1.2}X_{1i} + \beta_{y2.1}X_{2i} + \varepsilon_i \qquad (5.2)$$

can be represented pictorially in Figure 5.1.

Given any X_1 and X_2 means that we start from a point in the (X_1, X_2)-plane such as (X_{1i}, X_{2i}). For the given values of X_{1i} and X_{2i} we find the value of Y_i associated with it. This value of Y_i can be decomposed into two parts. There is, first of all, the part that is predicated by the true regression equation *excluding* the disturbance ε. This value we shall dub Y_i^* and it is given by

$$Y_i^* = \beta_0 + \beta_{y1.2}X_{1i} + \beta_{y2.1}X_{2i}. \qquad (5.3)$$

Now as we change to other values of the independent variable, say X_{1j}, X_{2j} we move to another point on the base of the diagram and find a Y_j^* associated with it. It is clear that the Y^* points will trace out a plane such as that shown in the figure. And if we hold one of the independent variables constant (say $X_2 = X_{20}$) the relationship is then simply a linear one between Y^* and X_1. It is just like cutting a thin slice out of the diagram in the Y, X_1-plane at a value of $X_2 = X_{20}$. The line revealed by this slice is then

$$Y_i^* = \overbrace{\beta_0 + \beta_{y2.1}X_{20}}^{\text{constant}} + \beta_{y1.2}X_{1i}. \qquad (5.4)$$

It shows how Y^* varies as X_1 varies for the *fixed* value of X_2, $X_2 = X_{20}$. An increase of one unit in X_1 gives rise to an increase of $\beta_{y1.2}$ units in Y^*, as we previously observed.

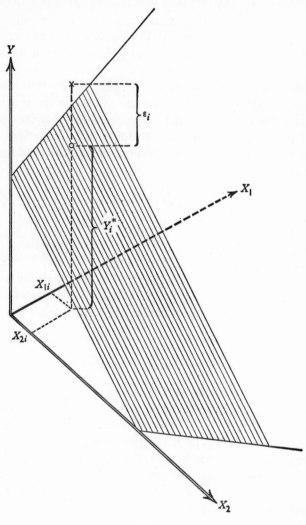

FIG. 5.1

The variable Y^* describes the regression plane. But actual observations deviate from the plane according to the value of ε. Again ε is measured in the Y direction and ε_i simply indicates the distance in the Y direction of Y_i from the plane i.e. from the value of Y^*, since

$$Y_i = Y_i^* + \varepsilon_i.$$

This is shown in Figure 5.1.

Exactly as in the case of simple regression the ε_i describes the deviation of the ith observation from the true theoretical or hypothetical plane. So far we have been describing purely the *theoretical* or *hypothetical or population* relationship. The plane and its coefficients and the variable ε are those which we suppose generate the actual observations of Y, X_1 and X_2 which we collect in practice. Now we must proceed to devise a method of obtaining *estimates* of these coefficients (and of the disturbances).

The method of getting estimators is exactly the same as in the simple case when there is only one (X) independent variable. We suppose that ε is distributed independently of the value of the independent variables i.e. ε is not correlated with X_1 or with X_2 in the population.

To simplify the exposition we shall suppose that all variables are measured as deviations from *sample* means, i.e. $x_{1i} = X_{1i} - \bar{X}_1$, $x_{2i} = X_{2i} - \bar{X}_2$ and $y_i = Y_i - \bar{Y}$, where ε_i is also *redefined* as the deviation from the sample mean, and that the plane goes through the origin. The theoretical equation is then written in lower-case letters:

$$y_i = \beta_{y1.2} x_{1i} + \beta_{y2.1} x_{2i} + \varepsilon_i. \tag{5.5}$$

Now we multiply this equation by x_{1i} and sum over the n observations, getting:

$$\sum x_{1i} y_i = \beta_{y1.2} \sum_i x_{1i}^2 + \beta_{y2.1} \sum_i x_{2i} x_{1i} + \sum_i \varepsilon_i x_{1i}. \tag{5.6}$$

It is clear that this operation can be done also for the second independent variable x_2 so that by multiplying Equation 5.5 throughout by x_2 and summing over all the n variables we obtain:

$$\sum x_{2i} y_i = \beta_{y1.2} \sum_i x_{1i} x_{2i} + \beta_{y2.1} \sum_i x_{2i}^2 + \sum_i \varepsilon_i x_{2i}. \tag{5.7}$$

The form of these two equations is exactly the same as that of the single equation of simple regression with one independent variable (x). In the simple case we formed an estimate by omitting the last term on the right-hand side, i.e. the cross-product (or the covariance when divided by n) of the independent variable and the disturbance. Let us do the same here, so that the equations we have which may be used for estimating $\beta_{y1.2}$ and $\beta_{y2.1}$ are (omitting the i subscript):

$$\left. \begin{array}{l} \sum x_1 y = \hat{\beta}_{y1.2} \sum x_1^2 + \hat{\beta}_{y2.1} \sum x_1 x_2, \\ \sum x_2 y = \hat{\beta}_{y1.2} \sum x_1 x_2 + \hat{\beta}_{y2.1} \sum x_2^2. \end{array} \right\} \tag{5.8}$$

These are called the *normal equations* (they are not, however, related to the normal distribution!). We can calculate from the sample each part of the terms after the sigma sign. For example, we note that the term $\sum x_1 y$ is simply the sum of the cross-product of x_1 and y, and $\sum x_1^2$ is the sum of squares of x_1. The sigma terms can be regarded as observed values. There are two unknowns, $\hat{\beta}_{y.12}$ and $\hat{\beta}_{y2.1}$, and with two equations there is some hope that one can solve to get the estimates of betas in terms of the known cross-products and sums of squares.

The simultaneous equations can be solved by the usual procedure of eliminating one variable. Multiply the first equation of (5.8) by $\sum x_2^2$ and the second equation by $\sum x_1 x_2$, and the last term of the two resulting equations will be identical.

$$\left. \begin{array}{l} (\sum x_1 y)(\sum x_2^2) = \hat{\beta}_{y1.2}(\sum x_1^2)(\sum x_2^2) + \hat{\beta}_{y2.1}(\sum x_1 x_2)(\sum x_2^2) \\ (\sum x_2 y)(\sum x_1 x_2) = \hat{\beta}_{y1.2}(\sum x_1 x_2)^2 + \hat{\beta}_{y2.1}(\sum x_1 x_2)(\sum x_2^2) \end{array} \right\} \tag{5.9}$$

Subtracting the second equation from the first we obtain

$$(\sum x_1 y)(\sum x_2^2) - (\sum x_2 y)(\sum x_1 x_2) = \hat{\beta}_{y1.2}[(\sum x_1^2)(\sum x_2^2) - (\sum x_1 x_2)^2].$$

Thus the estimate is given by the formula

$$\hat{\beta}_{y1.2} = \frac{(\sum x_1 y)(\sum x_2^2) - (\sum x_2 y)(\sum x_1 x_2)}{(\sum x_1^2)(\sum x_2^2) - (\sum x_1 x_2)^2}. \tag{5.10}$$

And in an analogous way, one can find an estimate for $\beta_{y2.1}$ by interchanging the subscripts 1 and 2, i.e.

$$\hat{\beta}_{y2.1} = \frac{(\sum x_2 y)(\sum x_1^2) - (\sum x_1 y)(\sum x_1 x_2)}{(\sum x_1^2)(\sum x_2^2) - (\sum x_1 x_2)^2}. \tag{5.11}$$

These somewhat forbidding formulae can be interpreted in a number of ways, for example, one may re-write them in terms of the simple regression coefficients $\hat{\beta}_{y1}$, $\hat{\beta}_{y2}$, $\hat{\beta}_{12}$, etc., by simply applying the formula

$$\hat{\beta}_{y1} = (\sum y x_1)/(\sum x_1^2), \text{ etc.}$$

Thus we find that

$$\hat{\beta}_{y1.2} = \frac{\hat{\beta}_{y1}(\sum x_1^2)(\sum x_2^2) - \hat{\beta}_{y2}\hat{\beta}_{21}(\sum x_1^2)(\sum x_2^2)}{(\sum x_1^2)(\sum x_2^2) - \hat{\beta}_{12}\hat{\beta}_{21}(\sum x_1^2)(\sum x_2^2)}$$

$$= \frac{\hat{\beta}_{y1} - \hat{\beta}_{y2}\hat{\beta}_{21}}{1 - \hat{\beta}_{12}\hat{\beta}_{21}} = \frac{\hat{\beta}_{y1} - \hat{\beta}_{y2}\hat{\beta}_{21}}{1 - r_{12}^2}, \qquad (5.12)$$

where r_{12} is the correlation coefficient of x_1 and x_2. This shows the relationship between the estimate of the simple regression coefficient $\hat{\beta}_{y1}$ and the partial coefficient $\hat{\beta}_{y1.2}$. To get the estimate of $\beta_{y1.2}$ one adjusts the $\hat{\beta}_{y1}$ by deducting the compound effect of x_1 on x_2 (i.e. the term $\hat{\beta}_{21}$) and the transmitted effect of x_2 on y (i.e. the term $\hat{\beta}_{y2}$). And this adjusted value is modified by the fraction of the variance of x_1 which is 'explained by' x_2 (i.e. the denominator $1 - r_{12}^2$).

Once one has calculated the regression coefficients one can easily return to the original equation where the variables do not have means of zero – i.e.

$$Y = \beta_0 + \beta_{y1.2}X_1 + \beta_{y2.1}X_2 + \varepsilon,$$

– and calculate an estimate of the constant β_0 by simply requiring the equation to fit the observed means. Taking averages of the *measured* regression equation, we have:

$$\bar{Y} = \hat{\beta}_0 + \hat{\beta}_{y1.2}\bar{X}_1 + \hat{\beta}_{y2.1}\bar{X}_2 \quad \text{or} \quad \hat{\beta}_0 = \bar{Y} - \hat{\beta}_{y1.2}\bar{X}_1 - \hat{\beta}_{y2.1}\bar{X}_2 \quad (5.13)$$

and note that the mean of the errors (or residuals) is zero. Since we now know all values in this equation except the $\hat{\beta}_0$, this gives us an estimate of this constant.

The verbal interpretation of the partial regression coefficients suggests that one can obtain these values in a different way. The partial coefficient $\hat{\beta}_{y1.2}$ is the regression of y on x_1 when 'the linear effect of x_2 has been eliminated'. If we 'eliminate the effect of x_2 on y' the obvious way to do this is by finding the regression of y on x_2, and then using the *residuals* in the y direction as a measure of the y variable with the effect of x_2 eliminated. The ith observation of this residual is simply

$$y_i - \hat{\beta}_{y2}x_{2i}, \quad \text{which we may call } e_{y.2}. \qquad (5.14)$$

In a similar way one can eliminate the effect of x_2 on x_1 by finding the regression of x_1 on x_2 and measuring the residual in the x_1 direction. The ith observation of this residual is

$$x_{1i} - \hat{\beta}_{12}x_{2i}, \quad \text{which we may call } e_{1.2}. \qquad (5.15)$$

We can then interpret the *partial* regression coefficient as the regression of $(y_i - \hat{\beta}_{y2}x_{2i})$ on $(x_{1i} - \hat{\beta}_{12}x_{2i})$ or of $e_{y.2}$ on $e_{1.2}$. In other words, we eliminate the effect of x_2 on both variables by taking the residuals from least-squares regressions on x_2, and finding the regression of the y residual on the x_1 residual. The partial regression equation may be defined as

$$(y_i - \hat{\beta}_{y2}x_{2i}) = \hat{\beta}_{y1.2}(x_1 - \hat{\beta}_{12}x_2) + \text{error or residual term.} \quad (5.16)$$

This is the *observed* equation and differs from the underlying theoretical equation. It is concerned with the regression of residuals, i.e. the regression of the observed deviations from simple regression lines.

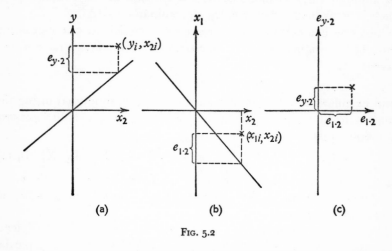

FIG. 5.2

Figures 5.2(a) and 5.2(b) show the simple *observed* regressions of y on x_2 and x_1 on x_2. Consider the ith observation, and plot the distances $e_{y.2}$ (Figure (a)) and $e_{1.2}$ (Figure (b)) of the points from the measured regression lines. Then the partial regression coefficient is found by fitting the ordinary simple regression of $e_{y.1}$ on $e_{1.2}$ in the scatter diagram (Figure (c)).

One might enquire under what circumstances the simple regression coefficient $\hat{\beta}_{y1}$ is equal to the partial coefficient $\hat{\beta}_{y1.2}$. Obviously a *sufficient* condition for this is that the variables x_1 and x_2 are not correlated in the sample; not only would $r_{12}^2 = 0$ but also $\hat{\beta}_{21} = 0$ as well. This is quite sensible since if x_2 is unrelated to x_1 eliminating the influence of

x_2 on x_1 will have no effect on x_1 at all, and so $\hat{\beta}_{y1.2} = \hat{\beta}_{y1}$. If, however, r_{12}^2 is not zero, $\hat{\beta}_{y1.2}$ will be equal to $\hat{\beta}_{y1}$ if

$$\hat{\beta}_{y1} = \frac{\hat{\beta}_{y2}\hat{\beta}_{21}}{r_{12}^2} = \frac{\hat{\beta}_{y2}}{\hat{\beta}_{12}}$$

or

$$\hat{\beta}_{y1}\hat{\beta}_{12} = \hat{\beta}_{y2}. \qquad (5.17)$$

This is the case when the total effect of x_2 on y can be decomposed exactly into two multiplicative factors – the total effect of x_2 on x_1 and the total effect of x_1 on y. This case is perhaps not so easy to recognise as the case when $r_{12} = 0$.

Multicollinearity

In simple regression of y on x we noted that one condition of getting an estimate of β_{yx} was that the x's were not all the same value. Now the obvious analogy of this situation in multiple regression is that all the x_1's have the same value and all the x_2's have the same value. Clearly, and for the same reasons, we cannot obtain estimates of $\hat{\beta}_{y1.2}$ and $\hat{\beta}_{y2.1}$. But there is also a less obvious analogue. Suppose that there is *perfect correlation* between the sample values of x_1 and x_2 – either perfect negative or positive correlation. Then in the equation

$$\hat{\beta}_{y1.2} = \frac{\hat{\beta}_{y1} - \hat{\beta}_{y2}\hat{\beta}_{21}}{1 - r_{12}^2} \qquad (5.18)$$

the denominator becomes zero – and the estimate $\hat{\beta}_{y1.2}$ is indeterminate. Similarly the estimate $\hat{\beta}_{y2.1}$ is not determinate.

This is, of course, the extreme case and it is useful as an archetype to show what happens as r_{12}^2 gets near to unity. Obviously the estimate then becomes very sensitive to the actual value of r^2. Consider, for example, an $r_{12}^2 = 0.98$ and $r_{12}^2 = 0.99$. The denominator is then 0.02 in the first case and 0.01 in the second case; this means that the effect is, *ceteris paribus*, to *double* the estimate of $\hat{\beta}_{y1.2}$.[†] For large r_{12}^2 there is, therefore, considerable instability in the estimates. We shall have occasion to take this up again when discussing the sampling properties of estimators.

† Assuming that the change in the estimate r_{12}^2 does not affect the numerator.

This effect when $r_{12}^2 \to 1$ may be described geometrically. The close correlation between x_1 and x_2 means that the points all lie above a line in the $x_1 x_2$-plane. There is little or no scatter in the $x_1 x_2$-plane, the only important scatter is in the y direction. When one tries to fit a plane to these observations one finds that we can easily locate the slope in the y direction – it is given by the broken line AO in the negative quadrant and

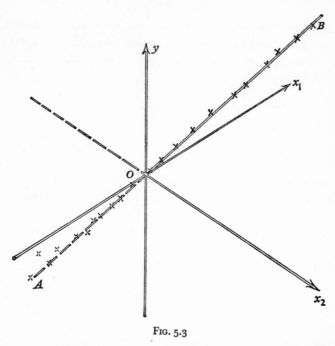

FIG. 5.3

continuous line OB in the positive quadrant. But it is impossible to get any idea of the slopes of a plane around the line; there are no observations to enable one to locate the plane. We can, as it were, spin the plane about the line as a hinge; and we still fit the observations.

It is as though when one carries out an experiment to determine separately the effect of x_1 and x_2 on y, we find that we cannot move the value of x_1 without at the same time moving the value of x_2 by the same proportionate amount, either positively or negatively. It is exactly like having two levers locked together – move one then both move. The essence of an experiment is to move x_1 separately from x_2 so that we can distil the separate effect of x_1 on y. If, however, every time we move x_1

we also move proportionately x_2, the effect on y of the two independent variables cannot be separately assessed. To forecast the value of y we need to know either x_1 or x_2. If we know either of the independent variables then knowledge of the other will not help at all in predicting y.

The Multiple Correlation Coefficient R^2

It might be surmised that there is a measure of correlation in the multiple regression case which corresponds closely to the correlation coefficient in the simple two-variable regression. In the latter case we defined the square of the correlation coefficient as that fraction of the variance of the dependent variable which was 'explained by' the independent variable. Similarly we labelled as the 'residual variance' that fraction of the variance which was not explained by the independent variable, i.e. $(1 - r^2)$. To get a similar measure for the multiple regression model, one proceeds in an exactly analogous way.

The *measured* regression plane in the three dimensions is described by the equation

$$\hat{y}_i^* = \hat{\beta}_{y1.2} x_{1i} + \hat{\beta}_{y2.1} x_{2i}. \tag{5.19}$$

This equation differs from the equation which describes the true or theoretical plane, where we omit the hats from y and β, i.e.

$$y_i^* = \beta_{y1.2} x_{1i} + \beta_{y2.1} x_{2i}. \tag{5.20}$$

Due to sampling errors we have only the measured values $\hat{\beta}_{y1.2}$ and $\hat{\beta}_{y2.1}$ instead of the *true* values $\beta_{y1.2}$ and $\beta_{y2.1}$. Except by the most fortunate accident, $\hat{\beta}_{y1.2} \neq \beta_{y1.2}$ and $\hat{\beta}_{y2.1} \neq \beta_{y2.1}$, so the measured or estimated plane will differ from the underlying theoretical plane. Similarly our value of y predicted by the measured regression $\hat{y}_i^*$ differs from the value of y_i^* predicted by the theoretical equation, hence the hat.

For the measured equation we may define the residual (or the error) as the difference between the observed value y_i and the value of y predicted by the equation $\hat{y}_i^*$.

$$\left. \begin{array}{l} y_i = \hat{\beta}_{y1.2} x_{1i} + \hat{\beta}_{y2.1} x_{2i} + e_i, \\ \hat{y}_i^* = \hat{\beta}_{y1.2} x_{1i} + \hat{\beta}_{y2.1} x_{2i}, \quad \text{so that } y_i = \hat{y}_i^* + e_i \end{array} \right\} \tag{5.21}$$

The e_i is the difference between the observed y_i and the value $\hat{y}_i^*$

E

predicted by the measured equation. (Again the observed e_i corresponds to the theoretical disturbance ε_i.) We find that

$$e_i = y_i - \hat{\beta}_{y1.2}x_{1i} - \hat{\beta}_{y2.1}x_{2i}. \tag{5.22}$$

Therefore the variance of the residual is given by

$$\text{var}(e) = \frac{\sum e_i^2}{n} = \left(\frac{1}{n}\right) \sum_i (y_i - \hat{\beta}_{y1.2}x_{1i} - \hat{\beta}_{y2.1}x_{2i})^2. \tag{5.23}$$

This can be expanded to give

$$\text{var}(e) = \frac{1}{n} \sum y_i(y_i - \hat{\beta}_{y1.2}x_{1i} - \hat{\beta}_{y2.1}x_{2i})$$

$$- \frac{\hat{\beta}_{y1.2}}{n} \sum x_{1i}e_i - \frac{\hat{\beta}_{y2.1}}{n} \sum x_{2i}e_i. \tag{5.24}$$

The last two terms are of particular interest. When we fitted the regression plane we assumed that there was no correlation between the disturbance and the independent variables; and the corresponding effect in our sample is that we fitted the measured regression plane by writing the covariances of the *observed* residual with the independent variables as zero. With the fitted regression plane there are zero correlations between the observed residual (in the y direction) and the x_1 and x_2. The last two terms are covariance (e, x_1) and covariance (e, x_2). Therefore they are zero.

The variance of the residual can then be simplified to

$$\text{var}(e) = \frac{1}{n} \sum y(y - \hat{\beta}_{y1.2}x_1 - \hat{\beta}_{y2.1}x_2),$$

omitting the i subscript, and

$$\text{var}(e) = \left(\frac{\sum y^2}{n}\right) - \hat{\beta}_{y1.2}\left(\frac{\sum yx_1}{n}\right) - \hat{\beta}_{y2.1}\left(\frac{\sum yx_2}{n}\right). \tag{5.25}$$

Thus, corresponding to the definition of $1 - r^2$, we define

$$\text{var}(e) = \frac{\sum y^2}{n} [1 - R^2]. \tag{5.26}$$

So that

$$\frac{\sum y^2}{n} [1 - R^2] = \frac{\sum y^2}{n}\left[1 - \hat{\beta}_{y1.2}\frac{\sum yx_1}{\sum y^2} - \hat{\beta}_{y2.1}\frac{\sum yx_2}{\sum y^2}\right],$$

or

$$R^2 = \frac{\hat{\beta}_{y1.2} \sum yx_1 + \hat{\beta}_{y2.1} \sum yx_2}{\sum y^2}. \qquad (5.27)$$

This can be put into words:

$$R^2 = \frac{\text{sum of squares of } y \text{ explained by } x_1 \text{ and } x_2}{\text{sum of squares of } y}.$$

This interpretation of R^2 is exactly analogous to that of r^2. We can therefore decompose the variance of y into two parts – one part of the variance of y is explained by the linear regression on x_1 and x_2 and the other part, which is the variance of the residual about the regression plane (and note that the variance we are talking about, is the variance of the *sample observations*)

$$s_y^2 \qquad = \qquad R^2 s_y^2 \qquad + \qquad (1 - R^2)s_y^2$$

$\uparrow$	$\uparrow$	$\uparrow$	
variance of	variance explained	residual variance	(5.28)
n sample	by regression of y	about the	
observations of y_i	on x_1 and x_2	regression plane.	

It must be noted that R^2 so measured is the *sample* value. Conventionally, like r^2, it does not have a kappa as one normally describes estimates from samples. The true or hypothetical value of the multiple correlation coefficient – let us call it $\Re^2$ – can be defined only in terms of the theoretical disturbances, i.e.

$$\begin{array}{l} \text{variance of } \varepsilon \\ \text{in population} \end{array} = \begin{array}{l} \text{variance of } y \\ \text{in population} \end{array} [1 - \Re^2]. \qquad (5.29)$$

Fortunately we rarely need to discuss the value of $\Re^2$ and it is then usually referred to simply as 'the population or true value of R^2, instead of using this Gothic symbol.

Partial Correlation Coefficients

The multiple correlation coefficient gives a measure of the closeness of fit of the regression plane to the observations. But, unlike the simple correlation coefficient, it does not measure how strong the correlation is between y and x_1, or the extent of the correlation between y and x_2.

There is, however, a natural definition of a *partial* correlation coefficient which one can develop exactly analogously to the simple correlation coefficient. We noted that

$$r_{1y}^2 = \hat{\beta}_{y1}\hat{\beta}_{1y}. \tag{5.30}$$

So we may define a *partial* correlation coefficient $r_{1y.2}^2$ as

$$r_{1y.2}^2 = \hat{\beta}_{y1.2}\hat{\beta}_{1y.2}. \tag{5.31}$$

This coefficient measures the correlation between y and x_1 *when the linear effect of x_2 on both variables has been eliminated*. In partial regression the way in which we eliminated the linear effect of x_2 on y and on x_1 was to measure the residuals in the regressions of y on x_2 and x_1 on x_2. This suggests that we can interpret the partial correlation coefficient as the correlation between these residuals of the elementary regressions, i.e.

$$r_{y1.2} = \text{correlation between } (y - \hat{\beta}_{y2}x_2) \text{ and } (x_1 - \hat{\beta}_{12}x_2). \tag{5.32}$$

Thus we have

$$r_{y1.2} = \frac{\sum (y - \hat{\beta}_{y2}x_2)(x_1 - \hat{\beta}_{12}x_2)}{\sqrt{[\sum (y - \hat{\beta}_{y2}x_2)^2 \cdot \sum (x_1 - \hat{\beta}_{12}x_2)^2]}}.$$

The values $r_{y2.1}$ and $r_{12.y}$ are defined in a similar way. It is also obvious that this definition satisfies also the previous formula (5.31).

As one might expect partial correlation coefficients satisfy all the conditions of ordinary coefficients. One property is that the correlation $r_{1y.2}$ is the same as $r_{y1.2}$, just as in elementary correlations. They lie between the values of -1 and $+1$. A zero value of $r_{1y.2}$ indicates that there is no correlation at all between the x_1 and y *when the linear effect of x_2 has been eliminated*; or, in other words, there is no correlation between the residuals of the regression of y on x_2 and the residuals of the regression of x_1 on x_2. It seems natural to interpret the partial correlation coefficient as an indicator of the 'importance' of a particular independent variable in predicting the dependent variable. For example, can one interpret the size of $r_{y1.2}$ as a measure of the importance of x_1 in determining y when the effects *via* x_2 are eliminated? One can use this interpretation only in experiments *where the dependent variable is the same*.

Two main tasks remain. One is to develop the relationship between the ordinary correlation coefficients and the partial coefficients of correlation. The second is to show how the partial correlation coefficients are related to the multiple correlation coefficients.

But before attempting these two developments it is convenient to develop a notation to describe the concept of sum-of-squares of residuals in the regression, and the variances associated with them. Let us begin with the *theoretical* or *true* regression

$$y = \beta_{yx} x + \varepsilon.$$

The disturbance term ε measures the deviation between observation and the true regression line in the y direction. But it is not obvious from the notation that the disturbance actually does this job. We might therefore invent a notation analogous to the notation used to describe regression coefficients and correlation coefficients, so that the role of the disturbance is perfectly easily seen. Obviously in this equation the natural definition to use is†

$$\varepsilon_{y.x}.$$

Thus the disturbance measures that part of the value of y which is not explained by the (true) regression of y on x. In other words, it is the disturbance of y when the effect of x has been eliminated. Analogously we may define the *measured* residual (or error) $e_{y.x}$ in the estimated regression of y on x, i.e.

$$y = \hat{\beta}_{yx} x + e_{y.x}. \tag{5.33}$$

Then we have proved that

$$\text{variance of } e_{y.x} = \text{var}(e_{y.x}) = \frac{\sum y^2}{n} [1 - r_{xy}^2], \tag{5.34}$$

where r_{xy} is the measured coefficient of correlation between x and y. Similarly the sum of squares might be expressed as

$$\text{SS}(e_{y.x}) = \text{SS}(y) [1 - r_{xy}^2], \tag{5.35}$$

where we use the notation SS( ) to describe the sum of squares of deviations from the mean value, which we have defined as zero in all our variables considered here.

For the equation with two independent variables x_1 and x_2, the obvious notation is therefore $\varepsilon_{y.12}$ for the theoretical disturbance, and $e_{y.12}$ for the measured or sample residual. Thus

$$e_{y.12} = y - \hat{\beta}_{y1.2} x_1 - \hat{\beta}_{y2.1} x_2.$$

† The reader will note that we used a similar notation in the previous section.

And

$$\text{var}(e_{y.12}) = \frac{\sum y^2}{n} [1 - R^2]. \tag{5.36}$$

This describes the residual variation in y when the linear effects of x_1 and x_2 have been eliminated. The reader may also observe that it would be a good idea to re-label R^2 – so that it describes precisely what is being measured. The natural notation is to call it $R_{y.12}^2$, so that

$$\text{var}(e_{y.12}) = \frac{\sum y^2}{n} [1 - R_{y.12}^2]. \tag{5.37}$$

There is then a nice symmetry between the definition of the residual and the notation of the multiple correlation coefficient.

Now we return to the definition of the partial coefficient of correlation. It may be simply defined as

$$r_{y1.2} = \frac{\text{covariance } (e_{y.2}, e_{1.2})}{\sqrt{[\text{var}(e_{y.2}) \cdot \text{var}(e_{1.2})]}} = \frac{\text{cross-product } (e_{y.2}, e_{1.2})}{\sqrt{[\text{SS}(e_{y.2}) \cdot \text{SS}(e_{1.2})]}} \tag{5.38}$$

This is simply the formula for the correlation between the residuals $e_{y.2}$ and $e_{1.2}$. The denominator is easily developed, by using the usual formula for the variance of the residuals in the simple regression:

$$\sqrt{[\text{SS}(e_{y.2}) \cdot \text{SS}(e_{1.2})]} = \sqrt{\{\text{SS}(y) \cdot \text{SS}(x_1) \cdot [1 - r_{y2}^2][1 - r_{12}^2]\}}. \tag{5.39}$$

The numerator requires a little more work. The cross-product is

$$\sum (y - \hat{\beta}_{y2} x_2)(x_1 - \hat{\beta}_{12} x_2).$$

So, on multiplying out the second bracket, we obtain

$$\sum x_1(y - \hat{\beta}_{y2} x_2) - \hat{\beta}_{12} \sum x_2(y - \hat{\beta}_{y2} x_2). \tag{5.40}$$

Now the second term in this expansion is the cross-product of x_2 and the residual $e_{y.2}$ [or $(y - \hat{\beta}_{y2} x_2)$]. But we know that the residual and the independent variable are always uncorrelated; our calculation of the least-squares coefficient makes them so. Thus the second term is zero, and so the expansion of the numerator reduces to

$$\sum x_1(y - \hat{\beta}_{y2} x_2) = \sum x_1 y - \hat{\beta}_{y2} \sum x_1 x_2.$$

If we now divide both numerator and denominator of $r_{y1.2}$ by $\sqrt{[\text{SS}(y) \cdot \text{SS}(x_1)]}$, and use the definition of r, we obtain

$$r_{y1.2} = \frac{r_{y1} - r_{y2} r_{12}}{\sqrt{[(1 - r_{12}^2)(1 - r_{y2}^2)]}}. \tag{5.41}$$

This, then, shows the relationship between the partial correlation coefficient and the simple correlation coefficients. It tells us how to eliminate the effect of x_2 from the ordinary correlation coefficient r_{y1} in order to obtain $r_{y1.2}$.

It will be observed that there is no simple relationship between the sign of $r_{y1.2}$ and r_{y1}. Thus the simple coefficient r_{y1} may be positive, but the term $r_{y2} . r_{12}$ may be larger than r_{y1} – so that $r_{y1.2}$ is negative. (Note that the denominator is always positive – we only take the positive root.) The positive effect of x_1 on x_2 (r_{12}) and of x_2 on y (r_{y2}) may be more than sufficient to explain away the simple positive relationship between y and x_1; so the partial coefficient is negative. An arithmetic example will make this clear.

y	x_1	x_2	y^2	x_1^2	x_2^2	yx_1	x_1x_2	yx_2
-2	-1	-2	4	1	4	2	2	4
1	4	2	1	16	4	4	8	2
1	-3	0	1	9	0	-3	0	0
0	0	0	6	26	8	$+3$	10	6

$$r_{y1} = \frac{3}{\sqrt{6 \cdot 26}} \qquad r_{y2} = \frac{6}{\sqrt{6 \cdot 8}} \qquad r_{12} = \frac{10}{\sqrt{8 \cdot 26}}$$

On inserting these values in the formula the reader will find that the partial coefficient of correlation $r_{y1.2}$ is negative, in spite of the fact that the ordinary coefficient r_{y1} is positive.†

The second task is to examine the relationship between $r_{y1.2}$ and $R_{y.12}$. It might be thought that, in some way, one could decompose the $R_{y.12}$ into constituent parts – and those constituents might be imagined to be the partial coefficients of correlation. A high $r_{y1.2}$ for example, may be thought to 'add to' the value of $R_{y1.2}$. Although it is an attractive idea, it is rather misleading. The analysis must proceed, as always, in terms of the residual variances or sums of squares of errors. Thus

$$SS(e_{y.1}) = SS(y) \, [1 - r_{y1}^2].$$

Now, we can do the same operation on the *residuals when the effect of x_1 has been eliminated*. Instead of analysing y and splitting up the sum of

---

† The reader should note that to fit a regression or correlation such a short series is quite pointless. It is presented here merely to illustrate arithmetic and principle – not to measure relationships.

squares of y into the two components, we analyse instead the sum of squares of the *residual* $e_{y.1}$ (or, $y - \hat{\beta}_{y1}x_1$), and split that residual into two components. We can therefore write immediately

$$SS(e_{y.12}) = SS(e_{y.1}) \left[1 - r_{y2.1}^2 \right]. \tag{5.42}$$

Thus we have begun with the $SS(e_{y.1})$ and then we have extracted the effect of x_2, by means of the partial correlation coefficient $r_{y2.1}$ in order to obtain the sum of squares of the 'residuals of residuals', i.e. $SS(e_{y.12})$. In terms of our notation, all one needs to do is to treat it as an equation in which the effect of x_2 is eliminated from the sum of squares of $e_{y.1}$. Incidentally it also gives us another way of defining the role of the partial correlation coefficient. And it is quite often useful to interpret the partial correlation coefficient in this way – exactly analogous to the interpretation of the simple correlation coefficient, except that it applies to the residuals instead of the variables themselves.

Clearly we can also substitute for the sum of squares of $e_{y.1}$ in the above equation. For we know that

$$SS(e_{y.1}) = SS(y) \cdot (1 - r_{y1}^2).$$

So, on putting these results into the above equation, we obtain

$$SS(e_{y.12}) = SS(y) \cdot (1 - r_{y1}^2)(1 - r_{y2.1}^2). \tag{5.43}$$

Or, on writing in the formula for the residual sum of squares in terms of $R_{y.12}$, we obtain

$$(1 - R_{y.12}^2) = (1 - r_{y1}^2)(1 - r_{y2.1}^2). \tag{5.44}$$

This expresses the correct relationship between $R_{y.12}^2$ (the multiple correlation coefficient) and the constituent $r_{y2.1}^2$ and r_{y1}^2. But the relationship is not a simple one. For a *given* value of r_{y1}^2 a higher value of $r_{y2.1}^2$ will give rise to a higher value of the multiple correlation coefficient. In common-sense terms this implies that if we fix the relationship between y and x_1, and then improve or increase the relationship between y and x_2, while holding the value of x_1 fixed, we shall improve the fit of the regression plane (i.e. $R_{y.12}^2$ will be higher). The reader may well conclude, however, that this is a somewhat contorted explanation.

The fact that there is no simple relationship between the fraction of the total variance of y explained by the x_2 variable (eliminating the effect through x_1) and the partial correlation coefficient $r^2_{y2.1}$ suggests that the role of the partial correlations in interpreting the results of regression analyses is rather limited. They have no simple role in the analysis of the components of the variance of the dependent variable. But there is a sort of step-wise interpretation which is suggested by the above argument. Suppose that we have measured the *simple* regression of y on x_1 and we have calculated the fraction of the variance not explained by that simple regression, $(1 - r^2_{y1})$. Now we might ask: 'suppose that the new variable x_2 were introduced, would that add much to the explanatory power of the regression?' Clearly we can give the answer that the addition of the x_2 variable will reduce the residual variance (or the sum of squares of the residual) by the fraction $(1 - r^2_{y2.1})$. This bracketed expression tells us the fractional reduction of the residual variance due to the addition of x_2 to the independent variables of the regression. But it should be noted that there is no simple relationship between the fraction of the variance explained by the regression $R^2_{y.12}$ and the partial coefficient. For we have

$$R^2_{y.12} = r^2_{y1} + r^2_{y2.1} - r^2_{y1}r^2_{y2.1}, \tag{5.45}$$

which is too complex to be useful.

Properly interpreted the partial coefficients can be used with advantage in many econometric studies. But again the reader will note that the interesting interpretations are usually connected with the value $(1 - r^2_{y2.1})$ rather than the simple coefficients themselves. It may well be sensible to record the values of $(1 - r^2_{y2.1})$ and $(1 - r^2_{y1.2})$ along with the regression coefficients. The former records the fractional reduction in the residual variance when we pass from a simple regression of y on x_1 to a multiple one of y on x_1 and x_2; the latter tells us the proportional reduction in the residual variance as we proceed from the simple regression of y on x_2, by adding the new variable x_2, to the multiple regression of y on x_1 and x_2. The partial coefficients, interpreted in this way, give us some guide on whether an additional variable is worth including in the simple regression model. The reader may well argue, however, that such a use is all very well, but one needs to know the sampling properties of the partial coefficients of correlation; how, otherwise, can one discover if the addition of another variable *really* adds to the explanatory power of the model, or whether it is a sampling effect only. Unfortunately the sampling properties of the partial correlation coefficients are very difficult to deal with, and complicated transformations are required. This intractability of the sampling characteristics of the coefficients is another reason why they are not extensively used, even in the interpretation discussed here. In practice the standard errors of the regression coefficients serves approximately the same purpose. When an additional variable is included in (or excluded from) the regression we can inspect the standard errors of the coefficients of regression and see how they behave. This concept of the standard error of the regression coefficient will have to be developed in the following chapter.

A Generalisation†

It is fairly clear that, although we have developed multiple regression and correlation for only three variables, it can readily be extended to any number of variables.‡ But, of course, we always add to the independent variables – the x's in the notation used here – and there is always only one dependent variable in this regression model. Thus for four-variable regression one may define the following equation,

$$y = \beta_{y1.23}x_1 + \beta_{y2.13}x_2 + \beta_{y3.12}x_3 + \varepsilon_{y.123}, \qquad (5.46)$$

where the variables y and x_1, x_2, x_3 and $\varepsilon_{y.123}$ are, as usual, measured in terms of deviations from their respective sample means. The notation is a natural development from the simpler three-variable case; the coefficient $\beta_{y1.23}$ tells us the effect on y of a unit increase in x_1 when the linear effects of x_2 and x_3 have been eliminated. In other words it tells us the consequences on y of a unit increase in x_1 when x_2 and x_3 are held constant. Similarly $\beta_{y3.12}$ tells us the effect of a unit increase in x_3 when x_1 and x_2 are held constant and the disturbance $\varepsilon_{y.123}$ reflects the fact that it is the disturbance in the regression of y on x_1, x_2 and x_3.

If it be supposed that the independent variables and the disturbance are independently distributed – so that they are uncorrelated in the population – we may proceed to estimate the parameters by forming the normal equations in exactly the same way as in the simple two- and

---

† This section may be skipped without loss.

‡ There is a limitation, however, on the fitting of the regression since there must be at least as many observations as there are variables. And such observations should not form collinear sets – they should be spread about throughout the space.

three-variable case.† Thus we multiply throughout by the independent variables and form the sums over the observations to produce the three normal equations

$$\sum x_1 y = \hat{\beta}_{y1.23} \sum x_1^2 + \hat{\beta}_{y2.13} \sum x_1 x_2 + \hat{\beta}_{y3.12} \sum x_1 x_3, \\ \sum x_2 y = \hat{\beta}_{y1.23} \sum x_1 x_2 + \hat{\beta}_{y2.13} \sum x_2^2 + \hat{\beta}_{y3.12} \sum x_2 x_3, \\ \sum x_3 y = \hat{\beta}_{y1.23} \sum x_1 x_3 + \hat{\beta}_{y2.13} \sum x_2 x_3 + \hat{\beta}_{y3.12} \sum x_3^2 \Bigg\}. \quad (5.47)$$

In these normal equations we suppose that the correlations between the residual and the independent variables are zero. This gives us three linear equations in three unknowns. Provided the equations are not collinear we can obtain estimates of the coefficients $\hat{\beta}_{y1.23}$, $\hat{\beta}_{y2.13}$, $\hat{\beta}_{y3.12}$ from the equations.

The computational process by which we obtain estimates is exactly the same as before. We eliminate variables one at a time from the equations. But this is somewhat tedious to do by hand, even in the three-variable case. Fortunately with the availability of large computers the need for extensive hand calculation has substantially diminished, and so we shall not pursue computational methods in the framework of this book.

The interpretation of the coefficients proceeds exactly as before. The multiple correlation coefficient $R^2_{y.123}$ is calculated in the usual way:

sum of squares of residuals about the regression $= \sum y^2 (1 - R^2_{y.123})$,

i.e. $$\mathrm{SS}(e_{y.123}) = \sum y^2 (1 - R^2_{y.123}). \quad (5.48)$$

The residual is defined as

$$e_{y.123} = y - \hat{\beta}_{y1.23} x_1 - \hat{\beta}_{y2.13} x_2 - \hat{\beta}_{y3.12} x_3.$$

When we form the sum of squares of the residual we observe that it will consist of

$$\sum y e_{y.123} = \sum y^2 - \hat{\beta}_{y1.23} \sum y x_1 - \hat{\beta}_{y2.13} \sum y x_2 - \hat{\beta}_{y3.12} \sum y x_3, \quad (5.49)$$

and terms such as $\sum e_{y.123} x_1$, $\sum e_{y.123} x_2$, and $\sum e_{y.123} x_3$. But by the assumptions of the normal equations, these last three summations are zero. So we may write

† To avoid misunderstanding it should be stressed that the necessary assumption is that the $\varepsilon_{y.123}$ and the x_1 are not correlated, the $\varepsilon_{y.123}$ and the x_2 are not correlated, etc.; but of course x_1 and x_2 and x_3 may be correlated.

$$SS(e_{y.123}) = \sum y^2 (1 - R^2_{y.123})$$

$$= \sum y^2 - \hat{\beta}_{y1.23} \sum yx_1 - \hat{\beta}_{y2.13} \sum yx_2 - \hat{\beta}_{y3.12} \sum yx_3 \quad (5.50)$$

and, of course, this is exactly analogous to the calculation of the sum of squares of residuals in the three-variable case.

It is natural to conjecture that the coefficient $\hat{\beta}_{y1.23}$ may also be interpreted as the regression of one residual on another. The residuals are, however, derived from three-variable regressions. Thus $\hat{\beta}_{y1.23}$ is the regression of $e_{y.23}$ on $e_{1.23}$. Similarly $\hat{\beta}_{y2.13}$ is the regression of $e_{y.13}$ on $e_{2.13}$, and so on.

The partial correlation $r_{y1.23}$ is defined in exactly the same way. It is the correlation between the two residuals $e_{y.23}$ and $e_{1.23}$. Thus we can also define

$$r^2_{y1.23} = \hat{\beta}_{y1.23} \cdot \hat{\beta}_{1y.23}$$

and

$$\hat{\beta}_{y1.23} = r_{y1.23} \cdot \sqrt{\left\{ \frac{SS(e_{y.23})}{SS(e_{1.23})} \right\}}.$$

Again these are exactly analogous to the simple correlation and regression coefficients; we merely work with the appropriate residuals instead. The student can easily check this; if we omit the subscripts after the dot, then the formulae are those of simple regression. (Note that e_y is simply y and e_1 is simply x_1.)

One further result is important – the link between the partial correlation coefficients and the multiple correlation coefficient. Clearly we can proceed one variable at a time:

$$\left. \begin{array}{l} SS(e_{y.1}) = SS(y)(1 - r^2_{y1}), \\ SS(e_{y.12}) = SS(e_{y.1})(1 - r^2_{y2.1}), \\ SS(e_{y.123}) = SS(e_{y.12})(1 - r^2_{y3.12}) \end{array} \right\} \quad (5.51)$$

The first equation simply eliminates x_1. The second equation works on the residuals when x_1 has been eliminated, and goes on to eliminate x_2. The third equation takes the residuals when both x_1 and x_2 have been eliminated and goes on to eliminate the effect of x_3. Again the simple notational rule enables us to write the equations down directly. Now we simply string them together to obtain

$$SS(e_{y.123}) = SS(y)(1 - R^2_{y.123}) = SS(y)(1 - r^2_{y1})(1 - r^2_{y2.1})(1 - r^2_{y3.12})$$

$$1 - R^2_{y.123} = (1 - r^2_{y1})(1 - r^2_{y2.1})(1 - r^2_{y3.12}). \quad (5.52)$$

And of course one could have proceeded to eliminate the variables in any order. For example, beginning with x_3 and then eliminating x_1 and lastly x_2, we should obtain

$$1 - R_{y.123}^2 = (1 - r_{y3}^2)(1 - r_{y1.3}^2)(1 - r_{y2.13}^2). \tag{5.53}$$

The reader will be able to form other combinations.

The interpretation of the partial correlation coefficient remains the same as before. If you have fitted a three-variable regression – using, say, x_1 and x_2 as the independent variables – then the term $(1 - r_{y3.12}^2)$ describes the fraction by which the residual variance is reduced by adding the variable x_3 to the independent variables in the regression.

The generalisation to five, six, ... variables proceeds exactly analogously to the cases considered so far. No new point of principle emerges; we merely have a longer set of subscripts.

This completes our survey of the basic features of regression and correlation. It is worth stressing once more that these methods are useful for analysing relationships that are approximately linear. We must have some grounds for believing that the relationships are linear before we put any faith in regression analysis. It should never be used as a mechanical method of analysing data. The intelligent use of graphical methods can often avoid serious misrepresentation.

Two main problems remain to be discussed. The first is concerned broadly with the sampling properties of regression and correlation coefficients. This will be the subject of the next chapter. The other main problem is to integrate the analysis of regression with the theory of economics. This will be the concern of Part III of this book.

Questions for Discussion

1. The quantity of a commodity purchased y is linearly determined by two variables, the relative price x_1, and the level of real personal income x_2, i.e. in deviations from means:

$$y = \beta_1 x_1 + \beta_2 x_2 + \varepsilon,$$

where ε is the disturbance and accounts for 'other effects' omitted from the model.

(i) Describe the pattern of observations and the results of calculating the regression when x_1 and x_2 are nearly perfectly correlated.

(ii) Suppose, however, that x_1 and x_2 are not perfectly correlated but that y represents ice-cream consumption and ε represents a 'weather index'. If personal income is also affected by the 'weather index', discuss the effects of this assumption on your estimate of β_2.

2. The following matrix shows the simple correlations between the three variables X_1, X_2 and X_2:

	X_1	X_2	X_3
X_1	1·00	0·78	0·59
X_2		1·00	0·02
X_3			1·00

Wheat	Standard deviation	Means
X_1 = Production (mill. bu.)	124·68	2,506
X_2 = Acreage (mill. acres)	7·36	99
X_3 = Yield (bu. per acre)	1·40	28

Calculate $r_{12.3}$, $r_{13.2}$ and $r_{23.1}$ and interpret your results.

3. Using the data in Question 2 relating to annual data for the United States for the period 1894–1930 (i.e. 37 observations) estimate the parameters of the equation $X_1 = \beta_{1.23} + \beta_{12.3}X_2 + \beta_{13.2}X_3 + \varepsilon$ and interpret your results. (Note the notation used for the intercept.)

4. (i) From the following data find the regression of value added per worker on the wage of production workers and the capital–labour ratio.

PETROLEUM AND COAL PRODUCTS

State	Value added ($ per man-hour)	Wage of production workers ($ per hour)	Capital–labour ratio ($ per man-hour)
Massachusetts	7·12	2·96	14·99
New York	8·28	3·29	15·20
New Jersey	6·70	3·64	20·09
Pennsylvania	7·16	3·37	21·89
Indiana	6·78	3·73	22·71
Illinois	9·24	3·41	17·72

Source: Hildebrand and Liu. (Note: a calculating machine should be used for these calculations.)

(ii) Consider an alternative formulation in the logarithms of the variables.

(iii) Find the multiple correlation coefficient and find the 'improvement' in the regression due to adding the capital–labour ratio as a second variable.

5. (i) From the following data compute the regression of automobile expenditure on consumer expenditure and other travel expenditure.

		Av. automobile exp. ($) p.a.	Other travel exp. ($) p.a.	Av. consumer exp. ($) p.a.
1935	Atlanta	212	29	2,437
	Chicago	158	46	2,476
	Omaha	180	28	2,132
	Portland	253	26	2,256
	Providence	175	29	2,258
1950	Atlanta	429	64	3,566
	Chicago	437	119	4,486
	Omaha	419	81	3,602
	Portland	318	74	3,446
	Providence	355	66	3,736

Source: Walter Oi and Paul Shuldiner, *An Analysis of Urban Travel Demands* (Chicago, 1962), p. 164.

(ii) Interpret your results carefully. Would it be more sensible to calculate *two* regressions – one for 1935 and one for 1950?

(iii) Examine the suggestion that we might *pool* the data for the two years but distinguish the post-war from the pre-war data by using a *third* (dummy) variable x that takes on a value of 1 if the observation is for the post-war years and a value of zero if the observation refers to the pre-war years. The regression coefficient of x_3, therefore, will tell us the auto expenditure that is due to the fact that the year is 1950, rather than 1935. It adds to the regression a different constant for the two periods. This is often called the technique of *dummy variables*. See Johnston, *Econometric Methods* for a further development.

6. It is thought that the investment of a firm as a ratio of its capital is a linear function of the expected rate of change of output. But the investment requirement is negatively related to the rate of technological progress, and technical improvements in turn are positively associated with the growth rate of outputs. Examine the regression of the investment capital ratio on the rate of change of output. Can the coefficient be interpreted as an *accelerator*? Calculate the bias in the estimate of the accelerator. (See A. Walters, 'Technical Progress and the Accelerator', *Review of Economic Studies* (1963)).

7. Consider an equation of the form:

$$M = \beta_0 + \beta_1 Y + \beta_2 P + \varepsilon,$$

where M is the quantity of money and Y is the nominal income and P is the price level. Examine the problem of 'deflating' the money and income variables by the price level. Under what conditions would deflation be a good idea?

Consider also the equation

$$\log M = \beta_0' + \beta_1' \log \Upsilon + \beta_2' \log P + \varepsilon',$$

and consider also the problem of deflation. Discuss the relationship with the 'money illusion' and examine the probable correlations between Υ and P.

8. From the data in Friedman and Schwartz,† compute the regression of the velocity of circulation on the rate of interest and the level of *real* income for the *United States* for the years 1920–1938. (Note that there are many definitions of money, the rate of interest and income. The student must choose those definitions that are appropriate.) Find the regression for the *differences* of the variables and interpret the results.

9. (*Orthogonal transformations*)

Consider the equation (in deviations from means):

$$y = \beta_1 x_1 + \beta_2 x_2 + \varepsilon$$

and examine the definition of two new variables (u, w) which are linear functions of x_1 and x_2 so that the two new variables are uncorrelated (i.e. $\sum uw = 0$), and $\sum u^2 = 1$, $\sum w^2 = 1$.

Show then that in the equation

$$y = \gamma_1 u + \gamma_2 w + \eta$$

we can estimate γ_1 by regressing simply y on u, and we can estimate γ_2 by regressing y on w.

10. Many monetary economists argue that the level of deposits is determined by the stock of bills and the liquidity ratio. Discuss the statistical evidence for this hypothesis.

	Stock of Bills ($£$ m.)	Liquidity ratio (%)	Deposits ($£$ m.)
Aug 1956	3,390	35·3	6,294
Aug 1957	3,070	35·1	6,447
Sep 1958	3,270	33·5	6,682
Mar 1959	3,170	32·7	6,817
Jun 1960	3,500	32·1	7,207
Mar 1961	2,890	32·2	7,818

Source: R. L. Crouch, 'A Model of the U.K.'s Monetary Sector' (to appear in *Econometrica*).

† See Bibliography.

6 Sampling – Correlation and Regression

Two-Variable Regression

We know that the fitted regression line that one derives from a particular sample differs from the true or theoretical regression line. There are two constants, α and β_{yx}, in the regression equation

$$Y_i = \alpha + \beta_{yx}X_i + \varepsilon_i \tag{6.1}$$

and we form least-squares estimates of these constants $\hat{\alpha}$ and $\hat{\beta}_{yx}$ to get the estimated equation

$$Y_i = \hat{\alpha} + \hat{\beta}_{yx}X_i + e_i. \tag{6.2}$$

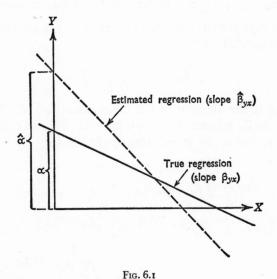

FIG. 6.1

The estimated line will differ from the theoretical line because (i) the intercept on the y-axis is different, i.e. $\hat{\alpha} \neq \alpha$, and (ii) the slope of the estimated line $\hat{\beta}_{yx}$ differs from the true slope β_{yx}.

In examining the sampling variation of the estimated line about the true line one must therefore analyse the two components of 'error' – that of the slope error and the part due to the intercept error. Obviously these two components are *necessarily* not independent since we used the value $\hat{\beta}_{yx}$ in estimating $\hat{\alpha}$ (i.e. $\hat{\alpha} = \overline{Y} - \hat{\beta}_{yx}\overline{X}$). As before, we shall first concentrate on the estimate $\hat{\beta}_{yx}$ and we shall later examine the variation of $\hat{\alpha}$. There is also one other sampling problem which we must defer until later – these are sampling properties of *predictions* of the value of Y for a given value of X. The estimated regression equation is used as a mechanism for predicting a value of Y for any given value of X. The variation of the predicted value of Y will obviously depend on both the slope and position of the line, and also on the particular value of X we choose. This third task is the most complicated of the sampling problems. But the first job is to examine the sampling variation of $\hat{\beta}_{yx}$.

As we found in Chapter 4, the sampling distribution of $\hat{\beta}_{yx}$ will have a mean equal to the true value β_{yx}. Thus the *mean* value of $\hat{\beta}_{yx} - \beta_{yx}$ is zero. We also saw that

$$\hat{\beta}_{yx} - \beta_{yx} = \sum x_i \varepsilon_i / \sum x_i^2, \quad \text{where } x_i = X_i - \overline{X} \text{ etc. as before.} \quad (6.3)$$

This can be expressed as a *weighted average of the ε_i's*. Given that the x_i's are fixed in repeated samples,

$$\hat{\beta}_{yx} - \beta_{yx} = \sum_i \left(\frac{x_i}{\sum x^2} \right) \varepsilon_i. \quad (6.4)$$

The 'weight' of the ith value of ε_i is the constant $x_i / \sum x^2$. The sampling variance of the $\hat{\beta}_{yx}$ is given by a simple formula: if k_1 and k_2 are constants, then, since ε_1 and ε_2 are independently distributed,

$$\text{var } (k_1\varepsilon_1 + k_2\varepsilon_2) = k_1^2 \text{ var } \varepsilon_1 + k_2^2 \text{ var } \varepsilon_2. \quad (6.5)$$

So that the variance of $\hat{\beta}_{yx} - \beta_{yx}$ is given by

$$\text{var}\left[\sum_i \left(\frac{x_i}{\sum x^2} \right) \varepsilon_i \right] = \frac{x_1^2}{(\sum x^2)^2} \text{ var } \varepsilon_1 + \frac{x_2^2}{(\sum x^2)^2} \text{ var } \varepsilon_2 + \dots$$
$$+ \frac{x_n^2}{(\sum x^2)^2} \text{ var } \varepsilon_n. \quad (6.6)$$

Now provided that we assume that the variance of ε does not vary – it is constant for all drawings – we may then write

$$\text{var } (\varepsilon_1) = \text{var } (\varepsilon_2) = \dots = \text{var } (\varepsilon_n) \quad (6.7)$$

as a constant var (ε).

So that

$$\text{var}\,(\hat{\beta}_{yx} - \beta_{yx}) = \frac{\sum x^2}{(\sum x^2)^2}\,\text{var}\,\varepsilon,$$

i.e.

$$\text{var}\,(\hat{\beta}_{yx} - \beta_{yx}) = \frac{\text{var}\,(\varepsilon)}{\sum x^2}. \tag{6.8}$$

The sampling variance of $\hat{\beta}_{yx}$ is given by the variance of the disturbances divided by the sum of squares of x.

Now we can easily calculate the denominator of this expression. The sum of the squares of deviations of the independent variable from its mean is a normal routine calculation in estimating $\hat{\beta}_{yx}$. The numerator is more involved. We do not know the variance of the disturbances – this is a theoretical value which one cannot observe. Evidence is, however, available from the observed residuals e_i, and we may use the sum of squares of the residuals in the estimate. The number of degrees of freedom in the variation of the e_i is two less than the number of observations. One degree of freedom is lost because the average of the e_i's is fixed (at zero) and one more is lost because the slope of the regression is fixed in calculating the e_i's. Thus

$$\text{estimate of var}\,(\varepsilon) = \sum e_i^2/(n-2)$$

$$= \sum (y_i - \hat{\beta}_{yx}x_i)^2/(n-2), \tag{6.9}$$

or, from Chapter 4 above,

$$= \sum y_i^2(1 - r^2)/(n-2). \tag{6.10}$$

Inserting this value in the above formula we obtain an estimate of sampling variance

$$\text{estimate of}\,\{\text{var}\,(\hat{\beta}_{yx} - \beta_{yx})\} = \frac{\sum y_i^2(1 - r^2)/(n-2)}{\sum x_i^2}. \tag{6.11}$$

Various alternative forms are available. For computation purposes the most convenient is

$$\text{est}\,\{\text{var}\,(\hat{\beta}_{yx} - \beta_{yx})\} = \frac{\sum y_i^2 - \hat{\beta}_{yx}\sum y_i x_i}{(\sum x_i^2)(n-2)} = \frac{1}{n-2}\left[\frac{\sum y_i^2}{\sum x_i^2} - \hat{\beta}_{yx}^2\right]$$

or

$$= \frac{\text{sum of squares of residuals}}{(\sum x_i^2)(n-2)}. \tag{6.12}$$

This can be quite easily calculated from the analysis of variance. The estimate of the residual variance is divided by $\sum x_i^2$.

It is easy to rationalise intuitively this formula for the sampling variance of $\hat{\beta}_{yx}$. The larger the variance of the residuals the more difficult it is to locate the slope of the true regression line. The observations will be dispersed widely about the true regression line and we need a very large number of observations to find a line with a slope of a given accuracy. The denominator increases with the number of observations of x – so the larger the number of observations the smaller the estimate of the sampling variance of $\hat{\beta}_{yx}$. Furthermore, in the deviations of x from the mean value (in this case zero) the denominator

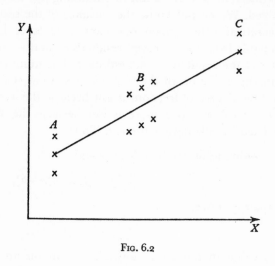

Fig. 6.2

will increase according to the *square* of the deviation. A wide dispersion of x will thus give rise to a small sampling variance. This corresponds, in an experimental situation, to a wide range of values for the independent variable – the wider the range the larger the importance of the systematic linear element relative to the experimental error. Diagrammatically we see that the group of six observations A and C enable us to locate the line much more accurately than the six observations labelled B. And it is also obvious that the greater the variance in the Y direction *about* the regression the more difficult it will be accurately to find the slope of the regression line.

Now we can return to the problem of finding the sampling variance of $\hat{\alpha}$. The estimate $\hat{\alpha}$ was formed by

$$\hat{\alpha} = \bar{Y} - \hat{\beta}_{yx}\bar{X}. \tag{6.13}$$

It is therefore clear that the sampling variance of $\hat{\alpha}$ involves the $\bar{X}$, the sampling variance of $\bar{Y}$, and the covariance of $\hat{\beta}_{yx}\bar{X}$ and $\bar{Y}$ as well as the variance of $\hat{\beta}_{yx}$. The variance of $\hat{\alpha}$ is given by

$$\text{var}(\hat{\alpha}) = \text{var}(\varepsilon)\left[\frac{1}{n} + \frac{\bar{X}^2}{\sum (X_i - \bar{X})^2}\right]. \tag{6.14}$$

The higher the value of $\bar{X}$ the higher the variance of $\hat{\alpha}$. The larger the sum of squares of x the smaller the variance.† Finally the larger the number of observations both terms in the square brackets diminish − so the variance becomes smaller. All these interpretations are clearly consistent within common-sense views of sampling properties of statistics. We can get an estimate of the variance of $\hat{\alpha}$ by simply substituting an estimate of the variance of ε in the formula, thus

$$\text{estimate of variance of } \hat{\alpha} = \frac{\sum e_i^2}{n-2}\left[\frac{1}{n} + \frac{\bar{X}^2}{\sum (X_i - \bar{X})^2}\right], \tag{6.15}$$

where the $\sum e_i^2$ is the sum of squares of the observed residuals. The denominator $n-2$ is the number of degrees of freedom in the residuals − we lose one for fitting the average and one for the regression slope. This expression outside the bracket is exactly the same as the estimate of the residual variance in the analysis of variance.

Prediction

Now we can turn to find the variance of values of Y which we predict from a knowledge of the *estimates* of the variance of $\hat{\beta}$ and $\hat{\alpha}$ and the given value of X. Clearly we can examine the variance of the value of $\hat{Y}*$ − the value of Y on the observed regression line. Thus, in the diagram, we observe that for a given X, X_0, the *true* regression would give a value of $Y*$ whereas the *observed* regression gives a predicted value $\hat{Y}*$. The sampling variance is then measured as the variance of

† For a proof and development of this formula see Johnston, *Econometric Methods*, pp. 16 ff.

$\hat{Y}^*$'s for all the sample regression lines about the true value Y^*. The variance is given by

$$\text{var} \, (\hat{Y}^*) = \text{var} \, (\varepsilon) \left[\frac{1}{n} + \frac{(X_0 - \bar{X})^2}{\sum (X_i - \bar{X}^2)} \right]. \tag{6.16}$$

Thus the farther the value of X_0 is from the mean of X the greater the variance of $\hat{Y}^*$. Again this is a reasonable result since as $X_0 - \bar{X}$ increases, so also we find that, on the average, that part of the error

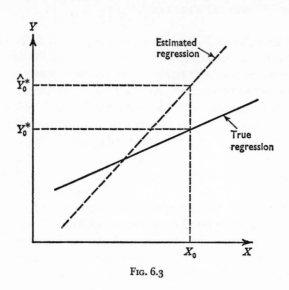

FIG. 6.3

which is due to the fact that the estimated slope differs from the true slope also increases. The lines 'fan-out', so the further one goes the greater the probability of a large difference between $\hat{Y}^*$ and Y^*.

Up to now we have been concerned with predicting the value *on* the regression line. The variance arises because the regression line we measure differs from the true regression line. Now we know that actual realised values of Y vary: in particular they do not lie *on* the true regression line. By our hypothesis they are distributed about the theoretical regression with a constant variance, i.e. var (ε). Now it is obvious that if one wanted to predict a value of Y (as distinct from the value on the true regression line Y^*) one must take into account that it inevitably involves the variance of ε. Even if one knew the *true* regression one would only be able to predict with certainty the value Y^*. The actual value of Y would invariably involve the variation in ε_0. The value of ε_0 can never be predicted. It constitutes a variability inherent in our model and cannot be reduced or eliminated by taking a larger sample. All we can do is to get better estimates of the variance of ε_0 by increasing the size of sample. The chance distribution of ε's always remains.

If, then, the task is to predict the actual value of Y we must consider it in two stages: first we predict the value on the regression line, i.e. $\hat{Y}^*$, and then we assert that the actual value of Y will be distributed about that $\hat{Y}^*$ as mean with a variance given by the estimate of the variance of ε. Thus if we consider the sampling variance of the predicted actual value of Y we must add var (ε) to the sampling variance of $\hat{Y}^*$, i.e. since ε_0 is independent of the sample values $\varepsilon_1, \varepsilon_2 \ldots \varepsilon_n$ which determine $\hat{Y}^*$,

$$\text{var } (\hat{Y}) = \text{var } (\hat{Y}^* + \varepsilon_0) = \text{var } (\hat{Y}^*) + \text{var } (\varepsilon_0)$$

$$= \text{var } (\hat{Y}^*) + \text{var } (\varepsilon),$$

$$\text{var } (\hat{Y}) = \text{var } (\varepsilon) \left[1 + \frac{1}{n} + \frac{(X_0 - \bar{X})^2}{\sum_i (X_i - \bar{X})^2} \right]. \tag{6.17}$$

As one can see, the last two terms in the square brackets become smaller as the sample size increases; but even if $n \to \infty$ the variance of $\hat{Y}$ would still be equal to the variance of ε. The *estimate* of the sampling variance of $\hat{Y}$ is given by simply writing in an estimate of the variance of ε. This is exactly the same as before:

$$\text{est. of var } (\hat{Y}) = \frac{\sum e_i^2}{n-2} \left[1 + \frac{1}{n} + \frac{(X_0 - \bar{X})^2}{\sum (X_i - \bar{X})^2} \right]. \tag{6.18}$$

Example

From a family budget survey we obtain the following data:

$$N = 1,190$$

$$\Sigma X = 60,258 \qquad \Sigma (X - \bar{X})^2 = 1,145,740$$

$$\Sigma Y = 5,345 \qquad \Sigma (Y - \bar{Y})^2 = 80,451$$

$$\Sigma (Y - \bar{Y})(X - \bar{X}) = 101,867.$$

Find the estimate of the regression of Y (expenditure on fish and meat in £ a month) on X (total household expenditure a month).

$$\hat{\beta}_{yx} = \frac{101,867}{1,145,740} = 0.0889.$$

The correlation between X and Y is

$$r_{yn} = \frac{101,867}{\sqrt{(1,145,740 \times 80,451)}} = 0.335643.$$

The standard error of $\hat{\beta}_{yx}$ may be obtained by first calculating an estimate of the residual variance:

$$\text{estimate of var } (\varepsilon) = \frac{80,451}{1,188} [1 - (0.3356)^2] = 60.1.$$

So then the estimate of the standard error of $\hat{\beta}_{yx}$ is found by

$$\text{estimate of sampling variance of } \hat{\beta}_{yx} = \frac{\text{est of var } (\varepsilon)}{\sum(X - \bar{X})^2}$$

$$= \frac{60.1}{1,145,740} = 0.0000525$$

$$\text{estimate of standard error of } \hat{\beta}_{yx} = 0.0072.$$

In this example the sample is large enough to ignore the nice adjustments of small sampling theory; the number of degrees of freedom in the residual variance is approximately the same as the number of observations. Find the standard error of the predicted Y for $X_0 = £75$.

Regression with Three Variables

The extension of the sampling theory to regressions with more than two variables is conceptually straightforward, though it is algebraically messy. With simple regression we saw that the variance of $\hat{\beta}_{yx}$ was given by the ratio of the var (ε) to the sum of squares of $X - \bar{X}$. Now we seek the analogous magnitudes in the true regression

$$Y = \beta_{y1.2}X_1 + \beta_{y2.1}X_2 + \beta_0 + \varepsilon \tag{6.19}$$

and the estimate of the regression plane

$$\hat{Y}^* = \hat{\beta}_{y1.2}X_1 + \hat{\beta}_{y2.1}X_2 + \hat{\beta}_0. \tag{6.20}$$

Let us consider the problem of finding the sampling variance of $\hat{\beta}_{y1.2}$.

The numerator in the sampling variance of $\hat{\beta}_{y1.2}$ is clearly going to be var (ε), just as in the simple two-variable case. The denominator is, however, more troublesome. In the two-variable case it was simply the sum of squares of the deviations $(X - \bar{X})$. But in the three-variable case we have two X's, X_1 and X_2 and it is clear from the formula for $\hat{\beta}_{y1.2}$, i.e.

$$\hat{\beta}_{y1.2} = \frac{(\sum yx_1)(\sum x_2^2) - (\sum x_2 y)(\sum x_1 x_2)}{(\sum x_1^2)(\sum x_2^2) - (\sum x_1 x_2)^2}, \qquad (6.21)$$

that both x_1 and x_2 (which are the deviations $x_1 = (X_1 - \bar{X}_1)$ and $x_2 = (X_2 - \bar{X}_2)$) enter into the calculation. The natural way of finding an analogue to the denominator in the simple case is to divide numerator and denominator by $\sum x_2^2$, i.e.

$$\hat{\beta}_{y1.2} = \frac{\sum yx_1 - \{(\sum x_2 y)(\sum x_1 x_2)\}/(\sum x_2^2)}{\sum x_1^2 - (\sum x_1 x_2)^2/(\sum x_2^2)}. \qquad (6.22)$$

The denominator is now analogous to the sum of squares of residuals in the simple case, i.e.

$$\sum x_1^2 - \frac{(\sum x_1 x_2)^2}{\sum x_2^2} = \sum x_1^2 \left[1 - \frac{(\sum x_1 x_2)^2}{(\sum x_1^2)(\sum x_2^2)} \right]$$

$$= \sum x_1^2 [1 - r_{12}^2]. \qquad (6.23)$$

This expression reflects the sum of squares of x_1 when we have deducted that fraction (r_{12}^2) of the sum of squares of x_1 that is explained by x_2. In other words, this is the residual sum of squares in the regression of x_1 on x_2. This constitutes then the denominator in the sampling variance of $\hat{\beta}_{y1.2}$, i.e.

$$\operatorname{var} \hat{\beta}_{y1.2} = \frac{\operatorname{var}(\varepsilon)}{\sum x_1^2 - (\sum x_1 x_2)/^2 (\sum x_2^2)}$$

$$= \frac{\operatorname{var}(\varepsilon)}{\sum x_1^2 \{1 - r_{12}^2\}}, \qquad (6.24)$$

where r_{12} is the simple correlation coefficient between X_1 and X_2, or

$$\operatorname{var}(\hat{\beta}_{y1.2}) = \frac{\text{variance of disturbance}}{\substack{\text{residual sum of squares of } X_1 \text{ in the} \\ \text{simple regression of } X_1 \text{ on } X_2}}.$$

In the denominator instead of the sum of squares of x we have the sum of squares of the residual in the simple regression of x_1 on x_2. Similarly we have

$$\text{var}\,(\hat{\beta}_{y2.1}) = \frac{\text{var}\,(\varepsilon)}{\sum x_2^2\{1 - r_{12}^2\}}. \qquad (6.25)$$

Now we can turn to the problem of obtaining an *estimate* of the variance of $\hat{\beta}_{y1.2}$. The denominator presents no problem – it is calculated directly from the sample just as in the case of simple regression. The numerator, the variance of ε, can be estimated from the sum of squares of residuals in the multiple regression. The measured residual is

$$e_i = Y_i - \hat{\beta}_0 - \hat{\beta}_{y1.2}X_{1i} - \hat{\beta}_{y2.1}X_{2i}$$

or

$$e_i = y_i - \hat{\beta}_{y1.2}x_{1i} - \hat{\beta}_{y2.1}x_{2i}. \qquad (6.26)$$

Now we know that the sum of squares $\sum e_i^2$ is given by

$$\sum y^2 - \hat{\beta}_{y1.2}\sum yx_1 - \hat{\beta}_{y2.1}\sum yx_2$$

or by

$$\sum y^2(1 - R^2), \qquad (6.27)$$

where R is the multiple correlation coefficient.†

The next problem is to find the number of degrees of freedom in this sum of squares. We have lost one degree of freedom on fitting the mean (or β_0) and one degree of freedom each for the two partial regression coefficients $\hat{\beta}_{y1.2}$ and $\hat{\beta}_{y2.1}$, so the degrees of freedom left are $(n-3)$. The estimate of the variance of   is given by

$$\text{est. of var}\,(\varepsilon) = \frac{\sum e_i^2}{\text{degrees of freedom}} = \frac{\sum y^2 - \hat{\beta}_{y1.2}\sum yx_1 - \hat{\beta}_{y2.1}\sum yx_2}{n-3}.$$

$$(6.28)$$

Thus, putting the pieces together, we have

$$\text{est. of var}\,(\hat{\beta}_{y1.2}) = \frac{\sum y^2(1 - R^2)}{(n-3)\sum x_1^2(1 - r_{12}^2)}$$

† See Chapter 5.

or

$$\text{est. of var } (\hat{\beta}_{y1.2}) = \frac{\sum y^2 - \hat{\beta}_{y1.2}\sum yx_1 - \hat{\beta}_{y2.1}\sum yx_2}{(n-3)\{\sum x^2 - (\sum x_1 x_2)/(\sum x_2^2)\}}. \quad (6.29)$$

In practice, of course, we calculate the estimate of the variance of ε separately since it is used frequently in various aspects of the analysis.

One particular use of the multiple regression approach is to examine whether the fraction of the variance of Y explained by X_1 and X_2 is significantly different from zero. Here we are not examining individual regression coefficients one at a time to see how they vary with different samples. Instead we are examining the *whole* regression plane to see whether the configuration of observations could have arisen by chance from a population in which X_1 and X_2 have *no* systematic (and linear) effect on Y. The larger the fraction of the variance of Y explained by X_1 and X_2 in the sample the more likely it is that the result could not have arisen by chance from a population where X_1 and X_2 had no effect on Y. To examine this problem we can put the results in the form of an analysis of variance table. The sum of squares is split between that due to the regression and the remainder called here the 'residual'. We can then form the ratio of the estimate of the variance

Source of variation	*Sum of squares*	*Degrees of freedom*	*Estimate of variances*
Regression	$\hat{\beta}_{y1.2}\sum yx_1$ $+\hat{\beta}_{y2.1}\sum yx_2$	2	$\left(\hat{\beta}_{y1.2}\sum yx_1 \atop +\hat{\beta}_{y2.1}\sum yx_2\right)\Big/2$
Residual	$\sum y^2 - \hat{\beta}_{y1.2}\sum yx_1$ $-\hat{\beta}_{y2.1}\sum yx_2$	$n-3$	$\left(\sum y^2 - \hat{\beta}_{y1.2}\sum yx_1 \atop -\hat{\beta}_{y2.1}\sum yx_2\right)\Big/(n-3)$
Total	$\sum y^2$	$n-1$	$\sum y^2/(n-1)$

due to the regression to the estimate of the variance of the residuals (or errors). This ratio is distributed as F with 2 and $(n-3)$ degrees of freedom. We thus compare our experimental F

$$\text{experimental } F = \frac{\text{SS due to regression}/2,}{\text{SS in residual}/(n-3)} \quad (6.30)$$

with the F given by the null hypothesis where the X_1 and X_2 have no effect on Y. The normal kind of significance test is applied.

One interesting aspect is the relation between the analysis of variance table and the multiple correlation coefficient. We defined

$$\text{residual SS} = (\text{SS of } \Upsilon)(1 - R^2). \tag{6.31}$$

Now it is clear that the R^2 is not defined in terms of the degrees of freedom. For we know that the left-hand side residual sum of squares has $(n-3)$ degrees of freedom, and the sum of squares of Υ has $(n-1)$ degrees of freedom. So it is sensible to redefine a new concept of multiple correlation which does take into account the degrees of freedom involved. We define $\bar{R}^2$ as the 'coefficient of determination' by dividing both sides by the appropriate degrees of freedom

$$\frac{\text{residual SS}}{n-3} = \frac{\text{SS of } \Upsilon}{n-1} (1 - \bar{R}^2)$$

or

$$\text{est. of residual variance} = [\text{est. of variance of } \Upsilon](1 - \bar{R}^2). \tag{6.32}$$

Similarly

$$\frac{\text{SS due to regression}}{2} = \bar{R}^2 \cdot \frac{\text{SS of } \Upsilon}{n-1}.$$

So that

$$\text{experimental } F = \frac{\bar{R}^2}{1 - \bar{R}_2}. \tag{6.33}$$

This explains the close relationship between F and $\bar{R}^2$.

For 4 variable regression the only difference arises when we make adjustments for degrees of freedom. For, in addition to fitting the mean, we have now fitted *three* other constants in the form of the regression coefficients. Thus the residual variance has $n-4$ degrees of freedom. Three degrees of freedom are used up in fitting the three regression coefficients – and there is one used in fitting the mean. Thus the analysis of the variance table will look as follows:

	Sum of squares	*Degrees of freedom*
Regression	$R^2_{y.123}\sum y^2$	3
Residual	$(1 - R^2_{y.123}) \sum y^2$	$n-4$
Total	$\sum y^2$	$n-1$

Again we can define the coefficient of determination $\bar{R}^2_{y.123}$

$$1 - \bar{R}^2_{y.123} = \frac{\text{SS}(e_{y.123})/(n-4)}{\text{SS}(y)/(n-1)} \tag{6.34}$$

as the appropriate ratio of sums of squares adjusted for the number of degrees of freedom. The numerator is simply an estimate of the residual variance, and the denominator is an estimate of the variance of y.

It will be observed that $\bar{R}^2$ is always less than R^2. $\bar{R}^2$ is a better estimate of the true value of the multiple correlation coefficient in the population $\mathfrak{R}^2$. Oddly enough, it is conceivable that $\bar{R}^2$ may be *negative*, i.e. it is conceivable that, for example,

$$\frac{\text{residual SS}}{\text{SS of } Y} \cdot \frac{n-1}{n-3} \quad \text{may exceed unity.}$$

This will occur if the regression explains a very small fraction of the total sum of squares. We will give a practical example of this later. On reflection it will be observed, however, that if $\bar{R}^2$ is a good estimator of $\mathfrak{R}^2$ and the latter value is zero we should expect some of the sample $\bar{R}^2$'s to be less than zero. In fact $\bar{R}^2$ is an *estimate* of a population value which cannot be negative; but clearly the estimate may be negative. In this sense the squared sign of $\bar{R}^2$ is misleading.†

The statistical interpretation of R^2 and $\bar{R}^2$ is fairly straightforward. We now have to deal with the more difficult econometric interpretation. The first point to be borne in mind is that the R^2 tells us only how efficient the statistician has been in fitting a plane to the observations. A high R^2 tells us that the residual variance about the plane is relatively small. It does not tell us that the theory is a 'good one'. For example, we know that one can produce a high R^2 but not necessarily a high $\bar{R}^2$ by adding independent variables; but, of course, this is a confession of failure of the theory. There is little difference between saying that you need a large number of independent variables to predict y and that the theory is useless.

Even if the number of independent variables is small a high R^2 may be achieved quite easily if there are dominant trends in the Y, X_1 and

† It might reasonably occur to the reader that it is really inefficient to estimate negative $\bar{R}^2$'s. The best procedure would clearly be to rule out this possibility in setting up the estimating method. This can be demonstrated – but it does involve more complicated methods of estimation.

X_2. These trends might be over a time series – as, for example, where Y is output in a year, X_1 is the labour force and X_2 is the quantity of capital at the beginning of the year. Examples of this kind will be examined in later chapters. A high R^2 is then evidence of dominant trends in all time series. The same effects might be observed over a cross-section of firms – large firms will have large Y, X_1 and X_2 and small firms small values. The high R^2 then reflects the fact that firms vary in size from being very large to very small.

In practice, one normally wants to use data not merely to predict trends but also to estimate the reaction to *changes* in the independent variables. One example is the problem of the effect of money on income. A regression of income on money produces a very high R^2 (or r^2) because of the trends in the series. But the important problem is to predict the *change* in income due to a *change* in the quantity of money. If we regress the *change* in income on the *change* in money we shall get a much lower r^2 (or R^2) because the trend in changes is not so dominant as in the original series. But this does not mean that the theory is inferior; it merely reflects the fact that it is more difficult to predict changes in income from changes in money because there is not such a large constant trend element in these series.

The interpretation of R^2 must be carefully adjusted according to the data it describes. One important example in econometric applications is when we have a cross-section of firms (or persons or families) of approximately the same size and attempt to interpret the resulting $(1 - R^2)$ in terms of sampling theory. Normally we should interpret deviations of observations from the regression plane as random drawings from a population. The ith family, for example, will have an ε_i or e_i attached to it which will vary randomly from one sample to another. But this is clearly not the way in which the families behave. Part of the ε_i associated with the ith family is clearly a constant and not a random variable; if, for example, we are explaining variations in money holdings with income as the independent variable, it may well be that one particular family is ultra-cautious and always keeps a very large stock of cash on hand. This 'ultra-cautiousness' is clearly a *constant* associated with the ith family and is not a random variable. We might then imagine that each family has a certain *constant* associated with it. But the value of $(1 - R^2)$ will measure the variation of these constants as well as the truly random variations. As a measure of the random variation $(1 - R^2)$ is clearly too large (i.e. R^2 is too small). In other words the high value of $(1 - R^2)$ is clearly the result of *specification errors*. These arise because we did not in fact attach a special constant to each family, and we have interpreted these as part of the random variations. In this case, therefore, we get the result that a low R^2 in a cross-section of units of a similar size may *overestimate* the true sampling variation because of the mis-specification of the model.

The reader may, at this stage, wonder whether there is any value at all in R^2 or $\bar{R}^2$. As with all other statistical measures they need to be used and interpreted with caution. The numerical interpretation is straightforward but the economic inferences are rarely easy to draw.

Questions for Discussion

1. From the various regressions calculated in Question 3 of 'Questions for Discussion' in Chapter 4 (p. 115), find the standard errors of the coefficients. Compare the coefficients with the estimates of the standard errors. Give a general interpretation of the strength of monetary multipliers in this period.

2. From Question 4, p. 142, find the standard error of the parameter α_1 of the equation, and use analysis of variance techniques to interpret the regression.

3. Using the data in Question 2, p. 142, on multiple correlation, find the standard error of the estimated regression coefficient $\hat{\beta}_{y1.2}$.

   Estimate the multiple correlation coefficient and complete the analysis of variance table. Discuss the 'significance' of the regression equation.

4. Consider two alternative models of income determination:

   $$\text{Keynesian} \qquad Y = aA + a_0,$$
   $$\text{Monetary} \qquad Y = bM + b_0,$$

   where Y is private disposable money income, A is 'autonomous expenditure', and M is the stock of money. Note that $Y = C + A$, where C is consumption (or more accurately, consumer expenditure). The a, b and a_0, b_0 are constants to be estimated.

   Investigate the possibility of spurious correlation in the Keynesian model. How could this be eliminated?

   Suppose further that autonomous expenditure includes private capital formation and the budgetary deficit of public authorities (i.e.

public expenditure minus taxes). Note that *disposable* income excludes taxes, and discuss the implications for the expected values of the coefficients of correlation. [See C. R. Barrett and A. A. Walters, 'The Stability of Keynesian and Monetary Multipliers', *Review of Economics and Statistics* (Nov 1966).] (This example emphasises the importance of deriving the appropriate model and inferring the appropriate tests – avoiding spurious correlation.)

5. Consider the use of likelihood methods in discussing the plausibility of hypothetical regression coefficients.

6. Examine the effect of using lagged values of the dependent variable as independent variables in a regression equation – (i) on the values of R^2, and (ii) on the standard errors of the regression coefficients of the other independent variables, when there is a strong trend in the series of the dependent variable. Find some illustrations of the principles.

7. A regression equation of y on x is calculated from n observations. Consider an alternative model where y is regressed on x and on z. Can you suggest the conditions under which the first estimate of $\hat{\beta}_{yx}$ will be a better estimate of the effect of x on y, *even holding z constant*, than will the partial coefficient $\hat{\beta}_{yx.z}$. (Note that one requires a definition of what one means by 'better'; it might be suggested that the appropriate definition should take into account both the error of specification as well as the sampling error.)

Part Three

Econometric Models

In Part II we were concerned with models which could easily be expressed in the form of a single equation – given certain independent variables we saw that the purpose was to predict the value of the dependent variable. In Part III the problem is extended to consider the case where there is *simultaneous* dependence – where two variables, for example, are connected by *two* equations (such as price and quantity linked by both an equation representing the demand curve and another representing the supply curve). One of the main problems is to discover whether the observations will enable one to measure one or both of these simultaneous equations. This is the problem of *identification*, which we discuss, largely in an informal way, in Chapter 7. Much of the problem of identification, however, is concerned with the *economics* of the process that generates the data; and we shall turn to examine these problems in Part IV of this book. Chapter 8 discusses the problem of describing the structure of models of simultaneous equations, examining their properties, and estimating the coefficients. Many people would regard this topic, the estimation of simultaneous equations, as the central core of econometric theory. Nevertheless one can understand much of applied econometric work without an intimate acquaintance with the problems of estimation of equation systems. The emphasis in this Part is on the character of the systems themselves, their dynamic properties, and the various forms in which they can be expressed.

7 Identification

A Simple Case of Demand and Supply

It is common to use an equation to express the essence of an economic theory. Thus we use the equation

$$\text{quantity} = f(\text{price})$$

to express the demand relationship. In order to confront the theory with data we specify that the observations are described by a simple relation – usually linear or linear in the logarithms – and an additive 'disturbance'. Thus we may have

$$Y_1 = \beta_0 + \beta_{12} Y_2 + \varepsilon, \qquad (7.1)$$

where

Y_1 is the quantity or logarithm of the quantity,

Y_2 is the price or logarithm of the price,

ε is the disturbance, and

β_0, β_{12} are the constants

as the demand equation which predicts quantity for a given price.

This equation supposes that the price is given – but it cannot be controlled by experiment or, normally, by administrative fiat. In normal economic theory the price is generated by the interaction – 'the scissors' is Marshall's famous phrase – of demand and supply. Consider then a supply process in which the quantity put on the market is determined by the ruling price. This might be expressed through the supply equation

$$Y_1 = \alpha_0 + \alpha_{12} Y_2 + \eta, \qquad (7.2)$$

where η is the disturbance and α_0, α_{12} are the constants of the supply equation. Normal theory would predict that $\beta_{12} < 0$ and that $\alpha_{12} > 0$; the demand curve slopes downwards and the supply curve upwards.

Now we have observations on Y_1 and Y_2 – quantities and prices on the market. The question which naturally arises is whether the observations group themselves around the demand curve or around the supply curve – or are they simply some hopeless mixture of both.

First let us suppose that there are *no* disturbances in each of the equations. What would the observations reveal? Figure 7.2 shows the two lines – the downward sloping one the demand curve and the

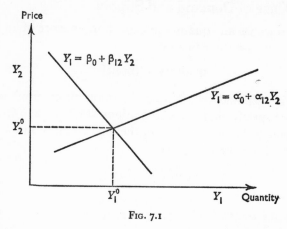

FIG. 7.1

upward sloping one the supply curve. Obviously if these conditions hold we shall simply observe the quantity Y_1^0 and the price Y_2^0. Unless the constants, β_0, β_{12}, α_0, α_{12}, change the observed price and quantity will be the same in each period. We record the unchanged equilibrium values Y_1^0 and Y_2^0 and that is all. (The algebraic solution is derived from the fact that we have two unknowns (Y_1, Y_2) and two linear equations.)

Now consider a situation where the demand line has *no* disturbance but where a random element enters into the supply relation. In particular let us imagine (Fig. 7.2) that the weather has a random influence on the supply. Examples of this are readily available – yields of many crops are related intimately to rainfall. If, therefore, the random rainfall affects the supply let us suppose that this can be represented by the variable η. Let us therefore start off in equilibrium (with $\eta = 0$) where the demand line and the true supply regression line intersect, i.e. where the price is Y_2^0 and the quantity Y_1^0. In the next period, however, the rainfall is particularly heavy and the quantity supplied rises to Y_1^1 [i.e. η for this period is $(Y_1^1 - Y_1^0)$]. But if the quantity Y_1^1 is put on the market the price will fall to Y_2^1, thus we shall observe the market relationship represented by the price Y_2^1 and the quantity Y_1^1. In the following period a drought occurs. The supply which would be offered for sale if there were *normal* or *average* rainfall would be Y_1^0. But due to the drought the amount which is actually available for sale is only Y_1^2 (i.e. the η in this period is $Y_1^2 - Y_1^*$). This quantity on the market will give a price of Y_2^2. So we see Y_1^2, Y_2^2 as the observation of this period.

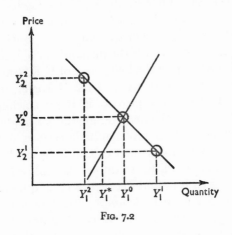

FIG. 7.2

The result is that we collect the statistics in the three periods represented by the circled points in the Figure. These describe the demand curve exactly (indeed if we *know* that the demand relationship was linear, two observations would be sufficient!). Paradoxically it is *variability in the supply relation* which enables us to measure the *demand* line. It will be readily seen that if we postulate that the demand curve stays in one place while the supply curve itself moves from one period to another the observations generated will describe the demand curve.

Is this description of the ideal state useful as a model of reality? Clearly this depends on the circumstances; each case must be judged on its *a priori* merits. With consumer expenditure on food, for example, it seems reasonable to suppose that the demand for food does not change rapidly over time; it moves, if at all, only slowly over time. As an approximation then it may well be sensible to treat the demand curve as fixed. On the other hand it is clear that the supply of food may be determined by random factors – apart from the price the weather is probably one of the main determinants of the quantity supplied.

Another example of conditions of identification which may be readily argued on *a priori* grounds is when the *price* is determined by factors outside the country. Consider, for example, the demand for rubber in the United Kingdom. It is clear that there is a world-wide market for rubber. The fraction of the world's supply of rubber that is consumed by the United Kingdom is very small Quite large variations. in the consumption of rubber by the United Kingdom will have very little influence on the world market and on the price set for rubber. Traders in the United Kingdom can import as much rubber as they wish at that given world price. If the demand curve is stable, variations in the world price will cause the behaviour of U.K. traders to trace out the market demand for rubber in the U.K. However, the reader might be struck by the fact that the proviso 'if' is extraordinarily important in this case. Variations in the demand for rubber might well be due to variations in income, the price of synthetic rubber, of motor cars etc. The demand curve for rubber may exhibit little stability *per se*, but it may be a stable function of, for example, the stock of motor cars. The natural approach then is to find the regression of quantity of rubber on price of rubber and the stock of motor cars. This would be a sensible form of analysis provided that the stock of motor cars was not itself dependent on the quantity of rubber consumed this year. Obviously this condition is normally satisfied.†

The addition of a variable to a demand function is quite a common procedure when it is thought that price by itself is not the dominant variable involved. Most economists would ascribe an important role to income. The demand curve might be described by the equation

$$Y_1 = \beta_0 + \beta_{12} Y_2 + \beta_{1x} X + \varepsilon, \tag{7.3}$$

where Y_2 is relative price and X is real disposable income. Now consider a simple supply equation

$$Y_1 = \alpha_0 + \alpha_{12} Y_2 + \eta, \tag{7.4}$$

and, as, before we assume that the amount demanded is equal to the amount supplied – both being denoted by the variable Y_1.

---

† During World War II, in the United States, the dire shortage of rubber tyres must have given rise to a considerable scrapping of motor cars. But clearly this involves a model where the *quantity* is fixed (by wartime shortages) and the price or ration is variable.

Let us now examine the question of identification. From observations of Y_1, Y_2 and X. What can be inferred about the slopes β_{12}, β_{1x} and α_{12}? To fix ideas, let us start off with the assumption that the disturbances ε and η are always zero. In this case the supply curve SS will be fixed as in Figure 7.3. If an increase in income results in an increased quantity bought, for any given price, we need to draw a different demand curve for each level of income. D_{100} represents the demand

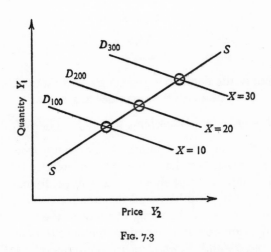

Fig. 7.3

curve when income $(X) = 100$, D_{200} the curve when income $(X) = 200$ etc. Now it follows that *provided there is variation in income*, the statistics will trace the supply curve as shown by the observations circled in the figure. The supply curve is identified but not the demand curve. The income acts rather like an independent control variable in an experiment – it creates a new environment (demand conditions) to which the suppliers react.

Oddly enough, of the two equations – the demand and the supply – it is the one with the additional variable (X) that is *not* identified. Adding additional variables to the demand equation enables us to identify the supply equation. This is because the additional variable moves the demand curve around and so gives rise to different price stimuli to the suppliers. In responding to these different prices the suppliers trace out the supply curve. If we had added income as a variable in the supply equation as well as in the demand equation we should not have been able to identify the supply curve since it would have moved whenever the demand curve moved.

A Formal Model

It is possible to express these ideas formally by examining the following equations (keeping the assumption that $\varepsilon = \eta = 0$):

$$\left. \begin{array}{ll} \text{Demand} & Y_1 = \beta_0 + \beta_{12} Y_2 + \beta_{1x} X \\ \text{Supply} & Y_1 = \alpha_0 + \alpha_{12} Y_2 \end{array} \right\}. \tag{7.5}$$

We can multiply the demand equation by a constant λ and the supply equation by $(1 - \lambda)$ and add the two sides to get

$$Y_1 = \lambda\beta_0 + (1 - \lambda)\alpha_0 + [\lambda\beta_{12} + (1 - \lambda)\alpha_{12}] Y_2 + \lambda\beta_{1x} X. \tag{7.6}$$

This is a 'mongrel' equation containing coefficients from both demand and supply equation. But the 'mongrel' is of exactly the same *form* as the demand equation, i.e. it shows Y_1 as a linear function of price (Y_2) and income (X). On the other hand the mongrel is quite different from the supply equation since the mongrel contains the variable X whereas the supply equation does not. When we measure the linear relationship between Y_2 and Y_1 and X, we measure the mongrel relationship. This depends on the arbitrary value of λ.

To see this geometrically we can represent the demand and supply equations as planes in Figure 7.4.

The supply plane is shown as that with close diagonal shading in the N.E.-S.W. direction. As price increases so the quantity supplied increases, thus the plane slopes upwards. The assumption that the supply does not depend on income means that, as we move along the income axis, the position (and of course slope) of the plane is unchanged. One illustration of this feature is that the distance d, which represents the quantity which would be supplied if the price dropped to zero, is the same for *all* levels of income. Similarly for any *given* price the quantity supplied will be the same for all incomes.

This is not true of the demand plane however. This has a positive slope in the income direction. As income increases, for a given price, the quantity demanded increases. One may here imagine the demand plane to be represented by a wedge-shaped piece of paper fitting into the box of the Figure. The thin end of the wedge (*CD* in the Figure) represents the price–quantity demand line at the lowest income. The

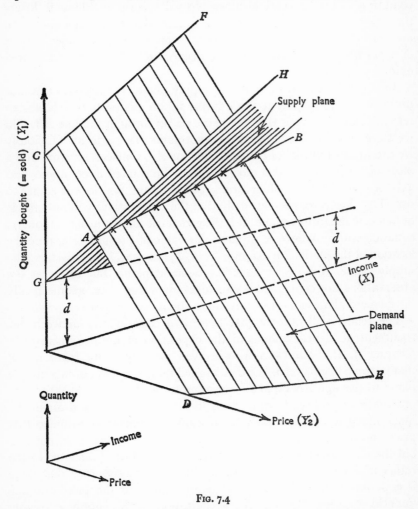

FIG. 7.4

sides of the wedge are represented by *CF* and *DE* – the *CF* edge represents the quantity bought (at zero price) as linearly increasing with income; and *DE* represents the price level at which no amount is bought and this price again depends on the level of income.

In the market we observe price–quantity–income situations which are represented by the crosses on line AB. This is the intersection of the two planes and these points satisfy both demand and supply conditions. The observations along AB will clearly enable us to locate the supply plane – because we are assuming that it does not vary with income. The AB line will enable us to locate the GH line since a piece of paper fitted to AB, such that the distance d is the same, will be in a unique position.

But this is not the case with the supply plane. We have no constant distance (corresponding to the d in the supply plane) to which we can refer. All we observe is that the plane passes through the line AB, and we have no other assumptions or information to guide us. Obviously we can fit any number of planes to the line AB. One can imagine that a piece of cardboard hinged along AB may be rotated freely about that axis; it will satisfy the observations at any of the positions it comes to rest. This illustrates geometrically that the observations will not enable us to locate the supply plane. It is the geometric analogue of the mongrel equation with unknown λ. A particular value of λ would determine the location of the plane. For example $\lambda = 0$, $Y_1 = \alpha_0 + \alpha_{12}Y_2$ and we have the supply plane. If $\lambda = 1$ we have the demand plane. But as far as the observations are concerned λ can take any value – i.e. geometrically the demand plane can rotate anywhere about the AB axis.

The reader will observe that there is a close affinity between our treatment of identification and the exposition of multicollinearity in Chapter 5. In both cases we observed price–quantity relationships that lay on a line like AB. We then argued that we could not fit a unique plane to the line AB because any number of planes would satisfy the observations – all we have to do is to rotate the cardboard about the hinge along AB. In our example of multicollinearity we assumed that price and income always moved linearly together so we could not seek out the separate effect of each variable on the quantity bought. In the rather different example of identification we have supposed that there is a perfect positive (linear) relationship between the price and the quantity supplied through the specification of the supply equation. Thus we cannot separately assess the effects of income and price on quantity in the demand equation.[†] This is, of course, the extreme case

† Oddly enough the two concepts were developed quite independently and are still treated as such in textbooks.

of multicollinearity and lack of identification because Y_1 and Y_2 are perfectly correlated in the supply equation when we assume $\eta = 0$.

Now let us return to the original two equation model of demand and supply and let us now assume that *the disturbances are not zero*. This means that the observations will not lie exactly on the planes but they will be scattered about or along the planes in a random manner. The question now turns on what one can adduce about the slope of the planes from the scatter of observations. This will, in turn, depend on the rules of behaviour of the random disturbances and upon their size.

Begin first with the simple example of the effect of the weather which we considered above. In a formal specification the demand and supply are given by the equation system

$$\left. \begin{array}{ll} \text{Demand} & Y_1 = \beta_{12} Y_2 + \beta_0 + \varepsilon, \\ \text{Supply} & Y_1 = \alpha_{12} Y_2 + \alpha_0 + \eta \end{array} \right\}. \tag{7.7}$$

We saw that when ε and η were always zero we could not identify either the demand curve or the supply curve. Now suppose that ε is still zero (i.e. the demand curve has no disturbances) but that η behaves like a random variable with a mean of zero. Thus any price–quantity observation must be exactly *on the demand curve* but it will not (except by an odd accident) lie on the supply line. This is exactly like the case where the random variable was a measure of the effect of rainfall on the crop. We can represent this formally by deducting the supply equation from the demand equation so that

$$(\beta_{12} - \alpha_{12}) Y_2 + (\beta_0 - \alpha_0) - \eta = 0,$$

i.e.

$$Y_2 = \frac{\eta - (\beta_0 - \alpha_0)}{\beta_{12} - \alpha_{12}}. \tag{7.8}$$

This means that Y_2 the price is a random variable since it is a linear function of η.† We can then feed it into the demand equation to find the quantity. Alternatively we could have found Y_1 as a linear function of η by eliminating Y_2, i.e.

$$Y_1 = \frac{\alpha_{12} \beta_0 - \beta_{12} \alpha_0 - \beta_{12} \eta}{\alpha_{12} - \beta_{12}}. \tag{7.9}$$

† There are a few difficulties we are skirting here. One condition is clearly that $\beta_{12} - \alpha_{12} \neq 0$; but this will be the case only if the two lines coincide. Secondly Y_2 must never be negative; price cannot sensibly be less than zero. This involves an upper bound on η and appropriate values for the constants in the equations.

This probably makes more economic sense in the weather example on p. 167; the quantity is now expressed as a random variable and we feed it into the demand equation to determine price *exactly*. But in principle the result is the same as before.

Now let us complicate the model by introducing a disturbance into the demand equation, i.e. ε is not always zero. Suppose also that ε and η are independently distributed so that they are also uncorrelated as well. The identification now crucially depends upon the size of the variance of the disturbances. Let us imagine that the disturbances in the demand equation are very small relative to the disturbances in the supply equations; for example suppose that $\sigma_\varepsilon = \sigma_\eta / 100$. Then common sense suggests that we may treat this case as *approximately* the same as the previous example. The observations will trace out the demand curve rather than the supply curve. If we fit a line by the normal regression technique we shall estimate approximately the true underlying regression line.

If, however, one cannot be sure that the variance of ε is very small relative to the variance of η there is no such comfort to be drawn. Consider again the simple model and let us ignore the constant α_0 and β_0 then

$$\left. \begin{array}{ll} \text{Demand} & y_1 = \beta_{12} y_2 + \varepsilon, \\ \text{Supply} & y_1 = \alpha_{12} y_2 + \eta \end{array} \right\} . \tag{7.10}$$

so that:

$$y_2 = \frac{-(\varepsilon - \eta)}{\beta_{12} - \alpha_{12}} . \tag{7.11}$$

Thus price is a linear combination of ε and η. If we attempt to measure the demand curve by regressing y_1 or y_2, one of the essential conditions will be violated. For consistent estimators of β_{12} it is required that y_2 the independent variable be independent of the disturbance ε.[†] But the variable y_2 is a linear function of the disturbance ε. Therefore ε and y_2 [$= (\varepsilon - \eta)/(\beta_{12} - \alpha_{12})$] are clearly correlated and not independent. The regression coefficient is found in the usual way:

$$\hat{\beta}_{12} = \frac{\sum y_1 y_2}{\sum y_2} = \beta_{12} - \frac{\sum \varepsilon (\varepsilon - \eta)}{(\sum y_2^2)(\beta_{12} - \alpha_{12})} ,$$

$$\hat{\beta}_{12} = \beta_{12} - \frac{1}{(\beta_{12} - \alpha_{12})} \left[\frac{\sum \varepsilon^2 - \sum \varepsilon \eta}{\sum y_2^2} \right] . \tag{7.12}$$

† See Chapter 4.

If ε and η are independently distributed $(\sum \varepsilon\eta)/(\sum y_2^2)$ will on the average tend to zero as the size of sample is increased. But $(\sum \varepsilon^2)/(\sum y_2^2)$ is a ratio of sums of squares and will not necessarily tend to zero as the number of observations is increased. It will always be positive. Since $\beta_{12} - \alpha_{12})$ is negative the second term will then always be positive. Thus

(estimate) = (true value) + (positive bias) + (covariance of ε, η which tends to become small as n increases).

In other words the estimate will tend to have a higher value than the true negative slope.

It is obvious that the greater the variance of ε the larger the bias. Indeed we can see that if the ε's are very large and the η's are quite tiny the regression of y_1 on y_2 will approximate to the supply coefficient α_{12}. For we have

$$\hat{\alpha}_{12} = \alpha_{12} + \frac{1}{\beta_{12} - \alpha_{12}} \left[\frac{\sum \eta^2 + \sum \eta\varepsilon}{\sum y_2^2} \right], \quad \beta_{12} - \alpha_{12} \neq 0, \qquad (7.13)$$

and if $\sum \eta^2$ is very small compared with $\sum y_2^2$, we can ignore the term $(\sum \eta^2)/(\sum y_2^2)$ as being trivially small. So the least-squares estimate $\hat{\alpha}_{12}$ approximates to the true value α_{12}.

We can introduce disturbance terms into our three-dimensional geometrical model also where, in deviations from means:

$$\left.\begin{array}{ll} \text{Demand} & y_1 = \beta_{12}y_2 + \beta_{1x}x + \varepsilon, \\ \text{Supply} & y_1 = \alpha_{12}y_2 \quad\quad + \eta \end{array}\right\}. \qquad (7.14)$$

As we saw in the three-dimensional Figure on p. 169, without disturbances ($\varepsilon \equiv \eta \equiv 0$) the two illustrated planes intersect in a line AB and we have not sufficient information to locate the demand plane. If now however we suppose that there is a disturbance η in the supply equation and that disturbance is a random variable (not always zero), a scatter of points will appear around the line AB. If ε the disturbance in the demand equation is always zero then the points will all lie on the demand surface and it is thereby identified. Generally we should expect some disturbance in the demand equation as well (i.e. ε is not always zero). This means that observations will then lie not on but *around* the demand plane. The identification then turns on the relative size of the disturbances. Suppose that ε is very small relative to the size of η. This will mean that there is now a wide scatter about the supply plane and a very small one about the demand plane. This will enable us to measure approximately the demand plane. If on the other hand η is small relative to ε, we may measure approximately the supply relation but not the demand plane. It is instructive to interpret observations in this model in terms of the multicollinearity argument – but this we leave as an exercise for the reader.

Economics of Identification

The identification of a parameter is not a cut and dried property. We can sensibly talk about a parameter being nearly identified – or perhaps about it being nowhere near identified. Much hinges on our *a priori* knowledge of those factors which have been excluded from the model. Often of critical importance is the type of data we have collected – especially whether it is a cross-section of observations at a moment of time whether it is derived from observations on the same firm, industry, or household over time for different periods. We shall be looking at these problems in later chapters of this book. One example will illustrate the approach. Suppose that one had a cross-section sample of firms and there were observations on their capital stock, labour and the quantity of output. Can we from this data estimate a production function showing how labour and capital separately affect the output of the representative firm? Can we in fact measure the marginal rates of substitution between factors of production?

In this example identification depends on the market conditions. Suppose that the firms bought their capital and labour freely in a competitive market where the same prices are charged to each firm. Now the marginal rate of substitution depicts the reaction of entrepreneurs to different relative prices for labour and captial. But if the wage rate and capital cost are *the same* for each entrepreneur in the cross-section, there is no stimulus to give variations in the capital–labour ratio. If firms consisted of identical entrepreneurs producing identical products the capital and labour inputs over the cross-section will be exactly the same. If entrepreneurs were different from each other, (e.g. one being relatively efficient at making good use of labour, another at using machinery,) the observations would of course reflect different capital/labour ratios. But this would indicate differences in entrepreneural ability; it would not measure the slope of the production surface.

It is easy to see how one could generate a model where the substitution possibilities are measurable. Imagine that each identical entrepreneur exists in a separate region and that within each region he can purchase capital and labour competitively at the existing prices. If relative prices are different in different regions this will be sufficient to make the entrepreneur choose different points on their production surfaces and so the observations will enable us to measure the pattern of substitution.

In this example the lack of identification of the production surface was deduced from general economic arguments about the nature of the price system. This is, or rather should be, the nature of most arguments about identification. There are, however, many other aids to identification. Probably the most important is to use different kinds of data. If in the previous example we observed the firms over a number of periods it is likely that the prices of factors will change. We may therefore record a distribution of observations about the production surface, as the entrepreneur responds to different factor ratios. Another help in identification may be derived from *a priori* knowledge about the shape and movement of the function. With a demand function, for example, we may be able to specify a minimum price or perhaps a minimum quantity. With a smooth function this suggests that the function is convex. If the observations cluster around a concave function it is likely that they measure primarily some other relationship.

Up to now we have said very little about the use of *a priori* knowledge about the correlation (or lack of it) between the disturbances in equation systems. If we knew that the η and ε were distributed independently in the equations

$$\begin{matrix} \text{Demand} & y_1 = \beta_{12}y_2 + \beta_{1x}x + \varepsilon, \\ \text{Supply} & y_1 = \alpha_{12}y_2 \qquad\quad + \eta \end{matrix} \Bigg\}, \qquad (7.15)$$

then it would be possible to identify the coefficients β_{12} and β_{1x}. The easiest way to see this is to form the 'mongrel' equation

$$y_1 = [\lambda\beta_{12} + (1-\lambda)\alpha_{12}]y_2 + \lambda\beta_{1x}x + \lambda\varepsilon + (1-\lambda)\eta. \qquad (7.16)$$

Now the disturbance in the 'mongrel' is $\lambda\varepsilon + (1-\lambda)\eta$, whereas the disturbance in the demand equation was ε and in the supply it was η.

Clearly if we postulate that the disturbance in the demand equation is not correlated with that in the supply equation, we can always distinguish between the demand equation and the mongrel since the latter will have a disturbance $\lambda\varepsilon + (1 - \lambda)\eta$ which *is* correlated with the disturbance in the supply equation (η). Only when $\lambda = 1$, i.e. the mongrel turns into the demand equation, is required condition of zero correlation satisfied.

Unfortunately this aid to identification is not very useful in practice because one does not usually know very much about the ·correlation properties of the disturbance terms. As we shall see when we discuss the production function it is usually easier to specify that disturbance terms *will* be correlated. This then adds to the troubles of identification.

Questions for Discussion

1. Compare the problems of identification in studying the demand for rubber and the demand for strawberries.

2. In the text of this chapter it was shown geometrically that there is a close affinity, on the formal level, between the concept of multicollinearity and the idea of identification. Consider this problem algebraically for the simple case of three variables with two equations.

3. Discuss the identification of the so-called 'Phillips curve', relating the percentage change in wage rates to the level of unemployment. [See A. W. Phillips, 'The Relation between Unemployment and the Rate of Change of Money Wages in the United Kingdom, 1861–1957', *Economica*, n.s. xxv (Nov 1958), 283–99, and Ronald Bodkin, *The Wage-Price Productivity Nexus* (Philadelphia, 1966).] Attempt to relate the Phillips curve to the demand and supply curves for labour.

4. It is sometimes argued that, in econometric work, there are always many relevant variables omitted from the analysis, so that the coefficient or the whole equation is more likely to be not identified than appears superficially likely. Discuss this view. [See T. A. Chung Liu 'Under-identification Structural Estimation and Forecasting', *Econometrica*, vol. 28 (4) (Oct 1960).]

8 Equation Systems

The Structure of Econometric Models

SIMPLE MODELS

Many of the basic ideas in economics are expressed in the form 'given X we shall observe Y'. In demand analysis, for example, X is price and Y is the quantity sold; in the theory of the consumption function X is aggregate personal disposable income and Y is expenditure on consumption. This is a simple form of theory and can be expressed as

$$Y = F(X). \tag{8.1}$$

It can be made even simpler by specifying the exact form of the function $F(X)$. Consider for example the naïve quantity theory of money. The level of money income (Y) is proportional to the stock of money (X). Thus

$$Y = VX, \tag{8.2}$$

where V is the income velocity of circulation (in the usual notation $X = M$, $Y = VM$). This simple proportional model also appears in other areas of economic theory – such as input/output analysis, where inputs are proportional to outputs. For most models in econometrics we adopt the slightly more general form of a linear model:

$$Y = \beta_{yx}X + \beta_0 + \varepsilon. \tag{8.3}$$

Usually a disturbance (ε) is added to catch any influence which has been omitted from the model.

The essence of much economics is the interdependence between variables. Often we find it impossible to discover situations in which we may take one variable as given and then observe the effect on the other. For example the simple velocity equation is one where, given various levels of money, one can observe whether the level of money income varies proportionately. But in practice we know that there is an influence also running from income to money. High prices (and so high money income) may cause the government to impose a credit squeeze by *reducing* the quantity of money. Income depends on money, but also money depends on income.

The obvious way to describe this interdependence is to construct a second equation to describe the behaviour of the government. This suggests then that we have two equations describing a system with *two* dependent variables. If no more variables are considered in the model, we have two linear equations:

Quantity
Theory $\qquad Y = \beta_{yx} X + \beta_0 + \varepsilon,$ $\qquad$ (8.4)
Equation

Money
Supply $\qquad X = \alpha_{xy} Y + \alpha_0 + \eta.$ $\qquad$ (8.5)
Equation

The first equation 'explains' the value of income, the second equation 'explains' the quantity of money. But these 'dependent' variables also appear as so-called independent variables – money appears as such in the quantity theory equation. Obviously the old nomenclature of dependent/independent variables is not very useful in the context of equation systems. A new term is needed for variables which are predicted by the model. They are called 'endogenous' variables.

THE STRUCTURAL EQUATIONS

One rule of model-building is then simply derived. One must have as many equations as endogenous variables. This is simply the counterpart of the normal rule of linear equations that one must have as many equations as one has variables to explain.† (It is often convenient to set out each equation with a different endogenous variable with a co-efficient of unity on the left-hand side of the equation – but it is, of course, not necessary to express it in this form).

There may be, and usually are, other variables in the model that are not endogenous. But no variables other than endogenous ones appear in the monetary model discussed above. Many Keynesians, however, would argue that the model is unsatisfactory; the level of income is explained by investment which may be determined by factors other

---

† One might conceivably be satisfied with less equations than endogenous variables if one did not wish to predict *all* the endogenous variables of the model; but this is an unusual situation in model-building.

than current income or money stock. Investment is then usually called 'autonomous' – the level of expenditure on capital acquisitions is determined by causes *outside* the model.† The equation system then would include investment on the right-hand side of the quantity theory equation – which we should perhaps re-christen the multiplier equation.

It is useful to distinguish between endogenous variables that are explained by the model and other variables, like investment, which the model does not attempt to explain. It accepts them as determined by some 'outside' mechanism. These latter variables are called 'exogenous' variables. It is conventional to describe the *endogenous* variables as Y's and the *exogenous* variables as X's – each with suitable subscripts.‡ Thus the money–investment model may be described by the equations

$$Y_1 = \beta_{12}Y_2 + \gamma_{11}X_1 + \beta_1 + \varepsilon_1, \qquad (8.6)$$

$$Y_2 = \beta_{21}Y_1 \qquad\qquad + \beta_2 + \varepsilon_2, \qquad (8.7)$$

where Y_1 = income,

Y_2 = money stock,

X_1 = investment.

Equations of this kind that describe the structure of the economic model are usually called the *structural equations*, and the coefficients are called *structural coefficients*. These equations express the theoretical causalities and interactions which are to be tested against the data. The coefficients therefore are the traditional constants of economic analysis. The first equations says that money income Y_1 is determined by the quantity of money Y_2 and by the level of investment X_1 and by a disturbance ε_1. The second equation explains the quantity of money as determined through government monetary policy, by the level of income Y_1 and a disturbance ε_2. There is no equation to tell us how the level of investment is determined. We may argue that investment is determined by the 'animal spirits' of entrepreneurs (as Professor Joan

---

† Thus in this model there is no accelerator effect.

‡ Formally the main distinction between endogenous and exogenous variables is that the probabilistic character of endogenous variables cannot be ignored, whereas, if one is interested only in making conditional statements, one can ignore the stochastic or probabilistic character of the exogenous variables by simply dealing with their *given* values. Ideally, of course, an exogenous value is not probabilistic, but often the exogenous variables which are used in practical applications are in fact probabilistic; then the approach is simply to make the predictions of endogenous variables for given values of the (probabilistic) exogenous variable.

Robinson has suggested), or by innovation and invention which one cannot easily encompass in an econometric model. Investment is determined 'outside' the model and is thus classed as an exogenous variable. The implication is that the influence is from the exogenous variable investment *to* endogenous income and *via* income *to* the endogenous stock of money. There is no reverse influence of income and money on investment. The level of investment can be taken as given for the purpose of calculating the value of income and the stock of money.

In principle there is no upper limit to the number of exogenous variables we may consider in an econometric equation – except for the statistical limit imposed by the number of observations. One is not restricted, as with endogenous variables, to having as many equations as the number of exogenous variables to be predicted. The introduction of a large number of exogenous variables must however be avoided since it complicates the theory, reduces its sharpness and reduces the number of degrees of freedom. The larger the number of exogenous variables the more we need to know before we put our model to work; the smaller the fraction of experience which is predicted by the model. Exogenous variables then should be used with economy, discretion and discrimination. *See Desai on Ad Hoccery.*

EXOGENOUS, ENDOGENOUS AND PREDETERMINED VARIABLES

The essence of an exogenous variable is that it can be 'taken as given' for the purpose of determining the endogenous variables. There is another class of variables that are quite similar to exogenous variables in this respect, but for many purposes must be separately treated. These are the *lagged* values of endogenous variables. Let us suppose for example that in the multiplier-quantity-theory equation above we wished to include among the variables which determine the level of income the level of the money stock in the previous year.[†] Thus using the parenthesis (t) to indicate the observation in the tth period we have

$$Y_1(t) = \beta_{10} + \beta_{12}Y_2(t) + \gamma_{12}Y_2(t-1) + \gamma_{11}X_1(t) + \varepsilon_1(t), \qquad (8.8)$$

$$Y_2(t) = \beta_{20} + \beta_{21}Y_1(t) \qquad\qquad\qquad + \varepsilon_2(t). \qquad (8.9)$$

Here γ_{12} describes the direct effect of a unit increase in the quantity of money in year $(t-1)$ on the level of income in year t, *when the quantity*

[†] It may be argued that there is a lag in the reaction of income to the stock of money or that the demand for money depends on permanent income.

of money in year t is held constant. This lagged value of the endogenous variable $Y_2(t-1)$ behaves in some ways essentially like an exogenous variable. It is an historic value so it can clearly be taken as given for calculating $Y_1(t)$ and $Y_2(t)$. (As we shall see, however, the structure and properties of the model are fundamentally affected by whether a variable is exogenous or whether it is lagged endogenous). For some purposes we can lump together the lagged endogenous and the exogenous variables under one heading – called *predetermined* variables. Thus we have the classification:

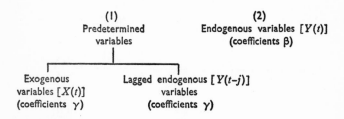

It is also useful to use a convention for labelling variables and their associated coefficients in any model other than a very small one. The convention suggested here does serve to identify readily the role of the variable and its coefficient. Thus

γ_{12} is the coefficient in the first equation (determining $Y_1(t)$) of the lagged endogenous variable $Y_2(t-1)$.

The first subscript locates the equation, the second identifies the (lagged) variable. (Note that we have called $Y_2(t-1)$ the 'second' predetermined variable).

STRUCTURAL SYSTEMS AND THE REDUCED FORMS

We now examine some of the properties of econometric models. We shall normally consider only very simple versions with few variables. The ideas, however, are the same whether we deal with two equations or two hundred and to deal with large models is merely more lengthy rather than illuminating.† Consider first of all the simple monetary model where we have no lagged endogenous variable such as $Y_2(t-1)$ (we omit the constants β_{10}, β_{20} throughout):

† Furthermore large models certainly require the use of matrix algebra in their presentation and analysis.

$$Y_1(t) = \beta_{12}Y_2(t) + \gamma_{11}X_1(t) + \varepsilon_1(t), \tag{8.10}$$

$$Y_2(t) = \beta_{21}Y_1(t) \qquad\qquad + \varepsilon_2(t). \tag{8.11}$$

The equations imply that we feed in from outside the model the exogenous investment X_1 and the two random disturbances $\varepsilon_1(t)$ and $\varepsilon_2(t)$. The values of Y_1 and Y_2 are determined by the interaction of the system.

One useful way of representing this structural system is by means of a flow diagram:

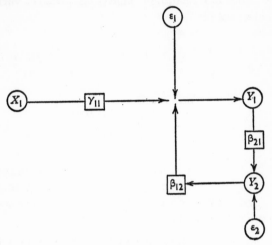

or in words:

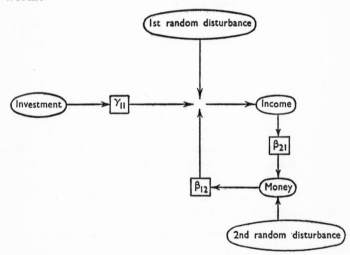

The circles enclose variables, the small squares describe the linear operations. The arrows describe the direction of the influence. We feed in the variables X_1 (investment) and the disturbances ε_1 and ε_2. They are given 'inputs' from outside the model and, in the diagram, they have only a one way connection to the model. The values of Y_1 and Y_2 (income and money stock) are determined by mutual interaction, and they receive as well as impart influences; arrows come and go.

Since ε_1, ε_2, and X_1 are the only 'inputs' or 'independent variables' in the model, it is sensible to rearrange the equations so that the endogenous variables are expressed in terms of the exogenous variable and the disturbances. We can substitute the second equation into the first to obtain Y_1 in terms of X_1, ε_1, and ε_2:

$$Y_1(t) = \beta_{12}\{\beta_{21}Y_1(t) + \varepsilon_2(t)\} + \gamma_{11}X_1(t) + \varepsilon_1(t), \qquad (8.12)$$

$$Y_1(t) = \frac{1}{1 - \beta_{12}\beta_{21}} \left[\gamma_{11}X_1(t) + \beta_{12}\varepsilon_2(t) + \varepsilon_1(t) \right], \qquad \text{provided that } \beta_{12}\beta_{21} \neq 1.$$
$$(8.13)$$

Substituting this relationship into the second equation we obtain

$$Y_2(t) = \frac{\beta_{21}}{1 - \beta_{12}\beta_{21}} \left[\gamma_{11}X_1(t) + \beta_{12}\varepsilon_2(t) + \varepsilon_1(t) \right] + \varepsilon_2(t). \qquad (8.14)$$

These two equations are the *reduced form* equations of the model. They express Y_1 and Y_2 as linear functions of X_1 and ε_1 and ε_2. They might be written as follows:

$$\left.\begin{array}{l} Y_1(t) = \pi_{11}X_1(t) + \text{disturbances,} \\ Y_2(t) = \pi_{21}X_1(t) + \text{disturbances} \end{array}\right\}, \qquad (8.15)$$

where

$$\left.\begin{array}{l} \pi_{11} = \dfrac{\gamma_{11}}{1 - \beta_{12}\beta_{21}}, \\[2mm] \pi_{21} = \dfrac{\beta_{21}\gamma_{11}}{1 - \beta_{12}\beta_{21}} \end{array}\right\}. \qquad (8.16)$$

The constant π_{11} measures the effect of a unit increase in X_1 on the value of Y_1. The effect consists of two parts – first there is the direct effect on Y_1 through the coefficient γ_{11} as set out in the quantity-theory-multiplier equation. Secondly there is the additional effect due to the fact that an increase in X_1 changes Y_1 and Y_1 influences Y_2 through the government monetary policy equation; and Y_2 will then have effect on Y_1 via the coefficient β_{12} in the quantity-theory-multiplier equation. The sum of these two effects appears in the coefficient π_{11}. In fact we have

direct effect on Y_1 when Y_2 is fixed $= \gamma_{11}$

indirect effect through Y_2 on Y_1 $\quad = \gamma_{11}\beta_{12}\beta_{21}/(1 - \beta_{12}\beta_{21})$

total effect $= \pi_{11}$ $\qquad\qquad = \gamma_{11}/(1 - \beta_{12}\beta_{21})$

These two effects can be easily distinguished in the circuit diagram; the direct effect is the arrow feeding in X_1, and the indirect effect is the clockwise loop through Y_2 and back again to Y_1.

The economics of this are also easily seen. An increase in investment increases income directly. But as income increases the government adjusts the quantity of money. This change in the quantity of money will have an additional effect on income.

The reduced form equations may be interpreted like ordinary regression relationships. The variable X_1 is given exogenously; it is multiplied by π_{11} and a disturbance is added to get the value of Y_1. This suggests that we can obtain a consistent estimate $\hat{\pi}_{11}$ of π_{11} by least squares – provided that the disturbances are not correlated with levels of investment.† A similar argument can be used for the estimate $\hat{\pi}_{21}$. These problems of estimation will be taken up later.

UNDER- AND OVER-INDENTIFICATION

This example also illustrates the formal properties of identification. By regression methods we can obtain estimates of π_{11} and π_{21}. The question which we normally ask, to see if coefficients are identified, is: can we calculate estimates of γ_{11}, β_{12} and β_{21} from estimates of π_{11} and π_{21}? We can readily see how to obtain an estimate of β_{21}; we simply divide $\hat{\pi}_{21}$ by $\hat{\pi}_{11}$. Since

$$\pi_{11} = \frac{\gamma_{11}}{1 - \beta_{12}\beta_{21}} \qquad (8.17)$$

† If there were such correlation between investment and the disturbance term, one should not treat investment as an exogenous variable; it should be considered as endogenous.

and

$$\pi_{21} = \frac{\beta_{21}\gamma_{11}}{1 - \beta_{12}\beta_{21}} \qquad (8.18)$$

we have

$$\frac{\hat{\pi}_{21}}{\hat{\pi}_{11}} = \text{estimate of} \left[\frac{\gamma_{11}\beta_{21}/(1 - \beta_{12}\beta_{21})}{\gamma_{11}/(1 - \beta_{21}\beta_{12})} \right] = \text{estimate of } \beta_{21}. \qquad (8.19)$$

But from the equations relating π's to the coefficients γ and β, we cannot deduce the values of γ_{11} or β_{12}. No amount of juggling with the equations will enable us to express estimates of the parameters γ_{11} and β_{12} in terms of the known estimates of π_{11} and π_{21}. In other words the coefficients of the first equation (the multiplier) are not identified. The coefficient of the second equation however is identified. *of by Rank Conditions*

These are of course exactly the same conclusions we shall have arrived at by using the elementary arguments of the last chapter. Examining the reduced form equations is just another way of exploring the formal identification properties of the model. In general the problem is to determine whether we have sufficient information in the π's (the coefficients of the reduced form) to enable us to determine the estimates of the *structural* parameters in the original equations.

Identification as we have so far presented it is seen to be a Good Thing. But surely one can have too much of a Good Thing – and indeed one can have too much identification. This is then a condition of *over-identification*. Let us extend the model of monetary multipliers discussed above by considering that the multiplier equation has another exogenous variable – suppose that it is government expenditure. And furthermore let us suppose that the direct effect of government expenditure on the quantity of money can be safely ignored (the government, of course, still indirectly affects the quantity of money because their expenditure affects income and this also determines the quantity of money created). Thus we have an equation system [with $X_2(t)$ as government expenditure in year t]

$$\left. \begin{array}{l} Y_1(t) = \beta_{12}Y_2(t) + \gamma_{11}X_1(t) + \gamma_{12}X_2(t) + \varepsilon_1(t), \\ Y_2(t) = \beta_{21}Y_1(t) \hphantom{+ \gamma_{11}X_1(t) + \gamma_{12}X_2(t)} + \varepsilon_2(t) \end{array} \right\} \qquad (8.20)$$

The reduced form equations are obtained by eliminating Y_2 and Y_1 from the right-hand side, thus:

$$\left.\begin{aligned}
Y_1(t) &= \frac{1}{1 - \beta_{12}\beta_{21}} \left[\gamma_{11}X_1(t) + \gamma_{12}X_2(t) \right] + \text{disturbances,} \\
Y_2(t) &= \frac{\beta_{21}}{1 - \beta_{12}\beta_{21}} \left[\gamma_{11}X_1(t) + \gamma_{12}X_2(t) \right] + \text{disturbances}
\end{aligned}\right\} . \quad (8.21)$$

If this is expressed in the form

$$\left.\begin{aligned}
Y_1(t) &= \pi_{11}X_1(t) + \pi_{12}X_2(t) + \text{disturbances,} \\
Y_2(t) &= \pi_{21}X_1(t) + \pi_{22}X_2(t) + \text{disturbances}
\end{aligned}\right\}, \quad (8.22)$$

we observe that

$$\left.\begin{aligned}
\pi_{11} &= \gamma_{11}(1 - \beta_{12}\beta_{21})^{-1}; \quad \pi_{12} = \gamma_{12}(1 - \beta_{12}\beta_{21})^{-1}, \\
\pi_{21} &= \beta_{21}\gamma_{11}(1 - \beta_{12}\beta_{21})^{-1}; \quad \pi_{22} = \beta_{21}\gamma_{12}(1 - \beta_{12}\beta_{21})^{-1}
\end{aligned}\right\} . \quad (8.23)$$

Now this gives us four equations and four unknowns γ_{11}, γ_{12}, β_{12}, β_{21} (note that estimates of the π's are all calculated from the regression) and it might look as though a neat solution is possible. But not so. By forming the ratios π_{21}/π_{11} and π_{22}/π_{12} we see that *both are equal to* β_{21}. That is to say we have *two* separate ways of estimating β_{21}, one by forming the ratio $\hat{\pi}_{21}/\hat{\pi}_{11}$ and another by forming the ratio $\hat{\pi}_{22}/\hat{\pi}_{12}$. There is no reason why these two estimates should have the same values; normally one would expect them to differ considerably. So now we have *too many* different ways of estimating β_{21}, thus we regard the β_{21} coefficient as *over-identified*. (It will be observed that although β_{21} is over-identified the structural coefficients in the first equation β_{12}, γ_{11}, γ_{12} are still not identified. We, so-to-speak, 'waste' our information in over-determining β_{21} and we cannot then derive estimates of the other parameters.)

Over-identification was once thought to be the common problem with many economic relationships. If there are many predetermined variables in the system which do not appear in the equation in question (in the above case the equation describing money being determined by the authorities), then it is likely that the equation will be over-identified.† But some econometrists have argued that under-identification is likely to be the more common occurrence. It may be claimed, for example, that we have omitted many predetermined variables from

---

† Formally a necessary condition for over-identification of an equation is that the number of endogenous variables in the equation is less than or equal to the number of predetermined variables in the system but not in the equation.

the second (money-creating) equation. There are in fact many exogenous variables that influence the quantity of money which we have simply not specified in this equation. A 'correct' specification may well reveal an under-identified not an over-identified equation. From the arguments so far it does not seem to be possible to decide on *a priori* grounds whether equation systems are likely to be under- or over-identified. Indeed this discussion does illustrate the dangers of adopting an unduly rigid and formal algebraic attitude. A detailed exploration of the data and the circumstances which gave rise to it would normally tell us much more than a formal listing of identification conditions.

TWO-STAGE LEAST SQUARES

Over-identification does however present a problem in estimating the coefficients of the structural equations. We know that the two ratios $\hat{\pi}_{21}/\hat{\pi}_{11}$, $\hat{\pi}_{22}/\hat{\pi}_{12}$ give different estimates of β_{21}. The simplest approach might be to consider various ways of combining the two to give a 'mean' estimate. For example we might write an estimate of β_{21} as $k(\hat{\pi}_{21}/\hat{\pi}_{11}) + (1-k)(\hat{\pi}_{22}/\hat{\pi}_{12})$ where $0 < k < 1$, or perhaps one may take the geometric mean. This natural technique has not been adopted by econometricians partly because of the difficulties of dealing with ratios of this type.†

A technique for dealing with this problem is the *two-stage* least squares method. In this approach, again using the above example, we first form the regression of Y_1 on all the predetermined variables in the system, which we may write as

$$Y_1(t) = \hat{b}_1 X_1(t) + \hat{b}_2 X_2(t) + \text{estimate of disturbance}, \qquad (8.24)$$

where the estimated regression coefficients are $\hat{b}_1$ and $\hat{b}_2$. If we write the estimate of the disturbance as $V(t)$, we can then write

$$\hat{Y}_1^*(t) = Y_1(t) - V(t) = \hat{b}_1 X_1(t) + \hat{b}_2 X_2(t) \qquad (8.25)$$

as the *estimate* of the non-stochastic or systematic part of $Y_1(t)$ derived from the regression line for given $X_1(t)$ and $X_2(t)$ thus $\hat{Y}_1^*(t)$ or $Y_1(t) - V(t)$

---

† This difficulty occurs with other seemingly simple methods. For example another obvious idea is to find an estimate of the regressions π_{11}, π_{12}, π_{21}, π_{22} when at the same time the ratios $\pi_{21}/\hat{\pi}_{11}$ and $\hat{\pi}_{22}/\hat{\pi}_{12}$ are *constrained to be equal.*

is inserted in the second equation (the money-creating equation) instead of the value $Y_1(t)$. The equation is then

$$Y_2(t) = \beta_{21}[Y_1(t) - V(t)] + \varepsilon_2'(t),$$

or
$$Y_2(t) = \beta_{21}\hat{Y}_1^*(t) + \varepsilon_2'(t). \tag{8.26}$$

Now we compute the regression of $Y_2(t)$ on $\hat{Y}_1^*(t)$ and this will give a *two-stage least-squares* estimate of the coefficient β_{21}.

The important property of this estimation method is that it avoids the simple one-stage leasts-quares bias and lack of consistency which appears if we simply regressed $Y_2(t)$ on $Y_1(t)$. By using a two-stage method we have eliminated from the variable Y_1 that part of the variation due to the disturbance. The $\hat{Y}_1^*(t)$ has had the estimated disturbance (or error) removed by the definition

$$\hat{Y}_1^*(t) = Y_1(t) - V(t). \tag{8.27}$$

This removes the least-squares bias and inconsistency which we examined in Chapter 4.

This technique is of quite general application. If we have an equation that is over-identified the first stage proceeds by taking the endogenous variables on the right-hand side and finding the regression of each in turn on all the predetermined variables. Then the values of the endogenous variables predicted by these first-stage regressions are inserted in the equation in place of the original Y's. Then the coefficients are estimated by the normal regression techniques.†

In practice two-stage least-squares methods are easy to use and are probably at least as good as any of the more complicated alternatives. The two-stage method has not completely replaced the ordinary least-squares techniques. This is partly because of the simplicity of the ordinary regression method and especially because of the simplicity of interpretation.

PREDICTION

One real advantage of ordinary least squares is in the use of the model for prediction. Let us suppose, for example, that we are not particularly

---

† This is not the only method of estimating over-identified equations. The two major alternatives are the *least-squares limited-information* method and the *full-information maximum-likelihood* method. It can be shown that for very large samples these more complicated and lengthy methods give rise to similar results.

forecasting.

interested in the values of the structural parameters as such. Suppose that we are not much concerned about measuring the value of the monetary and investment multiplier nor in the way in which the monetary authorities respond to changes in the level of income. What we are really concerned about is *predicting* as accurately as we can the level of income for a *given* quantity of money, a *given* level of investment and a *given* level of government expenditure.† With these given conditions (and, of course, assuming that we have correctly specified the equation in its linear form), ordinary least-squares regression on money, investment and government expenditure will enable us best to predict the value of income Y_1. This is the basic theorem of least-squares prediction. It will be noted that it does not matter, as far as prediction is concerned, whether the Y_2 appears on the right-hand side of the equation (and we know that Y_2 is itself affected by the value of Y_1). Of course the least-squares estimate of the *coefficients* will be biased but this does not matter if we are *only* interested in predicting Y_1. Indeed the bias in the coefficients takes into account the observed effects of Y_1 on Y_2 through the equation describing the money-creating process, and paradoxically this bias in the coefficient makes the prediction efficient. We may set out the rules in the following way:

Purpose	Ordinary least squares	Two-stage least squares
To estimate structural parameters	Biased and inconsistent	Consistent (although biased in small samples)
To predict an endogenous variable	Unbiased and best	Biased and inefficient

It is not surprising that one uses different techniques to answer different questions. Most econometrists are usually interested in both predicting national income and also in estimating the effects of an increase in investment or in government spending on the level of income. To estimate the effects of an increase in government spending on income *with other variables held constant* we need to know the structural parameter, the coefficient of government expenditure, in the first equation. That

† In other words, the regression equation used for prediction is concerned with making *conditional* predictions in the sense discussed in Part I of this book.

is to say if we wish to estimate the effect of government expenditure on income, *ceteris paribus*, then an estimate of γ_{12} is the appropriate measure and two-stage least squares is a useful technique. But for predicting national income we should use a least-squares approach. First the regression of Y_1 on Y_2, X_1, and X_2 is computed for the years for which we have data. Then the resulting coefficients are used to predict Y_1 for the values of Y_2, X_1, and X_2 which are assumed to be operative in the future year. If, as we have assumed in this example, one cannot get useful information on the value of Y_2 likely to rule in that forecast year, then the best forecast of Y_1 will be given by the (reduced form) regression of Y_1 on X_1 and on X_2. We use what variables can be forecast accurately – or perhaps those variables which are subject to control by government – in order to predict, conditional upon the 'independent' variables, that value to be taken by Y_1.

THE FINAL FORM OF EQUATION SYSTEMS

In the examples so far we have used no lagged endogenous variable among the predetermined variables. For the statistical properties of very large samples in the models discussed so far this does not matter. Lagged endogenous variables can usually be considered the same as exogenous variables; in the time period under consideration, last year's income may be taken as given and not affected by present values of the variables. Take, for example, the following monetary multiplier model:

$$\left.\begin{aligned}
Y_1(t) &= \beta_{12}Y_2(t) + \gamma_{11}X_1(t) + \gamma_{12}Y_2(t-1) + \varepsilon_1(t), \\
Y_2(t) &= \beta_{21}Y_1(t) \qquad\qquad\qquad\qquad + \varepsilon_2(t)
\end{aligned}\right\}. \qquad (8.28)$$

This is the same as the model discussed in the previous two Sections except that instead of $X_2(t)$ on the right-hand side of the first equation the lagged endogenous variable $Y_2(t-1)$ appears.

The reduced form of this model is then the same as before, with $Y_2(t-1)$ replacing $X_2(t)$, i.e.

$$\left.\begin{aligned}
Y_1(t) &= \frac{1}{1-\beta_{12}\beta_{21}}\left[\gamma_{11}X_1(t) + \gamma_{12}Y_2(t-1)\right] + \text{disturbances}, \\
Y_2(t) &= \frac{\beta_{21}}{1-\beta_{12}\beta_{21}}\left[\gamma_{11}X_1(t) + \gamma_{12}Y_2(t-1)\right] + \text{disturbances}
\end{aligned}\right\}, \qquad (8.29)$$

or
$$Y_1(t) = \pi_{11}X_1(t) + \pi_{12}Y_2(t-1) + \text{disturbances,}$$
$$Y_2(t) = \pi_{21}X_1(t) + \pi_{22}Y_2(t-1) + \text{disturbances}$$

(8.30)

The procedure for estimation is exactly the same as before. The properties of the estimators are also the same as before for *large* samples. For small samples, however, the properties do differ. But this is too complicated a matter to be examined here and the reader is referred to the problem of *auto-regressive systems* in Kendall and Stuart.†

The main aspect to be discussed here is the form of the model itself. Let us therefore ignore the disturbances and suppose that the equations are exact. Can we then specify the time path of income as a function of the exogenous variable X_1? Can we in other words trace the effect of a unit increase in X_1 on the value of Y_1 in the current and subsequent periods? The first point to be made is that one can no longer use the reduced form coefficients as measures of the effect of predetermined variables on the current exogenous variables. Consider, for example, a unit increase in X_1 in period t; this will affect Y_1 also in period t *via* the coefficient π_{11} (1st equation). But a unit increase in X_1 will also affect Y_2 in period t (π_{21} in second equation). And this will then be fed into the *first* equation in the *next* period when Y_2 with one period lag affects the value of Y_1 through coefficient π_{12}. In words an increase in investment (X_1) will increase income in the current period. The government then changes the quantity of money in response to an increase in income, and this change in the money stock will affect income in the *subsequent* period because there is a lag in the monetary multiplier.

Clearly in order to examine the *total* effect of a unit increase in X_1 we need to 'get rid of' the troublesome $Y_2(t-1)$. But, to simplify, first write the equations without disturbances

$$Y_1(t) = \pi_{11}X_1(t) + \pi_{12}Y_2(t-1),$$
$$Y_2(t) = \pi_{21}X_1(t) + \pi_{22}Y_2(t-1)$$

(8.31)

The problem is really to substitute away the values of $Y_2(t-1)$. We can do this by writing $(t-1)$ for t in the second equation; i.e.

$$Y_2(t-1) = \pi_{21}X_1(t-1) + \pi_{22}Y_2(t-2).$$

(8.32)

Substituting in the first equation we obtain

$$Y_1(t) = \pi_{11}X_1(t) + \pi_{12}\{\pi_{21}X_1(t-1) + \pi_{22}Y_2(t-2)\}.$$

(8.33)

† See Bibliography.

Substituting for $Y_2(t-2)$

$$Y_1(t) = \pi_{11}X_1(t) + \pi_{12}[\pi_{21}X_1(t-1) + \pi_{22}\{\pi_{21}X_1(t-2) + \pi_{22}Y_2(t-3)\}].$$ (8.34)

And so we continue substituting for the values of Y_2 and finally we obtain

$$Y_1(t) = \pi_{11}X_1(t) + \pi_{12}\pi_{21}X_1(t-1) + \pi_{12}\pi_{21}\pi_{22}X_1(t-2)$$
$$+ \pi_{12}\pi_{21}\pi_{22}^2X_1(t-3) + \pi_{12}\pi_{21}\pi_{22}^3X_1(t-3) + \dots \text{ and so on.}$$

Or

$$Y_1(t) = \pi_{11}X_1(t) + \pi_{12}\pi_{21}[X_1(t-1) + \pi_{22}X_1(t-2) + \pi_{22}^2X_1(t-3) + \dots].$$ (8.35)

This expression is an infinite series in powers of π_{22} with the associated lagged value of X_1 (investment). In economic terms it means that an increase of one unit in investment will increase income by an amount π_{11} in the current year. Next year income will change by an amount $\pi_{12}\pi_{21}$, and after a two-year lag income will change by an amount $\pi_{12}\pi_{21}\pi_{22}$ – and so on.

It is useful to give names to these concepts. The π_{11} might be called the *impact multiplier* of investment on income. It tells us the magnitude of the current effect on income. Now what are the effects on income if we increase investment by one unit and hold that new level of investment for a very long time? This requires all the X's to increase by one unit.† If this happens then the effect on Y_1 will be given by the whole series: the result is called the *total multiplier*. As t becomes large, $Y_1(t)$ will increase by:

$$\pi_{11} + \pi_{12}\pi_{21}(1 - \pi_{22})^{-1}.$$ (8.36)

This is then the impact multiplier π_{11} plus $\pi_{12}\pi_{21}(1 - \pi_{22})^{-1}$. The *total multiplier* is defined as the sum of the effects for all periods of a unit increase in X_1 and is given in this example, by the above expression. This describes the permanent effect of an increase in X_1 of one unit in period o which is maintained until period t; starting from an initial value $Y_1(o)$ at time o, $Y_1(t)$ gets nearer and nearer to the value: $Y_1(o) + \pi_{11} + \pi_{12}\pi_{21}(1 - \pi_{22})^{-1}$ as time elapses i.e., as t gets larger.

† In this equation it looks as though the X's increase by one unit from initial values of zero. The reader will recall, however, that for convenience of exposition we have ignored the constants β_{10}, β_{20} throughout, so that the reader may imagine that all X's are being increased from initial positive values.

Since we have summed an infinite series it is like a Keynesian multiplier – it approaches the new level of income asymptotically. In the same way it is reasonable to define *interim multipliers* which summarise the effects of a unit increase in investment for (say) a period of three years. This would then be defined as the sum of the first three terms of the series, i.e.

$$3\text{-year interim multiplier} = \pi_{11} + \pi_{12}\pi_{21}(1 + \pi_{22}). \qquad (8.37)$$

These are useful if our horizon is limited to short-run policy problems.

We must now return to one important question which was ignored in deriving the *final form* equations. Is it legitimate to substitute for $Y_2(t-1)$ in the first equation, and does one then get a sensible representation of model? From the total multiplier one sees immediately that a senseless result occurs if π_{22} exceeds or is equal to unity. With this value the terms in the infinite summation get larger and larger as we go back through time for $\pi_{22} < \pi^2_{22} < \pi^3_{22}$ etc. The sum (ref. (8.36) above) is then infinite. Another explosive case is where π_{22} is less than or equal to -1. Then again the sum does not settle down to any finite value as we increase the number of terms. These 'explosive' cases cannot be simply dismissed on *a priori* grounds. Indeed the case where π_{22} is approximately unity or perhaps a little more may be seen as perhaps a not very odd case of 'sustained growth' and inflation.† An increase in investment is enough to set money income on its upward path.‡ The case of $\pi_{22} < -1$ is one of swings in income which increase in violence over time! These are explosive oscillations.

The n-year interim multiplier is given by

$$\pi_{11} + \pi_{12}\pi_{21}\frac{1 - \pi^n_{22}}{1 - \pi_{22}}, \qquad (8.38)$$

† It may well be argued that many of the trends observed in economic time series arise from 'explosive' equations of this kind. Probably when the values of income (or prices or money stock) get too large, or increase at too fast a rate, the coefficients are changed to slow down or even reverse the process. Unfortunately little is known about the properties of explosive series, and virtually nothing about the 'adaptive' process of changing coefficients. But close approximations to the study of such processes appear in the work of Allais on the theory of inflations.

‡ Sir John Hicks used an explosive multiplier – accelerator model for *real* income in his *Contribution to the Theory of the Trade Cycle* (1950). Restraints on the behaviour of this explosive model were imposed by limitations of real resources. This would be a sensible limitation to impose on the present model – but since we are interested in the methodology rather than results these complications are avoided.

G

whatever the value possessed by π_{22}. If $0 < \pi_{22} < 1$ then income will increase monotonically to its new equilibrium value. There are no oscillations.

One may examine the value of π_{22} in terms of the structural parameters

$$\pi_{22} = \frac{\beta_{21}\gamma_{12}}{1 - \beta_{12}\beta_{21}},$$

where

γ_{12} is the investment multiplier when the effect of money on income have been eliminated,

β_{12} is the monetary multiplier when the effects of investment have been eliminated,

β_{21} is the reaction of the monetary authorities in adjusting the stock of money to a change in income.

We assume that γ_{12} is positive and in order to get arithmetical results let us suppose that the value is unity. Let us also suppose that β_{12} is also unity. In order to have 'non-explosive' results, it is clear that the necessary and sufficient condition is

$$-1 < \pi_{22} < +1.$$

i.e. reduced form in first order difference equation

Or, in terms of β_{21},

$$-1 < \beta_{21}/(1 - \beta_{21}) < +1.$$

And this will be satisfied by all $\beta_{21} < \tfrac{1}{2}$.

Now let us suppose that γ_{12} and β_{12} are not unity – but both are positive. Then we must have

$$-(\gamma_{12} - \beta_{12})^{-1} < \beta_{21} < (\gamma_{12} + \beta_{12})^{-1}.$$

The student may easily explore different values of the parameters that satisfy this relation. (Try the non-Keynesian case where $\gamma_{12} \to 0$.)

After this excursion into the stability of econometric models, let us now return to the estimation problems of the *final form*. For many purposes we may be interested in the final form of the equations. If one regarded the money-creating machine as autonomous (or working to a counter-cyclical *rule*) then we may be interested in the effects of investment on income when account is also taken of the behaviour of the monetary authorities according to their fixed rule. If that is the problem, then the sensible procedure is to find the regression of income on present and past levels of investment. The estimates will then measure the coefficients of the final form directly. But, *ex hypothesis*, these are the values required for policy purposes. They describe the income path for any given levels of investment.

Alternatively – and most people would argue more realistically – we may be concerned with finding an 'optimum' monetary rule to counter any oscillations caused by investment. [Note that we continue to suppose that all variables are deviations from constant (or perhaps trend) values. This simplifies the exposition.] Then we must examine the reduced form and the structural parameters. Consider the final form

$$Y_1(t) = \pi_{11}X_1(t) + \pi_{12}\pi_{21}[X_1(t-1) + \pi_{22}X_1(t-2) + ...]. \qquad (8.39)$$

Now if the effect on $Y_1(t)$ is to be zero after two periods this requires $\pi_{22} = 0$. But we see that this requires

$$\pi_{22} = \beta_{21}\gamma_{12}/(1 - \beta_{12}\beta_{21}) = 0, \qquad (8.40)$$

i.e.

$$\beta_{21} = 0 \quad \text{or} \quad \gamma_{12} = 0.$$

The monetary authority should not try to counter the investment cycles.† The model becomes one equation. All the effect of investment then appears in the current year through the coefficient $\pi_{11} = \gamma_{11}/(1 - \beta_{12}\beta_{21})$. Nothing is transmitted via the money creating equation to the following years. It is obvious however that one could shift some of the effects to future years and reduce the effect in the current year by having a negative value for β_{21} (granted $\beta_{12} > 0$). This would reduce π_{11} and would make $\pi_{12}\pi_{21}$ and π_{22} non-zero, so we should have various effects in subsequent periods. For estimation purposes it is important to note that we *do* need to know the structural parameters of the model for making policy decisions of this kind. In particular we need to know the functional form of the π's. Structural parameters then are required.

† An ultra-conservative *laissez-faire* solution indeed! The reader, however, should note that as this conclusion is the consequence of a model in which we have ignored disturbances. Much of the work of a counter-cyclical policy may be in terms of *offsetting disturbances* from outside the model.

SPECIAL SYSTEMS – TRIANGULAR AND RECURSIVE MODELS

Equations systems are so complex it is natural to see if there are any special systems that are both theoretically appealing and at the same time fairly simple to deal with. One such system is the *triangular* or *recursive* *model*. Consider the following system of equations (again we omit the constants):

$$\left.\begin{aligned}
Y_1(t) &= \qquad\qquad\qquad\quad \gamma_{11}X_1(t) + \varepsilon_1(t), \\
Y_2(t) &= \beta_{21}Y_1(t) \qquad\qquad + \gamma_{21}X_1(t) + \varepsilon_2(t), \\
Y_3(t) &= \beta_{31}Y_1(t) + \beta_{32}Y_2(t) + \gamma_{21}X_1(t) + \varepsilon_3(t).
\end{aligned}\right\} \qquad (8.41)$$

We use Y to denote endogenous variables and X to describe exogenous variables. Now the structure of this system is such that Y_1 depends only on an exogenous variable; Y_2 depends on Y_1 and exogenous variables whilst Y_3 depends on Y_1 and Y_2 and on exogenous variables. This means that given X_1 (and ε_1 and ε_2) one can calculate Y_2; given Y_2 (and ε_3) one can calculate Y_3. One never has to go backwards to Y_1 again since it is not affected by Y_2 or Y_3, likewise Y_2 is not affected by Y_3. A flow or circuit diagram will make this clear.

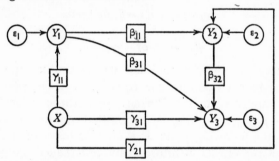

It will be observed that Y_2 does not feed back into Y_1 and Y_3 does not feed back into either Y_2 or Y_1. This is called a *triangular* form of relationship between the Y's. If the coefficients of the Y's are set out as in the equations we get a triangle of values with zeros above the diagonal, as follows:

Equation no.	Coefficient of Y		
	Y_1	Y_2	Y_3
1	1	0	0
2	β_{21}	1	0
3	β_{31}	β_{32}	1

(Note that it would be better to change the sign of the one's along the diagonal to *minus* one then we can interpret the variables as though they were all on the same side of the equation.)

An inspection of the form of the basic equations (above) of the triangular or recursive model, however, shows that there is no need to estimate the reduced form. One can estimate the coefficients directly by applying least-squares regression to each equation separately, provided that the disturbances are independently distributed. Consider for example the second equation. The endogenous variable $Y_1(t)$ involves the disturbance $\varepsilon_1(t)$, from the association in the first equation. But, in the second equation, the disturbance $\varepsilon_2(t)$ is independent of $\varepsilon_1(t)$; therefore it is independent of $Y_1(t)$. The crucial minimum condition for least squares is that the variable 'on the right-hand side' of the equation be distributed independently of the disturbance $\varepsilon_2(t)$ in the equation. This condition is satisfied in the second equation; and by an analogous argument it is also satisfied in the third equation, etc. Thus we can apply least-squares regression methods directly to each equation and obtain estimates of the coefficients directly.

One of the features of the triangular system is that it can be interpreted as a *causal* system.† There is one way relationship between the endogenous variables, i.e., the variables which the system explains; Y_1 is *caused* by exogenous variable X_1. Since Y_2 does not affect Y_1 we can use the word *cause* to denote the sense of this one-way effect from Y_1 to Y_2. The triangular system is usually called a *recursive system* because of the causal-chain relationships between the endogenous variables. One may prefer the name *triangular system* because it directly describes the structural form of the model.

SPECIFICATION ERROR

Although they often receive little attention in current literature, the errors caused by an incorrect or poor specification of a model are often far more important than errors due to poor techniques of estimation. The specification of a model is the job of economic theory. But it is clear that in modern theory there is much room for manœuvre and much potential work for Occam's razor. For example, suppose we were

† The reader is, however, warned that there is much dispute about this.

interested in measuring the demand for potatoes, then we might consider a simple model such as

$$Y(t) = \beta_0 + \beta_{yx}X_1(t) + \varepsilon'(t)$$

where $Y(t)$ is the quantity of potatoes bought in the tth period, $X_1(t)$ is the price of potatoes in that period, and $\varepsilon'(t)$ is a disturbance. We may measure the parameters in the above model by least squares techniques to get estimates $\hat{\beta}_0$ and $\hat{\beta}_{yx}$. (For simplicity we shall drop the parenthesised t in the remainder of this section. The reader is asked to remember however that the observations are for different time periods.)

Now suppose that this model is specified wrongly. Let us imagine that there is another variable which has an effect roughly as important as the price of potatoes, and which has been omitted from the model. Suppose that the missing variable and the only one that has this property is the price of bread. Then an adequate specification would be

$$Y = \beta_0 + \beta_{y1.2}X_1 + \beta_{y2.1}X_2 + \varepsilon, \tag{8.42}$$

where X_2 is the price of bread and ε is a random disturbance. With this specification ε is a random disturbance with a mean of zero and is independent of the values assumed by X_1 and X_2.

The question arises: what effects are introduced into our estimates if we choose the 'wrong' specification? In our case what effect does it have on the estimate of the reaction of consumers to the potato price if we do not take into account variations in the price of bread. Thus if we measure β_{yx} in the first equation – instead of estimating $\beta_{y1.2}$ in the second or 'correct' equation, what will be the difference between them? Under what circumstances will mis-specification be serious?

To simplify the problem let us transform all variables to deviations about means so that $y = Y - \bar{Y}$, $x_1 = X_1 - \bar{X}_1$, and $x_2 = X_2 - \bar{X}_2$, with sample mean $\bar{\varepsilon}$ and $\bar{\varepsilon}'$ assumed to be zero:

$$\left.\begin{array}{ll} \text{Incorrect} & y = \beta_{yx}x_1 + \varepsilon', \\ \text{Correct} & y = \beta_{y1.2}x_1 + \beta_{y2.1}x_2 + \varepsilon \end{array}\right\} \tag{8.43}$$

If we estimate β_{yx} in the incorrect equation by least-squares methods we multiply throughout by x_1 and sum each of the terms over the observations, i.e.

$$\sum yx_1 = \beta_{yx}\sum x_1^2 + \sum \varepsilon' x_1$$

leading to

$$\sum yx_1 = \hat{\beta}_{yx}\sum x_1^2$$

and
$$\hat{\beta}_{yx} = \frac{\sum yx_1}{\sum x_1^2}. \tag{8.44}$$

Now suppose we did the same calculation with the *correct* specification

$$\sum yx_1 = \beta_{y1.2}\sum x_1^2 + \beta_{y2.1}\sum x_1x_2 + \sum \varepsilon x_1. \tag{8.45}$$

Thus one obtains, by dividing throughout by $\sum x_1^2$,

$$\hat{\beta}_{yx} = \frac{\sum yx_1}{\sum x_1^2} = \beta_{y1.2} + \beta_{y2.1}\frac{\sum x_1x_2}{\sum x_1^2} + \frac{\sum \varepsilon x_1}{\sum x_1^2}. \tag{8.46}$$

The left-hand side is the estimate $\hat{\beta}_{yx}$ from the incorrect specification. The first term on the right-hand side is the correct population value of the coefficient we are estimating $\beta_{y1.2}$. The second term on the right-hand side contains two parts the first is the correct population value of the effect of the price of bread on the quantity of potatoes bought $\beta_{y2.1}$ when the effect of the price of potatoes is eliminated. The second part $(\sum x_1x_2)/(\sum x_1^2)$ is the *measured* or estimated *regression* coefficient of x_2 (the price of bread) on x_1 (the price of potatoes). We might write this as $\hat{\beta}_{21}$, so we have

$$\hat{\beta}_{yx} = \beta_{y1.2} + \beta_{y2.1}\hat{\beta}_{21} + \frac{\sum \varepsilon x_1}{\sum x_1^2}. \tag{8.47}$$

Now since the ε is uncorrelated with x_1, we may assume, as in ordinary regression theory, that the last term, a random variable, tends to get smaller and smaller on the average as the sample size increases. From the normal equation for estimating $\beta_{y1.2}$ and $\beta_{y2.1}$ we have

$$\sum yx_1 = \hat{\beta}_{y1.2}\sum x_1^2 + \hat{\beta}_{y2.1}\sum x_1x_2 + \sum ex_1,$$

or by dividing throughout by $\sum x_1^2$,

$$\hat{\beta}_{yx} = \hat{\beta}_{y1.2} + \hat{\beta}_{y2.1}\hat{\beta}_{21}, \tag{8.48}$$

when the term $\sum ex_1/\sum x_1^2$ is written as zero. This can obviously be repeated in the equation above so that the final result is simply the normal equation written in the form of regression coefficients. In words

$$\begin{bmatrix} \text{estimate of} \\ \text{slope of } y \text{ on } x_1 \\ \text{from incorrect} \\ \text{specification} \end{bmatrix} = \begin{bmatrix} \text{estimate of} \\ \text{slope of } y \text{ on } x_1 \\ \text{from correct} \\ \text{specification} \end{bmatrix} + \begin{bmatrix} \text{estimate of} \\ \text{slope of } y \text{ on } x_2 \\ \text{in correct} \\ \text{specification} \end{bmatrix}\begin{bmatrix} \text{estimate of} \\ \text{slope of } x_2 \\ \text{on } x_1 \\ \ \end{bmatrix}$$

Now it will be observed that if the price of bread and the price of potatoes were not correlated, the slope β_{21} would be zero. And, even though the price of bread had an appreciable effect on the purchases of potatoes, there would be no error of specification if we took the simple regression of y on x_1 as an estimate of the effect of the price of potatoes on the quantity purchased. Similarly one can show that if x_1 and x_2 are not correlated, the simple regression of y on x_2 will give an estimate of the cross effects of the price of bread on purchases of potatoes with no errors of specification.

This is of course a solution consistent with common sense since the partial regression coefficient of y on x_1 measures that relationship when the effect of x_2 has been eliminated. But if x_2 does not affect x_1 at all then we might as well take the simple regression of y on x_1 as a measure of that relationship. When the variables x_1 and x_2 are not correlated they are often said to be *orthogonal*.† With orthogonal variables the specification error caused by missing out variables is of no importance. We can assess the effects of each variable separately taking then one at a time.

In practice, however, it is rare that one encounters orthogonal (independent) variables. With the example used above, it is likely that the prices of potatoes and bread would move in the same direction. They are probably positively correlated so that $\hat{\beta}_{21}$ would be greater than zero. Let us suppose that $\hat{\beta}_{y1.2} = -\hat{\beta}_{y2.1}$, i.e. that the effect of the price of potatoes is the same as that of bread and that $\hat{\beta}_{y1.2}$ is negative whereas $\hat{\beta}_{y2.1}$ is positive. Then we have

$$\hat{\beta}_{yx} = \hat{\beta}_{y1.2}(1 - \hat{\beta}_{21}). \tag{8.49}$$

The value of the reaction of the demand to the price of potatoes will be estimated by the factor $(1 - \hat{\beta}_{21})$. In other words the incorrect specification (i.e. without the price of bread) will indicate too small an elasticity of demand for potatoes with respect to their price. By mis-specification

† Strictly speaking orthogonality also requires that $\Sigma x_1^2 = 1$, $\Sigma x_2^2 = 1$, i.e., the variables should also be standardised. But for our purpose this is of little importance.

we have included in the reaction to the potatoes price the effect of the associated movement in the price of bread which has the opposite effect on the quantity of potatoes purchased. An increase in the price of potatoes reduces potato purchases, but an increase in the bread price takes place (on the average) at the same time and this *increases* the potatoes bought as people switch from eating bread to eating potatoes. Of course one is also tempted to consider the extreme cases here: Suppose that $\hat{\beta}_{21} = 1$, then it would follow that the incorrect specification would show that there was no own-price elasticity of demand for potatoes. And if $\hat{\beta}_{21}$ exceeded unity we would get a *perverse* positive elasticity of demand from the wrong specification.

This is probably the simplest form of specification error to deal with. It can easily be extended to include more than one omitted variable and more than one included variable. The essence of the result is, however, the same. It depends on the regression of the omitted variables on those which are included. In practical applications one can often calculate (or perhaps even guess) the sign and size of the regression coefficients of excluded or included variables. This gives us some check on the extent and character of specification bias.

Omitting variables is, however, only one form of specification error and probably the most tractable. There are many others. One suspects that the most common type of specification error is due to the stipulation of linear or linear logarithmic relationships when the true functional form is more complicated. Not much is known about this sort of error. A general approach is to examine how the fit of an equation changes as we vary the specification. This method has been employed in many fields of econometrics – in Engel curves, in demand curves, in fitting production functions, in the demand for money, and so on. It may be dangerous, however, to use such methods unimaginatively since a few particular observation may give one cause for choosing one specification rather than another; and it may be quite clear that these observations were in fact subject to certain particular influences (e.g. war years) which were not explicitly considered in the model. A safer method is to graph the data (or the residuals) or build suitable three-dimensional models that will enable one to examine visually the confrontation of the theory with the data. Graphical methods are, however, very difficult and require considerable experience before they can be employed with any great confidence.

Questions for Discussion

1. It is thought that the rate of interest in year t is determined (linearly) by the amount of money in year t and by the level of income in year t, and the level in year $(t-1)$. On the other hand it is alleged that the level of income in year t is determined linearly by the rate of interest in year t. Money is an exogenous variable determined independently of income and the rate of interest. Set up the two equations of the model. Find the reduced form, and so set out the final form of the equations. Discuss the dynamic effects of monetary change.

2. Examine the equation system for a simple Keynesian model where there is some autonomous investment. Find the reduced form, and, if there are lagged endogenous variables, the final form.

3. Discuss the contention that errors of economic specification are far more important than errors that arise from sampling characteristics of data.

4. Consider the problem of finding a monetary 'rule' to stabilise the path of income growth in the economy with the model of Question 1 above.

5. Why is it not necessary to use two-stage least squares for models that are *just* identified?

6. Consider the following model of the Keynesian type:
$$C(t) = 0.5\,Y(t) + 0.25 + \varepsilon_1,$$
$$I(t) = 0.1\,Y(t) + 0.3\,Y(t-1) + 0.15 + \varepsilon_2,$$
$$Y(t) = C(t) + I(t) + Z(t),$$

where C is consumption, Y is income, I is induced investment, and Z is 'autonomous expenditure' which is a linear function of time. Examine which are the endogenous and which the exogenous variables in this system.

Construct the reduced form and examine the identification properties of the system. Show what is meant by the 'over-identification' of the consumption function.

Find the final form of the equations and discuss the properties of the system as it reacts to a once-and-for-all change in the trend rate of autonomous expenditure.

7. ('Reducing' an equations system to a 'one-period-lag' system.)
Consider an equation system such as
$$Y_1(t) = \beta_{12}Y_2(t) + \gamma_{11}Y_1(t-1) + \gamma_{12}Y_1(t-2) + \gamma_{13}X_1(t),$$
$$Y_2(t) = \beta_{21}Y_1(t) + \gamma_{21}Y_2(t-1) + \gamma_{22}Y_1(t-2) + \gamma_{23}X_1(t).$$

This involves the three predetermined variables in Y. For many purposes of analysis, however, one would like to reduce the system so that the maximum lag in the system is one period; 'then one may write the values in period t as a linear function of the lagged endogenous variables of the previous period $(t-1)$. Then one does not have to worry about the reaction of $Y_1(t-2)$ on $Y_1(t-1)$ and so again on $Y_1(t)$.

In order to do this we resort to a trick. We simply define a new endogenous variable $Y_3(t) = Y_1(t-2)$. We pretend that the Y_3 is this year's observation of Y_1 two periods backwards in time. Then we simply add another equation to the system:

$$Y_1(t) = \beta_{12}Y_2(t) + \gamma_{11}Y_1(t-1) + \gamma_{12}Y_3(t) + \gamma_{13}X_1(t),$$

$$Y_2(t) = \beta_{21}Y_1(t) + \gamma_{21}Y_2(t-1) + \gamma_{22}Y_3(t) + \gamma_{23}X_1(t),$$

$$Y_3(t) = Y_3(t).$$

Now this system has only a one period lag, and we have fewer formal complications in dealing with it. We have, as it were, reduced the lag but added to the equations. [For the use of this procedure see H. Theil and J. Boot, 'The Final Form of Econometric Equation Systems', *Review of the International Statistics Institute* (1962).]

(i) Examine the model if there has been a variable $Y_2(t-3)$ in the first equation.

(ii) Show that a single-equation model with the lagged endogenous variable among the predetermined variables may be transformed into an equation system.

8. Consider a macro-economic model, about which the following information is given.

Jointly dependent variables
(a) $Y_t =$ gross domestic production at market prices,
(b) $I_t =$ gross investment in fixed assets, stocks and work in progress,
(c) $M_t =$ import of goods and services.

Current exogenous variables
(a) $C_t =$ consumption by families and government together (= all other domestic expenditure),
(b) $E_t =$ exports of goods and services.

The index t indicates the current period. Lagged influences of dependent variables of earlier periods:

$$Y_{t-1} \text{ and } Y_{t-2}.$$

Structural Equations
(a) Accounting identity,

(b) investment-demand equation (accelerator)

$$I_t = 3\Upsilon_{t-1} - 3\Upsilon_{t-2},$$

(c) import function

$$M_t = 0{\cdot}2I_t + 0{\cdot}1C_t.$$

You are now asked:

(i) to complete the model by writing down the missing accounting identity (a).

(ii) to compute the reduced form.

(iii) to examine the final form.

Part Four

Applications

The purpose of Part IV is not to illustrate the techniques of econometrics with 'examples'. We shall be concerned with two basic areas of economic thought – the theory of consumer expenditure and the theory of production – and we shall examine the quantitative formulation and testing of hypotheses. The main task with all applied econometric research is to link the observations (the data) with the theoretical filing system. Somehow we must find the economic process that generates the data and relate that process to the theoretical problem in which we are interested. This requires an intimate intermingling or integration of economic theory, economic statistics and theoretical econometrics, together with a substantial intuitive 'feel' for the situation. The account of the studies of consumer expenditure and of production functions in Chapters 9 and 10 are not by any means complete surveys of the field. They are merely meant to give the student some of the taste of applied econometric research and to provide the reader with some of that informed scepticism which is so necessary in interpreting the results of econometric enquiries.

9 Consumer Expenditure

INTRODUCTION

In this chapter we review some of the applications of econometric techniques in the field of consumer expenditure. There are two main fields of enquiry. First there is the analysis of market demand for commodities and services. The purpose of the theory is to predict the pattern of expenditure of a consumer as he responds to the stimuli of income and price changes.

The great classic law of demand is that a reduction in the price of a commodity will give rise to a larger quantity being purchased. The demand curve slopes downward from left to right. But since the first formulation of the theory of demand much has been added to this simple law – mainly to expand it to deal with special cases. For example, the Slutsky and Hicks–Allen development emphasised the importance of the income term; they showed that, if a particular item was important in the budget of the consumer, it was quite conceivable that a fall in the price of one commodity with all other prices held constant would lead to a decrease in the consumption of the commodity in question. And this has lead to the use of the concept of the *compensated* demand curve, which measures the reaction of consumers to changes in relative prices, holding real income constant.

In the first part of this chapter we shall quickly review the main results of modern demand theory. This will then lead naturally to a formulation of the demand curve which can be tested against the data. The emphasis of this approach, however, is not on the theory – but rather in terms of formulating hypotheses which can be tested against the facts. The abstract predictions of pure theory have to be put into a statistical form – to take account of the inevitable deviations between fact and theory. The most important task of all is to relate data and theory.

The second part of this chapter will be devoted to the *macro*-economics of consumer behaviour, as expressed in the theory of the consumption function. The theory of aggregate consumption has undergone many developments in recent years. The classic formulation in Keynes' *General Theory* suggested that there was great stability in the relationship between aggregate income and aggregate expenditure. Furthermore Keynes argued that the marginal propensity to consume was always less than the average. In our review of the statistics we shall show how the Keynesian model was tested, apparently confirmed, but then found to be inefficient in prediction. We then review the new theories of consumption – in particular we shall be examining in some detail the 'permanent income hypothesis' and the 'life-cycle hypothesis'. These models show how one can employ a wide variety of data and indirect information in order to test hypotheses.

Inevitably the statistics that are available, or that may be collected, are generated by an economic process in action – not in a laboratory experiment. The precise character of the data will depend entirely on the process that generated them – and it is most unlikely that the process will correspond neatly to the model which we are interested in testing. In other words it is necessary to develop at least some broad model of the data generating process.

This is an important problem in all areas of applied econometrics. Unfortunately there is no formal set of rules that can be applied to determine the relevance or use of a set of statistics; one must rely on intuition, general knowledge, inferential data and, not least, one's judgement. The studies of demand and the consumption function will serve as a useful introduction to the peculiar amalgam of analysis, intuition and judgement that is the very stuff of applied econometrics. But in this field, as in many others, the reader will only learn by doing. Try it and see.

Expenditure – The Demand Function

THE THEORY AND FORM OF THE DEMAND CURVE

First let us review the context of the law of demand. We imagine an idealised situation where the individual is only one of a very large number that are purchasing the commodity in the market. Thus, the quantity purchased by the individual consumer will have only a very tiny effect on the market – so small indeed that we can ignore it.

Effectively the individual consumer can take the price as given; just as one takes the price of cigarettes as fixed and purchases any desired quantity.

We also normally take the income of the consumer as given, and for a similar reason. In a competitive world the price at which he can sell his productive resources (his labour and any property he may own) is given; so it is natural to include the level of income of the individual as a datum of the demand analysis. In its simplest form, therefore, the demand function for the ith individual may be expressed

$$\begin{array}{c}\text{quantity of the} \\ \text{commodity purchased} \\ \text{by the } i\text{th individual} \\ \text{in a specific period}\end{array} = \begin{array}{c}\text{function} \\ \text{of}\end{array} \left[\begin{array}{c}\text{price of the} \\ \text{commodity}\end{array} \text{ and } \begin{array}{c}\text{income during} \\ \text{the period of} \\ i\text{th individual}\end{array}\right]$$

This then records the reaction of the ith consumer to the price of the commodity and to his income.

Of course one is rarely satisfied with such a simple formulation; for it is known that many other influences play a role, and perhaps an important role in the real world, and it may well be quite misleading to omit them from consideration. The theory of consumer demand points to the prices of complements and substitutes as possibly important influences on the quantity purchased. Clearly if the price of margarine changes we would anticipate that there would be some effect on the quantity of butter purchased – even though the price of butter does not change. The theory tells us that relative prices are the variables that matter – and in particular the relative prices of substitutes and complements. Unfortunately we cannot hold the prices of other commodities constant as we vary the price of butter. We have to be content with the actual data generated by the economic process, and the prices of other goods may well vary over this period considered.

One other important assumption of the theory of demand is that 'tastes do not change'. But of course we never observe the behaviour of an individual with unchanging tastes; we know that they change frequently over time. Clearly if they change erratically, it will be difficult to take them into account. (This seems to be the case with women's clothes.) But if there is a steady continuous change in tastes over time, it is possible to take them into account by including a 'trend' term in the analysis. In so far as tastes vary smoothly with time one would expect that the trend term would account for their smooth movements over time.

Before going any further it is useful to put the theory into a form suitable for statistical testing. Let us first examine the postulated demand curve – and ignore for the time being the deviation between actual behaviour, on the one hand, and the theory on the other. In other words let us imagine that the demand curve is an absolutely accurate description of behaviour – and so let us ignore the difficulties associated with disturbances and errors. The first task is to devise a suitable notation for dealing with demand curves. We shall attempt to retain the standard notation; using the Y for the dependent variable and X_i's for the independent variables – just as we did in the linear regression analysis. But as we pointed out in Chapter 4, the relationships of demand curves are unlikely to be best described by a linear form.

If, for example, we used a simple model of

$$q = \alpha + \beta p, \quad \beta < 0, \quad \alpha > 0 \tag{9.1}$$

where q is the quantity and p the price (we ignore for the moment income, tastes, other prices, etc.), obviously such a linear relationship could hold only over a certain limited range; for it is easy to see that both price and quantity could become negative. For a very high price (p exceeding $|\alpha/\beta|$) the quantity would be negative, and for a very large quantity the price would be negative (if q exceeds α). Furthermore, with the linear formulation, the elasticity changes as the price varies; with the lower prices the elasticity becomes smaller. It is not at all obvious why the elasticity should vary this way.

The natural approach is to define a curve with *constant* elasticity – with the same proportional relationship between price and quantity over the whole range. And at the same time one can ensure that the curve does not trespass in the range of negative outputs or negative prices. A curve that is consistent with these requirements is the 'log-log' relation

$$Q = B_0 P^{\beta_{yx}},$$

where B_0 and β_{yx} are constants or on taking logarithms of Q and P

$$\log Q = \log B_0 + \beta_{yx} \log P. \tag{9.2}$$

$$\text{elast} \ \frac{dq}{dp} \ \frac{p}{q}. \quad \longrightarrow \quad \beta_{yx}$$

This is, of course, a linear function in the logarithms of price and quantity. So that in order to use consistent terminology we write

$$\Upsilon = \log Q, \qquad X = \log P, \qquad \beta_0 = \log B_0.$$

So the equation that describes the demand curve becomes:

$$\Upsilon = \beta_0 + \beta_{yx} X, \qquad (9.3)$$

and this is then the familiar form of the regression equation. This form of the demand curve has some interesting properties. One of the first points to notice is that there is no difficulty about the possibility of negative values for either price of quantity; one cannot define a logarithm of a negative number. For any price the quantity predicted by the equation will be non-negative. A second feature is that the elasticity of demand is constant. This is easily demonstrated by finding the elasticity

$$\frac{P\,dQ}{Q\,dP} = \frac{d\log Q}{d\log P} = \beta_{yx}. \qquad (9.4)$$

Thus the elasticity of demand with respect to the commodity's price is given by the constant β_{yx}. And it is specified that the elasticity is constant at β_{yx} for the whole range of the demand curve. Whatever the price, the proportional change in quantity due to a proportional change will be the same.

One of the great advantages of this form of the demand curve is that it provides an immediate measure of one of the critical parameters of demand theory – the elasticities; and this is not the case with, for example, the linear form of the demand curve.† The value of the parameter. β_0 depends on the units of measurement (as distinct from β_{yx}, the elasticity, which is a pure number and independent of units of measurement). If, however, we compare two curves with the same elasticities when the units of measurement are the same, the one with the higher β_0 will have the higher demand; that is to say the demand curve with the larger β_0 will lie to the right of the other.

STATISTICAL SPECIFICATION

In order to approach the data of the real world, we must turn this economic specification into a statistical form. The data will not exactly

† If $q = a + bp$, then the elasticity is given by calculating $(bp)/q$. In practice this can be troublesome; and there are statistical problems of 'ratio estimation' in measuring (p/q). And, of course, there are as many values of the elasticity as there are ratios (p/q).

conform to the model, and we need to specify formally the deviation between theory and observation. Such a deviation is called the *disturbance*. Of course this seems to be merely giving a name to our ignorance. But we are not entirely ignorant of the processes that generate the disturbance. And we must now proceed carefully to interpret the disturbance term and its role in the analysis of demand of the individual.

As we saw in the discussion in Chapter 4, one could regard the *statistical* character of the equation as being either 'error in equation' or an 'error in variable' type. The error-in-equation type is still the most popular in econometrics and it is worthwhile attempting an interpretation on those lines first of all.

Formally we should specify that the relationship between the quantity purchased and the price is not exactly (logarithmically) linear. Other factors enter into the decision. We have indeed sketched some of those influences above: income, tastes, prices of substitutes and complements and so on. We might imagine that if only we could hold these factors constant in an ideal type of experiment we might reasonably expect to measure the *true* log-linear relationship between price and quantity. If, somehow, we could eliminate variation in tastes, income etc., then we could simply measure the relation of Equation (9.4) above. The disturbance term might then simply be used to account for the effect on Y of all other variables which have been omitted from the model. It then serves as a sort of 'catch-all' term – a label for our ignorance of the effect of the other factors omitted from the model.

Unfortunately this interpretation is not quite good enough. It implies that if we only held constant these other variables omitted from the model we would then observe the *true* log-linear relation above. But this is not correct. For we do not *know* that the true relationship of price and quantity is of the log-linear form. There are an infinite number of relationships that could serve as demand curves – and the logarithmic-linear form is only one of them. So we may even be wrong – and indeed badly wrong – about the form of the relationship. The log-linear form is only a working hypothesis, not a revealed truth, and we cannot expect the behaviour of the consumer to conform exactly to this theoretical pattern. Thus the disturbance will also have to encompass any deviation between the true relationship between price and income and the particular log-linear form assumed in the regression model. To sum up, therefore, the 'error in variable' model supposes that the disturbance term describes

(i) the effect of those variables which have been omitted from the model, and

(ii) any deviation between the shape of the assumed function and the true demand relationship.

The reader then may well regard it as a catch-all, but it must be noticed that in the 'error in equations' model we have supposed that there is no error of measurement, i.e. errors in any of the measurements of the variables themselves.

In practice this assumption of no errors of measurement must surely be unrealistic. But it will be recalled that there is no difficulty in assuming that there are errors of measurement in the *dependent* variable Y. These can be treated in exactly the same way as an error in the equation, although one must remember to interpret the results properly. But of course there are also likely to be errors in the observations of the independent variable. We know that we may measure the wrong price, perhaps because no account was taken of a 'sale special' or because there was a subtle change in quality, or perhaps because the time at which we observed the price did not properly represent the price over the period during which we measured the quantity. There are indeed good reasons why we should examine the consequences of errors in measurement of price. But we shall defer these problems for the time being, and concentrate attention on the 'error in equation' model.

The *simpliste* error-in-equation model then may be written as

$$Y = \beta_0 + \beta_{yx}X + \varepsilon, \qquad (9.5)$$

where the epsilon term represents the catch-all effect of (i) and (ii) above. But now we must further specify the behaviour of the disturbance term. How will it vary from one observation to another?

SUBSTITUTES, COMPLEMENTS AND INCOME

During our discussion of the regression model in Chapter 4 above, we saw that there was one fundamental property required for disturbance terms. In order to provide good estimates of the parameters β_0 and β_{yx}, the crucial condition is that the disturbance must be distributed independently of the independent variable X. In words this means that the effect of the variables excluded from the model (and errors of specification of the form of the relationship) must be independent of the price of the commodity. There must certainly be no correlation between the price of the commodity and the 'catch-all' disturbance.

This is, of course, quite a powerful assumption and we might see what it implies by illustrating with a simple case. Suppose that the log-linear form were a correct one, and suppose further that the only other variable omitted from the model were the price of a substitute (of say margarine in the demand equation for butter). Income has no effect (or does not change) and tastes remain constant. Thus the disturbance term represents only the effect of variations in the price of margarine on the purchases of butter; and since they are substitutes, the effect of changes in the price of margarine on the consumption of butter is positive. A higher price of margarine will lead to a substitution of butter for margarine – so the quantity of butter purchased will increase.

Now this effect of the price of margarine on the consumption of butter would not matter if the price of margarine was independent of the price of butter. For then the disturbance term (the price of margarine) would be independent of (and so uncorrelated with) the price of butter – the independent variable.† But it is in practice difficult to imagine that these two variables will be uncorrelated. They are intimately connected with one another in the grocery market. If for example we imagine that the price of butter in a country falls – let us say because of 'dumping' by a foreigner – then the switch of consumers generally from margarine to butter will reduce the market demand for margarine – and so its price will tend to fall also. In other words, with substitutes like margarine and butter, we would expect their prices to be correlated positively. They would in general go up and down together on the market.

Now let us calculate the least-squares regression of Y on X, assuming incorrectly that the disturbance and the price of butter are inde-

---

† It must be recalled however that the larger the effect of the margarine price on butter purchases, the greater the variance of the disturbance – and the smaller the fraction of the variance of Y explained by variations in X. The important point in the present context is that the fact that the disturbance term is wholly 'price of margarine effect' does not alter the fact that the regression estimate $\hat{\beta}_{yx}$ will tend to β_{yx} the population value in the limit as the size of sample increases: provided that in the price of butter and the price of margarine are independent of one another.

pendently distributed. (Note that we use the convention $x = X - \bar{X}$ and $y = Y - \bar{Y}$ as in Chapters 4, 5 and 6.)

$$y = \beta_{yx}x + \varepsilon. \tag{9.6}$$

So that we find the regression coefficient in the usual way:

$$\sum yx = \sum \beta_{yx}x^2 + \sum \varepsilon x$$

$$\hat{\beta}_{yx} = \frac{\sum yx}{\sum x^2} = \beta_{yx} + \frac{\sum \varepsilon x}{\sum x^2}. \tag{9.7}$$

Now as the sample becomes larger and larger the last term tends not to zero, but to some positive value reflecting the positive association between the price of butter and the effect of margarine price on the consumption of butter. The estimator $\hat{\beta}_{yx}$ on the left-hand side will then overstate the effect of the price of butter on the quantity of butter purchased.† It will include the true effect – the coefficient β_{yx} on the right-hand side – and also the effect due to the fact that generally the price of margarine rises when the price of butter rises, i.e. the term $(\sum \varepsilon x)/(\sum x^2)$.

Thus we can set out the result in words:

estimated negative effect of the price of butter on purchases	=	true negative effect of butter price on purchases	+	positive effect of margarine price on purchases of butter

And this result conforms to common sense. If we do not hold the price of margarine constant in the exercise, then the effects on purchases of butter of an increase in the price will be to some extent offset by the fact that the price of margarine will also rise and this will damp down the substitution of margarine for butter. If only we had been able to hold the price of margarine constant we would have observed much more substitution of margarine for butter, and so the purchases of butter would have declined much more. But we could not do this so the effect of the change in margarine price is included in the estimate.

Now such a confounding of the effects of changes in the prices of both margarine and butter is clearly inefficient if we are interested in

† Note that the estimator $\hat{\beta}$, and the true value β, are both negative (*ex hypothesis*), so a positive effect in the last term on the right-hand side will mean that the absolute value of the estimator will tend to be less than that of the true value.

estimating the parameter β_{yx}, i.e. the effect of the price on the purchases of butter. The obvious technique to get rid of the effect of the price of margarine is to include it as a variable in the analysis. But before doing that, it is worth observing that the estimation of β_{yx} may be only one purpose of the model. In practice one may be more interested in simply *predicting* the purchases of butter as the price of butter is changed. We may not be primarily interested in the value of β_{yx} at all – except in so far as it helps us to predict the quantity of butter purchased. Now it is clear that an economist interested only in prediction will *want* to include the effect of the change in margarine price. This is part of the past experience which can be supposed to be projected into the future. The predictionist will be concerned with all the consequences of changing the price of butter – and a change in the price of margarine is one of them. If then one is concerned only with using the model to predict the consequences of a change in the price of butter in the real world, it is efficient to use the biased estimator $\hat{\beta}_{yx}$, since this will already take into account the fact that the price of margarine will also change and damp down some of the effects of the change in the price of butter.

But economists and econometrists are not always interested in fore-casting; they are usually more concerned about testing their theories. And clearly this does involve obtaining estimates of β_{yx}. To continue our butter–margarine example, then, we could eliminate the effect of the price of margarine on the purchases of butter only by obtaining observations of the price of margarine and including it as another variable in the regression analysis. Formally this is easily done

$$y = \beta_{y1.2}x_1 + \beta_{y2.1}x_2 + \varepsilon, \tag{9.8}$$

where x_1 is now the price of butter and x_2 is now the price of margarine.†
The reader must also note that although we have used the same symbol ε for the disturbance, it is of course quite different from the disturbance in the *simpliste* equation (9.5). If, indeed, we stick strictly to the illustration used above the disturbance in this equation would be identically zero – because we specified that the *only* component of the disturbance in the *simpliste* equation was the effect of the price of margarine on the quantity of butter purchased by the individual.

But that limited model has served its purpose, and we can now con-

---

† To be accurate one should say that the lower-case letters describe the variables as deviations from means; note also that ε is a deviation from a sample mean.

sider the more realistic case where there are many other influences on the quantity of butter purchased by the individual. Income, prices of substitutes (besides margarine) and complements, tastes, weather, and so on. Clearly we cannot consider all these effects – it would be much too complicated and time consuming obtaining the data and doing the analysis. Theory, combined with a large slice of intuition, must help us choose which variables to include and which to reject (or to lump together in the disturbance term). As we argued above, economic theory suggests that income will be an important factor. So we might then add a third variable X_3 representing the *disposable income* of the individual. This represents the (money) income which he can spend during the period on goods and services and still be as well off at the end of the period as he was at the beginning. (Let us continue the fiction that all other prices are held constant, so that if butter and margarine are a small fraction of the individual's budget, we can suppose effectively that the general price level facing him is constant.) So we can write the demand equation for the individual (in terms of variables measured in deviations from sample means)

$$y = \beta_{y1.23}x_1 + \beta_{y2.13}x_2 + \beta_{y3.12}x_3 + \varepsilon, \tag{9.9}$$

and we should insert again the warning about the different interpretation of the disturbance term.

HOUSEHOLD SIZE, PRICE LEVEL AND TASTES

Now this is the demand curve facing the *individual* and it describes his behaviour on the aggregate market. But of course in practice goods are often purchased by *households* rather than by individuals. The household acts as a sort of corporate purchasing agency for almost all items of consumer expenditure. The purchase or renting of accommodation is an expenditure which is clearly not divisible between individuals in the same household unit. Food is a major item for which there is a common 'kitty'. Even items which one would normally regard as purchases of an individual kind – such as clothing and car – often turn out to have certain communal properties, as any parent will readily testify. For most items of consumer expenditure the typical unit is the *household*; and this may be defined as a group of people with 'common' housekeeping arrangements. The definition is pragmatic rather than logical, but it will serve well for a wide variety of applications.

Households, however, vary considerably in composition and size. If, therefore, we adopt the houshold as the unit of analysis, rather than the individual, we shall have the additional problems of eliminating the nuisance variables of size and composition of the household. The nature of the household will vary over time. And in comparing results for different households we must somehow eliminate the effects of household size on income and expenditure.

The simplest way to do that is to add another variable to the analysis which reflects the size and composition of the household. One might record simply the number of adults (over 16 years) in the household, or one might measure the weighted composition of the household – counting adults as 1 and children as $\frac{1}{2}$'s. This latter measure would give a crude indicator of the number of 'equivalent adults'. Of course there are many more sophisticated methods of determining scales of equivalent adults; a 16-year-old boy will eat as much (or more) than his father, but, one hopes, he will consume much less liquor. The ideal is obviously to adopt different equivalent adult scales for different commodities. There are indeed complicated procedures for determining appropriate equivalent adult scales.

One may ask, however, whether it is necessary to treat household size and composition as an independent variable. For clearly we lose one degree of freedom as a consequence. It might be more efficient to divide the quantity purchased and the household income by the number of equivalent adults – thus standardising for household size and composition. (Note that we do not standardise the price variables – these are independent of household composition and are given by the exogenous market forces as far as the individual is concerned.) Whether this technique is more efficient than adding another variable depends on the extent to which purchases and income are proportionately influenced by family composition and size. This is a matter of fact.

Another important nuisance variable is the general price level. The theory of demand is couched in terms of the *relative* prices of commodities. Thus a 10 per cent increase in the price of butter which is accompanied by a 10 per cent increase in all other prices and incomes will have no effects on the quantity of butter purchased – unless there is a 'money illusion', which we specifically exclude from the theory of demand. The homogeneity of demand functions with respect to the 'general' level of prices suggests immediately a procedure for dealing

of degree zero

with variations in the general price level; we simply divide all money measures in the model by a general price index for households. This is easier said than done – because there is no price index available that nicely corresponds to the purchases of a particular household, or even a fairly broad class of households. And index numbers are notoriously brittle tools.

In practice index numbers have to be used for many other purposes. Consider our example of the demand for butter. Clearly this is not a homogeneous commodity; there are many different qualities and prices of butter – from my own observations I find that the most expensive butter is more than twice the price of the cheapest brand. If all butter prices changed proportionately and if the consumption pattern of butter of different qualities did not change, one price and one quality would be good enough to indicate the movement of all. But in practice the mixture changes, and relative prices change. One must therefore use index numbers to measure the price of butter and the quantity of butter purchased.

As we remarked above, some of the nuisance variables may be swept into a trend term. Probably most people would regard the trend term as partly representing the slow systematic movement in tastes over the years. The reader may find it difficult to believe that tastes move in such a steady systematic manner. But it is one important variable in economic analysis about which little is known either in theory or fact. He is a brave man who tries to predict the trend in taste in ostrich feathers (as wearing apparel, not food). A trend term is rather like a disturbance term – it is a confession of ignorance, but perhaps not so great an ignorance as in the case of a random variable. There are, of course, a number of practicable choices for the portrayal of a trend relationship. For example one may use a linear trend, a logarithmic-linear trend, a logistic trend, a geometric trend, etc. Again choice must depend on what a priori knowledge is available. No ground rules can be supplied.

MARKET (AGGREGATE) DEMAND CURVES

Up to this point we have been concerned with the demand curve for the individual or, as we have rephrased the problem, the household as the spending unit. But often our interest is not in the individual but in *aggregate market behaviour.* Although the theory of demand postulates the indifference curves of the representative individual, and deduces from them, and from market prices, the downward sloping demand curve, it is primarily the aggregate or market demand curve in which we are interested. The market demand curve determines the market price.

The first task is therefore to convert the demand curves for the individuals or households into a market demand curve. The arithmetic rules of aggregation are easy to apply; we simply add together the incomes and the quantities. In some cases it may be worth while considering the *per capita* quantities and incomes by dividing by the number of persons or the number of equivalent adults. Alternatively we may treat population as an additional term in the model.

Even price involves certain problems of aggregation – we need to combine the price measures appropriate to each family. (We add quantities and incomes, but of course we do not add prices.) But these difficulties are trivial in practice. The aggregation clearly makes ordinary economic sense. Each household does not take into account the reaction of any other households. Each will behave independently of the others – unless there be some emulation effect. It was clearly sensible to take the price as given for the individual for the purpose of predicting the quantity he buys. If we then construct the aggregate demand curve from these individual demand curves by adding them together, it is clear that we may interpret the result as the market demand curve. In a sense we have built up the market demand curve from the 'individual experiments'.

But in practice we are often – indeed almost always – confronted by the problem of measuring the aggregate demand curve directly by using aggregate data on incomes, prices and quantities. The question arises then whether we can use these data to estimate the aggregate or market demand curve. Can we take price as given for the purpose of predicting the quantity purchased? Can we take income as given – independently of the quantity bought? In other words can we *identify* the market demand curve from aggregate data generated by the economic process?

DATA

As we saw in the general discussion on identification, much depends on the particular process and its determinants. But first we must describe the data of aggregate studies. The basic information consists of *time series* of quantities, prices and incomes. Often the series are annual observations, but sometimes quarterly and even monthly data are available. These data embody all the difficulties and problems of index numbers of prices and quantities – of particular importance are quality variations and the conventions used for dealing with them.

It is also clear that the observations of the time series reflect various kinds of dynamic adjustment processes. Even if it were true that the supply conditions varied enough to make the demand conditions easily identified, the data will not conform to the essentially static conditions required for the tracing of a demand curve. Suppose for example that adjustments to new prices take place over time. Two situations are possible; either the period of adjustment is longer than the period of observation or it is smaller. If the period of adjustment is longer than the period of observation a price in period t will have part of its effect in period $t+1$, $t+2$ etc. Provided that we can make some reasonable guess about the period of reaction this case does not involve many serious problems. But the demand curve must be formulated in terms of overlapping reaction periods. The quantity adjustment in period t will be a function of price and incomes in period t, $t-1$, $t-2$, etc. The second case is more difficult to sort out. Within the period of observation, a number of price and quantity movements take place – but our observations aggregate (quantity) or average (price) them. This will result in a smoothing out of the demand curve – straightening out the curves etc. Certainly it will not give the sort of curve one would obtain with data for the adjustment period.

In practical cases, it is probably true that the majority of products exhibit some dynamic adjustment effect over time. For certain products there are associated developments that also take time. And these are particularly important for household durable goods, and for those commodities, such as motor fuel, associated with them. For example a fall in the price of petrol will induce people to use their existing cars more intensively, but it will also encourage people to buy more cars since the price of motoring has gone down. This takes time. Furthermore the adjustment process will be affected by the costs of carrying inventories.

For certain of the main sectors of household spending, however, one can largely ignore these complications of dynamic adjustment and inventory holding. Even with a period of observation as short as a month, it seems that there are unlikely to be significant problems of this kind in the purchase of food.† And for most studies the period of observation is usually the year – so it seems that with food we shall be smoothing out the demand curve rather than leaving any loose ends of an adjustment process.

IDENTIFICATION

The important question is, however, one of identification in the aggregate data. To illustrate with a ridiculous example, it would be silly to try to measure the price elasticity of demand for 'old masters'. The stock is given, and all we can discover is the relationship between price and aggregate income. But for many items of consumer expenditure there is a good case for regarding the price as fixed exogenously and for the quantity being the dependent variable. The common case is where the price is determined by the demand and supply on the world market and by transport costs to the country of consumption. The price of oranges in Britain, for example, is determined by world market conditions, including the cost of transport to the British market and the distribution costs in Britain. Suppose that there is a glut of oranges on the world market, so the price falls. If transport and distribution costs remained the same, the price on the British market would reflect the world price reduction – and the quantity bought would increase. It is likely that the cost of transport or distribution may change as the number of oranges imported into Britain increases; the price may therefore change as a consequence of the increased consumption. But this will still enable us to plot the demand curve from the aggregate time series data on price and quantity. The world market conditions – together with the relationship between transport and distribution costs and quantity – will enable us to identify the demand curve.

This sort of argument may be used for many types of food. Even when the price of fresh fruits and vegetables is not determined on the world market, one often finds that the weather plays an important role in

† One may wonder about this generalisation as the cost of household freezers declines, and they become more and more common. Much depends on the form of the oscillation in prices – in particular the amplitude.

determining supply – and perhaps only a trivial part in influencing demand. The weather shifts the supply curve around so much that it traces out the more-or-less stable demand relationship.

For other commodities however it is not at all plausible to suppose that the demand curve stays stable while the supply conditions vary. For example in the demand for ice-cream, it is clear that the demand conditions vary with the weather while the supply conditions hardly change at all. We can find the variation in consumption according to the temperature, but not much can be determined about the variation of demand with price. Indeed one must beware because the aggregate statistics would tend to trace out the supply curve – as the changes in the weather call forth different prices and levels of production and supply. The limited local market for ice-cream ensures also that we cannot use the argument that the price is fixed exogenously on the world market.

It is obviously difficult to make any firm generalisations about any particular category of expenditure. Each study must be judged in terms of the particular circumstances. Intuition, outside knowledge and inferential evidence must all be used; there are no settled rules of procedure.

INCOME ELASTICITIES FROM HOUSEHOLD BUDGETS – EXTRANEOUS ESTIMATORS

One of the main general problems with aggregate time series data is that there are few degrees of freedom and there are at least two variables (price and income) for which we require good estimates of their coefficients. The main disadvantage of aggregate time series is that there is often some strong correlation over time in the independent variables – relative price and real income. A dominant trend may appear in both series. This means that it is difficult to sort out the effects of each variable separately from the other. In other words there is the classic problem of multicollinearity (Chapter 5).

The usual way of dealing with this problem in demand studies is to use a so called *extraneous estimator* for the income coefficient. To see the nature of this technique, we might imagine what would be the reaction of an experimental scientist who found that he could not measure the effect of one factor because, in his experimental set up, another factor always moved as well. He would of course design another experiment when he could move one factor at a time. And this is analogous to the approach used in the study of demand. There exist other forms of evidence that can be used to estimate the income coefficient; a cross-section of household budgets.

In the course of administration the authorities often require to know the pattern of expenditure of households. Sample enquiries of household budgets are fairly common in most countries; and in most advanced countries they have become frequent, regular and more or less routine statistics. They record the expenditure on particular items, and sometimes the quantities bought, the total expenditure of the household, occasionally total income, and various features of the household composition – such as number of persons in the family, their ages and occupations.

Clearly one can record therefore the expenditure on items (such as butter) and the total expenditure (or income) – both suitably deflated by the number of equivalent adults – for each household in the sample. A plot of expenditure on butter against total expenditure (or income) will therefore tell us the effect of an increase in income on the amount spent on butter. The price of butter will not have any influence on this relationship. For if the budget enquiry refers to a particular year (and they usually do) all families will have experienced the same price conditions in the year. Any variation in the quantities of butter purchased will be due to income and particular effects associated with families. In other words the price variable may be supposed to be constant, while, over the cross-section of families (or strictly households), we measure the effect of income per equivalent adult on butter consumption p.e.a. (p.e.a. is short for per equivalent adult).

These relationships have been popular subjects among statisticians for many years. The curve describing expenditure on a particular commodity (or commodity group) is known as an Engel curve.† There has been much debate about the best form of the curve; generally opinion and data seem to favour the semi-logarithmic form

$$\text{expenditure on butter p.e.a.} = \text{constant} + (\text{constant} \times \text{log of income p.e.a.}) \quad (9.10)$$

† This name is derived from the prominent Saxon statistician who was foremost in measuring these relations – there is no connection with the more famous Engels of Marxian memory.

Thus successive increments of income have a smaller and smaller effect. This seems to be a good representation over certain wide ranges of income.† For our purposes, however, it is best to fit a slightly inferior alternative – a log-log relationship of the same form as the demand curve. Obviously this will then give exactly the measure we require – the elasticity of expenditure on butter with respect to income.‡

This value might then be inserted into the equation as an *extraneous estimator*. Let us write the subscript h to indicate the variables are for a household, and we can indicate that a coefficient is derived from the household cross-section – suitably deflated by an equivalent adult scale – by a superscript h. Thus our extraneous estimator is derived from a regression equation (in logs)

$$y_h = \beta_0^h + \beta_{y3}^h x_{3h} + \varepsilon^h. \tag{9.11}$$

Thus we obtain an estimator $\hat{\beta}_{y3}^h$ by least squares in the usual way. We may take it that in this cross-section the prices are constant – so we may ignore the effects of x_1 and x_2

Formally we now put the above estimator into the market demand equation. If $\hat{\beta}_{y3}^h$ were *exactly the same* as the true value $\beta_{y3.12}$ then the equation would take a very simple form

$$y = \beta_0 + \beta_{y1.23} x_1 + \beta_{y2.13} x_2 + \hat{\beta}_{y3}^h x_3 + \varepsilon. \tag{9.12}$$

Since we know the value $\hat{\beta}_{y3}^h$ from the cross-section of household budgets, we can transform the equation to

$$y - \hat{\beta}_{y3}^h x_3 = \beta_0 + \beta_{y1.23} x_1 + \beta_{y2.13} x_2 + \varepsilon. \tag{9.13}$$

We can treat the left-hand side simply as another dependent variable. It describes the quantity which would be purchased if there had been no variation in income. In other words it eliminates the income effect on the quantity variable, so that the residual on the left-hand side tells us the quantity when the income effect has been 'washed out'. It can be interpreted as a 'residual' in the sense in which we used that term in

† Many critics consider it a bad form because it does not conform to the 'adding-up' criterion i.e., the total of the individual expenditures will not equal the total expenditure. But this seems to be a somewhat artificial constraint to impose, and we shall ignore it here.

‡ In practice we often obtain only the elasticity of expenditure on butter with respect to *total expenditure*, not income. But the two measures are likely to be similar. In practice one finds that research workers often take the income elasticity as $\frac{9}{10}$ of the total expenditure elasticity.

the partial regression analysis of Chapter 5.† It is the deviation between the observed value of y and the value predicted by the regression equation. In principle we treat this residual as a new dependent variable – which we might call z – and proceed to find the regression of z on x_1 and x_2 using the *time series observations* of y, x_1, x_2 and x_3.

$$z = \beta_0 + \beta_{y1.23}x_1 + \beta_{y2.13}x_2 + \varepsilon \quad \text{where } z = y - \hat{\beta}^h_{y3}x_3. \qquad (9.14)$$

The estimates of the coefficients from this equation will be more accurate, on the average, than those obtained from the original equation. The coefficients of x will not be affected by the multicollinearity with income, and there will be a larger number of degrees of freedom.

ie this one way of treating multicollinearity. Cf Christ

SAMPLING AND SPECIFICATION ERRORS WITH EXTRANEOUS ESTIMATORS

But of course this may be considered a misleading interpretation – for we have supposed that the cross-section results from household surveys enables us to estimate *exactly* the *true* income coefficient in the time series realisation. Obviously this can never be the case. At the very least there will be sampling errors involved in the estimation of β^h_{y3}, and even if it were true that the population values were the same, i.e.

$$\beta^h_{y3} = \beta_{y3.12}, \qquad (9.15)$$

it would necessarily follow that the *estimate* $\hat{\beta}^h_{y3}$ would differ from the true population value β^h_{y3} and so from $\beta_{y3.12}$ because of sampling errors. Of course it is hoped that the sampling errors will be relatively small, and indeed smaller than those which would occur if there were a direct estimate from the time series itself (i.e. $\hat{\beta}_{y3.12}$). In practice it does seem that the standard errors of cross-section estimates of Engel curves are relatively low, and the estimates of the coefficients of x_1 and x_2 in the time series regressions of equation (9.14) are improved.

More important than the sampling variation, however, is the fact that the two measures β^h_{y3} and $\beta_{y3.12}$ are likely to be different magnitudes. The former records how butter purchases vary between one household

---

† It must be recalled however that we have assumed that this coefficient here measures the true one exactly – so that the correct term for the difference on the left-hand side of the equation is a 'disturbance'.

and another according to their income level. Low-income families will buy less butter than high-income families. But supppose that the low-income family enjoyed an increase in income – would it buy the same amount of butter as the high-income family? One would hesitate before replying 'yes' to such a question. It seems intuitively likely that the tastes of low-income families would differ from those at high levels of income. The choices of the working-class family differ considerably from those of a settled middle-class family, because of different social norms, standards and so on. (Some evidence is available on this aspect; probably the best known is that relating to winners of football pools!)

It might be thought that, although the Engel curve cannot be used to predict the consequences of large changes in income on expenditure, we can surely use it to predict the effects of *small* movements in income, and these are usually what one requires in the time series since income will not change by a very large amount from one year to another. But unfortunately little comfort can be obtained from such arguments since the slope of the Engel curve is largely determined by the widely dispersed incomes in the cross-section. Indeed this is one of the main advantages of using the family budgets – it does give us a large range of incomes from which we can determine the butter expenditure pattern. But there is surely a different 'process' at work in this cross-section of different families for a particular year from that which takes place for (broadly) the same families from one year to another.†

Unfortunately there are good grounds, therefore, for believing that the two coefficients – the one from the family budgets and the other from the time series – are not equal in the population. The difference may be large or small – there is at present little evidence to decide. Many investigators however appear to feel that the difference is small relative to the advantages to be gained from using the cross-section results as extraneous estimators. The errors of bias in the income coefficient may be more than offset by the reduction in the sampling variances (and standard errors) of the coefficients of x_1 and x_2 – the price elasticities. There is fairly clear evidence of the reduction in the measured standard errors of estimates of elasticities when extraneous

† It would be possible to investigate the processes together if we had budget studies for the same families for a number of years. We could then study the 'class' effect, that arises because of one's relative place in the income scale, and the 'time' effect, that arises as a family moves from one income class to another over time. In a few years the data will probably be sufficient to enable such a study to be carried out.

estimators are used but we do not know the extent to which this is offset by the unknown bias.†

If our purpose is, however, to *predict* a value of y for given prices and incomes, then the issue is quite clear. The prediction of future values of a time series of aggregate purchases and quantities for given aggregate income and levels of prices is much more efficiently and accurately done by using only the time series data themselves. It is best not to use an extraneous estimator. (See Shupak in Bibliography.)

This concludes our discussion of extraneous estimators and their use in the analysis of market demand. In practical application one always begins with a calculation of the extraneous estimator from the cross-section of household budgets. Then we eliminate the variation in the quantity variable in the aggregate time series data by calculating

$$z = y - \hat{\beta}_{y3}^h x_3, \tag{9.16}$$

where y is the aggregate quantity in the time series and x_3 is aggregate disposable income in the time series. The $\hat{\beta}_{y3}^h$ is of course the extraneous estimator from the cross-section. Thus z represents the quantity in the time series when the effect of x_3 has been eliminated. So we go on to regress the values of z on x_1 and x_2 in the time series. The worked example on page 230 will show the steps by which this calculation is carried out.

DIFFERENCING AND THE PATTERN OF RESIDUALS

In examining past studies of demand curves, it will be observed that in many – and perhaps most cases – in the aggregate time series analysis the regression is fitted to the *differences* of the variables from one period to the next. Let us return to the convention of labelling the period of observation in parenthesis after the variable; thus $y(t)$ refers to the observation of y in period t, and $y(t-1)$ to the observation of y in period $(t-1)$. And in the variable z, we should have $z(t)$ to refer to the period t and $z(t-1)$ to the period $(t-1)$. The x's are defined similarly

† There are many other problems associated with the use of cross-section data. But the household budgets do enable one to investigate many detailed and important problems in demand analysis. One of the most interesting uses is to measure the variations in *quality* of purchases and the variation over the income scale. Another is the relative incidence of employment, location (urban rural etc.) and other socio-economic variables on household budgets. The reader is referred to the Bibliography.

in the relevant time period. Thus the regression of differences would take the form of

$$z(t) - z(t-1) = \beta_0 + \beta_{z1.23}[(x_1(t) - x_1(t-1)]$$

$$+ \beta_{z2.13}[(x_2(t) - x_2(t-1)] + \varepsilon \qquad (9.17)$$

(The reader must note again that the constants in this equation – including the regression coefficients – are strictly defined for differences and they are not the same as those in the undifferenced equation.)

Or by using the notation

$$\left.\begin{array}{l} \Delta z(t) = z(t) - z(t-1) \\ \Delta x_1(t) = x_1(t) - x_1(t-1) \text{ and so on} \end{array}\right\} \qquad (9.18)$$

we can express the equation more succinctly as

$$z(t) = \beta_0 + \beta_{z1.23}\Delta x_1(t) + \beta_{z2.13}\Delta x_2(t) + \varepsilon. \qquad (9.19)$$

We simply transform our variables by taking differences over time and then perform the regression as before.

It is obvious that this procedure will eliminate the trend to a large extent. But in consequence we lose one degree of freedom: for if there are twenty time periods for which we have observations, there will only be nineteen periods for which we may observe differences. The main reason, however, for regressing differences instead of the observations themselves, is that there is often some marked positive time pattern in the residuals. This phenomenon – known as positive serial correlation in the residuals – was illustrated diagrammatically in two dimensions in Figure 4.10. The actual observations describe 'loops' about the regression line. The fact that there was a positive residual in year (t) will tend to give rise to a positive residual also in year $(t+1)$. If on the other hand there was a negative residual in year $(t+m)$ then there is likely to be a negative residual also in year $(t+m+1)$. When we take differences from one period to another, this positive serial correlation will be reduced. We shall, for example, subtract the positive residual at $(t+1)$ from the positive residual at (t).

Although this technique of regressing differences has been much employed in demand studies, further research has shown that it is efficient to employ only when the serial correlation is very high – probably over 0·8 is a good working rule. And it is intuitively clear why this sort of rule might be used. If the serial correlation is rather low (but positive) taking differences may make matters *worse.*†

Probably more important than the formal statistical manipulation, however, is the task of attempting to account for the particular pattern in the residuals. It is not unlikely that the time form of the residual variation is due to some factor which we have not considered in the analysis, but which can be observed and taken into account. It may well be that movements in the price of an unsuspected substitute or complement may account for the time pattern of the residuals. Thus in our Figure 4.10 it may well be that the high purchases of year (t) and $(t+1)$ are explained by the high price of the unsuspected substitute.

It is important to emphasise that in demand theory and measurement, as well as in every other branch of econometrics, sophisticated or indeed crude techniques are no substitute for a sensitive interpretation of data, for imaginatively seeking causation, and for bringing all peripheral and inferential evidence to bear. The interrelation of theory and data is a job for a skilled artist, rather than an unthinking computer. Rigid application of 'accepted' techniques will probably always obscure more than it illuminates.

Worked Example

PART I – CROSS-SECTION

Family Budgets

Family number	Expenditure on butter (£ p.a.)	No. of equivalent adults	Aggregate expenditure (£ p.a.)	Expenditure on butter. p.e.a.	Aggregate exp p.e.a.	Y_h log of exp. on butter p.e.a.	X_h log of agg. exp. p.e.a.	X_h^2	Y_h^2	$Y_h X_h$
1	4·2	2·00	800	2·1	400	0·32222	2·60206	6·77072	0·10383	0·83844
2	6·3	3·16	945	2·0	300	0·30103	2·47712	6·13612	0·09062	0·74569
3	10·0	2·00	1,400	5·0	700	0·69897	2·84510	8·09459	0·48856	1·98864
4	12·0	4·00	2,000	3·0	500	0·47712	2·69897	7·28444	0·22764	1·28773
5	3·0	3·00	900	1·0	300	0·00000	2·47712	6·13612	0·00000	0·00000
						1·79934	13·10037	34·42199	0·91065	4·86050

p.e.a. = per equivalent adult.

† The reader may guess that there is surely a middle way – by taking, as it were, a *partial* difference such as

$$y(t) - by(t-1), \quad x_1(t) - bx_1(t-1), \quad \text{etc.,}$$

where b is a value between zero and unity. If b is zero, then it is the original series, and if b is unity we are regressing the differences. Some value between may be just right. This conjecture is correct – but it is not easy to obtain an estimate of b. The reader is referred to the Bibliography.

CALCULATION OF $\hat{\beta}^h_{y3}$

$$\sum x^2_h = \sum (X_h - \bar{X}_h)^2 = \sum X^2_h - \left(\frac{1}{n}\right)(\sum X_h)^2$$

$$= 34 \cdot 42199 - \left(\frac{1}{5}\right)(13 \cdot 10037)^2$$

$$= 34 \cdot 42199 - 34 \cdot 32410.$$

$$\sum x^2_h = 0 \cdot 09789.$$

$$\sum y_h x_h = \sum X_h Y_h - \left(\frac{1}{5}\right)(\sum X_h)(\sum Y_h)$$

$$= 4 \cdot 86050 - \left(\frac{1}{5}\right)(13 \cdot 10037)(1 \cdot 79934)$$

$$\sum y_h x_h = 0 \cdot 14610.$$

Thus the extraneous estimator is

$$\hat{\beta}^h_{y3} = \frac{\sum y_h x_h}{\sum x^2_h}$$

$$= \frac{0 \cdot 14610}{0 \cdot 09789}$$

$$= 1 \cdot 49.$$

Thus we see that the budget studies suggest that there is a high income elasticity of demand for butter. Let us take the value as approximately $1 \cdot 5$ so that the reader can more easily check the working.

PART II – TIME SERIES

Year	Retail price index	Exp on butter (£ m.)	Disposable income (£ m.)	Quantity index of	Price index of margarine
1958	100	50·0	12,200	100	100
1959	102	51·0	12,900	105	107
1960	105	52·0	12,900	102	98
1961	106	53·0	13,500	103	99
1962	107	56·0	14,000	110	105
1963	109	59·0	14,200	118	104

(1) CALCULATE REAL DISPOSABLE INCOME AND z

Log of disposable income	Log of retail price index	Log X_3 of index of real disposable income	Log Y of quantity of butter	$\hat{\beta}^h_{y3} \cdot X_2$	$Z = Y - \hat{\beta}^h_y X_3$
4·08636	2·00000	3·08636	2·00000	4·62954	−3·62954
4·11059	2·00860	3·10199	2·02119	4·65300	−3·63181
4·11059	2·02119	3·08940	2·00860	4·63410	−3·62550
4·13033	2·02531	3·10502	2·01284	4·65753	−3·64469
4·14613	2·02938	3·11675	2·04139	4·67513	−3·63374
4·15229	2·03743	3·11486	2·07188	4·67229	−3·60041

(2) CALCULATE RELATIVE PRICE OF BUTTER

A Log of exp on butter	B Log quantity index of butter	C Log retail price index	Log relative price index $A - B - C$
1·69997	2·00002	2·00000	$\bar{1}$·69897 or −0·30103
1·70757	2·02119	2·00860	$\bar{1}$·67778 or −0·32222
1·71600	2·00860	2·02119	$\bar{1}$·68621 or −0·31379
1·72428	2·01284	2·02531	$\bar{1}$·68613 or −0·31387
1·74819	2·04139	2·02938	$\bar{1}$·67742 or −0·32258
1·77085	2·07188	2·03743	$\bar{1}$·66154 or −0·33846

(3) REGRESSION OF z ON x_1 AND x_2 OR OF Δz ON Δx_1, AND Δx_2

Year	Z	X_1	X_2
1958	−0·62954	−0·30103	1·00000
1959	−0·63181	−0·32222	1·02938
1960	−0·62550	−0·31379	0·99123
1961	−0·64469	−0·31387	0·99564
1962	−0·63374	−0·32258	1·02119
1963	−0·60041	−0·33846	1·01703

(Note that we have omitted −3 in the Z variable and so we should take this into account later.)

Year	ΔZ	ΔX_1	ΔX_2
1958			
1959	−0·00227	−0·02119	+0·02938
1960	+0·00631	+0·00843	−0·03815
1961	−0·01919	−0·00008	+0·00441
1962	+0·01095	−9·00871	+0·02555
1963	+0·03333	−0·01588	−0·00416

The regression proceeds in the normal way.

Regression of Z on X_1 and X_2

$$\sum X_1 = -1{\cdot}91195 \qquad \bar{X}_1 = -0{\cdot}318658$$

$$\sum X_2 = 6{\cdot}05447 \qquad \bar{X}_2 = 1{\cdot}009078$$

$$\sum Z = -3{\cdot}76569 \qquad \bar{Z} = -0{\cdot}627615.$$

Sums of Squares

$$\sum (X_1 - \bar{X}_1)^2 = \sum X^2 - \frac{1}{n}(\sum X)^2$$

or

$$\sum x_1{}^2 = 0{\cdot}610{,}036{,}36 - 0{\cdot}609{,}258{,}80 = 0{\cdot}000{,}777{,}56,$$

and similarly

$$\sum x_2{}^2 = 6{\cdot}110{,}637{,}14 - 6{\cdot}109{,}434{,}49 = 0{\cdot}001{,}203{,}65$$

$$\sum z^2 = 2{\cdot}364{,}498{,}49 - 2{\cdot}363{,}403{,}52 = 0{\cdot}001{,}094{,}97.$$

Cross-products

$$\sum (X_1 - \bar{X}_1)(X_2 - \bar{X}_2) = \sum X_1 X_2 - \frac{1}{n}(\sum X_1)(\sum X_2)$$

or

$$\sum x_1 x_2 = +1{\cdot}929{,}895{,}86 + 1{\cdot}929{,}307{,}31 = -0{\cdot}000{,}588{,}55,$$

and similarly

$$\sum x_1 z = 1{\cdot}199{,}363{,}36 - 1{\cdot}199{,}986{,}49 = -0{\cdot}000{,}605{,}13,$$

$$\sum x_2 z = -3{\cdot}799{,}610{,}03 + 3{\cdot}799{,}876{,}18 = 0{\cdot}000{,}266{,}15.$$

Solutions

$$\hat{\beta}_{z1{\cdot}2} = -0{\cdot}969{,}806,$$

$$\hat{\beta}_{z2{\cdot}1} = -0{\cdot}253{,}083,$$

$$\hat{\beta}_0 = (-0{\cdot}969{,}806)(-0{\cdot}318{,}658) + (6 - 0{\cdot}253{,}083)(1{\cdot}009{,}078)$$

$$= -0{\cdot}681{,}271.$$

The estimated regression equation is, therefore

$$Z = -0{\cdot}681{,}271 - 0{\cdot}969{,}806 X_1 - 0{\cdot}253{,}083 X_2$$

$$R^2 = \frac{1}{\sum z^2} \left[\hat{\beta}_{z1\cdot2} \sum zx_1 + \hat{\beta}_{z2\cdot1} \sum zx_2 \right]$$

$$= \frac{1}{0\cdot001095} \left[(-0\cdot969,806)(-0\cdot000605) + (-0\cdot253,083)(0\cdot000266) \right]$$

$$= 0\cdot474,442.$$

$$1 - R^2 = 0\cdot124,070$$

$$1 - \bar{R}^2 = (1 - R^2)[(n-1)/(n-3)] \qquad \text{where } n = 6$$

$$= 0\cdot525,558(5/3)$$

$$\bar{R}^2 = 0\cdot124,070$$

$$s_{z\cdot12}'^2 = \text{estimate of residual variance} = \frac{\sum z^2}{n} (1 - \bar{R}^2)$$

$$= (0\cdot000095/5)(0\cdot875,930) = 0\cdot000,191,82$$

$$s_{\hat{\beta}z1\cdot2}'^2 = \text{estimate of sampling variance of } \hat{\beta}_{z1\cdot2} = s_{z\cdot12}'^2 \bigg/ \left[\sum x_1^2 - \frac{(\sum x_1 x_2)}{\sum x_2^2} \right]$$

$$= 0\cdot000,191,82 \bigg/ \left[0\cdot000,777,56 - \frac{(-0\cdot000,588,55)^2}{0\cdot001,203,65} \right]$$

$$= 0\cdot391,647,$$

and similarly

$$s_{\hat{\beta}z2\cdot1}'^2 = 0\cdot253,044.$$

Regression of ΔZ on ΔX_1 and ΔX_2

(Note that $\Delta Z(t) = Z(t) - Z(t-1)$, $\Delta X_1 = X_1(t) - X_1(t-1)$ etc.)

$\sum \Delta X_1 = -0\cdot03743$	$\overline{\Delta X_1} = -0\cdot007,486$	
$\sum \Delta X_2 = 0\cdot01703$	$\overline{\Delta X_2} = 0\cdot003,406$	
$\sum \Delta Z = 0\cdot02913$	$\overline{\Delta Z} = 0\cdot005,826$	
$\sum (\Delta X_1)^2 = 0\cdot000,848$	$\sum (\Delta X_1)(\Delta X_2) = -0\cdot001,101$	
$\sum (\Delta X_2)^2 = 0\cdot003,008$	$\sum (\Delta X_1)(\Delta Z) = -0\cdot000,522$	
$\sum (\Delta Z)^2 = 0\cdot001,644$	$\sum (\Delta X_2)(\Delta Z) = -0\cdot000,251.$	

Solutions

(Note that, for typographical convenience, we have dropped the Δ sign in the subscripts.)

$$\hat{\beta}_{z1.2} = -1 \cdot 702070, \qquad \hat{\beta}_{z2.1} = -0 \cdot 680,468$$

$$\hat{\beta}_0 = -0 \cdot 004,598$$

$$R^2 = 0 \cdot 512,614 \qquad \bar{R}^2 = 0 \cdot 025,228;$$

$$s'^2_{z1.2} = 0 \cdot 000,359,2$$

$$s'^2_{\hat{\beta} z1.2} = 1 \cdot 457,573 \qquad s'^2_{\hat{\beta} z2.1} = 0 \cdot 280,625.$$

(The student is urged to work out these solutions. Note that $n = 5$ for differences.)

DURABLE GOODS

So far our discussion of the empirical estimating of demand curves has been concerned mainly with the demand for *non*-durables by households. When one examines the demand for durable household goods – including houses – one finds all the difficulties associated with the demand for non-durables, and some additional problems as well. With non-durables it was possible normally to ignore the stocks of goods held by households. When one buys a basket of strawberries, it is very likely that they are gone by the end of the week; but when a car is purchased one confidently expects that it will give useful service for a number of years. The distinction between durable and non-durable goods, however, is indeed murky; it will depend primarily on the purposes for which the analysis is required. (But as a general rule it is best to regard a commodity as durable if there is any doubt). In the analysis of consumer demand there are obvious borderline cases – such as clothing. But there is surely no doubt that household equipment such as refrigerators, vacuum cleaners, cooking stoves, etc., should properly be regarded as durable goods. We cannot here deal with the detailed analysis of the demand for durable goods; for that account the reader is referred to the Bibliography. Some of the particular problems and the way in which they have been met, if not solved, may give the reader some 'feel' of the work.

Decisions are made with respect to the *stock* of durable consumer goods. But because it is difficult to adjust the stock quickly – because of liquidity considerations and because correlated purchases also require time (such as building a garage to accommodate another car) – the actual change in stock in any year is less than that which would be realised in the long run. Thus only a fraction of the total adjustment takes place in the year in question; let us suppose that the fraction is in fact γ. Then if we write $s^*(t)$ as the desired stock in year t and $s(t)$ as the actual stock, we have

$$s(t) - s(t-1) = \gamma[s^*(t) - s(t-1)] \qquad 0 \leqq \gamma \leqq 1. \qquad (9.20)$$

Thus we imagine that the consumer looks at all the relevant variables and decides on the increase of his stock to the desired level by the end of the year (this is the value in the squared brackets on the right-hand side). His actual stock however is increased over the previous periods actual stock only by the fraction γ. This suggests that the consumer is always in the process of catching up on his purchasing programme by a process of continuous adaption. Indeed this may be called an *adaptive process*, and it is often applied to expectations as well as planned and actual purchases.

A second feature of durable consumer goods is the need for depreciation accounts. In principle the household changes its stock of equipment by retiring (or selling) goods on the one hand and purchasing new (or second hand) equipment on the other. While there are fairly good data on the depreciation of cars and houses, there is very little information on the depreciation rates of furniture, washing machines, televisions etc. in use in the household. In principle it is possible to determine the implied 'life' of equipment from data on purchases and stocks but the errors in the process are obviously large – and it would be most useful if there were independent information on depreciation and the 'life' of equipment (see Stone and Rowe, 1960, in Bibliography).

It should be emphasised that quality changes are particularly important and intractable with consumer durables. And most of the characteristics of 'quality' are intangible – such as the neighbourhood of a dwelling house, the riding comfort of a car, and so on. Many consumer durables are notoriously heterogeneous and it is very difficult to find any satisfactory means of reducing them to a common scale. For combining different qualities of goods at any particular time, the market price is an ideal indicator of relative quality. But of course the main questions concern the changes in quality over time. And as the quality changes so does the price – part of the change in price may be due to the change in quality, but it is not easy to see how much. Various devices are adopted in practice, such as measuring the cubic capacity of refrigerators, the brake-horse-power of cars, and so on. Unsatisfactory as these techniques have been, it is surely better to take some account of quality than to ignore it completely.

PERMANENT INCOME

A third feature of the analysis of durable household goods is that, in practice it has been found that the disposable household income is not very important as a determinant of the purchases of these goods. This seems to be due largely to the fact that there are a number of random elements in income receipts – sometimes income will be up and sometimes down. In fact households tend to adjust their stocks of durable consumer goods – and in particular houses – to their *long-run expected income streams*, rather than the actual income receipts in any particular year. Clearly a man who enjoys a windfall income in a particular year will not purchase another house consistent with this unusually high income level. He will know that in future years his income is going to be much lower and not so high as to sustain a large expensive dwelling. His house purchase will be determined by his long-run expectations, and not by the short-term oscillations in income.

This concept of long-run expected income will play a large part in the discussion of the aggregate consumption function, to be discussed in the second part of this chapter. The accepted term for this concept is the *permanent income*. In practice this is often measured by a weighted average of past incomes – with the weights declining over time. It is hoped that this will be a good surrogate for the average level of income to be expected in future years. It smooths out the wide oscillations in behaviour which would be predicted by the use of ordinary income concepts.

This completes our brief survey of the demand for durable household goods. All we have done here is to indicate some of the building bricks, and the difficulties of cementing them together. For a description of the actual studies it is best to read Harberger *et al.* or one of the other studies mentioned in the Bibliography.

There are many other major areas of demand analysis that remain to be considered, such as the demand for raw materials by firms; but this is perhaps best considered as part of the theory of production. There are, of course, also specialist fields of demand analysis such as the demand for imports and exports in international trade, the demand for paper assets, the demand for money, etc. All these demand functions require somewhat specialised treatment. But the basic approach is similar to that for consumers or household demand. It is simply that certain problems and difficulties become much more important. For example in the demand for money and paper assets, the speculative character of the demand requires special treatment. Nevertheless the similarities are striking, and it is often useful to proceed on the basis of an analogue of consumer demand – modifying it where necessary.

EMPIRICAL EVIDENCE

Over the past twenty years many empirical studies of the demand curve have accumulated. Naturally there has been a concentration on those single-use commodities that are relatively homogeneous – such as food and power – and the studies of non-homogeneous goods (such as womens' hats – which I suppose also might be classed as single-use) are relatively rare. For the United Kingdom the most extensive study of demand is that of Richard Stone and his colleagues.† Nearly all their results were for food (including alcoholic beverages now classified as food). Stone broadly followed a model similar to that which we have described, and so his results can be easily interpreted.

Table 9.1

Elasticities of Demand

| | Elasticity | | |
Commodity	Income	Own price	Domestic beef and veal price
Home produced mutton and lamb	0·70 (±0·12)	−0·56 (±0·43)	
	0·70 (±0·12)	−1·74 (±0·44)	1·61 (±0·44)
Imported mutton and lamb	0·70 (±0·12)	0·43 (±0·50)	
	0·70 (±0·12)	−0·60 (±0·40)	1·94 (±0·45)

† *Measurement of Consumers' Expenditure and Behaviour in the United Kingdom, 1920–1938*, vol. i.

Table 9.1 (cont.)

Elasticity

Commodity	Income	Own price	Fresh milk price
Condensed milk	−0·53 (±0·18)	−0·60 (±0·55)	
	−0·53 (±0·18)	−0·78 (±0·55)	1·40 (±0·95)
Cream	1·71 (±0·29)	−1·26 (±0·50)	*Imported eggs price*
	1·71 (±0·29)	−0·69 (±0·36)	−1·06 (±0·25)
Tea	0·04 (±0·04)	−0·19 (±0·07)	
			Coffee price
	0·04 (±0·04)	−0·27 (±0·08)	0·18 (±0·08)

Source: Stone *et al.*, *Measurement of Consumers' Expenditure and Behaviour in the U.K.*, table 106, p. 322.

The overwhelming impression from all demand studies is the validity of the broad law of demand. The relationship between quantity purchased and price is negative. A glance down Table 9.1 shows the predominance of negative own-price elasticities. It is true that some of the demand equations exhibited positive own-price elasticities – but these were always near zero and not significant in the narrow statistical sense.

The most impressive feature of these studies, however, is that the values of the coefficients accord with *a priori* reasoning. The closer the substitutes the greater the (absolute) elasticity of demand. But in order to measure the effects of changes in the price of substitutes, as well as changes in the own-price, some measures of the relative price of substitutes must be included with the independent variables in the regression.

In the theoretical discussions above, we showed that the omission of the price of a substitute from a demand equation would tend to bias the estimate of the own-elasticity. We showed that the estimate of own-elasticity would be biased upwards (i.e. if there were a negative elasticity the result would be a smaller absolute elasticity – or perhaps even a positive relationship). This result can be illustrated in the table of selected coefficients from Stone's study. The first equation in each set is the simple demand curve without including substitutes or complements. The second equation includes a close substitute for four of the commodities; the odd one is cream where we have shown instead a complement. In each case the own-price elasticity is changed in the predicted direction when the substitute is included in the analysis. For example we see that the own-price elasticity of imported lamb and mutton is actually *positive* when no substitute is included. The inclusion of the price of domestically produced beef and veal shows that there is a negative own-price elasticity, and that there is a high substitution elasticity with respect to the price of beef and veal. With cream, on the other hand, where the omission is a price of complement, the effect is to give a negative bias – and so the measured elasticity is (absolutely) larger in the simple equation.

The income elasticities were found from cross-section surveys of household budgets. Again they conform quite closely to expectations. Tea consumption, for example, varies hardly at all as income varies. Condensed milk one might reasonably expect to be an inferior substitute for fresh milk; and so it turns out in the statistics. The income elasticity is markedly negative; and an increase in income gives rise to a smaller amount of condensed milk purchased.

It would be wrong to infer that there were no surprises in this study of demand. It did not simply confirm all expectations. There were great subtleties of interpretation and of further analysis into which we cannot enter here. The student must pursue the original texts.

LINEAR EXPENDITURE MODELS

The model of demand which we have explored here is the typical form derived from the neo-classical economists. Although the specific form of the demand curve is specified, the model is of a very general form; the elasticities are not constrained to any particular subset of values, except perhaps the non-positive set. In many respects and for certain purposes it is indeed *too* general – and the modern drift of both economic theory and econometric research has been towards narrower and more specific hypotheses.

The most important of these modern theories postulates that the consumer allocates a certain fraction of his expenditure to each broad commodity group, and that these percentage allocations are stable from one year to another. Substitutions of one commodity for another take place *within* the broad expenditure category – but not between one category and another. Thus this theory views the consumer as though

is this correct?

he *fixed* the percentage allocation of his budget between clothes, rent, food, entertainment, etc. But within these categories he substitutes the cinema for the theatre, pork for beef, nylon for cotton, according to the relative prices on the market. One of the remarkable features of these models is that they are consistent with a very wide class of utility functions; they are not merely so restrictive as one might suppose.†

The concept of committed expenditure is obviously very useful for econometric model building and forecasting on a macro-economic scale. The practical models at present differ considerably from the formal theoretical constructs. The practical models find that amount of expenditure that is committed, and then allocate the remainder on a relative price and trend basis.‡ Of course the purpose to be served by such models is usually quite different from the classic micro-economic demand curve. But each can be used to reinforce the other (see D. A. Rowe in *British Economy in 1975*).

One of the main determinants of demand in these aggregate demand models is the amount which is to be spent in total on goods and services. This is determined, according to most economic theories, by the total amount of income – together with the rate of interest, the natural thriftiness of society (i.e. the extent to which future as against present consumption is valued) and so on. The consumption function itself plays an important role in determining the individual demands. And so in the second part of this chapter, we examine the theoretical and empirical aspects of the aggregate consumption function.

The Macro-Economics of Consumer Expenditure – The Consumption Function

THEORY

In this section we examine the *aggregate* behaviour of households as their incomes are increased. The consumption function of households

---

† The same sort of conclusion applies to the distribution of expenditure over time – to be discussed next in connection with the consumption function. The allocation of a constant expenditure per period is consistent with a large class of utility functions.

‡ For a description see Stone, 'Linear Expenditure Systems'; and for extensive application see W. Beckerman *et al.*, *The British Economy in 1975*, Cambridge, 1965.

has a central place in the Keynesian theory of income determination, and in the theory of economic growth. The behaviour of savings as income increases is also one of the lynch-pins of modern development theory. Of course households are not the only source of saving. Indeed in many countries the main form of saving consists of the undistributed profits of corporations – often called business saving. In developing countries the principal source of saving is the budget surplus of central government. Although the accounting contribution of personal (or household) saving may be very small, it must be recognised that the free choice of individuals may indeed offset the attempts to increase government saving by increased taxation. People may simply pay increased taxes by dis-saving, by dis-hoarding, rather than by reducing consumption. Therefore whatever the accounting figures, the free decisions of households – whether to spend or save and add to their wealth – will be of critical importance.

In the theory of consumption, hypotheses abound – much more so than in the theory of consumer market demand for commodities – and there are probably more hypotheses than truly independent bodies of data! Most theories predict that an increase in income will give rise to an increase in consumption – but some actually predict (with a finite and non-trivial probability) that consumption may actually go down!

We begin at what many people would regard as the beginning – the Keynesian hypothesis advanced in the *General Theory of Employment, Interest and Money* (1936):

Our normal psychological law that, when the real income of the community increases or decreases, its consumption will increase or decrease but not so fast ... (p. 114)

or

The fundamental psychological law ... is that men are disposed, as a rule and on the average, to increase their consumption as their income increases, but not by as much as the increase in income. (p. 96)

and later

This is especially the case where we have short periods in view ... (p. 97)

Keynesians have normally argued that as income increases a larger fraction of income will be saved, and the hypothesis may be specialised to some linear form such as that shown in Figure 9.1.†

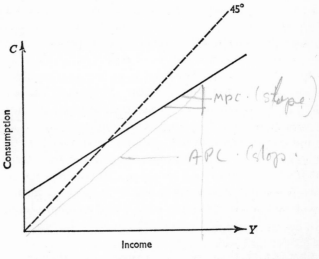

FIG. 9.1

Such a hypothesis is a simple one and can easily be confronted by suitable data. As with the investigations of micro-demand functions, the main forms of data are the cross-section of budgets of consumers and the time series of aggregate income and expenditure over the last 100 years or so. In the budget studies the households are arranged according to their income and their total expenditure. Two outstanding features emerged from these studies. First the marginal propensity to consume was always less than unity. Secondly the marginal propensity to consume was always less than the average propensity to consume.

Taken by themselves these findings appear to be quite consistent with the Keynesian concept of the consumption function. Indeed not only is the marginal propensity to consume less than unity, but also the

† The scholar will observe, however, that although Keynes thought that '. . . as a rule, . . . a greater proportion of income (will be) saved as income increases', he emphasises that all that is required for his model is that the *marginal* propensity as a ratio of absolute money values be less than unity (p. 97). Nevertheless it is often convenient to measure also the linear logarithmic relation as well.

elasticity of consumption with respect to income is less than unity.†
But if this consumption function holds over the long run, there would
be an observable increase in the fraction of income saved. Higher
incomes would result in a smaller fraction of consumption, and the
savings ratio would increase and consumption ratio would decline.

Evidence from the time series, however, shows clearly that this
hypothesis is discredited. Over very long periods there has been no
great change in the fraction of income that is saved. For the United
States, the country for which we have the most reliable and extensive
data, it appears that over the last 100 years saving on aggregate has
always amounted to about 10 per cent of income. Thus it seems that
the evidence from the time series, interpreted as a consumption
function, is not consistent with a similar interpretation of the cross-section
results.‡ It is clear, for example, that if the time series relationship
were the true consumption function, and one used the cross-section for
predicting consumption for a future increase in income, one would
predict too low a level of consumption and too high a level of saving.§

PERMANENT INCOME AND LIFE-CYCLE HYPOTHESES

Clearly the simple linear or log-linear consumption function as
formulated above does not reconcile the time series and cross-section
data. A satisfactory theory should be able to explain both forms of data,
and should indicate which coefficients should be used in each set of
circumstances. In order to meet this need several theories have been
suggested, few of which have been convincingly discredited by the data.
Here, however, we shall review what we believe are the two most
useful formulations: the *permanent income hypothesis* of Milton Friedman,
and the *life-cycle hypothesis* of Modigliani and Brumberg.

Both these theories stem from a common attitude about the important
elements in economic decisions. The basic determinant of an individual's

† This arises by fitting the logarithmic regression, or by multiplying the slope of the linear
regression by the ratio of income to consumption at each point on the income scale.

‡ The reader will note however that the marginal propensity to consume $\Delta C/\Delta Y$ is less than
unity in the time series results – and this is the minimum required by the Keynes' psychological law. But the elasticity is unity – and is clearly greater than the elasticity in the cross-
section.

§ Such predictions were characteristic of both Britain and the United States for the years
following World War II. Fears of too low a level of demand and of a stagnating economy
proved to be groundless.

consumption in a given year is not his income but his *wealth*. The wealth of an individual may be conceived such that it encompasses his *non-human wealth*, such as property titles etc., including expected inheritances and so on, but also his *human wealth*, which one may consider as the present value of his expected sales of labour services for the rest of his life. Thus a person will plan to spend these assets over his life span – with perhaps the proviso that a sum will be available at his death for his children.

How would a person plan to spend his assets over his lifetime? In principle this depends on the marginal utility of consumption in each period, and on the rate of interest. Let us assume for simplicity that the rate of interest is zero, then it seems to be the simplest hypothesis to suppose that the marginal utility of consumption is constant in each time period. Thus this would lead to the individual spreading out his assets so that he consumes them in equal portions in each year.

Now let us ask what is the effect of an increase in income of £100 this year – and let us assume that it is a windfall income that is not expected to persist for future years. Obviously the effect depends on the number of years of expected life of the individual and whether he wants to leave an inheritance. Let us therefore suppose that the individual, *knowing* that he will die in 50 years' time, wishes to leave no inheritance, and let us also assume as above that the marginal utility of spending is the same in each year. Clearly he will simply divide the £100 equally between the fifty years. So the effect of an increase of income of £100 is to induce him to increase his consumption in *this* year by only £2.

This is, of course, a far cry from the orders of magnitude of statistical consumption functions as well as from the values conjectured by theorists. The explanation is obvious; if the income receipt is a windfall and is not expected to recur he would be better off spreading the consumption over all expected future periods. It is best to characterise the receipt as a once-and-for-all increment to wealth, and then examine the effect of the increased wealth on the consumption pattern – on the assumption that the marginal utility of consumption does not change. The effect on assets is the critical determinant of the consumption effects. If the increment in income of £100 had been expected to be *permanent* rather than a once-and-for-all windfall, then it would have meant an increase of wealth of £5,000 – and, on our assumption, an increase of annual consumption of £100 per annum. Such a result more closely approximates to the empirical findings and the conjectures of theorists.†

This simple view of the world may be complicated in many ways. The additional effects of a positive rate of interest are simply seen by redefining wealth to include the expected interest receipts. In practical terms this means that during the early period of life we live primarily off the interest receipts, whereas in later life we live more and more off capital. (This is exactly like the repayments to a building society – but note that we have included *human* wealth in this calculation.) In formal terms we can convert an income stream expressed in terms of interest receipts into an equivalent amount of wealth, and proceed as before.‡ This does, of course, involve the assumption that one may borrow and lend as much as one likes at the going rate of interest. This might be taken as an extreme case. Probably the most realistic case in practice is where the amount of borrowing one may do is limited by the amount of non-human wealth. When money receipts are very erratic it may well be that in the attempt to smooth out the flow of consumption expenditures, the individual will bump up against this borrowing constraint. But for most capitalist and developed economies, where there is a well-developed loan market, this restraint may be presumed to be of less than dominating importance.

Further one may vary the assumption about the constancy of the marginal utility of spending. Needs will sometimes rise and fall at various periods – or perhaps randomly over time. So presumably the marginal utility of spending will vary randomly over time also. But it is difficult to believe that the high needs will be coincident with the high money receipts – and this is what is required by a 'normal' Keynesian consumption function. For then an increase in income of a

---

† A querulous critic asked: 'Surely if I had a good day at the races, I would buy myself and my friends a drink'. Such casual observation, however, does not discredit the theory – since buying a drink for one's friends is like buying drinks for oneself in the future. One will share in one's friends' good fortune in the future, when the horses will, on the average, run well for them!

‡ In our example above, the *permanent* increase of £100 per annum will be entered into today's wealth as

$$100 + \frac{100}{(1+r)} + \frac{100}{(1+r)^2} + \frac{100}{(1+r)^3} + \frac{100}{(1+r)^4} \cdots + \frac{100}{(1+r)^{49}} = 100\left[\frac{1-d^{50}}{1-d}\right],$$

where $d = (1+r)^{-1}$, and r is the rate of interest.

windfall kind would be associated with the accident of great need to spend and an unusually high marginal utility of spnding. A curious accident with surely a very low probability of occurrence.†

Over the long run a constant marginal utility of money spending seems the most sensible sort of assumption to make. And it must be observed that such a pattern of behaviour – constant spending in each period – does *not* imply that there is necessarily a utility function which is homogeneous in goods. Indeed the equal fraction spent in each year is a consequence of a wide variety of utility functions.

It is clear that this 'life-cycle' theory of consumption gives a large number of hypotheses about observed behaviour. The fraction saved will vary according to the age of the person. In early years he will dis-save and invest in education. Then when he becomes employed saving will begin – and gradually increase as his income increases. Towards the end of his working life saving will probably start falling and, in retirement, he will dis-save once more. This is a typical or average pattern. But one would expect to see wide divergences around such an average. People differ according to the extent to which they wish to leave inheritances. The effect of this would be to drive up or down the total amount of saving over the whole life cycle; but the *pattern* would remain the same.

Another sort of complication is introduced by the fact that, in most countries of the world, the date of death cannot be predicted with certainty. It still remains a chance event. On the average however deaths are sufficiently regular to enable advanced forms of insurance to be possible. With an endowment policy, for example, one buys the certainty of an estate whenever one dies. With a life annuity one purchases a guaranteed money income for the remainder of one's days. These arrangements to some extent provide a sort of 'hedge' against the uncertainty of the time of death; but taking out insurance does not remove the fundamental problem of this basic uncertainty in the human estate.‡

† It is as though I only have a win at the races when I have a great thirst.
‡ There are many similar uncertainties which do not have quite the finality of death, such as the unplanned birth of a child, the unexpected acquisition of a dependent relative, an (uninsured) illness, and so on. Part of one's wealth must be earmarked for such contingencies. But it is likely that the probabilities of events such as these will change with information and with the simple passage of time. This may in turn generate quite large changes in the pattern of savings.

Up to now we have been concerned with describing the implications of the life-cycle hypothesis on the behaviour of an individual. When we examine the *aggregate* behaviour of persons in total, there are aggregation effects to be taken into account. The age-structure of the population will influence not merely the aggregate saving ratio, but also the marginal propensity to save. If for example the population is old, one would expect a higher fraction of consumption and a lower fraction of saving than in a young population. The marginal propensity to consume would be lower in the young than in the old population. In general, it is clear that the life-cycle hypothesis suggests many hypotheses about consumption and demographic factors, some of which are pursued in the exercises at the end of this chapter.

PERMANENT INCOME – A FORMAL DEVELOPMENT

One of the critical elements in the life-cycle hypothesis is that the reaction of consumption to an increase in income depends on the expectations about whether that increase in receipts will continue for future years. The question turns on whether the income receipt is permanent or transitory. This distinction constitutes the main element in the development of the formal *permanent income hypothesis*.

Let us write

Y_p as the permanent income,
Y_t as the transitory income,
$Y = Y_p + Y_t$ as the measured income,
C_p as the permanent consumption,
C_t as the transitory consumption,
$C = C_p + C_t$ as the measured consumption.

We may conveniently interpret these as aggregates – perhaps for the country as a whole or perhaps for a particular area or occupation. The particular definition of what income is to be considered transitory and what permanent, and which part of consumption is to be defined as permanent are problems which are left to be decided by the data. No prior definitions are imposed.

The fundamental stability postulated is that between permanent income and permanent consumption. This describes the steady long run, planned relationship between the stable expected receipts and the stable consumption outlays. The determinants of this relation are: the 'normal' rate of interest that measures the rewards of saving, the ratio of human to non-human wealth – which determines the extent to which borrowing on non-human collateral is possible – and a variety of sociological and institutional factors, such as political and social stability, religion, etc. These factors or determinants do not change erratically from one period to another – except under easily identified conditions such as war or revolution. Thus there is a presumption of fundamental stability in this relationship.

The particular algebraic form of the relationship between permanent income and permanent consumption needs to be specified before approaching the data. Friedman has suggested that we adopt the simplest possible one: a line through the origin. This implies that people on the average always plan to save a constant fraction of their permanent income. The marginal permanent propensity to consume is less than unity, since the increment of permanent consumption is always less than the increment of permanent income – both measured in absolute terms. The permanent income elasticity of permanent consumption is however always unity; and the average permanent propensity to consume is constant and equal to the marginal propensity to consume out of permanent income. Thus

$$C_p = kY_p, \tag{9.21}$$

where k is the constant depending on the rate of interest, the ratio of human to non-human wealth, etc.

The permanent income hypothesis asserts that this is the only systematic relationship between the variables Y_p, Y_t, C_p, and C_t. There are six possible correlations between these four variables; thus we assert that the one between C_p and Y_p is positive, and all the others are zero. Thus the correlations between Y_p and Y_t, Y_p and C_t, C_p and C_t, C_p and Y_t, C_t and Y_t are zero. In fact, however, we need to specify that only *three* of these correlations are zero. With the specification that $C_p = kY_p$ the number of independent variables is reduced from four to three. (The reader will note however that the relationship between permanent consumption and permanent income is supposed to be *exact* without error or disturbance.) With three variables there are only three possible correlations, so it is sufficient to specify $C_p = kY_p$, and that the correlations Y_t and Y_p, C_t and C_p, and C_t and Y_t are all zero. The two other zero correlations automatically follow. The hypothesis is stated in this quite correct abbreviated form by Friedman in his path-breaking study (see *Theory of the Consumption Function*). It is, however, important to observe that the abbreviation is a consequence of specifying that the relationship between permanent consumption and permanent income holds *exactly without any disturbance and without errors of measurement*. Such an extreme hypothesis is bound to be discredited by the data, so that we may as well prepare for a disturbance or errors of measurement in this simple proportional relationship. With errors or disturbances in the equation, i.e.

$$C_p = kY_p + \text{disturbance}, \tag{9.22}$$

it is necessary to specify that the correlations between C_t and Y_p and between C_p and Y_t are also zero.

Obviously such a hypothesis is a strong one. To propose that of six possible correlations, only one is positive – the remaining five are zero – is to limit the outcomes drastically. Thus it provides a set of sharp predictions that can be examined against the data to see whether they are discredited. Before examining the plausibility of these assumptions and the evidence on the hypotheses, however, it is necessary to convert the theory into the standard regression equations of consumption on income.

The question which we now ask is what do we measure when we find the regression of *measured* consumption (C) on *measured* income (Y)? These are typically the variables observed in practice – and the regressions have been used for the purpose of testing theories of the consumption function. Using the usual least-squares formula we have

$$\hat{\beta}_{CY} = \frac{\sum(C - \bar{C})(Y - \bar{Y})}{\sum(Y - \bar{Y})^2},$$

or, using the standard convention of $c = C - \bar{C}, y = Y - \bar{Y}$,

$$\hat{\beta}_{cy} = \frac{\sum cy}{\sum y^2}. \tag{9.23}$$

Now let us suppose that $c_t = C_t - \bar{C}_t$, $y_p = Y_p - \bar{Y}_p$, etc. (It is also convenient to measure transitory income and transitory consumption such that they have a mean of zero, i.e. $\bar{C}_t$, $\bar{Y}_t$ are both zero.) Thus we can write

$$\hat{\beta}_{cy} = \frac{\sum (c_p + c_t)(y_p + y_t)}{\sum (y_p + y_t)^2} \tag{9.24}$$

so that

$$\hat{\beta}_{cy} = \frac{\sum c_p y_p + \sum c_p y_t + \sum c_t y_p + \sum c_t y_t}{\sum y^2}. \tag{9.25}$$

By the assumpsions listed above, however, we can write the last three terms in the numerator as zero. (These are the cross-products of variables that have no correlation.) Thus we obtain

$$\hat{\beta}_{cy} = \frac{\sum c_p y_p}{\sum y^2}. \tag{9.26}$$

But the strict permanent-income hypothesis above states that $C_p = kY_p$, so that $c_p = ky_p$, so we may substitute to obtain

$$\hat{\beta}_{cy} = k \frac{\sum y_p^2}{\sum y^2} = k\mathbf{P}_p \tag{9.27}$$

The ratio $(\sum y_p^2)/\sum y^2$ – which we call $\mathbf{P}_y$ – is the fraction of the total variance of income regarded as permanent. It is the ratio of the variance of permanent income to the variance of measured income.

This ratio $\mathbf{P}_y$ is always less than unity – by virtue of the assumption that y_p and y_t are uncorrelated. For we can write

$$\sum y^2 = \sum (y_p + y_t)^2 = \sum y_p^2 + \sum y_t^2 + 2\sum y_p y_t \tag{9.28}$$
$$\sum y^2 = \sum y_p^2 + \sum y_t^2.$$

Therefore the variance of measured income is equal to the sum of the variance of the permanent component and the variance of the transitory component.

The important conclusion is that the regression of measured consumption on measured income will produce a coefficient of regression which is always lower than the parameter k. The downward bias in $\hat{\beta}_{cy}$ as an estimate of k will be the more important the smaller the variability of permanent income relative to the total variance of income.

Before going on to discuss the implications of this result, we might now review some of the assumptions that have been made in order to derive it. The first is the proportionality between permanent consumption and permanent income – the factor k. Surely, it might be argued, incomes and consumption are not related proportionately – if we suppose that the relationship is linear, there is likely to be a positive intercept on the consumption axis. Thus we might write

$$C_p = a + bY_p \tag{9.29}$$

instead of the simple proportional relation used above.

The only substantial theoretical objection to such a formulation is that it gives rise to much more complicated results than the assumption of proportionality. It seems best to stick to the simple version until it has been convincingly discredited by the evidence.† It is important to emphasise that the proportionality assumption is not an essentially integral part of the permanent income hypothesis at all. The theory can take it or leave it.

The other major assumptions relate to the lack of correlation between the various components (other than the two permanent components) of consumption and income. The hard case is clearly the statement that there is no correlation between the two transitory components C_t and Y_t, and the assumption that there is no correlation between C_p and Y_t is only slightly less difficult to swallow. In our discussion of the life-cycle hypothesis we showed that an increase of transitory income *did* give rise to a small increase in consumption over all future periods. (One buys a drink for oneself as well as a round for one's friends.) Superficially the life-cycle and permanent-income hypotheses seem to be inconsistent.

The explanation of this inconsistency lies in the definition of the concept of permanent income, and its relationship to transitory income receipts. An increase of income, however transitory, increased wealth and so increased permanent planned consumption. All transitory components of income gave rise to changes in wealth, permanent income and consumption in the life-cycle hypothesis. Thus permanent income is bound to change in response to transitory receipts; it is true that the change will be very much damped, but movements in transitory

† I believe that the weight of evidence currently available does tend to discredit the proportionality assumption – but the issue is not yet clear cut.

and permanent components of income will be correlated. After all receipts do add to wealth.

It must be emphasised that these observations in no way discredit the theory of the permanent income hypothesis. Only the facts can do that. But it does suggest that this hypothesis must be viewed as an archetype; if, for example, the individuals who comprised the society had very distant horizons then in the limit they would behave as postulated by the permanent income hypothesis.

[handwritten: i.e. in the limit Yt would have no effect on current cons. - see eg. with spreading $100 over 50 yrs]

MEASURING PERMANENT INCOME

The practical importance of this point may be observed in the actual measurements of permanent income. We suggested (following Friedman) that the actual measure of permanent income be determined largely by the data. But some formulation is necessary, and the one that is often used in practice is to define permanent income as a weighted sum of past measured incomes. The simplest weighting system to use is the so-called geometric series:

$$Y_p(t) = \beta[Y(t) + \lambda Y(t-1) + \lambda^2 Y(t-2) + \lambda^2 Y(t-3) + \ldots], \quad (9.30)$$

where the β and λ comprise the weighting system. One of the conditions is that $0 \leqslant \lambda \leqslant 1$, for otherwise, either measured income would have an oscillating effect on the permanent component (if $\lambda \leqslant 0$) or permanent income would be indefinitely large (if $\lambda \geqslant 1$). And it is also obvious that β must be strictly positive, for we suppose that there is no admissible concept of negative income. With these restrictions the values of the paramenters are to be determined by the data.

But we might first consider the problem of the correlation between permanent income and transitory income in this model. We may find the transitory component for period t by deducting the permanent income from measured income:

$$Y_t(t) = Y(t) - Y_p(t)$$
$$= (1-\beta)Y(t) - \beta[\lambda Y(t-1) + \lambda^2 Y(t-2) + \lambda^3 Y(t-3) + \ldots]. \quad (9.31)$$

Thus, with this measure of permanent income, transitory income is also a weighted average of past incomes. Now it is obvious that since permanent income and transitory income are both weighted averages of past incomes, it is most unlikely that they would be uncorrelated – for they contain the same ingredients.†

One of the most useful features of this specification of permanent income is the ease with which one may manipulate the model. Since it is essentially in the form of a geometric series, one can readily 'add up' the elements:

$$Y_p(t) = \beta[Y(t) + \lambda Y(t-1) + \lambda^2 Y(t-2) + \lambda^3 Y(t-3) + ...]. \qquad (9.34)$$

Thus multiplying this equation by λ, and writing it for the period $t-1$ instead of t, we find

$$\lambda Y_p(t-1) = \beta[\lambda Y(t-1) + \lambda^2 Y(t-2) + \lambda^3 Y(t-3) \doteq ...]. \qquad (9.35)$$

Looking at these two equations we see that the right-hand sides are the same, except that the first equation has the additional term $\beta Y(t)$. Thus we subtract the second equation from the first to obtain

$$Y_p(t) - \lambda Y_p(t-1) = \beta Y(t), \qquad (9.36)$$

or

$$Y_p(t) = \lambda Y_p(t-1) + \beta Y(t).$$

In words permanent income in period t is a linear function of income in period t and permanent income in period $(t-1)$.

The interpretation is, however, even more interesting and informative. The coefficient of current income β tells us the effect of current measured

---

† Readers who are not afraid of a little formal statistics may easily check that a zero correlation would be most fortuitous. We may write

$$\left.\begin{array}{l} Y_p(t) = \lambda Y_p(t-1) + \beta Y(t), \\ Y_t(t) = -\lambda Y_p(t-1) + (1-\beta)Y(t) \end{array}\right\}. \qquad (9.32)$$

If we can express the correlation between $Y(t)$ and $Y(t-j)$ as r^j, i.e. if the income series is generated by a first-order auto-regressive process, we can show that the correlation between permanent income and transitory income is zero if, and only if

$$P_y = \frac{\beta}{\lambda^2}\left[(1-\beta) + \frac{r(1-2\beta\lambda)}{1-r\lambda}\right]. \quad 0 \leqslant r \leqslant 1 \qquad (9.33)$$

If we insert values of $\beta = 2/3$ and $\lambda = 1/3$ which are those suggested by empirical evidence in the United States, we find that if $(2/3) \geqslant r \geqslant 1$, $P_y > 1$ and this is clearly inadmissible; if $r = 0$, $P_y = 1/2$. Thus between $0 \geqslant r \geqslant (2/3)$ the required value of P_y rises from $1/2$ to unity. Values below 0 are not consistent with positive r. And this implies that they are not consistent with the facts since the first order approximation of an auto-regressive process always produces a positive r. Indeed one should observe that the value of r in practice is in the region of 0.9. So this clearly points to the very high likelihood of inconsistency.

income in calculating the permanent component. An increase of £1 will have the effect of adding to permanent income an amount of £β in the current year. Next year this will induce a further addition of £$\lambda\beta$ and the year after that £$\lambda^2\beta$, and so on.†

The perceptive reader will observe a marked similarity between the permanent income hypotheses and the 'errors-in-variables' model of regression. The permanent components of measured income and consumption are the analogues of the true values; the transitory components are the 'errors' of observation or measurement. Indeed we postulate the same correlations between the permanent and transitory terms that were used for the errors-in-variables model; all correlations are zero except that between the two (true) permanent variables. Not surprisingly one obtains the same sort of results – a downward bias in the least squares estimation of the true (permanent) linear relation.

But this formal similarity should not be interpreted to mean that the permanent income hypothesis is the 'same' as the errors-in-variables model of regression. It is not. The economic and even the statistical interpretation is quite different. The transitory components are not errors of observation or measurement of some true or exact magnitude. We suppose in theory that there are *no* errors of observation in the measurement of both transitory and permanent concepts. The transitory income itself is not an error of measurement; it constitutes real money income and is not a slip of the statistician or accountant. Nor can the transitory component be regarded as an 'experimental error'. Indeed the only way to interpret these concepts is within the terms of the economics of the permanent income hypothesis itself!

The most useful feature of the two theories of the consumption function surveyed here is that they provide many hypotheses suitable

† To show, once more, that with this formulation a correlation between transitory income and permanent income, together with the correlation between permanent income and permanent consumption, automatically implies a correlation between transitory income and permanent consumption, we may write

$$C_p = k\Upsilon_p + \text{disturbance}, \quad k \neq 0,$$
$$\Upsilon_p = b\Upsilon_t + \text{disturbance}, \quad b \neq 0,$$

so that
$$C_p = k(b\Upsilon_t) + \text{disturbance}.$$

And if k and b are both positive, as we specify in practice, then the correlation between C_p and Υ_t is necessarily positive.

for direct and indirect testing against the data. We cannot do justice in these pages to the great variety of tests to which the theory may be put, to the re-arrangement of old data and the collection of new information which the theory has induced. We review here only the broad outlines; for a masterly account of the relation between theory and data, the reader is referred to Friedman's *Theory of the Consumption Function*, chapter iv in particular.

DATA

One of the awkward problems of empirical work on the consumption function is that of defining 'consumption'. Clearly the most useful definition is that which treats all consumer durables as additional saving and capital at the time of purchase. 'Consumption' then records only the depreciation relevant in a particular year. If one buys a car in 1960, one 'saves' the £1,000 required to purchase it, and one consumes the depreciation over the 10-year life of the car.

Unfortunately the data on depreciation accounts and second-hand prices of consumer durables are notoriously scarce and poor. Consequently in much statistical work one is forced to work with a concept of 'consumers expenditure' – which includes the price of the durable in the year of purchase. Thus 'consumer expenditure' would include the £1,000 in 1960, whereas consumption would include only the annual depreciation in 1960 – say it is £100 – and the remaining £900 would be regarded as part of saving. In other words the concept of 'consumer expenditure' treats consumers' assets as if they were completely written off in the year of purchase. Obviously the importance of this error of measurement of consumption depends on the 'smoothness' over time of the purchases of durable consumer goods. The evidence of time series suggests, however, that there are durable consumer-good booms and slumps, and this will give rise to oscillations in consumer expenditure which do not appear in consumption.

With the definition of income there are probably not so many important difficulties. Income here is a short way of describing the personal disposable income of households. Direct personal taxes are excluded. In practice, however, it is often found that studies, particularly in the United States, tend to include both personal taxes in income and personal taxation in consumer expenditure also. There are, of course, the perennial shortcomings of income statistics, that they do not or at least very rarely, reflect capital gains – either realised or unrealised. With these idiosyncracies of definition in mind, let us now examine the data in the light of the permanent income hypothesis.

TIME SERIES AND CROSS-SECTIONS

One of the main difficulties with the old theories of the consumption function was the reconciliation of the cross-section results with those from the time series. Over the long run the average propensity to consume has always been in the neighbourhood of 0·9 for the United States. Yet from cross-section studies of household budgets, the marginal propensity to consume has been in the region of 0·57 to 0·79. Let us use the permanent income to see if this difference can be explained.

Clearly the time series of aggregate data for the United States will have very small transitory components. In the aggregate statistics we should expect transitory components largely to cancel out. Thus we may write the aggregate time series relationship as approximately that of the stable function between permanent income and permanent consumption;

$$C_p = 0 \cdot 9 Y_p, \qquad (9.37)$$

where we have inserted $k = 0 \cdot 9$ into the formula.

The cross-section results are however of a different kind. Observations are not aggregates; each observation relates to a particular family (or in some cases an income class). Transitory components cannot be supposed to be small – for some families will have had a good year and some will have had a bad year. Some will find themselves well up the income scale, whereas others will find themselves near the bread line. The fact that in a particular year a family finds itself with a relatively high income may reflect the fact that it has a high permanent income; but families classified as having high income in a particular year will on the average have a large *positive* transitory component to their income. It is indeed partly this positive transitory income that causes them to have high incomes. Conversely, persons or families classified according to the income in a particular year as poor, are on the average likely to be down on their luck – and likely to have a negative transitory income.

cf. Friedman's diagram.

Table 9.2

Relation between Consumption and Income based on Budget Data, for different Countries, Dates, and Groups of Consumer Units

Date	Consumer units	Average income	Average propensity to consume	Marginal propensity to consume	Income elasticity of consumption
		United States *(income given in dollars)*			
1888–90	Selected wage-earner families	682	·90	·67	·74
1901	Selected wage-earner normal families	651	·92	·68	·75
1917–19	Selected wage-earner families	1,513	·91	·78	·86
1935–36	Non-relief-non-farm families	1,952	·89	·73	·82
1941	Urban families	2,865	·92	·79	·87
1944	Urban families	3,411	·82	·57	·70
1947	Urban families	3,323	·92	·78	·85
1950	Non-farm families	4,084	·91	·73	·80
1950	Spending units of one or more persons, urban plus rural	3,220	·92	·75	·82
1935–36	Non-relief farm families	1,259	·87	·57	·65
1941	Farm families	1,680	·83	·57	·69
		Great Britain *(income given in pounds sterling)*			
1938–39	Middle-class families with one earner				·89
1951–52	Income units of one or more persons, urban plus rural	369	·99	·86	·87
		Sweden *(income given in Swedish kronor)*			
1913	Industrial workers and low-grade employees	744	·99	·90	·91
1923	Industrial workers and low-grade employees	1,232	1·00	·96	·96
1923	Middle-class families	2,692	1·00	·92	·92
1933	Industrial workers and low-grade employees	1,236	·98	·94	·95
1933	Middle-class families	2,341	·96	·88	·91
1933	Small farmers	577	·95		
1933	Farm and forestry workers	504	·99		

Source: Friedman, *A Theory of the Consumption Function.*

An extreme example will illustrate the idea. Suppose that the cross-section consisted of two families – both of which enjoyed the same permanent income of, say, 100 a year. But in the particular year in which the cross-section is observed, one family has a negative transitory component of – 20, and the other family a positive transitory income of + 20. Thus the distribution of income will be solely due to transitory components.

If it were true that the distribution of income were caused only by the transitory income component, then of course there would be a perfectly random distribution of income and consumption around the point reflecting the *same* permanent income and consumption for each family. In practice, however, the distribution of income reflects differences in permanent income as well as the year to year variations of the transitory component. Both vary over the income scale.

The coefficient of regression of measured consumption on measured income for the cross-section $\hat{\beta}_{cy}$ may be expressed in the form of the product of the ratio of the variance of permanent income to the variance of measured income and the coefficient k,

$$\hat{\beta}_{cy} = k\mathbf{P}_y \qquad (9.38)$$

Inserting $\hat{\beta}_{c2}$ from the cross-section (we take a typical value from the peace-time range, i.e. 0·75) and the value of k from the aggregate time series we obtain

$$0·75 = 0·9\mathbf{P}_y \qquad (9.39)$$

Thus we can find the implied ratio of the variance of permanent income to the variance of measured income as 0·82. Thus about 18 per cent of the variance of income may be regarded as transitory.

A comparison of these results with those for Great Britain may illuminate this result. Unfortunately we have not such a wealth of savings statistics as the United States, but one might reasonably suppose that the average propensity to consume out of permanent income is 0·99. From the cross-section, the marginal propensity to consume out of measured income is 0·86. Thus

$$0·86 = 0·99\mathbf{P}_y.$$

This implies that about 13 per cent of the variation in measured income was considered to be due to transitory components. This is considerably less than that in the United States in spite of the fact that the relative variance of income is roughly the same in the two countries. The higher value of k is no doubt explained by the 'cushioning' of welfare and national assistance in the United Kingdom – which is proportionately much more important than that in the United States. There is not so great a need to save for a rainy day. The smaller component of variance due to transitory effects is probably partly explained by the structure of industry (in particular a smaller farm sector) and the limitations on competition in much of the small business sector due to the prevalence of price maintenance arrangements (in 1951–2).

OCCUPATIONAL DIFFERENCES AND CHANGES IN INCOME

The permanent income hypothesis clearly has implications for the occupational behaviour of consumers. The effects appear in the two constants of the analysis, i.e. the average propensity to consume (k) and the fraction of the variance of income considered to be transitory (P_2). It is likely that the value of k will be lower (savings will in the long run be higher) for farm than non-agricultural families. Incomes from crops and animals vary considerably with weather and to some extent market conditions. They must prepare for dry years. There is, in other words, a large variance of the transitory component of income. Compared with about 18 per cent for the country as a whole, the transitory component of farmers is almost certainly more than 30 per cent of the total variance of measured income.

One would also expect similar results to hold for the small businessman. The variation in income is large and one would expect that a large fraction of it would be attributable to transitory components. Similarly civil servants should have a higher permanent income component and a very small transitory element. For the results of these tests the student is referred to Friedman's study of consumption.

The permanent income hypothesis has many implications for the analysis of the effects of *changes* in income. The classification of income units according to their change in income tends to sort out those with similar experience of transitory income receipts. Consider for example persons with the same permanent income in each year; then classification according to the change in income from one year to the next will simply measure the transitory component. The variance of the transitory component within each income-change class will be less than the variance of the transitory component for the whole group. Clearly we have put all those with high positive transitory components into one class, medium but positive transitory component into another, and so on. Within each class, therefore, there will be a relatively small variance of the transitory income. Now consider the realistic situation where people do not have the same permanent income, then there is the variance of the permanent component to be taken into account. But classification according to income-change class will not be concerned with a classification according to permanent income; for permanent income is not correlated with the transitory component. Thus the variance of permanent income would be the same for each income-change class.

Thus the hypothesis predicts that for each income-change class the fraction of the total variance explained by transitory components will be lower than for the group considered as a whole. Thus the regression of consumption on income for each income-change group will have a higher slope (a higher marginal propensity to consume) than for all the groups considered together. Again the evidence seems to conform to the pattern predicted by the hypothesis. For a sample of farms in the United States the regression for income-change classes was between 0·24 and 0·29, whereas the regression for all classes was 0·15.†

REGRESSION ESTIMATES OF PERMANENT INCOME

One of the important problems yet to be discussed is the method of measuring the permanent income. It is rather remarkable that so many tests of the permanent income hypothesis may be carried out without explicitly measuring the permanent income. One estimates instead the *variance* of permanent income as a fraction of the variance of measured income. But for some purposes a measurement of permanent income itself is desirable and one must devise means of estimating this concept. If we estimate permanent income by the geometrically weighted series of past, measured incomes:

$$Y_p(t) = \beta[Y(t) + \lambda Y(t-1) + \lambda^2 Y(t-2) + \lambda^3 Y(t-3) + \ldots +], \quad (9.40)$$

we must find values for the β and λ.

† See Friedman, *Theory of the Consumption Function*, p. 102. As an exercise in relating hypothesis and fact this account is probably one of the best in the literature.

From the fundamental proportional relationship between C_p and Y_p we have $C_p = kY_p$. And this can be written as

$$C - C_t = kY_p, \qquad C = kY_p + C_t. \tag{9.41}$$

But we know that, *ex hypothesi*, C_t is a random variable that is uncorrelated with Y_p. This equation can, therefore, be treated as a standard regression problem where the disturbance C_t is independent of the value of the independent variable.

Substituting for the value of Y_p, and writing the time periods in parentheses, we find†

$$C(t) \overset{?}{=} k\beta[Y(t) + \lambda Y(t-1) + \lambda^2 Y(t-2) + \ldots +] + C_t(t). \tag{9.42}$$

This equation holds for all periods. And so one might be tempted to fit a regression of $C(t)$ on $Y(t)$, $Y(t-1)$, $Y(t-2)$, etc. This is a sensible way of seeing whether the coefficients actually do conform to the predicted geometric pattern. If we have an independent estimate of k, we can obtain estimates of β and λ from the regression coefficients of $Y(t)$ and $Y(t-1)$. But the coefficients of $Y(t-2)$, $Y(t-3)$, etc. will give us estimates of λ^2, λ^3, etc. – and so we can check for the consistency of this specification with the facts.

Suppose, however, that we are interested only in estimation – we are, so-to-speak, quite certain that this specification is the best available. Then we can write

$$\lambda C(t-1) = k\beta[\lambda Y(t-1) + \lambda^2 Y(t-2) + \lambda^3 Y(t-3) + \ldots] + \lambda C_t(t-1). \tag{9.43}$$

Deducting this equation from the one in the above paragraph

$$C(t) - \lambda C(t-1) = k\beta Y(t) + C_t(t) - \lambda C_t(t-1). \tag{9.44}$$

And this may be re-written in the standard form of a regression equation

$$C(t) = \lambda C(t-1) + k\beta Y(t) + C_t(t) - \lambda C_t(t-1). \tag{9.45}$$

This suggests that we need simply to regress $C(t)$ on $C(t-1)$ and on $Y(t)$ to obtain measures of λ and β. The regression of current consumption on lagged consumption and on current income will give us estimates of the 'weights' (provided that we know k).

† It will be observed that it is easy to add constant terms to make the fundamental equation non-proportional. Similarly additional constant terms may be added to the equation defining permanent income. They add to the algebra but not to enlightenment.

But such an estimate of λ will have a downward bias. The disturbance term of the above equation is $C_t(t) - \lambda C_t(t-1)$. It is clear that $C_t(t-1)$ is correlated with $C(t-1)$, i.e. that the transitory component of consumption is correlated with the measured income. Thus the disturbance and the independent variable, last year's consumption, are not independent; they are positively correlated. The higher the transitory component of consumption, the higher the measured consumption. It is easy to show that the downward bias in estimating λ is the larger the greater the importance of the transitory component of consumption.†
Thus if the transitory component of consumption is very small and has a small variance compared with the permanent consumption, the bias will be small.

In words this means that a high transitory component of the variance of consumption will lead us to rely more on the recent measured income, rather than on past incomes, in calculating permanent income. If almost all consumption were permanent, then the historical weights to be attached to measured income would be more or less correct. In fact then the bias, if it exists, is towards a foreshortening of the income experience included in the formulation of permanent income.

The evidence suggests that the value of λ for the United States is in the region of $\frac{2}{3}$. For the United Kingdom however the value of λ is much lower – provably about $\frac{1}{3}$ or even $\frac{1}{4}$. This suggests that in the United Kingdom recent experience is given relatively more weight than past experience in reckoning permanent income. A larger fraction of a current income receipts is considered permanent than in the United States. This is of course consistent with casual observation.‡

† In fact the downward bias is a var (C_t) var (C).

‡ There is an intimate connection between $\mathbf{P}_y$ and the two parameters β and λ. For since

$$Y_p(t) = \lambda Y_p(t-1) + \beta Y(t)$$

$$\text{var } (Y_p(t)) = \lambda^2 \text{ var } \{Y_p(t-1)\} + \beta^2 \text{ var } (Y) + 2\lambda\beta \text{ cov } (Y_p(t-1) \cdot Y(t)).$$

Assuming that we may neglect 'end effects' so that var $\{Y_p(t)\}$ = var $\{Y_p(t-1)\}$, we may write

$$\mathbf{P}_y = \lambda^2 \mathbf{P}_y + \beta^2 + \frac{2\lambda\beta \text{ cov } (Y_p(t-1) \cdot Y(t))}{\text{var } (Y)}. \tag{9.47}$$

If the correlation between $Y(t)$ and $Y(t-j)$ is expressed as r_j, we may write

$$\frac{\text{cov } (\quad)}{\text{var } (Y)} = \beta[r_1 + \lambda r_2 + \lambda^2 r_3 + \ldots]. \tag{9.48}$$

[continued...]

The reader who has stayed with the argument up to this point may well wonder why the permanent income hypotheses is not tested directly by measuring the correlation between transitory income and transitory consumption. The obvious test is to examine 'windfall' income and to see whether the propensity to spend from windfalls exceeds zero – and in fact to see whether spending units really do discriminate between windfalls and permanent components so that the marginal propensities to consume of the former is much less than that from permanent income.

The great difficulty about this direct test is the absence of suitable data. Windfalls, suitably recorded, are a rather rare phenomenon and the opportunities for testing are limited. Nevertheless some of the evidence does appear to discredit the permanent income hypothesis. Bodkin, in a study of windfall income, showed that those who received the windfall had substantially the same propensity to spend as those who did not.[†] It would be proper to point out, however, that there are some doubts about the interpretation of the evidence – and other evidence on windfalls has shown that there is a very low propensity to spend.[‡]

If, furthermore, the income series is generated by a first-order auto-regressive process, we have $r_j = r^j$, so that

$$\mathbf{P}_y(1 - \lambda^2) = \beta^2 + 2\lambda\beta^2(r + \lambda r^2 + \lambda^2 r^3 + \ldots).$$

And so

$$\mathbf{P}_y = \frac{\beta^2}{1 - \lambda^2} \left(\frac{1 + \lambda r}{1 - \lambda r} \right). \tag{9.49}$$

This formula clearly shows that $\mathbf{P}_y$ is a function (but not a very simple one) of the parameters of the equation determining permanent income and the auto-correlation structure of the income series. We might simplify this result by supposing that $\beta = 1 - \lambda$. This ensures that the sum of the 'weights' is unity. Then we obtain the result

$$\mathbf{P}_y = \left(\frac{1 - \lambda}{1 + \lambda} \right) \left(\frac{1 + \lambda r}{1 - \lambda r} \right). \tag{9.50}$$

This is fairly sensitive to the coefficient r. But it is easy to see that if we insert empirical values for r, such as r in the region of 0.9 which we find in practice, and $\lambda = \frac{2}{3}$, we find that $\mathbf{P}_y = 0.80$ which is very near to the value found from a comparison of cross-section and time series results. As λ tends to quite small values, however, $\mathbf{P}_y$ tends to unity, e.g. with $\lambda = \frac{1}{3}$ and $r = 0.9$, $\mathbf{P}_y = \frac{13}{14}$. As $r \rightarrow 1.0$, $\mathbf{P}_y \rightarrow 1$.

[†] R. G. Bodkin, 'Windfall Income and Consumption', *American Economic Review*, vol. xlix (4) (Sep 1959), pp. 602–14.

[‡] R. Bird and R. Bodkin, 'The National Service Life Insurance Dividend of 1950 and Consumption: a further test of strict permanent income hypothesis', *Journal of Political Economy*, vol. lxxiii (Oct 1965), p. 499. This re-evaluation of the evidence suggests that the hypothesis is not discredited; but it seems difficult to discredit competing hypotheses also!

Some of the faith in the strong version of the permanent income hypothesis has been shattered by 'windfall evidence'. In particular it seems that although the correlation between transitory components is probably relatively low, it is usually positive, and not so trivial that it can be ignored. The basic idea of the permanent income concept and the broad framework of the theory has, however, passed the empirical tests – if not with flying colours then with enough correspondence to suggest that the theory is the best one we have.

Questions for Discussion

1. (i) From the following data, show *how* to estimate a log-linear demand function. Illustrate your argument by carrying out the calculations on these observations:

Family Budgets

Family no.	Expenditure on bread	No. of equivalent adults	Aggregate expenditure
	£ p.a.		£ p.a.
1	11·5	3·5	1,100
2	14·1	4·0	900
3	8·0	2·0	1,800

Time Series

Year	Index of retail prices	Expenditure on bread	Personal disposable income	Quantity Index of bread	Price Index of cakes
	1961 = 100	£m. p.a.	£m. p.a.	1961 = 100	1961 = 100
1961	100	60·1	12,300	100	100
1962	102	61·0	12,900	99	103
1963	105	61·1	13,800	97	107

(ii) Suggest possible diagrams you might plot in order to illustrate these results.

2. From the following data show *how* to estimate a demand function. Carry out the calculations on three observations.

Family Budgets

Family no.	Expenditure on beef £ p.a.	No. of equivalent adults	Aggregate expenditure £ p.a.
1	20·5	2·3	1,204
2	27·5	3·1	1,426
3	14·1	1·4	914

Time Series

Year	Index retail prices	Expenditure on beef £n.	Personal disposal income £m.	Quantity index of beef	Index of price of lamb
1951	100	320	8,500	100	100
1952	101	326	8,900	102	101
1953	102	359	9,700	108	107

3. Carry out an analysis of the consumer demand for one of the following commodities: eggs, beef, milk. (Note that the data are readily available for eggs and milk from the respective marketing boards in the United Kingdom. This data together with the official studies of consumer budgets should be used. For beef, suitable data can be obtained from Ministry of Agriculture statistics and the records of imports and exports.)

4. Consider the problems involved in measuring the demand for transport by passengers. (Note that this is a problem which is much complicated by the fact that there are so many 'qualitative' dimensions to passenger transport. The time spent on the journey, the degree of comfort and convenience, and the reliability of the service are all important aspects that should be taken into account.) See Fisher in Bibliography.

5. Although the normal theory of the consumer relates the quantity purchased to relative prices and income, examine the circumstances under which it would be better to use *consumer expenditure* (in aggregate) as an independent variable rather than income. (Hint: this is connected with the permanent income hypothesis.)

6. Examine the problem of finding the demand for steel and the demand for aluminium. Discuss how to forecast the substitution possibilities. (See Fisher in Bibliography.)

7. Take one of the equations from a demand study – such as that from Question 3 above, or from Stone – and use it, together with income and price data, to predict quantities in years other than those encompassed by the study. Compare the predicted values with the actual values. Also construct 'naïve predictors' – such as assuming that the change in quantity in a particular year will be the same as that in the previous year (irrespective of prices, incomes, etc). Compare the efficiency of the naive predictors with that of the demand equation. If this shows that the naive predictor is more accurate than the demand equation, does this mean that the theory of demand is discredited? As an additional exercise the reader might try the efficiency of prediction using a demand model with, and without, the use of an extraneous estimator of the income coefficient. (See Shupack in Bibliography.)

8. Consider other forms of equation which might serve as functions. For example consider

$$\log q = a + bp$$
$$q = (b + cp)^{-1}$$
$$q = a + bp + cp^2.$$

State clearly the limits and hypotheses you have about the signs of the constants. Consider the problem of adding a term for income effects and how this might be usefully done.

9. 'Consumption depends on wealth both human and non-human, and only depends on the flow of income insofar as this flow reflects changes in wealth.' Discuss.

   Describe the effect on consumption of

   (i) an influenza epidemic that results in the deaths, suddenly, of a large number of old people;
   (ii) everyone discovering a pot of gold in their garden;
   (iii) a non-contributory full pay pension financed by the State;
   (iv) the re-distribution of wealth through State lotteries.

10. It has been argued that the life-cycle hypothesis implies that the fraction of income saved is better considered as proportional to the rate of change of income, rather than the level.† Show that, by using the geometrical weighting system, one can write the permanent income hypothesis so that consumption is a linear function of the *change* in consumption and the *level* of income, together with transitory consumption.

    Examine critically the statement, and suggest an alternative formulation. Would you agree that this suggests that there is a critical difference between the life-cycle hypothesis and the permanent income hypothesis?

† See M. J. Farrell, 'The New Theories of Consumption Function', *Economic Journal*, vol. 69 (Dec 1959), pp. 678–96. The author calls this the 'Rate of growth hypothesis.'

11. Milton Friedman has suggested that the main determinant of the demand for money is the level of permanent income. Develop a suitable model and examine some of the empirical implications. See 'Professor Friedman on the Demand for Money', *J.P.E.*, LXXIII (Oct 1965).

12. Describe the effect on consumption over the next 20 years of:
    (i) a sudden rise in the birth rate;
    (ii) a redistribution of income by direct taxes from small families to large families;
    (iii) a progressive tax on the amount of capital owned;
    (iv) a capital gains tax.

13. It might be argued that, corresponding to the permanent-income concept there is a *permanent-wealth* concept. Thus people do not react fully to the change in their monetary measured wealth as the rate of interest changes (and share and bond prices change). Discuss the definition and use of the concept of permanent wealth; is it also possible to define an implied *permanent rate of interest*?

14. Discuss the implications of the following data:

Relation of Savings and Income to Age of Head of Income Unit, Great Britain 1953

Age of head of income unit	Income mean ratio	Mean savings as a percentage of mean income
18–24	62	1·2
25–34	114	0·9
35–44	134	2·9
45–54	126	1·2
55–64	93	2·2
65 and over	55	−6·0
All ages	100	1·0

Note that the income mean ratio is the ratio of the mean income in the age group to mean income of all ages. Source: Harold Lydall, 'The Life Cycle in Income, Saving and Asset Ownership', *Econometrica*, XXIII (April 1955). For the interpretation see Friedman, *Theory of the Consumption Function*.

15. Fit a consumption function to the income consumer–expenditure figures for the United Kingdom – preferably using quarterly statistics – over the last ten years. Discuss the relative advantages of using quarterly and annual statistics in this analysis. Enquire carefully into the method by which the quarterly data are prepared, (considering carefully the 'interpolated values').

10 Econometric Studies of Production

In the previous chapter we discussed the econometric studies of the behaviour of consumers, in the form of demand curves and consumption functions. 'Consumption' is one of the three main branches of economics – the others are 'distribution' and 'production'. If our survey of applied economics had pretensions to comprehensiveness, we should have to discuss in detail the models of distribution theory and their verification. Such a task has not been attempted here. We restrict our survey to production. But of course much of the theory of distribution is derived from the theory of production through the marginal productivity relationships. One cannot avoid measuring marginal productivity and associating it with the wage rate. Such analysis is, however, incidental to the main purpose of this chapter which is concerned with the empirical measures and tests of productive relationships.

Our procedure is broadly the same as in Chapter 9. We first examine the micro-economic theory of production. The key concept is the production function of the firm. The ingredients of the production function are the technical conditions – the knowledge and availability of techniques – and any limitations imposed on the supply of factors of production to the firm. The extent to which one presses back the analysis to consider the technological problems of choice in productive relationships depends (or at least should depend) on the sort of questions to which one seeks answers.

If the main purpose of the analysis of the productive relationships is to advise a particular firm on its output policy and its choice of processes, then, of course, the analysis must be concerned intimately with the detailed technology of production. The inputs of raw materials, the types and quantities of machines and labour absorbed into each process must be carefully specified; the expected outputs must also be listed. Then a choice must be made among the available processes.

This problem is best tackled by a linear programming approach, to be dealt with in some detail in the next chapter. The programming model enables one to explore in detail the problem of the best choice of available technical processes. And it also suggests an integrated engineering-accounting theory of the decision making process. But, strictly interpreted, this use of the linear programming model does not form part of the body of econometrics. We are prescribing which productive relationships *should* be used; it is a planning model. Econometrics, narrowly interpreted, is concerned with measuring the predictions of economic theories, with testing hypotheses against the facts, and not with 'teaching the businessman or the politician to maximise'. It is perfectly clear, however, that it is impossible to maintain such a purist attitude for very long – and so we have included an interpretative account of linear programming in this book.

But the main purpose of econometrics in production is still to test the hypotheses of economics, and some of these tests may be performed at the micro-economic level on the firm or perhaps on the industry. (In one sense these studies complement those that use the programming approach, since they are concerned with questions of indivisibilities, of scale effects etc. which the programming model assumes away.) The broad assumption is that the entrepreneur has chosen the most efficient method of producing the particular outputs; the technical problem, which is so intimately the concern of the programming method, is assumed solved – and solved correctly, although in practical applications one takes into account the inevitable 'disturbance'. We then examine the constellation of inputs and outputs in these 'efficient' situations. The classic problems are whether there are economies or diseconomies of scale, and the extent of substitution between factors of production. Many subsidiary questions also arise – such as the relationships between factor inputs and the prices of factor services, and the nature of technical progress – which can be put into the form of a production function.

Research on the production function of the firm – the *micro-production function* – comprises, however, only a small part of the total effort in this field. Most attention has been paid to the *aggregate* production function – perhaps for an industry, but more usually for a sector – such as the manufacturing sector – of the national economy. In principle it should be possible to aggregate micro-production functions to arrive at a macro-function; but as we shall see there is no simple interpretation of the parameters of such an aggregate production function.

The questions to which we seek answers with the analysis of aggregate production functions are broadly the same as those with the micro-functions. We measure the marginal productivity of capital and labour and the contribution to output caused by technical progress. This enables us to attribute the growth in output to the proximate causes – the growth in the labour force, the increase in the stock of capital, economies of scale, and the 'catch-all' of technical progress.

The big question with all applied econometric work – whether the data measure our theoretical constructs – applies with particular force to the work on production and cost functions. It is important to work out in each case the underlying market mechanism that generates the data. Then one can examine the relationship between observation and theory.

THE PRODUCTION FUNCTION

Production relationships are formally described by amounts of input associated with specified amounts of output. From the same list of inputs one may obtain a number of quantities of output. Let us consider the simple case where there is only one input – such as labour – so that the result can be represented in a two-dimensional figure, as in Figure 10.1. If the input of labour is fixed at L we can imagine that the productive possibilities with L may be described by a number of points, such as A, B and C in the figure. It may be that there are so many points of possible production associated with L that we can pretend that any output along the line AL can be achieved; but this would be a limiting case. The normal and general situation is clearly where there are a number of discrete outputs that may be produced. Thus the A, B, C, and L may describe the four outputs that are possible with a quantity of labour L. And so for other quantities of labour we may find associated output levels – each a discrete value or point represented in the output-labour plane.

It is clear that points such as A in some sense 'dominate' B, C, and L. If with that amount of input one can produce A, surely is it not possible to ignore the other possibilities B, C and L? One can simply produce

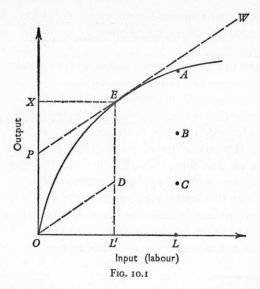

Input (labour)

FIG. 10.1

the output at A, and, if one wanted only the lower output represented by B, the balance could be simply thrown away. (The reader must observe that we can never throw away more than we have – so it is not possible to produce negative outputs; thus output must always be a non-negative number.) But it must be possible then to throw away output without cost; disposal must use no resources at all. This is obviously a very useful assumption and we shall return to it later in detail in the linear programming interpretation of production decisions. It is clear that, with this zero disposal cost assumption, the point A does dominate B and C and L.

It is possible to choose all points on the input axis and ask what is the maximum output that can be achieved with the particular input. Thus we shall obtain a series of points such as A in the figure. These points form the *efficient set of production possibilities*. There may be any number of points such as A in the efficient set – or conceivably there may be no points at all, in which case production cannot take place at any price.

We need to make this theory far less general (and less empty) than it appears in such an abstract formulation. One of the rather large assumptions is to suppose that there is such a vast number of choices of input spread over the whole range of the scale that we can treat it as a *continuous variable*. The associated efficient points (such as A) are also assumed to be continuous – and we suppose they can be represented by a smooth continuous function such as that plotted OEA in Figure 10.1. This is the *production function* of traditional theory; the reader might think that a better name for it would be a 'production frontier' but that name has been appropriated for other uses.

As we have drawn the production function in the figure, it implies that it is possible to employ no labour and produce no output. The production function goes through the origin. Thus there are no fixed costs; all inputs (and of course there is only one in this representation) are variable. The second feature of the function is that it defines a convex set. Any two points on the function's curve – such as E and A, for example – may be connected by a line which will lie below or on the production function. This will also hold for any other two points – such as OE or OA, and so on.

[It is worth a slight digression to explain the puzzling use of the words 'convex' and 'concave'. A *set* is described as convex if it has no 'dents' in it Thus the set of achievable input – output combinations enclosed by the curve OEA and the input axis is a convex set; a line joining any two points of the set will pass through only other points that are in the set, it will not 'go outside'. On the other hand, and quite confusingly, the *function* represented by the line OAE is described as a concave function. The criterion for a concave function is that a chord joining any two points on the function will contain only values of the dependent variable X that are *less* than the value of the function for the given variable (L) Thus although the *set* is *convex* the *function* is *concave*.]

The importance of the assumption of convexity of the set and concavity of the function may be illustrated by considering the behaviour of an entrepreneur who faces a given wage rate on the labour market and a given price on the product market. Thus we can draw the market opportunities open to the entrepreneur by depicting the price ratio – the (price of labour)/(price of output) – by a slope in the plane. We have plotted this slope for the special case through the origin – and the entrepreneur must give up DL' output in order to obtain OL' units of labour, so that DL'/OL' represents the real wage of labour in terms of the units of output.

Now consider the producer at O and let us ask whether he would produce any positive output. By employing OL' units of labour he can produce more than the real wages DL' needed to pay them. Clearly he can produce at E; and on drawing a line through E with the same slope as OD, we see that he could hire labour L', produce output OX and pay his wage bill (in units of output) of PX, and so enjoy profits of OP Now it will be observed that the line PW is at a tangent to the production function at E Clearly the entrepreneur cannot make any larger profit than OP. The (gross) output OX is the equilibrium output and this is associated with an equilibrium labour input of OL', and equilibrium profits of OP.

It is easy to see that there is only one equilibrium possible in this situation. If the production function is always curved in this concave fashion (if it is *strictly* concave in the mathematical sense) then there will be only *one* point at which a wage/price line coincides with a segment of the production function. If, on the other hand, over a part of the range the production function is linear (that is to say it is concave, but not *strictly* concave), then the wage/price line may coincide with this linear segment. But this merely means that a number of output and input combinations in that vicinity give rise to the *same* profits, so the entrepreneur will be indifferent over this range.

In both cases the equilibrium (or equilibria) is a consequence of the fundamental assumption of convexity of the production set or concavity of the production function. This ensures that a local equilibrium is also a global equilibrium. We know that if the point E gives the largest profit compared with outputs adjacent to it, then that is good enough to class it as the best one can do. There is no need to look at *large* changes of outputs; if it is the maximum profit for small changes then it is also the maximum for large changes as well. If the function were convex over some higher outputs, however, it may well be that although the wage-price line is tangent at E there will be another 'bump' in the production function beyond A such that the wage/price line PEW actually cuts the function; then profits at E are not the *maximum maximorum*, and the entrepreneur would make larger profits by increasing his output beyond A. Thus the great disadvantage of convexity over any range of the function is that we are forced to survey the *whole range* of possible outputs to see which is best, whereas when the function is concave it is sufficient to survey only the immediate neighbourhood.

The convexity of the production set and the concavity of the function is clearly a fundamental requirement in competitive markets. And in specifying particular algebraic forms of the function the nature of the concavity must be carefully specified. In general terms one may write a function

$$X = F(L, K, M), \qquad (10.1)$$

where X is the number of units of output and L the number of units of labour, K the units of capital and M the amount of input of raw materials. Then we must clearly specify that none of the variables may take negative values, and that the function is concave in all directions.

In econometric work the task has been first to find simple functions that satisfy these conditions. By far the most popular form is the Cobb–Douglas production function

$$X = AL^\alpha K^\beta, \quad A > 0, \quad X \geqslant 0, \quad L \geqslant 0, \quad K \geqslant 0 \qquad (10.2)$$

where, as before, L is the quantity of labour and K the amount of capital. (We assume for simplicity that there are no raw material inputs; production is completely integrated.) The reader will observe that this function is the same as that which was used for measuring empirically the market-demand curves, and it obviously has similar properties.

The function is a *linear one in the logarithms* of the inputs and output. Thus we have

$$\log X = \log A + \alpha \log L + \beta \log K. \qquad (10.3)$$

If, therefore, we measure the logarithms of output and inputs (all to the same base) we shall find a linear relationship with a slope of α in the labour direction and a slope of β on the capital axis. The constant α measures the *elasticity of response* of output to labour input. A one per cent increase in labour, with the amount of capital held constant, will add α per cent to output. Similarly a one per cent increase in the amount of capital, with no change in the labour employed, will add β per cent to the level of output. If both labour and capital are increased by one per cent, then output will expand by $(\alpha + \beta)$ per cent. This result can be checked by using the original equation; let us multiply the amount of labour by λ and the amount of capital by λ, and ask what is the effect on output. We find

$$\text{new output level} = A(\lambda L)^\alpha (\lambda K)^\beta = AL^\alpha K^\beta \lambda^{\alpha+\beta} = \lambda^{\alpha+\beta} X \qquad (10.4)$$

Thus if we multiply all inputs by 2, we shall increase output by multiplying $2^{\alpha+\beta}$ fold.

The coefficients α and β, and their sum $\alpha + \beta$, have an immediate interpretation in terms of the concepts of *economies of scale*, as well as in terms of the mathematical concepts of convexity. Consider first the coefficient α. Clearly if α exceeds unity, output will expand proportionately more than the input of labour required to produce it. This implies that if we plot the output against the labour input (holding the amount of capital constant) we shall obtain a convex function such as that illustrated in Figure 10.2. The function goes through the origin – since output cannot be produced without labour – and then there are no diminishing returns to labour; the absolute increase in output due to another man-hour increases as the level of employment increases. Thus it is impossible to have $\alpha > 1$ in a competitive labour and produce market – since it would imply that the entrepreneur could always make more money by hiring more labour to produce a larger output. Similarly we may show that with a competitive capital market – i.e. the entrepreneur may obtain as much capital as he likes at the going price – the condition is that $\beta < 1$.

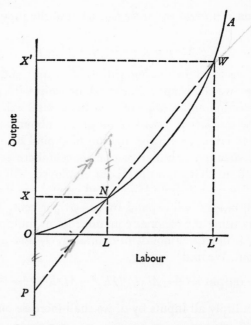

Fig. 10.2. Output-Labour Function with Constant Capital and $\alpha > 1$

The sum of the coefficients indicates the extent of economies or diseconomies of scale. If $\alpha + \beta > 1$, then a doubling of *both* inputs will give rise to a more than twofold increase of output. If $\alpha + \beta < 1$, then a doubling of *both* inputs will cause output to expand less than twofold. The case when the two coefficients just sum to unity is the 'knife-edge' case of constant returns. Proportionate expansions of both inputs are matched by the same proportionate increase in output. It will be observed that the same degree of economies of scale is experienced for all output levels. If the firm enjoys increasing returns over one section of the output scale it enjoys them over *all* other sections. There is no way in which we can use a *single* Cobb–Douglas function to describe the firm that enjoys increasing returns up to a certain level of output then experiences either constant returns or decreasing returns beyond that output level. We shall return to these problems of interpretation below.

Yet another way of examining the properties of the Cobb–Douglas is to find the marginal productivities of labour and capital.

$$\text{Marginal product of labour} = \frac{\partial X}{\partial L} = \alpha \frac{X}{L}$$

$$\text{Marginal product of capital} = \frac{\partial X}{\partial K} = \beta \frac{X}{K}$$

$$(10.5)$$

And it can be seen directly from this version that, if the expansion of output is proportionately smaller than the increase in input, then the marginal productivity will decline over the whole range of outputs.†

The equilibrium condition can be found by confronting the entrepreneur with prices on the competitive markets. Let the price of output be P, the wage rate W, and the price of capital R. Then the entrepreneur will maximise profits, $\Pi = PX - WL - RK$, subject to the restraint imposed by the production function.

$$\frac{\partial \Pi}{\partial L} = P\alpha \frac{X}{L} - W = 0 \quad \text{or} \quad \alpha \frac{X}{L} = \frac{W}{P}$$

$$\frac{\partial \Pi}{\partial K} = P\beta \frac{X}{K} - R = 0 \quad \text{or} \quad \beta \frac{X}{K} = \frac{R}{P}$$

$$(10.6)$$

These simply state that the marginal productivity of labour is equal to the real wage, and that the marginal productivity of capital is equal to

† The requirement for the output to expand proportionately less than input is simply that $\alpha < 1$ and $\beta < 1$, as we saw above.

the price per unit of capital divided by the price of output. They are the familiar marginal productivity conditions and they determine the capital labour ratio, and the capital output ratio

$$\frac{L}{K}=\frac{\alpha R}{\beta W}, \quad \frac{K}{X}=\beta\frac{P}{R}. \tag{10.7}$$

Thus we see the obvious economic fact that the ratio of labour to capital depends on the ratio of the factor prices, not their absolute levels. Similarly the capital output ratio depends only on the ratio of the price of output to the price of capital.

We can re-write the marginal productivity conditions as

$$\alpha=\frac{WL}{PX}, \qquad \beta=\frac{RK}{PX}$$

$$\alpha=\text{share of wages}, \quad \beta=\text{share of capital.} \tag{10.8}$$

Thus in equilibrium the coefficients α and β will measure the fractions of total receipts paid respectively to labour and to capital. The elasticity of response of labour also measures labour's share of total income.

These marginal productivity conditions give us the equilibrium ratio of factor inputs – but they do not tell us what level of output should be produced. To discover this, let us insert the marginal productivity conditions in the equation defining the profit

$$\Pi=PX-WL-RK=PX-\alpha PX-\beta PX$$

$$\Pi=PX(1-\alpha-\beta). \tag{10.9}$$

Now consider the maximisation of profit with respect to output:

$$\frac{\partial\Pi}{\partial X}=P(1-\alpha-\beta)=0. \tag{10.10}$$

This equation gives us the condition for a stationary solution. *But it does not involve the value of X at all.* Since P is strictly positive we can see that the solution is

$$\alpha+\beta=1. \tag{10.11}$$

The level of output is left undermined; but it is required that there be constant returns to scale in the production function.

Intuitively this can be seen to be a sensible result. For if there were economies of scale in production over the whole range of output and if the entrepreneur could purchase labour and capital on the market at fixed prices and sell his output without changing the price, then it would be profitable always to expand output. We may illustrate this argument where there is only one input – such as that in Figure 10.2. Suppose that the provisional production plan was to produce OX units of output with OL units of labour. Let us also suppose that the wage price ratio is given by the slope of PNW. At this output the entrepreneur is losing money measured (in terms of output) by OP. And for outputs between X and X' he would lose even more money; but for outputs in excess of X' he would reduce his losses, and make larger and larger profits – provided the output increases at a constant percentage rate that is greater than the percentage increase in input. There would be no limit to this process.

Correspondingly if there are *diseconomies* of scale over the whole range of outputs, it will always increase the profits of a firm to split itself into two, three, four, ... parts, until each firm is of an infinitely small size! Costs per unit of output decrease as the size of firm is reduced – so the entrepreneur is encouraged along the endless road of smaller and smaller units of production.†

† A diagrammatic illustration may help. Consider the horizontal axis as representing all inputs. As they are varied proportionately, let us write it in terms of labour units. The marginal conditions are satisfied at E, and at output X. But now consider splitting the firm into two so that we employ $L/2$ input units in each. But then we clearly get a larger output from the two together $2(OY) > OX$ – and so make larger profits. And so the process will go on *ad infinitum*.

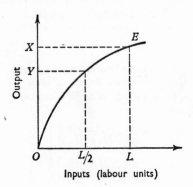

Thus we can see that the conditions of perfect competition require that $\alpha + \beta = 1$. In this limiting case, the size of firm is indeterminate – any size will do since there is no advantage or disadvantage to size. All the revenue of the firm is paid to factors; in our case this means that the wage bill and the returns paid to capital just exhaust the total revenue of the firm Nothing is left unallocated.

SIZE OF FIRM

This model of production, although internally consistent and useful for many analytical and empirical purposes, is of very limited use for analysing the production functions of *firms*. One of the most important aspects of the firm – its size – is indeterminate. Clearly a satisfactory theory would predict the size of firms from observable variables and we should be then able to test the theory in this respect. The question is, therefore, can we adapt the theory so that the size of firm is determinate?

Two approaches clearly suggest themselves. The first is to drop the assumption of perfect competition. Suppose instead that there are conditions of imperfection in some or all of the markets in which the entrepreneur participates. Formally this is easy to incorporate in the analysis.† But such a development does throw the baby out with the bath water. There are all the well-known difficulties of product definition, the concept of 'industry' and so on. We shall therefore not pursue this particular complication here – but the reader is referred to the literature in the Bibliography.

The second approach is to suppose that there is another type of input which is distinguished from labour and capital because it cannot be

---

† Specifying

ϵ_x for the elasticity of demand for output,

ϵ_l for the elasticity of supply of labour,

ϵ_k for the elasticity of supply of capital,

we obtain marginal conditions

$$\left. \begin{array}{l} \alpha\dfrac{X}{L} = \dfrac{W[1 + (1/\epsilon_l)]}{P[1 + (1/\epsilon_x)]} \\[2em] \beta\dfrac{X}{K} = \dfrac{R[1 + (1/\epsilon_k)]}{P[1 + (1/\epsilon_x)]} \end{array} \right\}. \qquad (10.12)$$

bought on the market. This input is called 'entrepreneurship'. Each individual is supposed to have this attribute in some degree; some people will find it profitable to employ their entrepreneurial capacity by setting up a firm, others will find that their capacity is so limited that it is not worth employing. It is the limitation of entrepreneurial capacity that determines the size of a firm. For one cannot buy entrepreneurship on the market; one can only employ one's own capacity.† Thus the distribution of the firm is 'explained' by the distribution of entrepreneurial capacity in the population.

The reader may think that this is a 'weak' sort of explanation of size. For we cannot readily observe entrepreneurial ability – except in so far as it manifests itself in output in a certain size of firm. Entrepreneurial ability cannot be measured independently of the output of the firm. Thus it is really no more than giving a name to one's ignorance of that process which determines the size of firm in a competitive market.

The limited supply of entrepreneurship to a particular firm means that there may be increasing returns to the variable inputs up to the point where the entrepreneurial capacity is fully employed, then decreasing returns to the variable inputs will appear. Thus we shall observe the typical U shape of the long-run average cost function. At the lowest point of this U – as the entrepreneurial capacity becomes fully employed – there will be constant returns to scale (to the inputs other than entrepreneurship). This limiting case is the equilibrium output for the firm.

The remarkable feature of this stylised description of competitive equilibrium is that the Cobb–Douglas with constant returns describes the production function *only within the range immediately adjacent to the equilibrium output*. The production function just passes from increasing returns through to decreasing returns as the entrepreneur uses up all his entrepreneurial capacity; but as we pass from increasing returns the firm experiences constant returns over a very small range of output before encountering increasing costs. The reader may well wonder about the usefulness of a production function which has such a limited interpretation. We return to this problem below.

---

† Some concept of this kind is required in order to rationalise the *existence* of firms. See M. Friedman, *Price Theory. A Provisional Text* (1962) Aldine.

THE CONSTANT ELASTICITY OF THE SUBSTITUTION (c.e.s.) PRODUCTION FUNCTION†

The Cobb–Douglas has done very valuable service as a production function both in theoretical explorations and in empirical fitting. But as a description of productive relations it has some shortcomings which, for certain uses, may be serious. The critical feature of the Cobb–Douglas is the extent to which it permits the substitution of one factor for another. We can see this by examining the marginal rate of substitution of labour for capital:

$$\text{m.r.s. of labour for capital} = \frac{\partial K}{\partial L} = \left(\frac{\partial X}{\partial L} \bigg/ \frac{\partial X}{\partial K}\right) = \frac{\alpha K}{\beta L}. \quad (10.13)$$

(This result is obtained by writing the marginal rate of substitution as the ratio of the marginal productivities of labour and capital.) Thus the marginal rate of substitution varies directly proportionately to the factor ratio.

The marginal rate of substitution is however in terms of units of capital divided by units of labour. It depends therefore on the units in which the inputs are measured; if for example capital were measured in dollars while units of labour were reckoned in man-years, the marginal rate of substitution of labour for capital is expressed in terms of dollars per man-year. It is more useful to find an expression for the substitution properties of a production function without having to trouble about units of measurement on each occasion. Thus one defines the concept *elasticity of substitution*, which is a pure number and is independent of the units of measurement.

It is clear that since the marginal rate of substitution is defined in units of (capital units ÷ labour units), the elasticity must be defined as the proportionate change in the ratio of factor inputs due to a proportionate change in the marginal rate of substitution. The elasticity of substitution is defined as

$$\frac{d \log (K/L)}{d \log (\text{m.r.s.})} = b = \text{elasticity of substitution.} \quad (10.14)$$

The reader might think this is the wrong ratio to measure; that we should instead measure the reciprocal to see how the marginal rate of substitution changes as we change the factor ratio. But it will be ob-

‡ See Arrow *et al.*

served that such a reciprocal would not be consistent with ordinary usage. A 'high' elasticity of substitution usually means that for a wide variation in the factor ratio, the marginal rate of substitution changes little. The isoquants are fairly flat. This will then mean that b is high – consistent with common usage. But if we used the reciprocal ($1/b$) as a measure of substitution elasticity we would find that it is low when elasticity is high, and vice versa. Thus the definition of b is more usefully associated with intuitive notions of substitutability.

One can see immediately that the elasticity of substitution of the Cobb–Douglas is unity. From the marginal rate of substitution equation

$$\log (\text{m.r.s.}) = \log (\alpha/\beta) + \log (K/L)$$
$$b = 1.$$

For all outputs and inputs of the Cobb–Douglas the elasticity of substitution is unity; one can always substitute capital for labour (or labour for capital) at this fixed elasticity of unity.

Thus when we approach the data with a Cobb–Douglas production function, we are, in a sense, forcing the data into a mould that implies the substitution elasticity of unity. But, it may be objected, the processes and productive relationships which we are investigating may not fit into that mould. For example, many processes appear to have very low elasticities of substitution, and indeed it may be better to fit the data to production functions that have *zero* elasticity of substitution. Thus one might prefer a function with fixed requirements of each input in order to produce a unit of output. This is the 'fixed proportions' case – sometimes called the Leontieff production function or the input-output production function. (We shall examine this model in more detail in the chapter on the linear programming interpretation of the production decision.) At the other extreme, it is perhaps possible to imagine processes where the extent of substitution is very high indeed. The isoquants may be nearly flat and the elasticity of substitution will be much in excess of unity. Again the Cobb–Douglas will not be appropriate for the data that arise from such a productive process.

It is natural to enquire whether there is not some simple production function that provides for elasticities of substitution other than unity (Cobb–Douglas), zero (fixed proportions), or infinite (a pathological case when only *one* input will be used). Obviously the simplest form of function will have a *constant* elasticity of substitution that may take any admissible value, that is any value between zero and infinity. A function that satisfies this condition and the various other conditions which one normally imposes on production functions (such as non-negativity), is

$$X = \gamma[\delta K^{-\rho} + (1 - \delta)L^{-\rho}]^{-1/\rho}, \qquad (10.16)$$

where X, L and K are output, labour and capital, as before, and γ, ρ and δ are non-negative constants. In addition we specify that δ must not exceed unity, i.e. $0 \leqslant \delta \leqslant 1$.

Before attempting to interpret the Greek constants γ, δ and ρ let us examine the properties of the function in the usual way. First, what happens when we increase labour and capital by the same percentage amount. Multiplying labour and capital by a factor μ (which must be greater than zero) we find

$$\text{new output level} = \gamma[\delta(\mu K)^{-\rho} + (1 - \delta)(\mu L)^{-\rho}]^{-1/\rho}$$

$$= \mu X. \qquad (10.17)$$

One concludes, therefore, that the function implies constant returns to scale; a 10 per cent increase of labour and capital will give rise to a 10 per cent increase in output. It is worth noting that it is easy to specify a function that has the same general form as the one considered above – but which exhibits either increasing or decreasing returns to scale. Consider:

$$X = \gamma[\delta K^{-\rho} + (1 - \delta)L^{-\rho}]^{-\nu/\rho}. \qquad (10.18)$$

The only difference between this function and the one above is that the exponent outside the square brackets is now $-\nu/\rho$ instead of $-1/\rho$. It will be observed that an increase in both inputs by a factor μ will give rise to an expansion of output of $\mu\nu$, and so when $\nu > 1$ there will be increasing returns to scale, and when $\nu < 1$ there will be decreasing returns. In the remainder of this section we shall confine the analysis to the case of constant returns, that is we shall assume that $\nu = 1$.

The easiest coefficient to interpret is γ. Clearly this varies according to the units in which output is measured. If it is measured in tons (long tons) instead of pounds, then the γ for tons will be $1/2,240$th of that for pounds. If, however, we use the same units for measuring labour, capital and output, and we compare production functions with different

γ's, clearly that with the highest γ will have the the highest *production parameter* (like A in the Cobb–Douglas).†

The marginal productivities can be found in the usual way:

$$\text{Capital} \quad \frac{\partial X}{\partial K} = \frac{\delta}{\gamma^\rho}\left(\frac{X}{K}\right)^{1+\rho}$$

$$\text{Labour} \quad \frac{\partial X}{\partial L} = \frac{1-\delta}{\gamma^\rho}\left(\frac{X}{L}\right)^{1+\rho} \tag{10.20}$$

Thus in equilibrium in a perfectly competitive market we find

$$\frac{\delta}{\gamma^\rho}\left(\frac{X}{K}\right)^{1+\rho} = \frac{R}{P},$$

$$\frac{(1-\delta)}{\gamma^\rho}\left(\frac{X}{L}\right)^{1+\rho} = \frac{W}{P}, \tag{10.21}$$

or we can write the latter equation in logarithms as

$$\log\left(\frac{X}{K}\right) = -\frac{1}{1+\rho}\log\left(\frac{\delta}{\gamma^\rho}\right) + \frac{1}{1+\rho}\log\left(\frac{R}{P}\right),$$

$$\log\left(\frac{X}{L}\right) = -\frac{1}{1+\rho}\log\left(\frac{1-\delta}{\gamma^\rho}\right) + \frac{1}{1+\rho}\log\left(\frac{W}{P}\right). \tag{10.22}$$

Thus we see that a 1 per cent increase in the real wage will be associated with a $(1+\rho)^{-1}$ per cent increase in labour productivity. The coefficient $(1+\rho)^{-1}$ therefore measures the response in terms of substituting capital for labour as the real wage rate rises.

The role of this coefficient $(1+\rho)^{-1}$ can be seen directly if we find the marginal rate of substitution of labour for capital from the ratio of the marginal productivities

$$\text{m.r.s. of labour for capital} = \frac{\partial K}{\partial L} = \frac{\partial X/\partial L}{\partial X/\partial K} = \left(\frac{1-\delta}{\delta}\right)\left(\frac{K}{L}\right)^{1+\rho} \tag{10.23}$$

† In analysis it simplifies matters considerably if we measure output in units such that $\gamma = 1$. This change of scale is always possible and it will obviously not affect the analysis that follows. Thus the 'standardised' production function may be written

$$X_s = [\delta K^{-\rho} + (1-\delta)L^{-\rho}]^{-1/\rho} \tag{10.19}$$

where we use the subscript 's' to denote standardised units of output. (One can always convert back to original units by multiplying each X_s by γ).

Finding the elasticity of substitution is now simple

$$b = \frac{\text{elasticity of}}{\text{substitution}} = \frac{d \log (K/L)}{d \log (\text{m.r.s.})} = \frac{1}{1+\rho}. \tag{10.24}$$

Thus ρ is a simple function of the elasticity of substitution (b), and

$$\rho = \frac{1}{b} - 1. \tag{10.25}$$

A suitable name for ρ is therefore the *substitution parameter*. The higher the value of ρ the lower the elasticity of substitution. Furthermore it can be readily seen that ρ cannot be less than -1. As ρ approaches -1 from above, the elasticity of substitution tends to infinity; this means that the isoquants gradually get flatter and flatter. At the other extreme, as ρ tends to infinity, the elasticity of substitution becomes smaller and smaller; essentially this is the case of fixed coefficients.

Another interesting case is when $\rho \to 0$, for then the elasticity of substitution will tend to unity. The reader will recall that the Cobb–Douglas function had an elasticity of substitution of unity, and it would be natural to conjecture that there is some connection between the limiting case of the constant-elasticity-of-substitution function and the Cobb–Douglas. There is. The Cobb–Douglas with constant returns to scale is the limiting form of the c.e.s. function as ρ tends to zero. Unfortunately this is not transparent from a glance at the c.e.s. function. If we write $\rho = 0$ it will be found that the function is indeterminate, that is to say we get a meaningless 'result'. We have to resort to trickery. Consider this version of the function

$$\left(\frac{X}{\gamma}\right)^{-\rho} = \delta K^{-\rho} + (1-\delta)L^{-\rho}. \tag{10.26}$$

We wish to convert these terms into expressions without involving the ρ variable either as a multiple or an exponent. One way is to take the logarithms, and then convert it back again by writing it as an exponent; for $\delta K^{-\rho}$, for example, we write

$$\delta K^{-\rho} = \delta \exp [\log \{K^{-\rho}\}]. \tag{10.27}$$

On expanding the exponent we have

$$\delta \exp [\log (K^{-\rho})] = \delta \exp [-\rho \log K]$$
$$= \delta \left[1 - \rho \log K + \rho^2 \frac{(\log K)^2}{2!} + \ldots \right]. \tag{10.28}$$

The other two terms in the equation may also be expanded in the same way. Clearly as ρ tends to zero, the values of ρ^2, ρ^3 will be very small compared with values of ρ, so let us ignore them in all expansions. We then find

$$1 - \rho \log (X/\gamma) = \delta[1 - \rho \log K] + (1 - \delta)[1 - \rho \log L], \qquad (10.29)$$

and this may be written as

$$X = (\text{constant}) \ K^\delta L^{1-\delta}, \qquad (10.30)$$

which is exactly the Cobb–Douglas form with constant returns to scale, that is $\beta = \delta$, and $1 - \delta = \alpha = 1 - \beta$.

This limiting form also gives as an immediate interpretation of the parameter δ. Clearly it is exactly analogous to the parameter that determines the distribution of income in the Cobb–Douglas case. We might therefore properly call it the *distribution parameter*. The role of this parameter can be further illustrated by examining the competitive equilibrium where the marginal rate of substitution is equal to the ratio of factor prices. We obtain after a little manipulation

$$\frac{\delta}{1 - \delta} = \left(\frac{R}{W}\right)\left(\frac{K}{L}\right)^{1+\rho} \qquad (10.31)$$

or

$$\frac{\text{wage bill}}{\text{profits}} = \frac{WL}{RK} = \frac{1 - \delta}{\delta} \cdot \left(\frac{K}{L}\right)^\rho.$$

The reader can readily check that with $\rho = 0$, these are the same values as those which occur with the Cobb–Douglas function. But with the c.e.s. production function δ is not sufficient to determine the distribution of income between factors; we require a knowledge of the substitution parameter (ρ) also.[†]

In the Cobb–Douglas we found that the distribution of income between labour and capital depended only on the coefficients of the production function; the distribution did not vary with the factor ratio. With the c.e.s. production function, however, we see that the distribution is a function of the factor ratio. The greater the deviation of ρ from zero, the greater the effect of factor ratios on the distribution of income. Suppose for example that the elasticity of substitution is rather low – say 0·5 – so that the value of ρ is unity, and let us imagine

[†] Note also that if $\rho \neq 0$, then δ is *not* independent of units in which K and L are measured.

that $\delta = \frac{1}{3}$. Then a 10 per cent increase in the quantity of capital with the same amount of labour will be associated with an increase in labour's share.†

This completes our survey of the c.e.s. production function. There are, of course, many other functions that may serve as production functions – but none have the attractive simplicity of the c.e.s. function, the Cobb–Douglas and the 'fixed coefficients' form. Nearly all research into empirical relationships have used one or other of these functions as a standard model. We shall follow this practice in the remainder of this chapter.

FITTING THE COBB–DOUGLAS TO DATA ON CROSS-SECTIONS OF FIRMS

We now examine the problem of fitting a Cobb–Douglas production function to a cross-section sample of firms. The basic presupposition is that each firm has had ample time to adjust its capacity in terms of capital equipment and plant to the particular circumstances (the level of entrepreneurial capacity) in each firm. Those entrepreneurs who can efficiently run large firms have had sufficient time to hire labour and build up their stocks of capital to the desired levels. Let us suppose that each firm has adjusted *exactly* and has made no mistakes and desires to adjust no further. Let us further suppose that the market conditions are those of perfect competition; each entrepreneur may buy as much as he likes or sell as much as he likes at the going prices. There are so many firms producing the output and buying and selling in the markets that the decision of any one of them has no finite effect on the prices.

---

† Using the factor share equation we may have a starting point where labour receives 200 and capital 100, and the number of units of labour is 100 and the number of units of capital is 100; so the factor share equation is

$$\frac{\text{wage bill}}{\text{capital receipts}} = \frac{200}{100} = \frac{2/3}{1/3} \left(\frac{100}{100}\right)^1.$$

On increasing the amount of capital from 100 to 110, we find

$$\frac{\text{wage bill}}{\text{capital receipts}} = \frac{220}{100},$$

which is an increase in the ratio by 10 per cent.

What will be the observations generated by such a process? If all firms had exactly the same amount of entrepreneurship and each enjoyed the same technological conditions of production (that is to say the firms had the same production function), then each firm will be reacting to the same set of absolute prices. Thus each firm in the cross-section will produce the *same* output with the *same* amounts of labour and capital. There would be no distributions of observations from which one may estimate the production function!

In this highly stylised account of the economic process we have assumed that each entrepreneur makes no mistakes. They adjust exactly to their circumstances so that they maximise their profits. We might then reasonably enquire whether the existence of errors and mistakes will help identify the production function. Will the deviations from the optimum give rise to observations that will enable us to measure the production function?

Clearly much will depend on what sort of mistakes are made. Let us suppose for example that the mistakes take the form of simply producing too much or too little. Let us, however, assume that the efficient production techniques and factor inputs are always employed. Thus each firm will have the same capital/labour ratio, but they will produce different outputs. This will enable us to observe economies of scale in the production function. Those firms which are producing large outputs (by mistake) will also be employing proportionately larger amounts of each labour and capital input. We shall record the proportionate expansion of output as both labour and capital are increased by the same percentage. This is then a perfect arrangement for measuring the existence of economies of scale – the response of output to the same percentage increase in all inputs. Therefore a logarithmic linear relation between inputs and output will yield an estimate of the economies of scale in firms in this industry.

It will be noticed, however, that the two (or more) inputs will change proportionately over the cross-section; the logarithm of labour and the logarithm of capital will be perfectly correlated in the cross-section. This is, of course, a classic case of multicollinearity (or alternatively we may call it a case of no-identification of the separate input effects). From the data on inputs and outputs one will not be able to measure α or β separately, but one will know the value of the *joint* effect $(\alpha + \beta)$. Indeed in calculating the regression we need only to take *one* of the inputs and find the simple (logarithmic) regression of output on that single input. This will then give us an estimate of $(\alpha + \beta)$.† From the cross-section of inputs and outputs it is not possible to measure the coefficients α and β separately.

Let us pursue this particular example still further and ask whether one might use the marginal productivity conditions in order to estimate α and β. Under conditions of perfect competition it is known that α is equal to labour's share, and β measures the share of capital. With full equilibrium in factor inputs one may use the observed values of labour's share and capital's share as estimates of α and β respectively. But it must be noted that such an estimation is consistent with the rest of the model only *if there are constant returns to scale* in the immediate region of the 'no-mistake' outputs. In other words the method of estimation *assumes* constant returns to scale at the 'no-mistake' equilibrium output.‡

The final question we ask of this 'mistakes example', is what form the returns to scale will take and whether they can be encompassed by a single Cobb–Douglas function? In the ordinary theory of the firm we suppose that there are increasing returns up to the lowest point of the U-shaped long-run average cost curve, and then for larger outputs there are decreasing returns to scale. Thus if mistakes are made by producing too much as well as too little, the sample values will be a mixture of increasing and decreasing returns to scale. In principle we should fit a Cobb–Douglas function to those firms that are producing too small an output and observe whether there are, or are not, in-

---

† It may be worth while showing that this is so. Write X_1 as the log of labour, X_2 as the log of capital and Y as the log of output. Then the Cobb–Douglas is

$$Y = \beta_0 + \alpha X_1 + \beta X_2. \tag{10.32}$$

But since labour and capital change proportionately, we have

$$X_1 = X_2 + \text{constant}.$$

So that

$$Y = \text{constant} + (\alpha + \beta)X_1$$

or

$$Y = \text{constant} + (\alpha + \beta)X_2. \tag{10.33}$$

‡ It will be observed that, nevertheless, we may use the labour and capital shares from the whole cross-section to estimate the values of α and β. The capital/labour ratio is constant over the cross-section, so obviously the shares are the same, and, in principle, information from one firm is good enough!

similar to what Nerlove does. Fits separate f" for small & large firms not "too small" & "too large" output.

ECONOMETRIC STUDIES OF PRODUCTION 291

creasing returns. If the $\alpha + \beta > 1$, then the theory is consistent with the data. Similarly a function fitted to the firms that have mistakenly produced too much should give rise to a sum of the coefficients less than unity – if the observations are to be consistent with the theory. But one conclusion must be emphasised: no *single* Cobb–Douglas can be consistent with the whole body of data.

But suppose that one did fit a single Cobb–Douglas function to the cross-section data; this is, after all, the most common procedure in practice. Roughly speaking, if there were as many firms over-producing as there were under-producing (and by the same amounts on the average) the regression of output on one of the inputs will show more or less constant returns to scale.† If, on the other hand, most of the mistakes were in under-producing, then we would have a relative concentration of points such as F and E in the figure (in the preceding footnote). Consequently we should measure apparently increasing returns in the cross-section. And it is quite true then that there are, on the average, increasing returns for firms in this industry. But it must also be observed that a general expansion of outputs of all firms in the industry would soon run into constant and then decreasing returns.

This 'mistakes-only' model is a useful one for examining the more realistic model – where it is supposed that entrepreneurship varies from one firm to another. The simplest possible version of entrepreneurship variation is to suppose that it manifests itself in a multiplicative constant in the production function. Let us suppose that U_i is

† A figure will make this clear: Imagine there are three typical firms – those just at equilibrium (E in the Figure) and those below (F) and those above (G). Clearly a regression through the three points (such as RR') is likely to be approximately a ray from the origin.

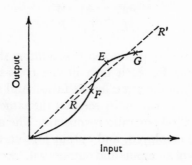

ie constant returns.

the entrepreneurial effect on output of the ith entrepreneur, so that

$$X_i = AL_i^\alpha K_i^\beta U_i, \qquad (10.34)$$

where we use subscript i to denote the ith firm; thus L_i is the labour input of the ith firm or entrepreneur. Note that the constant elasticities of response of output to inputs α and β are the same for all firms entrepreneurs.

The characteristics of U must be carefully specified. One point is that it can never be negative – for then it would imply that negative outputs were feasible, and we know that they are not. Second it is obviously convenient, though not essential, for it to have a mean of unity; then we can interpret the A as the constant for the *representative* firm. Third it is obviously tempting to interpret the U as a disturbance and to describe its realisation by means of a probability distribution. Just as entrepreneurship is a name for our ignorance – so the disturbance performs the same service. One must, however, be careful with such an interpretation, for the U_i is a *constant* for the particular ith firm, or entrepreneur. The U_i for that particular entrepreneur is not a number drawn out of a hat from one year to another; it represents his more or less constant relative efficiency as a businessman.

With perfectly competitive conditions in both factor and product markets, there will be the usual conditions of equilibrium for each individual firm. Outputs and inputs will vary over the cross-section, as in the 'mistakes-only' case. But there will be no variation in the capital/labour ratio. With the same prices of inputs for each firm, there will be no incentive to have different ratios of factor inputs. Formally we can see this from the marginal productivity conditions

$$\frac{\partial X_i}{\partial L_i} = \alpha \frac{X_i}{L_i} = \frac{W}{P}. \qquad (10.35)$$

This labour marginal productivity condition shows that the ratio $(\alpha X_i)/L_i$ is the same for each firm in the cross-section. So average labour productivity is the same for all firms. And from the analogous equation for capital we can easily see that the same statements may be made, so the capital/labour ratio is constant. The absolute amounts of labour and capital employed, and output produced, in each firm will vary, but the ratios of all inputs and outputs will be constant.

But effect of superior entrepreneurship likely to be reflected in labour productivity.

At first sight this 'entrepreneurship-variation' model looks as though it will give rise to the same observable effects as the 'mistakes-only' model. The ratio of inputs are the same and there is again the difficulty that the labour and capital are perfectly positively correlated so we cannot separate the effects of each in the production function. The conclusion is that we can measure the coefficients α and β by observing factor shares – provided that there are constant returns. The critical difference between this 'entrepreneurship variation' model and the 'mistakes only' model is that there is no opportunity for measuring the returns to scale above or below the equilibrium output.

Output will vary over the cross-section with the extent of entre-preneurial ability. But, from the marginal productivity conditions, we see that inputs will vary in proportionately the same way. There will be the *appearance* of constant returns to scale. The attempt of any firm to expand its output will give rise to decreasing returns, and, if the firm reduced output, increasing returns would appear.

Thus the 'entrepreneur variation' model provides less information than the 'mistake' model of the cross-section. Clearly it is possible to mix the two models and have both entrepreneurial variations and mistakes. And, of course, the observations will then depend on the relative importance of the two effects. The entrepreneurial variation will give rise to a downward bias in the measurement of the economies or diseconomies of scale generated by the mistakes. But again a simple regression over the cross-section is likely to give rise to the result $\alpha + \beta = 1$; and this must *not* be interpreted as evidence of constant returns over the range of outputs in the cross-section.

SEPARATE MARKETS WITH THE COMPETITIVE MODEL

The difficulties which we have encountered in interpreting cross-section results, with the competitive model suggest that possibly a profitable procedure may be to try to measure the productive relation-ships in a number of different market situations. The basic trouble with the cross-section in conditions of perfect competition is that each firm is subject to exactly the same stimuli – they each face exactly the same market conditions. Price, wage rate and the cost per unit of capital are the same throughout the cross-section – for all firms buy and sell in the same market. If, however, different firms were observed in *insulated* market situations, then there is at least the possibility that the observations will trace out the production function – or perhaps some average version of the productive relationships.

Insulated markets may be produced by many phenomena. Probably the simplest case is where there are prohibitively high transport costs and each firm has a local market. This is broadly the case with certain utilities, such as gas companies or bus companies. Let us imagine that these companies are controlled by a public authority and suppose that the control takes the form of requiring the firm to supply the local market with all its needs at a fixed price. The local markets vary in size so that there is an independent stimulus which was absent in the competitive market discussed above.

Let us first suppose that the local regulated monopolists buy factors of production on the national market at the same prices and that they can buy as much as they like without affecting the price. Assume also that there are no variations in entrepreneurial ability so that we may take it that the production function facing all these entrepreneurs is the same. The only thing that varies is the amount of output that they are required to produce.

What will be the pattern of observations produced by this process? The most important aspect is that it will be possible to observe increasing returns to scale, if they exist. The size of firm is fixed by the size of the market, at least up to the critical size when costs begin to increase and decreasing returns set in. Even in very large markets it is conceivable that we shall observe outputs on the increasing cost section (or decreasing returns section) of the production function. Diseconomies of scale may begin to show in the observations.† The second feature of the observations is that they will not enable us to measure the separate effects of labour and capital, because each firm faces the same relative prices of the two inputs.

Suppose now that we relax the supposition that the firms all face the same relative factor prices. Imagine that wage rates vary from one area to another, and this is not exactly matched by the variation in the

---

† The reason for this possibility is not obvious. For, it may be argued, surely if the entrepreneur found that at a certain size, smaller than that required to supply the whole market, there appeared diseconomies of further expansion, it would pay simply to start a new firm. But, of course, the new firm may have more diseconomies of small size than the over-large firm experiences. So it is profitable for the large firm to enter this range of diseconomies of scale.

controlled price of output. Then real wages will vary over the cross-section and so each firm will be induced to have a different marginal productivity of labour. Hence there will be some variation in the factor ratios so that we shall have observations to enable us to determine the values of α and β. $\alpha \frac{X}{L} = \frac{W}{P}$

Although it seems that there are good reasons for believing that this model will generate a suitably identified production function, it will be observed that we have left many questions unanswered – such as the method of price regulation used by the authority. If, for example, the firms were controlled by the authority regulating their price so that they earned only a certain percentage on capital invested (such a method is used for regulating utilities in the United States), then this will affect the substitution arrangements between labour and capital; and presumably it will affect directly the chosen marginal rate of substitution between capital and labour. The moral is that, when there exists a regulated non-competitive market, the process of regulation itself must be studied to discover the effects on the choice of production techniques, factor ratios and size of firm.

cf.
Nerlove

COMPLEX MODELS OF ENTREPRENEURSHIP VARIATIONS

So far we have dealt with only simple models of entrepreneurial ability. It has appeared as a simple multiplicative constant for the individual firm. It seems to be best to use this simple model until such a time as it is convincingly discredited by the data. But some econometrists have proposed more complicated models.

Probably the most difficult model to deal with is when the co-efficients of the production function vary from one entrepreneur to another. Thus for the ith entrepreneur the coefficients of capital and labour would be respectively β_i and α_i; and they would not be the same for all entrepreneurs. This may be rationalised by suggesting that some entrepreneurs are better, on the average, at more capital intensive production than others. Certain other entrepreneurs are more adept at organising labour intensive methods. This is equivalent to saying that there is no unique production function; there are as many production functions as there are entrepreneurs. However intuitively appealing such a concept may be, it is extraordinarily difficult to deal with in practice and we shall not further pursue it here.†

A less complicated way of elaborating the entrepreneurship assumptions is to suppose, as before, that the coefficients are the same for each firm, but that in addition to the entrepreneurial effect U_i in the production function, there are also similar entrepreneurial effects appearing in the marginal productivity conditions. In other words the efficiency of an entrepreneur is reflected not merely in his production function, it is also reflected in the precision with which he achieves the best employment of factors. An efficient entrepreneur, in this sense, will employ factors up to the amount when their marginal productivity is exactly equal to the price ratio. A relatively inefficient entrepreneur will miss by a mile – either overshoot or underemploy. To distinguish the accuracy with which an entrepreneur achieves his marginal conditions from the productive efficiency (U_i), we shall call the former *economic efficiency* and the latter *technical efficiency*. Let us use a variable V_{1i} to denote the economic efficiency of the ith firm in achieving its marginal productivity condition with respect to labour, and V_{2i} the analogous variable for capital. Then the marginal productivity conditions for the ith firm may be written

$$
\left.
\begin{aligned}
\frac{\partial X_i}{\partial L_i} &= \alpha \frac{X_i}{L_i} = \frac{W}{P} \cdot V_{1i}, \\[2mm]
\frac{\partial X_i}{\partial K_i} &= \beta \frac{X_i}{K_i} = \frac{R}{P} \cdot V_{2i}.
\end{aligned}
\right\}
\tag{10.36}
$$

If the entrepreneur achieves the peak of economic efficiency then both V's will be unity; the marginal productivity is exactly equal to the real wage or the real price of capital. Deviations from unity, in either the positive or negative direction, indicate inefficiency – and the greater the deviation the greater the economic inefficiency. Provided that it is specified that the coefficients α and β are not negative, it follows that the V's will never be negative.

† Regression models have been developed for dealing with situations of this kind: they are called 'regression models of the second kind'. Essentially they treat the coefficients as random variables, and then proceed to discover what can be adduced about the process from a random sample.

This model may be written simply in terms of the logarithms of the variables:

$$\log X_i = \log A + \alpha \log L_i + \beta \log K_i + \log U_i. \qquad \text{Production Function} \qquad (10.37)$$

$$\log X_i = \log\left(\frac{W}{P}\right) - \log \alpha + \log L_i + \log V_{1i}. \qquad \text{Labour Marginal Productivity} \qquad (10.38)$$

$$\log X_i = \log\left(\frac{R}{P}\right) - \log \beta + \log K_i + \log V_{2i}. \qquad \text{Capital Marginal Productivity} \qquad (10.39)$$

These three equations describe the production system. It will be observed that they are simultaneous equations with disturbances. They are linear in the logarithms of the variables. There are three 'unknown' variables in the system the logarithms of output, labour and capital. These are determined by the disturbances and the interaction of the constants in the system, that is by the production coefficients, and the relative prices.

The details of the structural characteristics and estimation problems with this model of the production system will not be pursued here. [The reader is referred to Walters (1963)]. It is, however, worth observing that there are basic difficulties of identification with this model. We have observations of X, K, L and the prices P, R, W, and from these we must see if the coefficients of the production function can be identified. The question is: can we produce an equation that looks exactly like a production function, that is a linear function of the logarithms of output, labour and capital, by simply adding together fractions of the two marginal productivity equations? If we multiply the labour marginal productivity condition (10.38) by λ, where $0 < \lambda < 1$ and the capital marginal productivity condition (10.39) by $(1 - \lambda)$ and add the two equations we shall obtain

$$\log X_i = \text{constant} + \lambda \log L_i + (1 - \lambda) \log K_i + \lambda \log V_{1i} + (1 - \lambda) \log V_{1i} \qquad (10.40)$$

Now clearly this equation is of exactly the same form as the production equation (10.37) – it is linear in the logarithms of output and the two inputs. Thus we shall not be able to distinguish between this 'mongrel' equation and the production function. Similarly the data will be unable to distinguish the production surface from this combination of the marginal productivity conditions.†

These difficulties of identification suggest that the model might be developed by including other exogenous variables. It is important, however, not to throw endogenous variables into the analysis merely to chase identification. They should be consistent with the economic theory of production, and at the same time provide information on aspects of economic adjustments. One of the most plausible additions is to suppose that the adjustment of the capital stock to the desired level does not take place immediately but takes place only over a number of years. This suggests that last years capital stock be included as a variable in the capital marginal productivity equation.

This obviously concerns intimately the dynamic process of the productive relationships. But clearly these problems can only be adequately tackled by using time series data. We might then consider briefly the use of time series data in fitting production functions for the individual firm – or perhaps the industry.

TIME SERIES DATA FOR MICRO-PRODUCTION FUNCTIONS

We have had occasion to stress the problems of interpreting the data from cross-section samples in attempting to fit or test hypotheses about production function. Most of these difficulties arise because the firms in the cross-section are all subject to the same stimuli of relative prices. Obviously one way out of these difficulties may be sought through time series data.

Consider, for example, the observations on an individual firm from one year to another. Clearly relative prices will change from one year to the next. It is most unlikely that the price ratio of capital and labour will remain the same, and furthermore the price of the output will change over time. Thus the firm will have an incentive to adjust its factor ratio as well as the total amount of output produced. Different

† The reader will notice, however, that the disturbance term in the 'mongrel' equation is different from the disturbance term in the production function equation. If it were possible to believe that economic efficiency and technical efficiency were uncorrelated (and independent) then it would be possible to distinguish between the mongrel equation and the production function. But the reader will soon satisfy himself that such an assumption is implausible – and indeed it has been discredited by the data.

factor prices and relative product prices will generate variations in the employment of factors and the amount of output.

At first sight, therefore, the time series observations seem to avoid all the difficulties associated with the cross-section. It appears that the observations of time series will provide much more promising material for the estimation of production functions. Unfortunately this promise is not fulfilled.

One of the main reasons is that adjustments of capital (and perhaps even labour) take a considerable time to work out. Factories are not built in a day or even a year. It is necessary to consider explicitly the dynamic process of a firm moving from one equilibrium towards another.† Formally this problem could be tackled by using an adaptive process similar to that which we discussed in connection with the demand for durable goods. Although some success has been achieved with this approach, it does require the data to yield additional results (the speed and form of adjustment) and of course it does soak up degrees of freedom.

One of the main disadvantages of time series data is that they incorporate technical change and progress that takes place over the period. In seeking for the constants of the production function, we have to try to eliminate the 'nuisance' variable of technological progress. It would not much matter if that nuisance were merely a trivial one, but evidence suggests that it is not. Technical progress is responsible, normally, for between 50 per cent and 90 per cent of the increase in output that takes place over time. Obviously technical progress then swamps the statistics. Unfortunately so little is known about the form of technical progress – there is very little economic theory which will help sort out the effects – that to distil it from the data is a formidable task. The effects of factor inputs, economies of scale and factor substitutions are, to a large extent, confounded in the statistics. We shall be returning to the analysis of technical change in the discussion of the *aggregate* production function later in this chapter.

† The reader might well object: surely the same problem was present in the cross-section; we simply ignored it. This is true. But *relatively* this effect is likely to be small in the cross-section. Large firms are very much larger than small firms – and the minutiae of variations due to these lagged dynamic adjustments are likely to be very small compared with the large range of variation of the cross-section sample. With time series, however, this is not the case. We are concerned with relatively small year-to-year variations in the output of a firm. Effects that could be ignored in the cross-section become of great importance in the time series.

TECHNICAL PROGRESS AND VINTAGE MODELS AND EX POST AND EX ANTE SUBSTITUTION

As we saw in the last section, many of the difficulties of time series estimates of production functions arise from the fact that technical progress is an important – indeed the *most* important – element in the statistics. Obviously we require to develop the production function so that it specifically takes into account and measures technological change. The simplest approach is to use a multiplicative trend term to represent technological progress. Thus in the Cobb–Douglas we should have

$$X(t) = Ae^{\lambda t}L(t)^{\alpha} . K(t)^{\beta}. \qquad (10.41)$$

We have used the parenthised t to show that the output is produced, the labour employed, and the capital used in the year t. If labour and capital are held constant, then output will grow at the rate of λ. We can write this equation as

$$\log X(t) = \log A + \lambda t + \alpha \log L(t) + \beta \log K(t). \qquad (10.42)$$

The interpretation is that a one per cent increase in labour will give rise to a α (100) per cent increase in output, a one per cent increase in capital will generate a β (100) per cent increase in output, and that output will grow over time, independently of what happens to labour and capital, at a rate of λ (100) per cent.

This sort of technical progress is often described as 'disembodied'. It goes on at the same rate, whatever the level of capital accumulation, or decumulation and does not require capital equipment to realise the gains in productivity. They can be implemented on old machines just as well as on new equipment. Furthermore we see that technical progress is *neutral* (in both the Hicks and Harrod sense). Thus the term $e^{\lambda t}$ does not affect either the marginal rate of substitution or the factor ratios over time; it simply results in a constant percentage addition annually to output.

This disembodied form is, of course, an extreme model of technological progress. It seems likely that many technological improvements do in fact require new machines and equipment. Progress is *embodied* in the new machine and the new process. Correspondingly there have been developed models of *embodied technical progress*; in their pure form these models allow technical progress to be implemented *only* through capital formation.

To see what this implies, let us imagine motor cars being built year after year; and each year's new motor cars can be labelled a *vintage* for that year. The motor cars built in 1966, that is of vintage 1966, will be the best that can be produced with the knowledge of 1966. By 1967 more knowledge or know-how will be accumulated and the 1967 vintage of automobiles will be better than the 1966 vintage. But this additional knowledge affects only the new cars produced in 1967; it does not affect at all the 1966 vintage. The latter reflect the technology of their year and new improvements in car production will not help their productivity.†

In principle this means that one has a production function for each vintage of capital. Let $L(t, v)$ indicate the amount of labour used on capital of vintage v in year t, let $K(t, v)$ be the amount of capital of vintage v available for use in year t, and let $X(t, v)$ denote the amount of output produced in year t from machines of vintage v. Then the production function for capital of vintage v in year t, with associated labour and output is

$$X(t, v) = Ae^{\lambda v}L(t, v)^{\alpha}K(t, v)^{\beta}. \qquad (10.43)$$

This is of the same form as the one of disembodied progress considered above – but there is a crucial difference. The term denoting technical progress, $e^{\lambda v}$, has the *vintage* of capital as its exponent – *not* time. The higher the vintage number, or the more recent the vintage, the larger will be the output from given amounts of labour and capital. (Solow 1959.)

Let us imagine an entrepreneur with a fixed stock of capital goods at time t. To each of these pieces of equipment we may attach a vintage year that will indicate the productivity of the machine; thus we can list his assets by their vintage. The question is how much labour will he employ with each vintage of machine?

Suppose that there are conditions of perfect competition in the markets facing him, then he will take the wage as given and employ labour on each machine vintage until the marginal productivity is

† It will be noted how specialised are the assumptions of the pure embodied vintage model. Improvements in organisational efficiency so that old vehicles are used more economically are excluded from the model.

equal to the real wage. Thus the marginal productivity of labour for each vintage will be the same, i.e.

$$\frac{\partial X(t, v)}{\partial L(t, v)} = \alpha \frac{X(t, v)}{L(t, v)} = \frac{W(t)}{P(t)} \qquad (10.44)$$

This equation will hold over *all* vintages at any time t. The real wage rate may normally increase through time, but at any time t all the marginal productivities on vintages will be the same.

The amount of labour employed on vintage v machines depends on the 'amount' of vintage v machine in existence. The capital services performed by a machine decline over time because of the rise of repair and maintenance costs, the increased probability of breakdown, and so on. The simplest assumption is to suppose that over time the amount of capital in a machine declines at a constant rate (sometimes called the 'radioactive decay' hypothesis). If we further assume that the firm buys only new machines and does not sell them second-hand, we can describe the amount of capital in year t of vintage v as the decayed new capital of year v of vintage v. Let us call the new capital of year v $N(v)$, which is of course the same as $K(v, v)$. If therefore this new capital decays at a constant rate δ we know that

$$K(t, v) = K(v, v)e^{-\delta(t-v)} = N(v)e^{-\delta(t-v)}. \qquad (10.45)$$

This then shows that the amount of capital of vintage v in year t is determined by applying the decay rate to the *new* capital created or bought in year v for the years of its life $t - v$.

Given the new capital purchases in each of the past years, one can therefore write down an inventory of the amount of capital of each vintage in any particular year. These quantities are determined exactly by the decay factor δ. Thus since the quantity of vintage capital is known in each year, the vintage production function coefficients are known, and the real wage rate is known, we can find the amount of labour that will be employed with each vintage machine – by applying the marginal productivity condition to each vintage. Formally this means that we insert the 'equipment decay' equation into the marginal productivity condition, so we obtain

$$\alpha Ae^{\lambda t} . L(t, v)^{\alpha-1} . N(v)^{1-\alpha} . e^{-\delta(t-v)(1-\alpha)} = W(t)/P(t). \qquad (10.46)$$

A little rearrangement will give a solution of $L(t, v)$ in terms of investment in year v, i.e. $N(v)$, and the real wage and the various rates of growth and decay.

Then output, labour and capital (duly decayed) can be added across vintages for any particular year. This will produce a production function as an aggregate for the vintages. But the concept of 'capital' in such a production function is an aggregate of different vintages and must reflect both the 'radioactive decay' (δ) as the machines gradually wear out, on the one hand, and, on the other, the increased productivity due to the embodied technological progress (λ). On adding the vintage production functions we obtain

$$X(t) = A e^{\delta(1-\alpha)t} L(t)^{\alpha} J(t)^{1-\alpha}, \qquad (10.47)$$

where
$$J(t) = \int_{-\infty}^{t} e^{v[\delta+\lambda(1-\alpha)^{-1}]} N(v) \, dv.$$

Thus $J(t)$ is the appropriate measure of capital to enter into the production function; it will be observed that it consists of the new investment in all previous periods depreciated by radioactive decay (δ in the exponent) and by the decline in old capital's efficiency, relative to new equipment, due to the pace of technical progress ($\lambda/(1-\alpha)$).

A number of features of this model call for comment. The first is that the coefficients α and $(1-\alpha)$ are the same for all vintages; the elasticities of capital and labour do not vary from one year to the next – from recent equipment to the antiques in the basement. Secondly machines never die; like old soldiers they only fade away gradually through time (this is because of the radioactive decay assumption). The labour employed with a given vintage machine will fall over time but the machine will always have a little labour associated with it – except at the limit. This result is, of course, a consequence of the choice of a Cobb–Douglas with its elasticity of substitution of labour and capital of unity.

This model is much more complicated than the ordinary Cobb–Douglas, but it does reflect the embodied aspects of technical progress in a production function with high substitution between labour and capital. Objections may be advanced against this formulation, however, since the possibilities for substitution of labour for capital may appear only before the capital is produced. Once a machine is created it may always require a certain amount of labour to keep it producing. An aircraft, for example, may be built to fly with a crew of three, and one cannot substitute capital for labour to bring the crew down to two. One can, however, produce new types of aircraft that have been designed for a two-man crew.

These reflections suggest that there should be a sharp distinction between the *ex ante* or design substitution possibilities before the machine is built and the *ex post* opportunities for substitution when the equipment exists and is in operation. We may think of this process, physically, in terms of putty and clay. Before the equipment is produced we have a great choice of factor proportions – capital is then essentially like putty and it can be fashioned to suit current and expected future conditions. But once the capital equipment is constructed it becomes similar to baked clay; the substitution possibilities are very limited and the restricted choice of factor ratios is embalmed for ever in this machine.

The simplest (and extreme) case of this *ex post/ex ante* model is when the factor ratios *ex post are fixed*. Each machine must have a certain amount of labour input in order to produce at all – and any labour in excess of the fixed amount required is simply wasted. The *ex post* question is whether to use the machine or not. And this will be decided by measuring the quasi-rent from using the machine – that is the difference between the revenues from sales of the output and the cost of the fixed amount of labour required to run the machine. If the quasi-rent is positive, the machine will be employed; if the quasi-rent is negative, the machine costs more to run than it earns in revenue, and so it is best left to rot. This distinguishes the model from that considered above; there we simply employed less and less labour on the equipment and it was never completely unemployed (except in the limit), whereas here the machine is either fully employed or fully idle.

The *ex ante* choice of technique is made in the year of installation. We need to specify the output–input combinations from which he may choose. And since substitution is possible *ex ante* we might use the Cobb–Douglas or the c.e.s. function to describe these possible choices of a labour-capital ratio. Obviously the technique will be chosen that is expected to give rise to the maximum expected discounted quasi-rents over the future expected useful life of the asset.†

This mixture of *ex ante* substitution with fixed *ex post* coefficients has many attractive properties. It explains the obsolescence of equipment in terms of its productivity and the real (output) wage rate. It demonstrates that only a fraction of capital in existence will be employed; the rest will not be worth employing at the going real wage.

Which of the various 'vintage' models is most useful depends much on the particular questions to which answers are sought. These models, however, have hardly been put through their paces. No doubt important developments are yet to be made.

Models of the Aggregate Production Function

FORMAL AGGREGATION THEORY

The basic economic theory of production is usually stated for the firm or perhaps for the process or the plant. The entrepreneur is the decision maker. He specifies the amount of resources he buys, how they are combined in the production processes, and how much output is produced. The entrepreneur chooses a particular production arrangement from among the many that are available to him; and the production function describes some of the alternatives – the efficient set as we called them above – between which he can choose. Similarly the marginal productivity conditions are properly defined for the individual firm; the owner of the firm makes decisions about factor employments on the basis of the price and the productivity.

In spite of the fact that the economic theory of production is strictly applicable only to the micro-unit – the individual firm – it is obviously tempting to attempt to apply the same sort of concepts to the behaviour

† For example, with the Cobb–Douglas formulation, we obtain a real rate of return on capital of

$$\frac{\pi}{PK} = A\left(\frac{K}{L}\right) - \frac{W}{P}, \quad \text{where } \pi = \text{'profits' or quasi-rent.} \quad (10.48)$$

This value will eventually zero and then negative as the real wage increases over time; when it is negative the machine is not employed. Non-negative values over the future are discounted and summed to obtain the rate of profit on each technique. The capital–labour ratio is chosen so that this future rental is maximised.

of firms as an *aggregate*. It seems that one may merely add together the inputs of each firm, and add the outputs; then we can interpret the result as an *aggregate production function* for the group of firms. One hopes that the aggregate production function may be interpreted in exactly the same way as the production function of the firm – just as we interpret the demand curve for a commodity on the market as the sum of the demand curves of the individuals who participate in the exchange.

If the aggregate production function is to be interpreted as a production function then it must have the same broad form and properties of the micro-functions from which it has been derived. It must have similar marginal productivity conditions, so that the marginal productivity of labour for the aggregate of firms is equated to the real wage, and that of capital is the same as the real cost of capital in equilibrium. And there is an obvious difficulty of 'external economies'; if, as the total output of the aggregate of firms expands, production expands proportionately more than inputs, then clearly the aggregate production function will reflect these external economies – but the micro-functions will not. To avoid this difficult problem let us first suppose that there are no external economies and that each firm enjoys constant returns to scale.

The problem is to find (i) a class of functional forms such that the aggregation gives rise to a sensible production function, and (ii) a rule of aggregation – i.e. whether one should take arithmetic or logarithmic means, what should be the 'weighting' system, etc. These are complicated problems and the general treatment of the 'aggregation problem' is far beyond the scope of this book. But we can state the broad result for our particular problem quite simply.

We can define an aggregate production function if, and only if, the micro-functions are of the form

$$X^{w_0} = aL^{w_1} + bK^{w_2} \qquad (10.49)$$

where the a and b are constants and the exponents w are also constants. (These constants are not arbitrary since they must satisfy the constant-returns condition, but it is clear that, even granted this condition, there is still a wide choice for particular values.) Interpreted in words this means that output can be broken down into two components – one that is due to labour and one that is caused by capital. There is no 'interaction' term reflecting, for example, the multiple of labour and capital. The production function is '*additively separable*' in its factor components.

Let us now review the two production functions which we have discussed at length above. First the Cobb–Douglas:

$$X = AL^{\alpha}K^{1-\alpha} \tag{10.50}$$

Now it is clear immediately that the Cobb–Douglas does not satisfy the conditions of the aggregation rule. No amount of juggling will enable us to put the Cobb–Douglas into the additively separable form. Of course if $\alpha = 0$ or $\alpha = 1$, then it would be of the same form as required by the aggregation condition (with either $a = 0$, or $b = 0$); but such a production function is of no interest for examining substitution possibilities, for output if a function of only one factor. With $\alpha \neq 0$, the Cobb–Douglas will not have a sensible aggregate production function of the Cobb–Douglas type.

Now consider the c.e.s. production function

$$X = \gamma[\delta K^{-\rho} + (1 - \delta)L^{-\rho}]^{1-\rho}. \tag{10.51}$$

A little rearrangement will soon put this into the additively separable form

$$X^{-\rho} = \gamma^{-\rho}\delta K^{-\rho} + \gamma^{-\rho}(1 - \delta)L^{-\rho}. \tag{10.52}$$

Thus the c.e.s. production function is additively separable, and so we can define a sensible aggregate function. (It may however be difficult to see that the c.e.s. does conform to the aggregation rule, whereas the Cobb–Douglas, which is merely a limiting case of the c.e.s. does not. But it will be observed that as one proceeds to the limit the quality of additive separability disappears; in the limit the function becomes multiplicative.)

On the aggregation criterion, therefore, the c.e.s. is clearly superior to the Cobb–Douglas. But this does not imply that the Cobb–Douglas is useless for fitting to aggregate data. The issue partly turns on how large the errors of aggregation are, and whether one can use a method of averaging (or aggregating) that minimises these errors. Unfortunately there has been no systematic examination of aggregation errors of the Cobb–Douglas function so one cannot give any reliable judgement of the magnitude. It has been shown, however, that probably the best method of aggregation is by using geometric, rather than arithmetic, means.† In practice we rarely have geometric aggregates or means available, and the practical issue depends on the relative variation of the geometric and the (available) arithmetic totals; again, however, there is little evidence on which one can draw to check the conjectures.

AGGREGATION IN PRACTICE

The formal (mathematical) conditions for aggregation are stringent enough, but we must now examine the typical forms of aggregation used in practice. Obviously aggregation may be done at various levels – from the narrow industry to the broad sectors of the economy, or, conceivably, for the national economy as a whole. Probably in most recent work in economics, the tendency has been to concentrate on broad sectors of the economy – such as the manufacturing and mining sector, or the agricultural sector, and the private sector of the national economy.

Intuitively it is likely that aggregation will not matter very much if the firms that are being added are very much alike – in their output (they all may produce one inch pins, for example), their inputs and their techniques of production. Yet, even in this simple case, one must be careful of the interpretation. The industry will expand its output by the growth of existing firms and by the birth of new firms as new entrepreneurs enter the industry or as old entrepreneurs transfer their efforts from other industries to this expanding one.‡ With an industry very narrowly defined, it is likely that there will be a very elastic supply of entrepreneurial talent entering the industry, and so it may well be that the main effect will be the birth of many new firms in the industry – and the existing firms may simply settle down eventually at their original size.

---

† Intuitively this can be seen to be sensible, since

$$\log X = \alpha \log L + (1 - \alpha) \log K + \log A.$$

Thus the Cobb–Douglas is additively separable *in the logarithms* of the variables. [Unfortunately although one can then express an aggregate in terms of the totals of the logarithms, the resulting aggregate Cobb–Douglas does not satisfy the marginal productivity condition. See Walters (1963)].

‡ The discerning reader will easily see that with new firms appearing it is impossible to use the geometric averages of the Cobb–Douglas aggregation (see previous footnote). If the firm produced nothing, the aggregation by geometric means is then not defined; output in aggregate is zero!

Now, by contrast, consider the aggregate production function for the whole economy. Clearly then the supply of entrepreneurial talent cannot be increased by switching it from other industries; the only opportunity is to employ entrepreneurial capacity which is at present unemployed.† Consequently the expansion of output as a whole in response to the larger inputs will be more inhibited by the lack of entrepreneurship than will that of the constituent industries.

The most important difficulty, however, with aggregation is in the interpretation of the aggregate relationship. In practice it must include industries with truly enormous capital–labour ratios – such as oil refining and petro-chemicals – on the one hand, and on the other it must encompass handicrafts such as handloom weaving and embroidery and bespoke gun-making. If, when capital and labour were expanded in aggregate, the petro-chemical industry expanded their inputs at the same rate as the bespoke gun-making industry, there would be few difficulties. But in practice this never happens; growth is characteristically unbalanced. Consequently the increase of inputs into industry as a whole will have an effect which depends on the distribution of the inputs among the constituent industries.

The normal rules of allocating inputs are, according to neo-classical theory, the equivalence of marginal productivities. Factors will flow to the uses where their marginal productivities are highest. But this model assumes conditions which are perfectly competitive. In industry we know that certain sectors and industries exhibit marked characteristics of monopoly. Marginal productivities are not brought to equality by the competitive process. Arrangements such as market sharing, price fixing, and restrictive entry ensure that marginal productivities are much in excess of the relative prices. Thus in order to predict the consequences on aggregate output of a change in the quantity of inputs, one must know all about the competitive conditions and how they respond to changes in factor supplies. Clearly this is an impossible task.

The essential conclusion, however, is that it is then impossible to write an aggregate production function which, like its micro-counterparts, is *independent of the prices of inputs and outputs*. We cannot formulate the aggregate production function as a *technical* relationship between

† Or, conceivably, import entrepreneurs. This is an important source of growth of aggregate production in some countries.

inputs and outputs. Relative prices must enter in order to explain the aggregate level of output. So the function that includes relative prices – and obviously they enter the function in a very complex way – must be interpreted as a hodge-podge of technological and market conditions.

In spite of these difficulties, the simplicity of the production function approach to aggregate data has apparently been sufficient to overcome the scruples of most investigators. And, in any case, no alternative treatment of the aggregate series has been suggested that is obviously superior to the production function approach. Much ingenuity has therefore been lavished on the 'disaggregation' of certain aspects of the aggregate production function. While this overcomes some of the objections to 'adding chalk and cheese' it does not much affect the fundamental objection raised above: but we might briefly review some of the methods that have been adopted.

Many objections to aggregate (and in many cases micro-) production functions are levelled at the concept of capital involved. Adding together old and new equipment is obviously going to give rise to errors of aggregation. But if we use a version of the vintage model – either the substitution model or the putty-clay model – we shall at least avoid some of these problems of aggregation. (The reader will recall, however, the assumption of perfect competition and constant returns in this aggregate model.) Indeed the main use of the vintage model has been, so far, in aggregate production function models of this kind.   It is also possible to disaggregate the labour force according to not only sex and age but also the educational level of the workers. One of the objectives of this approach is to measure the effects of education on the level of production. Thus it is hoped to take into account the effects of investment in human capacity as well as the effects of the accumulation of inanimate machines.

This completes our discussion of the basic concept of an aggregate production function. We must now enquire into the methodological problems of estimation, and we begin with the cross-section approach.

CROSS-SECTION STUDIES OF THE AGGREGATE PRODUCTION FUNCTION

Among the first studies of the aggregate production function the cross-section approach played an important role. At first sight it seems impossible to conceive of cross-section studies of the aggregate production function, analogous to the cross-section studies of firms.† And, in fact, the cross-section studies of aggregate production functions do not observe different economies at a particular time. They use the aggregate data for different *industries* as the observations. In other words the inputs and outputs are measured for the steel industry, the motor car assembly industry, the cotton spinning industry, and so on. A production function is then fitted to these industrial observations. It would, therefore, be more appropriate to call the function fitted to such observations an *inter-industry* cross-section. The question is whether it can be interpreted as a production function. Will the data trace out an 'average' or aggregate production function for the manufacturing sector as a whole?

Intuitively it seems that it cannot be interpreted as a production function. It tells us something about the structure of industries, but it says little or nothing of the consequences on output of increasing inputs. Let us first examine the question of economies or diseconomies of scale. If we interpreted the inter-industry cross-section as a production function, then we should say that if a large industry used twice the inputs of a small industry and produced more than twice as much output, then this was evidence of economies of scale. But one can see immediately that this result hinges entirely on the classification into industries. Suppose that one had split up the large industry into four equal parts – by using some finer classification. Clearly the result is now reversed! The small industries are proportionately more productive than the large ones. There are pseudo 'diseconomies of scale'. Such absurd results are merely a consequence of the statistical conventions of classification used in the Census of (Manufacturing) Industry.‡

But we can proceed one step further in interpreting the statistics. In competitive situations one would expect that the classification of firms into industries would be independent of the total productivity of factors. First there is an inherent tendency to equalise factor productivities through the migration of labour and capital to the employments with

† There remains, however, the possibility of cross-sections of aggregate production functions between states or countries. We discuss this approach later.

‡ It will be noted that there is no clear association between the size of an industry and the average size of its constituent firms. Small industries may have large firms and large industries small firms.

the highest rewards; so one would expect, on the average, constant returns. Second, when factor productivities to get out of line, due to demand changes or striking technological advance, there is no reason why these deviations should be associated with any particular size of industry. Consequently one would expect a more or less random pattern of deviations from the mean productivity over the industrial cross-section. The expectation would be, therefore, that one would observe more-or-less constant (pseudo) returns to scale over the cross-section. But such a result has nothing to do with the aggregate production function; like the interpretation of the cross-section of firms, the more-or-less constant total factor productivity over the cross-section tells us something about the competitive allocation of factors between industries. The deviations from this constancy must be explained in terms of lags in the process of dynamic adjustment or in terms of non-competitive conditions associated with the industry as a whole. The coarser the classification of industries, the more one would expect these deviations to be smoothed out by the process of aggregating firms into industries.

In our analysis of the fitting of production functions to cross-section samples of firms in a competitive industry, we noted that there was some doubt about whether the observations identified the production function. They may merely have been scattered about some linear combination of the marginal productivity conditions. It is clear that broadly speaking the same criticisms apply also to the inter-industry cross-sections as well. We can, however, put a further twist to the argument. One of the main hypotheses that emerges from the Cobb–Douglas function, under conditions of perfect competition, is that a one per cent increase in labour per unit of capital will give rise to $\alpha(100)$ per cent increase in output per unit of capital, where α is labour's share.

$$\left(\frac{X}{K}\right) = A\left(\frac{L}{K}\right)^{\alpha} \quad \text{or} \quad d\left(\log \frac{X}{K}\right) = \alpha d\left(\log \frac{L}{K}\right) \qquad (10.53)$$

where
$$\alpha = \frac{WL}{PX}$$

The question we might ask is: could we not have obtained this result without the specification of the Cobb–Douglas? The answer is yes, of course. But even more pointedly we can show that such a result is

simply a consequence of the condition that *all revenue from output is distributed either to labour or to capital.* Let us write

$$PX = WP + RK \qquad (10.54)$$

so that

$$d\left(\frac{X}{K}\right) = \frac{W}{P} \cdot d\left(\frac{L}{K}\right) + d\left(\frac{R}{P}\right). \qquad (10.55)$$

But since relative prices do not change over the cross-section, we write $d(R/P) = 0$. So that

$$\frac{X}{K} \cdot d\log\left(\frac{X}{K}\right) = \frac{WL}{PK} \cdot d\log\left(\frac{L}{K}\right) \qquad (10.56)$$

and

$$d\log\left(\frac{X}{K}\right) \equiv \left(\frac{WL}{PX}\right) d\log\left(\frac{L}{K}\right). \qquad (10.57)$$

This is exactly the same as the Cobb–Douglas hypothesis. But we have derived it from the simple convention that all the revenue is paid out to factors. This relationship between output per unit of capital and labour per unit of capital is simply a consequence of the accounting convention of allocating all the receipts to factors. Consequently it is consistent with *any* production function, not just the Cobb–Douglas, that is fitted to data in which the accounting convention has been employed.

In practice, of course, one would not get an exact fit of this form. Partly deviations would arise because of errors of measurement, errors of aggregation, etc., but one would also expect that there would be *some* variation in the ratio of the prices (R/P). These effects would give rise to some scatter about the logarithmically linear relation. They would give the impression of fitted statistical function rather than an accounting identity with errors of measurement etc. But appearances are deceptive and the results should be interpreted with care.

Analogues with the discussion of the fitting of a pseudo-production function to a cross-section of firms may easily be drawn. Suppose, for example, that there was considerable variation in the relative prices (R/P); then, paradoxically, this would enable us to distinguish the Cobb–Douglas form from the accounting identity. Under competitive conditions the Cobb–Douglas function would not have (R/P) as a variable, but, as we have seen above, the accounting identity would include this price ratio in all its forms. Thus the two equations could be distinguished, one from the other, and so there is the possibility of refuting the hypothesis of the Cobb–Douglas production function.† But, as we shall see, no aggregate cross-section (inter-industry) study has used such sophisticated methods.

It is not difficult to conclude that the inter-industry studies of cross-sections do not shed any light on the production function – neither on the 'aggregate' production function nor on the production function of the constituent industries. They are interesting as descriptions of the structure of industrial classification and, when one examines deviations (or 'error') around the regression line, of the variation of the cost of capital in terms of the price of output over the cross-section. The data simply do not enable one to discriminate between one production function and another.

TIME SERIES STUDIES OF THE AGGREGATE PRODUCTION FUNCTION

As one would expect from the discussion of micro-production functions, the problems that appeared with the cross-section inter-industry studies to a large extent disappear when one has time series data. One would expect that the price ratios would change over time – the relative price of capital moving in a different way from the relative price of labour. This provides a *deus ex machina* by which entrepreneurs are induced to choose different combinations of labour, capital and output. They are subject to different stimuli in different periods of time, so they trace out their own production function – and so, by aggregation, we observe the aggregate production function in the statistics.

The trouble is that we observe many other things as well. Technological change will be a large and important nuisance variable in aggregate as well as in micro-functions. Additional complications arise from the fact that the rate of technological advance differs between industries; and those industries which enjoy the highest rate of technical advance will also tend to give relatively large reductions in prices

---

† But, of course, one of the purposes of cross-section analysis is, in fact, to standardise for those characteristics – such as relative prices and technical progress – that change over time. One would suspect that the relative price of capital would be subject to small variations and those variations would be very difficult to observe. We return to this point in discussing the empirical evidence.

which will cause them to grow at a faster rate than industry as whole (electricity generation, for example). Part of the 'technical progress' in the aggregate function will be due to the distribution of resources from the relatively backward to the progressive industries.

The analysis of technical progress presents the most formidable difficulty with aggregate time series data. At one extreme (Solow 1957) it is identified as the residual trend in the data when the effects of factor inputs have been subtracted. Assume a Cobb–Douglas, constant returns to scale in the aggregate production function, perfect competition in factor and goods markets; then α will be measured by the fraction of income paid to labour. Thus we write

$$\log X(t) = \log A(t) + \alpha \log L(t) + (1 - \alpha) \log K(t) \qquad (10.58)$$

where $A(t)$ measures the 'constant' in the year t. With knowledge of $X(t)$, $L(t)$, and $K(t)$ and with observations each year on labour's share, we can calculate $\log A(t)$ as the residual.† Thus we calculate

$$\log A(t) = \log X(t) - \alpha \log L(t) - (1 - \alpha) \log K(t) \qquad (10.59)$$

for each year. So one may measure the change in the residual $\log A(t) - \log A(t-1)$ or $[A(t) - A(t-1)]/A(t-1)$ approximately as the proportionate contribution of 'technical progress' from year $t-1$ to year t. Thus we may state that $100[\{A(t) - A(t-1)\}/A(t-1)]$ per cent of the increase in output from $(t-1)$ to t was due to technical progress as here defined.

One may object, however, that technical progress is here merely a name for any change in output that cannot be explained separately by the acquisition of capital or increment of labour. It is merely a residual – a name for our ignorance – and it is misleading to call it technical progress. It encompasses random events (such as good luck with the weather), internal migration of factors of production (such as that discussed above, which might be interpreted as redistributive effects), the *interrelated* effects of factors of production (because of the lack of additive separability in the logarithms of the true production function), economies of scale (which might take the form of economies external to the firm), improvements in the education of the labour force, and

† Note that we should strictly calculate a new α for each period since labour's share changes over time; the change is, however, very small.

various kinds of non-neutral technical change that to some extent balance out. A rag-bag indeed!

It should be observed that one does not need necessarily to suppose that the production function is Cobb–Douglas. With the c.e.s. function one could do the same sort of analysis. One needs to know the elasticity of substitution, however: once that is specified or estimated, we can obtain an estimate of δ from the marginal productivity conditions. Consider for example the equation that describes the marginal rate of substitution as equal to the price ratio

$$\left(\frac{W}{R}\right) = \left(\frac{1-\delta}{\delta}\right)\left(\frac{K}{L}\right)^{1+\rho} \tag{10.60}$$

or

$$\left(\frac{WL}{RK}\right) = \left(\frac{1-\delta}{\delta}\right)\left(\frac{K}{L}\right)^{\rho}$$

or

$$\log\,(WL/RK) = \log\,[(1-\delta)/\delta] + \rho \log\,(K/L) \tag{10.61}$$

It is easy to see that the regression of the logarithm of the ratio of labour's income to that of capital on the logarithm of the capital-labour ratio will give an estimate of ρ. We should also obtain an estimate of the coefficient δ, for the constant in this regression equation is the log of the ratio $(1-\delta)/\delta$.†

Turning to the original c.e.s. equation

$$X = \gamma(t)[\delta K^{-\rho} + (1-\delta)L^{-\rho}]^{-1/\rho}, \tag{10.62}$$

where we write $\gamma(t)$ as a function of t to emphasise that it is a function of time; and although they have not been explicitly written as functions of time, the three variables X, K and L must be interpreted as time dependent. Clearly we can write

$$\gamma(t) = X(t)[\delta K(t)^{-\rho} + (1-\delta)L(t)^{-\rho}]^{1/\rho}. \tag{10.63}$$

With a knowledge of the time series of the three variables on the right hand side, and having calculated ρ and δ from the conditions defining the marginal rate of substitution, we can find $\gamma(t)$ as a residual. And so

---

† The reader will note that the term $\gamma(t)$, which is the term analogous to $A(t)$ in the Cobb–Douglas, does not appear in the equations. It cancels out on taking the ratio of the marginal productivities to obtain the marginal rate of substitution.

we can use the $\gamma(t)$ as an index of technical progress – and, of course, one must not forget all the other factors mentioned above that affect the value of this residual.

Of course the problem of measuring technical progress and eliminating it from the production function can be tackled by many of the procedures mentioned above. Probably the most successful approach has been to specify the *vintages* of capital equipment and use either the substitution model or the putty-clay models. Fitting these models is however a complex procedure and the reader should consult original sources if he wishes to pursue this topic further.

As with any aggregative process, one finds that relationships which are of a one-way causal form at the micro-level turn out to be more complicated interdependent relationships at the aggregate level. While at the micro-level we could take the view that the amount of labour employed was determined by the individual firm and that there was a one-way effect, from labour to output, it is not obvious that such an effect holds on aggregation. For example, suppose that in a particular year an unusual amount of technical progress takes place which results in an expansion of aggregate output which, in turn, increases the real wage of the existing labour force. But this increase in the real wage may induce people to give up their leisure time and go to work; so there will be an expansion of the quantity of labour along its aggregate supply curve.† If, therefore, we fit a least squares regression such as $\log(X/K)$ on $\log(L/K)$ (with $\alpha + \beta = 1$) we shall get a biased estimator of the coefficient α; and since the correlation between the residual and the independent variable (L/K) is positive, the bias will be positive. We shall over-estimate the labour coefficient.†

This raises the problems of statistical specification and estimation to which we turn in the next section. But the discussion up to this point should be seen in perspective. We have been concerned primarily with the *economic* specification of the model, on the one hand, and the nature of the data and what can be adduced from them, on the other. The conceptual fitting together of data and theory is an essential prerequisite before we approach the problems of statistical inference. In

† Formally we are suggesting that there are simultaneous relationships which are not brought out by the single equation approach. We should properly add an equation describing the supply of labour.

‡ It will be noted that if there is a *lag* (longer than a year) in the adjustment of the quantity of labour to the increased real wage, there may be no bias.

other words we must first ensure that the data are consistent, on a conceptual level, with the hypotheses of the theory; only then is it sensible to ask questions about the statistical precision with which the data conform to the predictions of theory.

In practice the economic specification of the model, and the specification of the process by which the data are generated are normally much more important than the formal statistical properties of sampling and significance. (It is, after all, not much use to know how precise one is in measuring the wrong parameter.) In order to avoid the common errors involved in misinterpreting data it is always wise to set up a model of the data generating process, and to subject it to critical examination. The confrontation of the data generating model with the model derived from theoretical reasoning will then shed some light on the extent to which one can use the data to attempt to discredit the theory.

STATISTICAL SPECIFICATION

During the course of the discussion of the economic theory of production we have had occasion to specify some of the deviations between theory and observation. Indeed a (large?) component of the 'disturbance' term in the production function is derived from the theory of the firm; this is the effect of entrepreneurship. It is important to attempt to find a theoretical rationalisation for disturbances – if there is one available – since we can then predict the behaviour of the disturbances more precisely than if they are unknown random variables. But unfortunately it seems that only a fraction of the deviation between theory and practice can be described by the formal theoretical concepts of economics; a part of the deviation must be ascribed to mistakes, variation in factors omitted from the model, errors of measurement, errors of specification of the functional form, and so on. Thus it is best to approach the statistical specification of production models with the view that, although part of the disturbance may be explained by the concepts of economic theory, a large fraction, and perhaps most, must be due to 'those factors which have been excluded from the model.' In other words, it is a name for our ignorance rather than our theoretical conceptions.

The simplest specification is to suppose that the disturbance enters as a multiplicative non-negative random variable U with a mean of unity. In the Cobb–Douglas, for example, we have

$$X = AL^{\alpha}K^{\beta}U \qquad (10.64)$$

Provided that U is never negative, output will never be negative. Taking logarithms,

$$\log X = \log A + \alpha \log L + \beta \log K + \log U \qquad (10.65)$$

Clearly $\log U$ will take negative values and, if U has a mean of unity, we may suppose that $\log U$ has a mean of zero. Thus $\log U$ plays the same role as the ordinary additive disturbance term.

This suggests that the simplest method of estimation is to carry out a least-squares regression of $\log X$ on $\log L$ and $\log K$. And indeed least-squares estimates have been the most popular approach in practical applications. Whether it is the 'best' form of estimation depends very much on the purposes for which the statistics are required. If we are concerned merely with making the best predictions of the value of X for given K and L the least-squares approach is likely to be the best.†
For forecasting future values of X it is probably best to use simple least-squares.

In many instances, however, one is not primarily concerned with forecasting the level of output; the prime purpose may be to check the hypothesis that α is equal to the labour's share, or that the sum of the coefficients $\alpha + \beta$ is unity. Then, of course, we need good estimates of the coefficients α, β themselves. We need to estimate the structural coefficients α, β of the model.

We know from the theoretical discussion in Chapter 5 that least-squares estimates of α and β will be the best estimates provided that the independent variables (L and K) may be taken as given constants, (that there is no feed-back effect from X on to L and K) and that the disturbance term is distributed independently of the values taken by

† This must be interpreted as a *conditional* statement, however, since it hinges on the fact that the true relationship between the variables is in fact linear in the logarithms. If it is not linear in the logarithms – if, for example, it has a quadratic form – then a linear prediction will involve errors of specification. Again it is important to examine graphically the form of the data to see whether they do conform to a linear pattern – and in particular to see whether particular observations exert a great influence on the results of fitting.

good first step always

L and K. We have pointed out above that there are various reasons why we should expect that the conditions required for least-squares estimation are not met.

The interpretation of the conditions required will, however, vary according to the nature of the data – whether cross-section or time series, whether aggregated or not. We might illustrate the argument by one example – leaving the reader to pursue the other arguments as an exercise. Suppose that we had cross-section data such as that illustrated on p. 297, where the firms have a disturbance term associated with their production function, and also two disturbance terms in their marginal productivity conditions – one each for labour and capital. Now it is clear that we cannot take factor inputs as determined independently. The level of factor inputs is determined by the quantity of output and the random disturbance that enters into the marginal productivity relationship.†

The methods of estimation which one might adopt, instead of the normal least-squares approach, encompass very simple approaches and most complicated and time-consuming computational schemes. The simplest – and one that has been extensively used – is the factor share method; we estimate α from the fraction of total income that is paid to workers. Simple though this approach may be, it also requires the *assumptions* of constant returns to scale (and perfect competition in factor and goods markets) and that the marginal productivity law holds. We cannot use such estimates to test these hypotheses.‡ Nevertheless the factor shares estimators are very useful as a basis for building models of other aspects of aggregate and micro-functions.

The estimation models for simultaneous equations systems are much more complex. The first stage is, however, to find the reduced form – that is to express the endogenous variables X, K and L in terms of the exogenous variables. The reader will observe that, oddly enough, there are *no* exogenous variables in the system of simultaneous equations considered in the system on page 297 above. If some method, such as two-stage least-squares is to be used, then at least one exogenous variable must be added to the model. The obvious candidates are the lagged value of the capital stock, since it is likely that the adjustment

† See Walters (1963) for further discussion.

‡ The factor shares estimator is, however, biased downwards. It seems, however, that the amount of bias is relatively very small.

process of capital stock takes longer than a year, or, perhaps in other models, the different price variables facing each individual. We shall not pursue these models any further – but the interested reader may like to try his skill with examples at the end of the chapter.

The complications that are involved in estimating the c.e.s. function are much greater than those of the Cobb–Douglas. It is not merely that there is another parameter to be measured – that would be a relatively easy task – the main problem arises from the non-linearity of the function. There is no simple transformation that will make the c.e.s. function of a linear form.† In practice most investigators use some version of the factor shares approach – such as we discussed above – and of course there are many variants of this basic approach depending on the data one has available. If, for example, one had available labour productivity in terms of output per worker, and the real wage, one could measure the relation

$$\log\left(\frac{X}{L}\right) = \left(\frac{1}{1+\rho}\right)\left[\log\left(\frac{W}{P}\right) - \log\left(1-\delta\right) + \rho \log \gamma\right]. \quad (10.67)$$

This is, of course, simply a version of the labour productivity equation. The regression coefficient then measures the elasticity of substitution b or $(1+\rho)^{-1}$.‡ The attraction of this approach is that it does not require data on capital or on the price of capital. But in order to obtain estimates of the other parameters of the production function we do require some knowledge of the quantity of capital. With these statistics one can estimate the two parameters δ and ρ from the condition that the marginal rate of substitution is equal to the factor price ratio.

$$\frac{WL}{RK} = \frac{1-\delta}{\delta}\left(\frac{K}{L}\right)^{\rho} \quad (10.68)$$

$$\log\left(\frac{WL}{RK}\right) = \log\left(\frac{1-\delta}{\delta}\right) + \rho \log\left(\frac{K}{L}\right)$$

† If one knew exactly the value of ρ then one could take the equation (writing $\gamma = 1$)

$$X^{-\rho} = \delta K^{-\rho} + (1-\delta)L^{-\rho} \quad (10.66)$$

and then take the $-1/\rho$th root of each variable X, K and L. Then we would have a linear relationship in the transformed variables. But of course in practice one does not know ρ.

‡ The reader should go on to enquire under what conditions one may take the wage rate as given for the purpose of adjusting the labour productivity. It will be recollected that many wage agreements and government 'guidelines' would require that *wage rates be determined by productivity* – rather than the other way around.

The remaining 'efficiency' parameter can then be estimated by substitution in one of the equations.

The formal problems of estimation with non-linear relationships are, however, of relatively small importance compared with the problems of the data themselves. As one might expect there are marked multi-collinearities in the time series. Indeed when the first Cobb–Douglas function was fitted critics claimed that it merely measured the dominant time trends in both series, and that it did not measure the aggregate production function at all. The attempt to eliminate the trend by moving average techniques or by linear or exponential terms (such as by estimating technical progress) tends to introduce spurious relationships and, of course, to magnify the errors in measurement of the variables.†

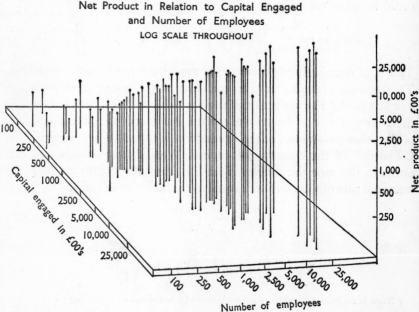

85 AUSTRALIAN FACTORY INDUSTRIES IN 1912:
Net Product in Relation to Capital Engaged
and Number of Employees
LOG SCALE THROUGHOUT

FIG. 10.3. *Source:* E. H. Phelps-Brown, 'The Meaning of the Fitted Cobb–Douglas Production Function', *Quarterly Journal of Economics*, LXXI (Nov. 1957)

† One of the simplest ways of eliminating the trend (and reducing the amount of serial correlation in the disturbances is to work with the differences (in the logarithms) of the variables. As one can see from the 'saw-tooth' example of Figure 4.11 the errors of measurement are relatively much more important in the correlations and regressions of differences.

It might be thought that this problem of multicollinearity would be avoided in cross-section samples; but not so. A glance at the Figure 10.3, will illustrate the degree of multicollinearity encountered in practice. In this three-dimensional model all scales are measured in logarithms and the vertical axis measures the value added, and the two horizontal axes measure the quantity of labour and the value of capital. All observations are for *industries* – so it is essentially an inter-industry cross-section. The observations are concentrated in a 'tube'; there is little variation in the capital-labour plane. Thus there is little information to enable one to fit a plane to these observations; one can give the fitted plane the same slope as the tube, but it is clear that the fitted plane can be rotated around the tube and still give a good fit to the observations. This is of course the typical case of multicollinearity. Industries which have large labour forces usually also employ large amounts of capital, and those with small labour inputs use little capital. There are very few industries that use large amounts of capital and small labour inputs, or have a very low capital-labour ratio. Size of industry, both of labour, capital and output is the dominant relationship in the data.

With intra-industry cross-sections the multicollinearity is even more pronounced. Technologies are similar, and the capital labour ratios and capital output ratios are more or less the same. Small variations exist – but they may be explained partly by errors of measurement, and mistakes. The important conclusion, therefore, is that one does not avoid multicollinearity by the use of cross-section data; one merely examines a different kind of collinear data.†

The Results

THE DATA

Undoubtedly the easiest variable to measure – and the one on which there is usually most information – is the labour input. But it is more complicated than simply counting heads. Labour should be measured

† The reader may well think: 'But why not use an extraneous estimator?' This technique has paid off with consumer studies, surely it is likely to help with the analysis of production. Some use has in fact been made of extraneous estimators. Broadly speaking there are two kinds: first the factor shares estimate of the coefficients of the production function, and second, information about the engineering or technological relations obtained from the engineering data. The mixture of engineering and economic data does pay handsome dividends – and we discuss one basic model of this kind in the following chapter.

in terms of a standardised unit; and so there is the problem of adding together labour units of different quality. Obviously the best indicator of man's 'quality' is his marginal product – and since, in equilibrium, this will be measured by the wage he earns in some reference or base year, this suggests that labour should be weighted according to its remuneration in the base year and then aggregated to find the quantity of labour measured in standard units. Any future additions to the labour force will be weighted according to their relative marginal productivity in the base year. In practice, of course, it is necessary to classify labour into broad groups according to age, sex, and perhaps education or skill. The weighting system can be adopted with these broad groups.† The second question is what sort of average should be used. The theory of aggregation suggests that a geometric average would be the best approach. But unfortunately the vast majority of statistics are published as arithmetic averages or totals, so the use of geometric averages is not a practical proposition. Indeed, for practical studies, investigators have often used some simple unweighted concept – such as number of persons employed or number of man-hours. Since skill and the composition of the labour force change over time, it is clear that biases – and almost certainly downward biases – are introduced into time series studies of the production function.

With the measurement of output, however, there are very few studies which do not employ weighted index number techniques. Even with apparently homogeneous commodities, such as tons of coal, it is found that different grades of even the same type of coal command quite different prices – and so the composite output has to be weighted. Again, because of the availability of the data, one uses arithmetic base-weighted (Lespeyres) indices.

The main problems occur in the measurement of capital. In production functions the concept of 'capital input' required should correspond to the 'capital service' which is performed during the period for which we calculate output and labour input. The problem is the old distinction between a stock and a flow. Consider for example two machines which produce identical services each year; but suppose that

† If, for example, an arithmetic average were used for two age-sex-skill categories, we should have

$$L(t) = \frac{L_1(t) \cdot W_1(0) + L_2(t) \cdot W_2(0)}{W_1(0) + W_2(0)}, \tag{10.69}$$

where the base period is 0 and a subscript refers to the age-sex-skill category.

one will last 20 years and the other 10 years. The machine with the longer life will command a higher price on the market than the machine with the short life. But the *rent* paid for one year's service from these two machines should be the same. And although one machine is more valuable than the other, the two machines have exactly the same effect on current production when they are combined with the same amounts of labour.

In addition to all the usual index number difficulties in combining heterogeneous goods into one measure, particular difficulties occur with capital because of the process of technical change and innovation over time.† The inventory of capital goods includes different kinds of machines, buildings and inventories at different stages of their life cycle, and of the process of technological change. To combine them into a single measure we reduce them to money values. But the value of a piece of existing capital equipment is determined by its expected rate of profit, and of course the existing rate of profit. Thus we cannot use K and R as though they were independent measures; the value of R enters into the computation of K.

Many other problems that enter into the measurement of capital can often be dealt with by using *ad hoc* methods. For example, the capital measures available in practice usually do not allow for the fact that certain machines are unemployed or under-employed. Since the labour statistics (especially if man-hours is used) do allow for the extent of unemployment in labour, it seems that some allowance should be made for the unemployment of capital also. Various techniques have been suggested. One is to take the period when labour is 'fully employed' as a standard for full employment of capital; then it is assumed that the employment of capital varies *pari passu* with the percentage employment in the labour force. There are, however, many alternative adjustment procedures which, with our present rudimentary state of knowledge of the idle time of machines, are just as defensible.‡

† Of course this problem is present in the aggregation of the labour inputs also; but it is thought that it is less important. Old dogs do learn new tricks – but old machines only eat more and break down.

‡ There is a contra case of course. It might be objected that the services of the capital equipment are not the quantities which the firm *buys*. It *buys* capital goods and transforms them into capital services as part and parcel of the process of production. The efficient employment (and indeed *un*employment at appropriate times) of capital equipment is part of the production decision. The fact that he can lay off labour and avoid paying wages but he cannot avoid his capital commitment is an important element in fixing his capital labour ratios. I find this contra case persuasive; but I believe that I am in a minority here.

In practical applications most investigators have used a concept of *net capital* (or net worth) rather than the *gross capital*.† The most common measurement of capital is by the perpetual inventory method. This takes the addition to the stock of capital each year and constructs notional depreciation accounts for each type of asset. Thus each asset is gradually written down in the accounts until it eventually disappears from the capital stock. Other methods of measuring fixed capital have been developed – but they are not much used in statistical production functions. The Giffen method – of capitalising the income from capital by using a 'year's purchase' measure – emphasises both the theoretical shortcomings of capital measures and the empirical crudities.‡ Yet another method is to use the valuations of plant and equipment for fire insurance; this probably gives a more promising approach to the net capital concept, but it has hardly been adequately tested yet.

At the arm-chair-in-an-ivory-tower level it is easy to be sceptical and even cynical about the estimates of production functions that are based on such an unsatisfactory measure of capital stock. But such reflections, though relevant, are not critical for judging the production function approach. The true issue is whether one can explain more and predict better with, rather than without, capital stock series. Unfortunately the facts are not entirely clear on this point – partly because they have not been organised in this way. But we turn to consider the empirical estimates in the next section.

---

† Net capital measures the capital stock by deducting depreciation (or capital consumption) each year. Gross capital does not take into account depreciation each year – but simply writes the machine off at the end of its life. It seems that the true measure for production functions should lie somewhere between the two extremes; the reader can argue the case as an exercise. (See Hogan 1958).

‡ Nevertheless the Giffen method was used in a famous study by Arrow, Chenery, Minhas and Solow (1962). They found the net rate of return on capital from the balance sheets, of certain firms in the industry then calculated

$$\frac{PX - WL}{R^*} = K(R^*) \tag{10.70}$$

where the estimated rate of return is R^* and the conceptual measure of capital derived from it $K(R^*)$. If, therefore, firms happened to make a loss in one year of measurement of R^*, the implied capital stock would be negative! Obviously a better measure requires some averaging process over time. But there is still the fundamental difficulty of measurement interdependence.

EMPIRICAL EVIDENCE

We review first the empirical evidence on *cross-section studies*. A list of *inter-firm* studies is shown in Table 10.1. All the studies used the Cobb–Douglas form of the production function so one can compare the values of the labour coefficient with the share of wages; and the sum of the coefficients indicates whether or not there are returns to scale. (We are assuming for the time being that the production function has been identified and measured by the cross-section data.)

The findings are fairly clear cut. The sum of the coefficients is near to unity in many – indeed most – of the reported results.† There appears to be constant returns to scale in most of the inter-firm studies. It would be useful to examine the standard errors of the sum of the coefficients and to test the hypothesis that the sum did not deviate from unity; but such a task is lengthy and is best left aside.‡ One may rely more on the weight of the evidence rather than its statistical quality.

The only striking exceptions to the general rule of constant returns to scale are the results for the United States railroads, and the co-efficients for agriculture in pre-war Japan. The results for United States railroads are roughly of the order one might expect. If there are increasing returns in the railway industry then it would certainly have appeared during the period of relatively low utilisation in 1936. Even in normal times, however, one would expect the railways to exhibit increasing returns to scale because of the relatively large units of plant and inherent indivisibilities. The odd result is clearly the *negative* coefficients for labour in agriculture in Japan; clearly the implication is that the family labourers actually get in one another's way! To contemporary observers this appeared to be a plausible finding.

The second main hypothesis is that the labour coefficient is equal to the wage earners share of income. We have detailed statistics for a number of Indian industries on a comparable statistical basis. A glance at the evidence suggests that this hypothesis is certainly not strikingly apparent in the data. Although there is a correlation between the

---

† However one has the uneasy feeling that many results which are reckoned to be 'unreasonable' are not reported and unconsciously suppressed. Claims of ubiquity or generality for the numerical results therefore should be made with much caution.

‡ It will be observed that the standard error is estimated from the sampling variances of $\hat{\alpha}$ and $\hat{\beta}$ *and* their covariance. Thus

$$\text{var}\,(\widehat{\alpha+\beta}) = \text{var}\,(\hat{\alpha}) + \text{var}\,(\hat{\beta}) + 2\,\text{cov}\,(\hat{\alpha},\hat{\beta}). \qquad (10.71)$$

Table 10.1 Values of Cobb–Douglas Coefficients

Inter-Firm Studies of Industries

	Labour α_1	Capital α_2	Raw materials α_3	Total $\alpha_1+\alpha_2+\alpha_3$
UTILITIES, RAILWAYS				
France				
1945 Gas	·83	·10	—	·93
	·80	·14	—	·94
U.S.A.				
1936 Railroads	·89	·12	·28	1·29
OTHER EXTRACTIVE AND MANUFACTURING INDUSTRIES				
U.K.				
Coal	·79	·29	—	1·08
Coal	·51	·49	—	1·00
U.S.A.				
1909 Clothing	·98	—·07	—	·91
Foods	·72	·35	—	1·07
Metals and machinery	·71	·26	—	·97

India	Labour α_1	Capital α_2	Raw materials α_3	Share of wages	Total
1951 Cotton	·92	·12		·63	1·04
1952 Cotton	·66	·34		·75	
1951 Jute	·84	·14		·60	·98
1952 Jute	·91	·34		·71	
1951 Sugar	·59	·33		·30	·92
1952 Sugar	·24	·94		·32	
1951 Coal	·71	·44		·57	1·15
1952 Coal	·58	·58		·55	
1951 Paper	·64	·45		·41	1·09
1952 Paper	·59	·49		·39	
1951 Basic	·80	·37		·37	1·17
1952 Chemicals	·82	·40		·48	
1951 Electricity	·20	·67		·30	·87
1952 Electricity	·02	1·00		·30	

Agriculture

	Labour	Land	Capital	Live-stock	Feeder cattle	Fertilizer	Machinery and draft animals	Units of productive livestock	Total
International									
1949 General agriculture	·28	·39				·29 (feed)		·05	1·01
Australia									
1955 Milk	·23					·13 (feed)		·62 (other)	·98
India									
1955 Arable	·56	·08				·25			·89
Japan									
1939 Rice	—·07	·73							·66
"	—·53	1·30							·77
South Africa									
1950–1951	·18	·21				·54	·13		·93
1951–1952	·13	·24				·60	·17		·97
Cow and calf ranches	·19	·19				·52	·31 (other)		·90
Growing and fattening ranches	·13	·28				·55	·03		·96

	Labour	Land	Capital	Live-stock	Feeder cattle	Fertilizer	Machinery and draft animals	Total
U.S.A. Arable and various								
1939 Cotton	·45	·29	—	·033	·011			·90
Corn-Hog	·37	·35	—	·095	·013			·99
Wheat	·41	·23	·08 (equipment)	·045				1·00
1939 Iowa (various)	·03	·23	·08	·48		·07 (fertiliser)	·03	·850
1942 Iowa (various)	·16	·29	·42					·87
1950 Crop	·33	·50	·38				·15	·93
Montana	·04	·91	·58					1·12
N. Iowa	·08		·17					1·16
S. Iowa	·09	·80	·39					1·28
Alabama	·32	·39	·46					1·17
1950 Iowa Crop Share	·12	·77	·32					1·21
Cash Leases	·10	·97	·31					1·38
1951 Iowa Crop	·09	·97	·15					1·21
1951 Iowa Crop Share	·10	·73	·20					1·03
1946 Minnesota (mixed)	·04	·20	·19		·29 (feed etc.)		·17 (current expenses)	0·72
1951	·06	·32	·32					0·84

	Labour	Land	Capital	Other	Total
U.S.A. Livestock and Dairy					
1950 Dairy and General (milk)	·15		·25		·94
1950 Livestock (Montana)	·08		·94	·54	1·02
N. Iowa	·08		·91		·99
S. Iowa	·12		·98		1·10
Alabama	·23		·74		

labour coefficient and the share of wages, the correlation is a weak one, and there are many perverse movements over time. For example in the cotton industry when the labour coefficient decreased from 1951 to 1952 the share of wages moved *up*. Indeed when one examines the Indian data in detail it is clear that there is some considerable instability in the estimates of the labour coefficient – in cotton, sugar and coal, for example.

To sum up the results of inter-firm cross-section studies, therefore, it seems that there is broad agreement that there are no marked diseconomies or economies of scale in manufacturing industry. Economies of scale were present in the railways and this finding confirms the age old conjectures about the shape of rail cost curves. On the other hand there was no convincing evidence that the labour coefficient was equal to the share of wages, and the coefficient did not appear to be strikingly stable.

The cross-section studies *between industries* – where the observations are aggregates for each industry – are reviewed in Table 10.2. The most remarkable result – and one that has caught the attention of all research workers – is the fact that the sum of the coefficients is very nearly unity in the great majority of the studies. The second result is that the labour coefficient is a close approximation to the share of labour in value added.

The interpretations of these statistical findings – both for cross-sections of the *intra*-industry kind and *between* industry, that is both *inter firm* and *inter industry* – is the critical task. As one may guess from the discussion above, it seems to me very doubtful indeed whether one may interpret *either* kind of cross-section result as evidence on the (average or representative) production function of the firm or 'the' industry. The inter-firm study gives us evidence primarily on entrepreneurial ability; but, there may be some evidence from which one may adduce a production function coefficient, if there are mistakes in choosing a capital labour ratio: but 'mistakes' seems to be a weak rationalisation for arguing that one has identified production coefficients. For the inter-industry studies, however, even this possibility does not exist. One is fairly certain that the inter-industry studies provide evidence on the grouping of firms into industries and its effects on outputs and inputs. The fact that the labour coefficient is equal to the labour share is evidence of the accounting convention that all income

Table 10.2

Inter-Industry Production Functions: Cross-Section Estimates

Year	Country	Labour α_1	Capital α_2	Sum $\alpha_1 + \alpha_2$
1889	U.S.A.	·51	·43	·94
1899		·62	·33	·95
1904		·65	·31	·96
1909		·63	·34	·97
1914		·61	·37	·98
1919		·76	·25	1·01
1912	Australia	·52	·47	·99
1922–3		·53	·49	1·02
1926–7		·59	·34	·93
1934–5		·64	·36	1·00
1936–7		·49	·49	·98
1910–11	Victoria	·74	·25	·99
1923–4		·62	·31	·92
1927–8		·59	·27	·86
1933–4	New South Wales	·65	·34	·99
1937–8	S. Africa 1	·66	·32	·98
	2.	·65	·37	1·02
1923	Canada	·48	·48	·96
1927		·46	·52	·98
1935		·50	·52	1·02
1937		·43	·58	1·01
1938–9	New Zealand	·46	·51	·97
1924	U.K. (industry)	·72	·18	·90
1930		·75	·13	·88
1946	India	·66	·31	·97
1947		·57	·50	1·07
1951		·59	·40	·99
1909	U.S.A. (industry)	·74	·32	1·06

Source: Walters (1963)

is allocated to one factor or another; it tells us nothing about the production function.

Let us now turn from these negative results to the *inter-state* cross-section studies. As we argued above, the fact that entrepreneurs in different states are confronted by different relative price ratios means that each will select different points on the production function, so there is a possibility that the data will enable one to estimate the underlying production coefficients. The observations here are normally aggregates for particular industries in each state. There are broadly two sub-classes of studies; the first is the truly international cross-section – such as that examined by Arrow, Chenery, Minhas and Solow (1967), and second the inter-state comparison where the states are constituents of a larger federal unit – such as the study by Hildebrand and Liu of the United States.

The first main use of international cross-sections was to test the hypothesis that the elasticity of substitution was unity. The c.e.s. function was fitted to international cross-section data. The first results suggested that the elasticity of substitution was in the region of 0·6 to 0·9 (i.e. $\rho > 0$). Recent additional work has, however, tended to suggest that the hypothesis of unit elasticity of substitution is not discredited by the data. The Cobb–Douglas function is therefore a good approximation. The data also enable one to analyse the variation in efficiency from one country to another; one may seek to account for the variation in output as due to variation in γ. This hypothesis – that variations in efficiency between countries were neutral – was not discredited by the data. Many other tests and estimates have been made with this international cross-section data – but the student is referred to the original studies for further analysis.

One of the problems with international comparisons is the fact that one must work in terms of a standard money unit – both in measuring output and in the measure of capital. One of the advantages of inter-state (within a federal union) comparisons is that they do not require transforming by use of the foreign exchange rates. In the United States all constituent states use the same currency. The disadvantage, on the other hand, is that if there is a *national* market for produce and factors there will be a tendency for price ratios to be equal. So, there will be a similar problem to that encountered in the cross-section studies of firms in a particular industry; with the inter-state comparison, however, the observations will be totals for particular industries in each state. But transport costs and other 'frictions' will prevent the achievement of full equalisation of factor price ratios. Whether this will provide sufficient variation to enable one to sample observations and trace out the production function is a large question.

Nevertheless an extensive study has been carried out of the inter-state, inter-industry production functions in the United States. by Hildebrand and Liu. Their model was complicated to include labour supply curves, lagged adjustment processes of factors to new 'desired' levels, and a unique method of allowing for technical change. The main result of this study was to suggest that there *are* economies of scale in manufacturing industry (p. 108). In 12 of the 15 industries studied the sum of the coefficients exceeded unity – as one can see in Table 10.3. These results are not so striking as they appear at first glance, for it is clear that the standard errors of the sums of coefficients are relatively large (though unfortunately they are not given by the authors) and it is likely that, at most, only two industries would give significant returns to scale at the conventional 95 per cent significance level. The second main result of this study is to show that the elasticity of output with respect to labour (the Cobb–Douglas coefficient) exceeds the labour share of income (or value added). Similarly the Cobb–Douglas capital coefficient exceeds the share of income going to capital. And of course both these results are consistent with the finding of economies of scale.

The Hildebrand and Liu results are consistent with common sense. In states where there is a relatively large amount of a particular industry one would expect that it was for a good reason – that is to say one would expect that it was relatively efficient to concentrate in that state. And in states where there was a relatively small amount of that particular industry one would again suspect that it was because it was more profitable to pursue other activities. (There *is* inter-state specialisation and trade.) So it does not follow that, if the amount of this particular industry were doubled in that latter state there would be increasing returns to scale. One would expect, on the contrary, some decreasing returns as the industry employed less efficient specialised factors of production. In other words one must again be cautious in interpreting the results from this cross-section study as evidence of the shape of the production function.

TIME SERIES STUDIES

There are comparatively few time series studies of the production function for particular industries; time series work is much more commonly associated with industry groups or whole sectors of the economy. We have, however, brought together some of the results of *industry studies* in Table 10.4. The most striking feature of these statistics is the difference between them and the cross-section studies. There is

Table 10.3
Inter-state Production Functions (U.S.A.)
Measurement of Returns to Scale under Constant Technology

Industry	Rank according to returns to scale	Labour-output elasticity	Production worker-output elasticity	Non-production employee-output elasticity	Capital-output elasticity	Returns to scale
	(1)	(2)	(3)	(4)	(5)	(6)
Food products	1		0·31	0·40	0·53	1·24
Chemicals	2		0·34	0·57	0·27	1·18
Primary metals	3	0·96			0·16	1·12
Instruments	4	0·67			0·44	1·11
Lumber products	5	0·79			0·31	1·10
Paper products	6		0·55	0·27	0·28	1·10
Stone, clay, and glass products	7		0·66	0·30	0·13	1·09
Rubber products	8	0·85			0·23	1·08
Machinery	9		0·47	0·27	0·33	1·07
Apparel	10		0·58	0·26	0·20	1·04
Fabricated metal products	11		0·53	0·34	0·15	1·02
Transportation equipment	12		0·41	0·28	0·32	1·01
Petroleum and coal products	13		0·27	0·50	0·23	1·00
Electric machinery	14		0·41	0·24	0·30	0·95
Leather products	15	0·85			0·07	0·92

Source: Hildebrand and Liu, p. 108

obviously great variation between one time series and another and between one industry and country and another. A comparison of the results for agriculture in the United States and in the United Kingdom provides an extreme case of wild results. And the fact that the elasticity of output with respect to labour is apparently near zero in textiles and metals and machinery in Japan is clearly too much to swallow. Of

Table 10.4

Production Functions for Industries: Time Series Estimates

Country and period	$\hat{a}_1$	$\hat{a}_2$	$\hat{a}_3$ (raw material)	$\hat{a}_1 + \hat{a}_2$ $(+\hat{a}_3)$	exp. trend
U.S. agricultural 1920–41	1·70	·81		2·51 with exponential trend	1·6% p.a.
U.K. agriculture 1924–47	·18	·37		·55	1·03% p.a.
U.K. cotton industry 1948–52	·33	·70 (loom hours)	·26	1·29	·45% p.a.
U.K. coal	·79	·21		(restricted)	—
Canada–automobiles 1918–30	·96	·41		1·37	exp. trend $-·034t$ $+·00134t^2$

Table 10.5

Production Functions for Aggregates of Industries: Time Series Estimates

Period	Country	$\hat{a}_1$	$\hat{a}_2$	$\hat{a}_1 + \hat{a}_2$
1899–1922	U.S.A.	·81	·23	1·04
		·78	·15	·93
		·73	·25	·98
1907–29	Victoria	·63	·30	·93 (trend eliminated)
1901–27	New South Wales	·84	·23	1·07
1915–16, 18–25	New Zealand	·78	·20	·98
1923–40		·42	·49	·91
1920–40	U.S.A. mining and manufacturing	·54	·46	(restricted)
		1·34	·93	2·27 (linear trend)
1909–49	U.S.A.	1·46	·49	1·95 (parabolic trend)
1909–49	U.S.A.	·65	·35	(restricted)
1900–55	Norway	·99	·23	1·22
1917–55	Norway	·76	·20	·96
1917–39	Norway	·51	·28	·79
1922–39	Norway	·62	·72	1·34 (exponential trends)
1925–52	Finland	·39	·62	1·01
		·78	·22	(restricted)

Source: Walters (1963).

course special explanations may be sought – and in many cases they have been found – for these 'odd' results. But it would be patently dishonest not to suggest that the simple production function has failed to prove itself a useful tool for the analysis of the time series of inputs and outputs for particular industries. In what way should the function be developed to improve its performance? Unfortunately there are no general guides at present available. One may however conjecture that the performance would be much improved by a lagged adjustment of factor inputs, and particularly capital, to the new desired level. Another important advance may be achieved by using one version or another of the 'vintage' model. These questions must, however, be left open at the present time.

The time series studies of the private sector of the economy as a whole – or of the manufacturing and mining sector – have, in the past, produced results which are much more consistent with *a priori* expectations. A selection of results is shown in Table 10.5. The early time series studies – and particularly those that used only data before the slump of the 1930s – show a remarkable conformity with expectations. The sum of the coefficients is approximately equal to unity and the labour coefficient is very nearly the same as the worker's share in value added. This was widely interpreted as evidence consistent with constant returns to scale, on the one hand, and with the marginal productivity theory of distribution on the other.

But the results for later years show that, to some extent, these results were a statistical accident of the period of investigation. If we examine the results for the United States for later years one finds that there is (i) convincing evidence of increasing returns to scale and (ii) a strong suggestion that the labour coefficient exceeds the share of wages and a rather weaker result that the capital coefficient exceeds the share of rentier incomes. Indeed in many studies not reported here it seems that the elasticity of output with respect to labour actually exceeds unity.†

Plausible explanations for these findings may be sought in the slowness of the adjustment processes. Aggregate output responds to the conditions of aggregate demand. If there is a sharp fall in aggregate demand the entrepreneur will not necessarily plan to reduce his stock

† See Marc Nerlove: 'Notes on the Production Relations included in Macro-econometric Models', *Studies in Income and Wealth*, vol. 31 (National Bureau of Economic Research, Princeton, N.J., 1967).

of equipment if he expects demand to get back to normal in the near future. The aggregate production function cannot easily encompass cases of this kind. It is to be expected only that it will explain output-input relationships when all inputs are 'fully-employed'. It cannot usefully be used when there is excess capacity. But these phenomena of under-employment of resources do not apply only to capital; when there is a fall in demand the entrepreneur will not make drastic reductions in his work force – since the cost of hiring and firing, although assumed to be zero in economic analysis, is in fact not trivial. Furthermore the retention of machines means that certain 'overhead' components of the labour force are profitably employed in the short run – which may last for years – whereas if the entrepreneur were convinced that the slump had come to stay he would fire them also. The complexities of these reactions over time are ignored in the simple production function approach – and this may account for the apparently enormous response of output (during the recovery) to very small increments of inputs – especially of labour. Essentially one is not taking into account the *under*-employment of labour within industry. Ideally one could incorporate these effects into the system by regarding the (representative) entrepreneur as maximising his profits over a horizon much longer than a year – taking into account the 'friction' costs of hiring and firing, of selling machines now and buying them back later, and so on. As one can see, however, the complications are great. Probably at this stage of our knowledge, and with the crude data that are available to us, it is best to use some blunter instrument – such as adaptive expectations.†

The analysis of technical progress has achieved its most sophisticated form in the studies of the aggregate production function. Early studies regarded it as simply a bonus – or manna from heaven – which went on from one year to the next. With the assumption of disembodied technical progress of this kind one finds that the term for technological progress explains on the average between 1·0 per cent and 2·0 per cent p.a. of the growth of output. In the United States, for roughly the first half of the 20th century technical progress accounts for about 1·5 per cent of the growth. There is some evidence that probably this percentage has increased for certain countries – Germany, France, Japan and Italy – since he early 1950s, and it may even exceed 2·0 per cent. But

† See the discussion of durable consumer goods in Chapter 9.

over the long run of 30 years or so the order of magnitude seems to be between 1·0 and 2·0 per cent p.a.

Research on technological change has developed in a number of ways. First there has been some preliminary empirical work on the vintage model of capital – so that technical progress is then embodied in the equipment. The natural result is that the rate of technological advance is estimated to be much greater on the new capital equipment alone than we found in the disembodied model applying to all equipment whatever its age. In fact Solow found that the percentage improvement of productivity on new equipment in the Cobb–Douglas version of the vintage model was 2·5 per cent per annum; and this is considerably higher than the disembodied figure of 1·5 per cent. The embodied progress, however, only applied to new equipment and the productivity increase of the economy is damped down by all the old equipment on which, in the vintage model, there is no productivity gain. Secondly, there has been a renaissance of the economics of education, and many investigators have attempted to link the productivity gains with the improvements in the quality of the labour force through education. Third there has been an attempt to examine the hypothesis that technical progress is not neutral. Indeed the first results of this work do suggest that there was non-neutrality in technical progress; but much remains to be done.†

CONCLUSIONS ON PRODUCTION FUNCTIONS

For the empirical econometrist or economist, the statistical estimation of production functions is a very challenging task. It is also an important one. One of the critical jobs in all macro-econometric models – and nearly all sector models of the economy – is to formulate the relationship between outputs and inputs, and to predict the course of technological progress. But the task is difficult – mainly because the observations we have of productive relationships normally do not trace out the production function. The data trace the conditions of competitive equilibrium, and thus sheds little light on the underlying relationships.

Again this field has emphasised the importance of relating data and

† At the time of writing, the most useful summary of current research is to be found in *Studies in Income and Wealth*, vol. 31 (1967).

theory. The need to set out formally the model that gives rise to the observations has been stressed almost *ad nauseam*. But only by exploring such a model can one see the relationship between the observations and the theory to which they should be fitted.

Our approach has been critical and sceptical; but one also hopes that it has been constructive. Let us briefly review the main results. First, there has been no convincing evidence that the marginal productivity law has been discredited for the micro-production relationship. One must add however that this is no very large claim since it has not really been strenuously tested. The presence of nuisance variables has prevented any sensitive test of the marginal productivity relationship. Second, at the macro-level there is some evidence to show that the variation in the marginal productivity of labour in the same industry in different countries or states varies predictably with the real wage rate. With intra-state, inter-industry cross-sections, however, the evidence on the share of wages and the Cobb–Douglas coefficients are irrelevant. With time series data on aggregate relationships the basic problem is one of the confounding of evidence on the marginal productivity changes with technical change and other trends in the series.

Third, the evidence on economies of scale at the micro-level is quite flimsy. The cross-section samples of firms have to be carefully interpreted – but there does appear to be evidence of economies of scale in precisely those industries where one would expect there to be increasing returns – the utilities.† The cross-sections of industries shed no light at all on economies of scale – either in the micro- or for the aggregate–production function.

The time series results gave no convincing evidence on economies of scale. Much depends on the time period of analysis. Indeed the results seem to depend considerably on the state of the trade cycle over the period. For slump periods the production function apparently exhibited increasing returns to scale. But we adduce this as evidence that the production function is merely reflecting the variation in aggregate demand, not that it is properly measuring the technical relationship between inputs and outputs. There is however some suggestion that

† One real test of economies of scale is, of course, the historical experience of industries – to see whether small firms either grow or go bankrupt, or whether the large firm is just a transitory phenomenon; but this research is outside the scope of production function analysis.

economies of scale do exist in the aggregate production function – but whether they are 'distribution-of-factors-among-industry' effects or whether they are true external or internal economies is not known. The confounding effect of economies of scale and technological progress prevents a subtle analysis of the residuals.

The last major finding has been the dominance of technical progress in accounting for growth. Existing evidence suggests that technological improvements account for about 50 per cent to 90 per cent of the growth in output per capita. The increased capital per worker has played only a minor role in the growth of production and national income per capita.

But this very conclusion emphasises how little we know about the process of technical change, its causes, its diffusion and its application. The imponderables of technical progress and the effects on production, growth and decay, are the really big unknowns in modern economics. The paucity of our analysis and knowledge in this supremely important area is probably the cause of more 'failures' of economic models than any other factor. One hopes of course for some brilliant new insight; but for the time being all one can do is painstaking research on existing models.

Questions for Discussion

1. Extend the Cobb–Douglas production function to the firm that makes *two* commodities. Show how to extend the C.E.S. function to deal with two commodities.

2. Consider the problems of estimating the multiproduct production function. (See L. R. Klein, *A Textbook of Econometrics*.)

3. It is known that labour varies considerably in 'quality' over time. Discuss methods of estimating these effects. (See Zvi Griliches, 'The Sources of Measured Productivity Growth in U.S. Agriculture, 1940–60', *Journal of Political Economy* (Aug 1963).

4. For the following data, find measures of technical progress using the assumptions that the production function is

$$X_t = A(t)L(t)^\alpha K(t)^\beta U(t), \quad \text{where} \quad \beta = 1 - \alpha$$

and that the marginal productivity condition for capital is satisfied in each period.

	L	K	X	Share of income to capital
1871	2·647	1·747	68	0·34
1881	2·961	2·214	81	0·35
1891	3·425	2·773	97	0·35
1901	3·916	3·698	111	0·33
1911	4·668	4·662	130	0·34

Source: E. H. Phelps Brown and Handfield-Jones, 'The Climacteric of the 1890's . . .', *Oxford Econ. Papers* (N.S.), 4 (1952).

Comment on your results.

5. Find the regression estimates of α and β from data of Question 4

$$X_t = A_t L(t)^\alpha K(t)^\beta,$$

where $\alpha + \beta$ is not restrained to be equal to unity.

Discuss whether there are or are not economies of scale in the aggregate production function.

6. Interpret the concept of aggregate economies of scale. Does it imply economies of scale to the individual firm or to industries?

7. Plot the data of Question 4 in suitable graphs.

8. Construct a three-dimensional model of the data of Question 4. [Use a plasticine base and wooden sticks.]

9. Consider the model

$$X_i = A K_i^\alpha L_i^\beta U_i$$

and

$$\frac{\beta X_i}{L_i} = \frac{W_i}{P} V_{1i}, \qquad \frac{\beta X_i}{K_i} = \frac{R_i}{P} V_{2i},$$

where the subscript i refers to the ith firm, W_i and R_i are the prices of labour and capital. Describe the conditions of competition in which such firms might exist.

Examine the problems of estimation.

10. Let the production be

$$X(t) = A L(t)^\alpha K(t)^{1-\alpha} U(t).$$

Consider now a model where the capital stock is adjusted over time to the desired level by the adaptive process.

$$K(t) - K(t-1) = \lambda[K^*(t) - K(t-1)],$$

where $K^*(t)$ is the *desired* capital stock.

11 Linear Programming – an Economic and Accounting Interpretation

Introduction

During the 1950s probably the most significant developments took place in economics since the Keynesian revolution of the mid-1930s. These new developments took the form of an immense simplification in the statement of economic problems and their solution. And this same simplification enabled one to extend the theory of economics back into the technological foundations on which it stands. We can now show how the economic decision can be cast in the form of a choice between various available technologies; the economics and the engineering are integrated and coordinated. Furthermore one can show how the economic-engineering decision can be interpreted in terms of the concepts of cost accounting. Indeed the linear approach enables one to erect a logical and consistent theory of cost accounting that fits neatly into the technological and economic theories of the process.

One of the great achievements of linear programming has been to integrate many areas of thought into a set of simple coherent postulates and procedures. Engineer and accountant (not to mention economist) can now talk 'the same language'. The area of communication is increased. Each discipline can be used to help the other.

The other main advantage is the fact that programming is a *practical* tool of analysis and calculation. To use the current jargon, it is an 'operational' theory. It does not merely tell us that there is a solution to the problem which we pose, it gives a practical rule for calculating the solution. Furthermore the theory is designed for dealing with large problems – with many variable and numerous constraints and conditions. The rules of arithmetic by which one attains a solution (the 'algorithm') are simple – and so they can easily and conveniently be fed into a computer. Thus the large problems where there are many outputs and many processes are reduced to the elementary simple operations which can be handled by the high-speed digital computer.

In this exposition, however, we shall not be concerned primarily with the problems of computing. These are best left to the computer experts. Our main concern is with the interpretation and application of the model, with the uses and extensions of the basic ideas. Then the reader will be able to think naturally in programming terms about the formulation of problems – and so he can enjoy the rich rewards that they can give.

If one were to be a purist in interpreting the word 'econometrics', I think it would exclude linear programming. But purity is never a virtue in the meritricious social sciences. Ideas and techniques spill over from very many disciplines. And the basic concepts of linear programming are so important that no student, who has read this far, should be able to escape them.

The Programming Analysis of the Firm

The analysis of programming is simply illustrated in terms of the decision of a firm on its production mix in the competitive environment. Later we shall show how this basic model may be used for a very wide variety of problems.

Consider a firm that has a certain fixed stock of equipment – let us suppose that it has 24 machines, 2100 square feet of floorspace, and 9 store racks.† This is all the fixed equipment (including floor space) which the firm commands. In the short run the firm cannot buy any more equipment, nor can it sell it on the market. We suppose, however, that the firm can buy variable factors at a constant price. Thus the firm can buy any amount of labour services it likes at the going wage rate. Similarly the firm may buy any quantity of raw material and fuel at the prices that rule on the market. Thus we suppose that there is a neat division between those productive resources that in the short run are fixed in supply – such as the floor space, machines and the store racks – on the one hand, and the factors of production that can be bought on the market, on the other, such as labour, raw materials, etc. This distinction roughly corresponds to the accounting dichotomy between fixed costs and variable costs.

† We shall work throughout in terms of 100 square feet of floor space as a unit – or h.s.f.

Now let us consider the output side of the production problem. For simplicity we shall suppose that there are only *two* kinds of goods that may be produced by this firm. Let us call them pipes and sheets. These products are homogeneous and may be made in infinitesimally small units – so that we may think of outputs as continuous variables. Furthermore pipes and sheets can be sold on the market at fixed prices. The market for the firm's output may be thought to be perfectly competitive – the firm may sell as much as it likes at the going prices. (The reader may also interpret the 'market conditions' as those of controlled prices; the firm may produce as much as it likes and sell it at the controlled price.) We suppose that there are no stocks or inventories in the model. All output is sold in the period in which it is produced.

One of the crucial assumptions of the model is that each unit of a particular output – let us imagine that the output in question is sheet – requires a certain specified quantity of inputs, both fixed and variable. Consider first the variable inputs such as labour and raw materials. Thus if it takes one man-hour to produce five sheets, it will take two man-hours to produce ten sheets, five man-hours to produce 25 sheets, and in general λ man-hours will produce 5λ sheets, where λ can take any non-negative value, i.e. any value of zero or above. A similar assumption is made for all other variable inputs.

It is clear therefore that a unit of output 'embodies' a specified fixed quantity of variable inputs. And since the price of output and the cost of units of variable inputs are both constant, we might conveniently measure the 'margin' of price over the cost per unit of output of all the variable inputs. Suppose for example that only two variable inputs go into the making of a sheet – labour and raw material. As before it takes one man-hour to produce 5 sheets – and suppose that it costs 10 shillings an hour for labour. Thus the labour cost of a sheet is 2 shillings. If each unit of output of sheet requires one-tenth of a ton (or two hundred-weights) of raw material which costs 30 shillings a ton, the raw material cost of a sheet is 3 shillings.

If we suppose that on the market the firm can sell sheets for 44 shillings, we see that the returns net of the variable input cost is then

$$45 - 2 \text{ (for labour)} - 3 \text{ (for raw material)} = 40 \text{ shillings} \qquad (11.1)$$

This 40 shillings might be referred to as the gross return from sheets, or the gross profits. It is, according to accountants, the fund from which the firm recovers its overhead costs and from which it pays out its profits. For the other product of the firm we can make a similar calculation; let us imagine that this has been done and that the net revenue (or gross profit) of a pipe is in fact 100 shillings.

We can then express the total 'net revenue' or 'gross profit' of the firm in £ as

2 × (no of sheets produced) + 5 × (no of pipes produced).

This then gives one the total sum from which overheads are 'to be covered' and from which the entrepreneur draws his reward. The two unknowns are of course the number of units of sheets and pipe produced. The product mix is the problem to be solved. It is therefore convenient to call the first unknown, the number of sheets, x_1 and the second unknown, the number of pipes, x_2. The 'net revenue' is then

$$£(2x_1 + 5x_2). \tag{11.2}$$

The task of the entrepreneur is to make this sum as large as possible.

This would, of course, lead to the entrepreneur selecting values of x_1 and x_2 as large as possible – if he were able to select each output independently of the other. But as one increases x_1 or x_2 we must take into account the fact that machines and floor space and store racks become occupied. Since these inputs are required for the production of both sheets and pipes, and since there are only limited quantities available, the constraints to the production of sheets and pipes are set by the required inputs of fixed factors of production.

To fix ideas let us continue the numerical example and suppose that

1 sheet requires 4 machines.

Now by our assumption of constant input requirements per unit of output we may write

x_1 sheets require $4x_1$ machines, where x_1 is any non-negative number.

Let us now examine the machines required for pipe production. Suppose that

1 pipe requires 1 machine.

So we have

x_2 pipes require x_2 machines

– by applying once more the fundamental assumption – where x_2 may be any non-negative value.†

With a production of x_1 sheets and x_2 pipes, therefore, we require a total number of machines of

$$4x_1 + x_2 \qquad (11.3)$$

These are the total machine requirements; but there are only 24 machines available. So the production of pipes and sheets must be limited to those quantities that occupy no more than the 24 machines available. They may occupy fewer machines than are available or all 24 machines may be employed; but we cannot use more than we have. So we specify that the production of pipes and sheets must be such that they do not use up more machines than are available, i.e.

$$4x_1 + x_2 \leqslant 24, \qquad (11.4)$$

which may be translated in words as

number of machines required for $\leqslant$ number of
producing x_1 sheets, x_2 pipes $\qquad$ machines available

It is convenient and instructive to illustrate this restriction imposed by the availability of machines in a figure.

In Figure 11.1 we represent the possible product mixes – measuring the number of sheets horizontally (x_1) and the number of pipes vertically (x_2). To express the limitation of production due to the limited number of machines, let us suppose that no sheets are produced (i.e. $x_1 = 0$) and that all the machines are employed producing pipes – no machines are left idle. Then by substitution we find

$$4(0) + x_2 = 24, \quad \text{so that} \quad x_2 = 24 \qquad (11.5)$$

We could produce 24 pipes; and we record this as point A in the figure. Now suppose that we used all the machines to produce only sheets, how

---

† The reader will notice that in order to specify the results in this way, all the variables and constants should refer to some unit of time – perhaps the week or the hour or day or year. We have omitted this from the text to save cluttering up the argument. The time dimension is however most important in practice – for it serves to define which factors may be taken as fixed and which may be considered variable. But once we have fixed the distinction between fixed and variable factors, we can then define the flows of goods and inputs according to any convenient time unit.

many could be produced? By the same argument (but with $x_2 = 0$) we find that $x_1 = 6$. This is shown as point B in the Figure.

The line AB then describes the equation

$$4x_1 + x_2 = 24 \tag{11.6}$$

i.e. the combinations of pipes and sheets that will be produced when *all* machines are employed. Of course one need not employ all machines – some may be left idle. Thus by leaving machines idle one can produce also any combination of pipes and sheets described by the triangle AOB. As far as the machine restriction is concerned we can choose any

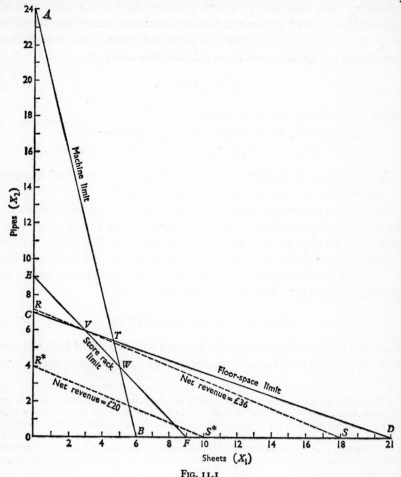

FIG. 11.1

combination of outputs in that triangle. It will be observed, however, that we cannot choose *negative* outputs of either pipes or sheets, and although this is an obvious constraint it is necessary to be tedious and specify it precisely. Geometrically we can choose outputs only in the positive quadrant.

One may specify the inputs of the amount of floor space required for producing pipes and sheets. Again we use the fundamental assumption that a unit of output requires a constant amount of input. For floor space, for example, one may find that one sheet requires one (hundred) square foot of floor space, so that x_1 sheets require x_1 (hundred) square feet of floor space. For pipes however more floor space is required; for one pipe we require 3 hundred square feet of floor space – so that x_2 pipes require $3x_2$ hundred square feet. There are 21 hundred square feet available, so we express the restrictions on output due to the limitation of floor space as

$$x_1 + 3x_2 \leqslant 21 \qquad (11.7)$$

or in words, the floor space used in producting x_1 and x_2 must be no greater than the amount available.

We record this floor space constraint in exactly the same way that we recorded the machine constraint in Figure 11.1. The floor space constraint is shown by the line DC and the output mixtures that may be produced without running out of floor space are represented by the triangle COD.

Now we can see that the two restrictions – of machines and floor space – appear together on the Figure as the overlapping triangles AOB and COD. The area of overlap is the polygon $OCTB$ – and this describes the possible product mixes that one can achieve without running out of either floor space or machines. Any output mix North of CT for example will require more floor space than there is available, and any combination of outputs to the East of TB will need more machines than exist in the firm.

The final limitation to consider is that of the store racks. Let us suppose that one sheet and one pipe each require one store rack. So we may express the constraints on production due to the limited supply of store racks as

$$x_1 + x_2 \leqslant 9 \qquad (11.8)$$

This can be represented diagrammatically as before; thus the line EF describes the output combinations when the store racks are fully employed. And the triangle *EOF* then represents the possible outputs one may produce without running out of store racks.

The fact that we have only a limited number of store racks has the effect of limiting still further the choice of output combinations which we considered when we took account only of the limitations of machines and floor space. Now we find that the combinations of outputs in the triangle *VTW* are no longer possible – for we need more store racks than we have available to produce these numbers of pipes and sheets. Thus the possible – or, to use the accepted nomenclature, the *feasible* – output combinations are represented by the polygon *OCVWB*.

The *feasible* set of outputs has a central place in the analysis of programming. These represent the choices of outputs available given the existing technology – as represented by the input requirements per unit of output and the available fixed resources of the firm. As it appears in our example each of the three fixed resources affect the feasible set of outputs. It is, however, quite conceivable that one or more resources may be in ample supply whatever combination of outputs one wishes to produce. For example if there were 12 store racks available, we would find that production was never influenced in any way by the availability of storage racks; there would always be plenty to spare. Geometrically this would mean that the store rack limitation would be a line North-East of the point *T*; it would not – as it were – cut off a corner from the feasible region. Thus there would be no restraint imposed by the store rack availability on the feasible sets of outputs; so we might describe the constraint as *redundant*. We can then just forget about it – at least for the existing technology.

Obviously in our numerical example all the constraints operate at some combination of outputs; none are redundant. Even the requirements that the outputs be non-negative are not redundant. In principle we should also describe the conditions $x_1 \geqslant 0$ and $x_2 \geqslant 0$ as two additional constraints. In geometic terms this means simply labelling the axes as constraints in addition to the three 'resources constraints' we have already discussed.†

† Although it appears to be a trivial point to specify the non-negativity conditions as constraints – it is not. For example, one may also impose another constraint on the model; it may well be that we have already contracted to supply a certain specified number of sheets during this period – let us suppose that we have to supply 2 sheets. Then the non-negativity constraint $x_1 \geqslant 0$ is indeed redundant – for it must be dominated by the constraint $x_1 \geqslant 2$.

Now the feasible outputs have been described as the area bounded by the straight lines OC, CV, VW, WB and OB. It is obvious that all we require to know in order to give an accurate description of the area are the location of the points O, C, V, W, and B. Once these points are known the area is uniquely described – and so the feasible combinations of outputs are accurately known. This property is a consequence of the assumption of linearity in our technology – and it greatly simplifies the analysis and computations. The points O, C, V, W and B are called the *corners* (or, sometimes, the *extreme points* or *extrema*) of the feasible region.

We have reviewed the possible outputs – in terms of the feasible region, it now remains for us to discuss which is the *best* or *optimum* combination of outputs. The best or optimum can be defined only in terms of some ultimate objective. Here we specify that objective simply as the maximum gross profit (or the minimum loss). And since the fixed resources are indeed fixed, this amounts to making as much net revenue as one can with the specified amount of floor space, machines and store racks. The object is then to maximise the expression

$$2x_1 + 5x_2 = \text{net revenue.}$$

We seek to find numbers for x_1 and x_2 such that net revenue is maximised. This expression is called the *objective function*.

But obviously we can only choose the combinations of x_1 and x_2 that lie in the feasible region. They must lie in (or on) the polygon $OCVWB$. We can therefore restate the problem

$$\text{Maximise} \quad 2x_1 + 5x_2 \quad\quad\quad (11.9)$$

$$\text{subject to} \quad 4x_1 + x_2 \leqslant 24, \quad\quad\quad (11.10)$$

$$x_1 + 3x_2 \leqslant 21, \quad\quad\quad (11.12)$$

$$x_1 + x_2 \leqslant 9, \quad\quad\quad (11.13)$$

$$x_1 \geqslant 0 \quad\quad\quad (11.14)$$

$$x_2 \geqslant 0. \quad\quad\quad (11.15)$$

This is then a complete statement of the problem to be solved in algebraic terms. All these inequalities are required to describe the feasible region which, in two dimensions can be described much more simply on a graph.

We have yet, however, to describe the objective function in geometric terms. We might conveniently begin by asking whether it is possible for the enterprise to earn a certain arbitrary gross profit or net revenue – let us say £20. It is easy to see that output combinations that satisfy the equation

$$2x_1 + 5x_2 = 20$$

will give rise to a net revenue of £20. This line can be plotted on the diagram and it is shown as $R*S*$ in Figure 11.1. Since this line goes through the feasible region it is clearly possibly to obtain a net revenue of £20; indeed it is obvious that one can make larger profits. We can imagine – as it were – a movement of the net revenue line North-East – as we increase the profits. The line will of course always be parallel to the line $R*S*$, since the net revenues per unit of outputs remains constant. The line may be written as $x_2 = -0·4x_1 + 0·2$ (net revenue); we simply vary the net revenue. As one moves North-East, so the profits or net revenues increase. But if we go further North-East than the line RS we shall leave the feasible region. For the line RS *just touches* the feasible region at the point V.

It is obvious then that the problem is solved when the firm reproduces the combination of outputs represented by the point V. From the Figure it will be observed that the point V represents $x_1 = 3$ and $x_2 = 6$. Thus the net revenue is a maximum at

$$2 \times (3) + 5 \times (6) = £36.$$

These are the earnings – the 'quasi rent' in Marshall's terminology of the fixed resources. We shall return to this interpretation later, but first it is worth while examining the solution in a little more detail.

The first point to observe is that the solution is always at a *corner*. The point V, for example, represents a corner of the feasible region. But, it might be alleged, this is merely an accident – due to the fact that the slope of the line RS differs from the slope of CV and VW. Suppose that the slope of RS were *just equal* to the slope of CV. The reader can easily check that this would occur if the net revenues were

$1\frac{1}{2}$ per sheet and $3\frac{1}{2}$ per pipe

or 3 per sheet and 7 per pipe

or some multiple of these figures.

Then the revenue line *RS* would coincide with the line *CV*. And so there is no *unique* corner solution. Any point along the line *CV* will satisfy the condition that it be in the feasible region, on the one hand, and that it give rise to maximum profits on the other.

But although there is no longer a unique solution, we can still use a *corner* as a maximum. Since any point on the line *CV* is as profitable as any other, we can express the solution as *either C or V*. It does not matter whether we choose the corner at *C* or at *V* – and we do not need to worry about possible combinations in between since they are just as profitable (and no more profitable) than the corner solutions.

One of the great simplifications of linear programming is that we need to concentrate only on the corners of the feasible region. The connecting links can be ignored. Thus the optimum will always be located at either *O* or *C* or *V* or *W* or *B*.

It is easy to see how a unique equilibrium might be located at *C*. Suppose for example that pipes were even more profitable relative to sheets than the 5 to 2 ratio assumed in the net revenue function (the objective function). It is easy to see that if pipes are more than 3 times more profitable than sheets, the revenue line *RS* will then be flatter than the line *CD* expressing the limitation of floor space. (The reader will recall that one pipe took 3 times as much floor space to produce as a sheet.) Thus the entrepreneur will maximise his net revenue by producing at the point *C*; i.e. since pipes are so profitable relative to sheets he will concentrate on producing only pipes.

It is obvious that by varying the relative net revenues of pipes and sheets we can show how each point such as *V*, *W* and *B* may be chosen. If, for example, sheets were more than 4 times as profitable as pipes, the point *B* would be chosen and the firm would produce only sheets.

But what about the 'origin' at zero. Would the firm ever stop producing at all? Would it ever leave the plant idle? One can see that would be the solution only if there were no positive net revenues from either of the two products. If the variable costs exceeded the price it would clearly be best to stop production – since the output makes no contribution to overheads and merely eats up the financial resources of the firm. It will be observed, however, that if one of the products has positive net revenue, while the other has a negative one, it will always pay to produce only the output with the positive contribution, and this would be represented by a corner solution at *C* or *B*.

Now let us return to the corner solution at V. It will be noticed that at V all the floor space is being used and all the store racks are occupied – for V lies on the two 'full-employment' lines for these two resources. But V lies well inside the limitations imposed by the availability of machines; at V there are machines to spare. The constraints of floor space and store racks are said to be *binding constraints* at V, whereas machines are a *non-binding constraint*. To be complete we should also add that the 'non-negativity' constraints are also not binding – outputs of both pipes and sheets are positive.

It is clear that any corner solution is the consequence of two – and only two – binding constraints. For example the point B is the solution of the constraint on machine availability and the constraint imposed by the non-negativity of the production of pipes. Even the zero point is the solution due to two binding non-negativity constraints. All the resource constraints are then non-binding.

This suggests a general way of approaching the solution. Obviously the fact that there are only two binding constraints is a consequence of the assumption that there are only two goods being produced – pipes and sheets. With two goods there are only two binding constraints in the solution; with three goods there would be three binding constraints; and so on. The general law is, therefore, that if there are more constraints than goods, the number of *binding* constraints in the solution will be equal to the number of goods.

This result enables one immediately to characterise a solution to our numerical problem; since there are two goods and three fixed resources, at least one of the resources must be under-employed. It is conceivable that two of the fixed resources are under-utilised – as at C and B – or that all three are not worth employing – as at O. Geometrically the solution is simply the intersection of two lines – and this is the solution of two simultaneous equations. Thus the point V is the solution of the two binding constraints

$$x_1 + 3x_2 = 21 \quad \text{floor space } CD \qquad (11.17)$$

$$x_1 + x_2 = 9 \quad \text{store racks } EF \qquad (11.18)$$

And the solutions are: $x_1 = 3$, $x_2 = 6$ – as we found in the Figure. Each of the corners of the feasible region may be found as the solution of two simultaneous equations. We only need to know the two equations in order to discover the output mix. Or to put the point another way, we need to discover which constraints are non-binding, i.e. which still appear as *in*equalities, which are the 'resources to spare'. For example in the solution of V we have

$$\left.\begin{array}{l} x_1 + 3x_2 = 21 \\ x_1 + x_2 = 9 \end{array}\right\} \text{binding constraints} \qquad (11.19)$$

$$\left.\begin{array}{l} 4x_1 + x_2 < 24 \\ x_1 > 0 \\ x_2 > 0 \end{array}\right\} \text{non-binding constraints} \qquad (11.20)$$

The non-binding constraints appear with a strict *in*equality sign ($<$ or $>$) whereas the binding constraints appear with an *equality* sign.†

In practical computational terms this means that one has only to determine which constraints are binding and then proceed to solve the simultaneous equations involved. One may begin at some corner of the feasible region – and quite a convenient place is the zero point. Thus we begin with $x_1 = 0$ and $x_2 = 0$. Now we ask should we increase either x_1 or x_2? It is clear that increasing either will give rise to larger profits – but it is obviously more profitable to move from O to C than from O to B, because pipes are worth much more on the market. (And we do not have to give up producing anything because we start from the zero point.) We move therefore to the corner at C.

From C we examine whether it would be profitable to move to V (which is the only alternative to either staying at C or moving back to O). The slope of the line CV indicated the rate at which one can exchange pipes for sheets in *production*. One more sheet costs $\frac{1}{3}$ of a pipe; but we calculate that one more sheet will bring in a net revenue of 2 pounds and losing $\frac{1}{3}$ of a pipe will reduce our net revenue by $1\frac{2}{3}$ pounds. In other words we compare the rate of exchange in production with the rate of exchange on the market; if we get more on the market than we have to give up in production, the move is profitable. So the expansion of sheet output at the cost of pipes is worthwhile and we proceed to V and increase profit by $\frac{1}{3}$ pound. Considering the move from V to W, we

---

† The reader will notice that there are 5 relationships (inequalities) and we select two for equalities. Now 2 can be selected from 5 in 10 different ways – but 5 of these different combinations give points outside the feasible region (e.g. F, E, A, T and D). We need to examine only the 5 in the feasible region.

see that to expand production of sheets by one unit would require a reduction of pipe output by one unit: so the result would be a gain of 2 pounds and a loss of 5 pounds – a net loss of 3 pounds per unit expansion of sheet output. So the move to the corner at W is not worthwhile – and it is best to stay at V.

These sorts of calculations are typical of the 'marginal revenue minus marginal cost' comparisons of economic analysis. At each corner we compare the marginal revenue – or in our terms the net revenue per unit of that output considered for expansion – with the marginal cost – which is the net revenue lost through contraction of the remaining output(s). This is exactly the same as the calculations of economic analysis. In programming we proceed one step at a time. For example we would never go from O to V, or from O to W. We always introduce one product at a time, And this makes the comparison a simple step-by-step process, and ideal arrangement for high speed computers as well as for the more elementary pencil-and-paper methods of computation.† At each stage of the calculation we can interpret the operations in terms of the ordinary postulates of economic analysis – by a comparison of marginal revenue and marginal cost.

This completes our statement and solution of the problem of maximising profits subject to the constraints imposed by the existence of fixed amounts of certain resources. It is typical of the sort of mixed technical and economic approaches that characterise many problems. It shows that the economist needs to build his model on the firm base of the technological specifications of the processes. We feed into the model information about the input requirements per unit of output. And from information about the availability of inputs, we compute the output combinations that are feasible, and then calculate which will be most profitable.

In other words the economist is concerned with the task of getting as much as possible from the fixed resources. But there is no longer any neat division between the technical problem of 'production' and the economic problem of 'which to produce and how much'. Both are aspects of the same decision. This approach contrasts with the old approach of economics – where it was assumed that the feasible outputs

---

† The reader interested in computational design should consult any of the basic textbooks on linear programming such as G. Hadley *Linear Programming* (Reading, Mass., 1962) for a description of the *simplex method* and its various derivatives.

were already known. Further it was usually specified that the *efficient* output combinations and processes were already known.† The engineering problems were assumed solved by the engineer. Thus the characteristic feature of this programming approach is to extend economic analysis backwards into the choice of technique and process. One does not take the engineer's problem as solved and given; instead we take only the data relevant to engineering processes and calculate efficient outputs as part and parcel of the procedure for maximising profits.

Thus we have shown the intimate relationship between the economic and the technological aspects of the firm as it appears in programming. We now must turn to consider the accounting problems of the production programme – and, most important, their interrelations with the economics and technology.

Accounting and the Dual

Our preoccupation in the above pages has been with the maximisation of profits (or net revenues). Given the resources available (or purchasable on the market) we have found the best that could be done in terms of making as large a profit as possible. But often in economic analysis we are concerned with *minimising costs*, and it seems natural to suppose that if we are doing as well as possible we must also be somehow producing at minimum costs. The question arises then: can we interpret the above problem as one of minimising costs? If we could then this would lead to natural accounting concept of the problem. We must also ask whether the accounting interpretation would give the same results as the technological interpretation – for it is clearly not much use if the results are not consistent one with the other.

The first question to arise is: what are costs in this model? Clearly the variable factors – labour, raw materials, etc. – are costs but since they are constant per unit of output there is no problem at all in dealing with these items. More interesting are the fixed resources. In one sense, of course, fixed resources do not have a cost; they are simply there and the cost of constructing them is a byegone. But the resources do earn

† Efficiency here means that with a given level of inputs one cannot produce more of one good without also producing less of another; it specified the maximum outputs available from given inputs.

revenue.† All these resources between them earn a net revenue of 36 pounds; so we might reckon the *total value* of the floor space, machines and store racks at this sum.

But we do not know how to distribute this sum between the various fixed factors. There is no obvious rule of allocating (to use the accounting term) the total sum between one fixed resource and another. But it is easy to develop such a rule – by using the concepts of the 'profitability' of a unit of a fixed resource. If we were to obtain another small unit of floor space [say one more (hundred) square foot, assuming that is very small], by how much would net revenue be increased? This value then measures the value of floor space at V. Similarly one can calculate the additional revenue which one would obtain through acquiring an additional store rack; this then measures the value of the store rack at V.

These valuations are of critical importance in the following analysis; and they are usually called the *shadow prices* of the resources. They represent the maximum amount one would be willing to pay to acquire a (small) unit of the resource in question.‡ Furthermore they also measure the amount by which net revenue would be reduced if we lost a unit of the fixed resource at V. There is a useful symmetry of valuation. The shadow prices measure the values of resources to the firm, whether in (small) expansion or in (small) contraction. It will be observed that if any other corner be selected the shadow prices will be different, and of course, in sum they will give us a smaller net revenue.

Let us now value the fixed resources at their (unknown) shadow prices, and let us specify the total costs of the firm as the sum of each of the quantities of fixed resources multiplied by its shadow price. There are three fixed resources, so we use

£p_1 for the shadow price of machines,

£p_2 for the shadow price of floor space,

£p_3 for the shadow price of store racks.

Thus the total costs of the firm are then, in £,

$$C = 24p_1 + 21p_2 + 9p_3 \qquad (11.21)$$

† The money which they make might be called a 'quasi rent' in the old Marshallian terminology, see below.

‡ It is necessary to emphasise that the conjectural change is always in terms of infinitesimal units; but the unit of record may however be quite large. It is always wise to think in terms of analytic infinitesimal changes – although one may talk in terms of the unit of record.

The p might be thought to be analogous to the accounting concept of allocated costs in this calculation. But the rules of definition are quite different from those which accountants normally employ. One of the critical conditions is that *all net revenue must be allocated to one fixed factor or another*. There will be no net revenue which is spare and unallocated.

This is best put in terms of a comparison of allocated costs and revenue for each product. Consider for example the production of one sheet. This requires four machines, one hundred square feet of floor space, and one store rack. These are the inputs required for the production of one sheet. With the (unknown) shadow prices we can value the costs as

$$4p_1 + p_2 + p_3 \qquad (11.22)$$

This is the total *allocated cost* of one sheet. Now the requirement that all net revenue be allocated to one fixed factor or another means that the costs must be *at least as great* as the net revenue obtained from one unit of sheet. So we can express the requirement as

$$4p_1 + p_2 + p_3 \geqslant 2 \qquad (11.23)$$

Or, to express it in words,

allocated cost of a sheet $\geqslant$ the net revenue of a sheet.

In the same way we examine the allocated cost of a pipe. Thus one pipe requires one machine, three hundred square feet of floor space and one store rack. The net revenue per pipe is 5, so we have

$$p_1 + 3p_2 + p_3 \geqslant 5 \qquad (11.24)$$

And since there are only two outputs specified in this model these two equations, combined with the restrictions on non-negativity, $p_1 \geqslant 0$ $p_2 \geqslant 0$ $p_3 \geqslant 0$, are all that are required.†

Clearly there is not so obvious an interpretation to be attached to these inequalities as there was to the ones in the production problem. But in order to examine further their interpretation we shall first state the problem again in extensive form. We seek to find non-negative values for the p in the cost function: $C = 24p_1 + 21p_2 + 9p_3$,

---

† Note that the restrictions on the p that require them to be non-negative are quite natural ones from the economic point of view – since it is always possible to close down the firm and take all shadow prices as zero. Or we may simply not use one resource to its full employment level. But the least one can do is not to use it. One cannot sell it in the short period.

so that the cost is minimised subject to the requirement that all costs have been allocated to one fixed factor or another.

$$\text{minimise} \quad C = 24p_1 + 21p_2 + 9p_3 \qquad (11.25)$$

$$\text{subject to} \quad 4p_1 + p_2 + p_3 \geqslant 2, \qquad (11.26)$$

$$p_1 + 3p_2 + p_3 \geqslant 5, \qquad (11.27)$$

$$p_1 \geqslant 0, \qquad (11.28)$$

$$p_2 \geqslant 0, \qquad (11.29)$$

$$p_3 \geqslant 0. \qquad (11.30)$$

Thus the objective is to find those shadow prices that minimise costs, and at the same time allocate all the net revenue to fixed factors.

Now consider the numerical solution to the production case discussed above. We saw that at V in the figure the machines were not fully employed; there were machines to spare and no restrictions were imposed on production by the shortage of machines. Thus more machines would have no value to the firm and a (small) reduction in the number of machines would not affect profits. Clearly the shadow price of machines must therefore be put at zero. Writing $p_1 = 0$ in the two inequalities and in the cost function, we find:

$$\text{minimise} \quad 21p_2 + 9p_3 \qquad (11.31)$$

$$\text{subject to} \quad p_2 + p_3 \geqslant 2 \qquad (11.32)$$

$$3p_2 + p_3 \geqslant 5 \qquad (11.33)$$

$$p_2 \geqslant 0, p_3 \geqslant 0.$$

And it is immediately obvious that the solution is found by writing the two inequalities (11.32–3) as equations, for these values will clearly minimise costs, i.e.

$$p_2 + p_3 = 2, \qquad (11.34)$$

$$3p_2 + p_3 = 5, \qquad (11.35)$$

and so the solution is

$$p_1 = 0, \quad p_2 = \tfrac{3}{2} \quad \text{and} \quad p_3 = \tfrac{1}{2}. \qquad (11.36)$$

These values may be substituted into the cost function to obtain

$$C = 24(0) + 21(\tfrac{3}{2}) + 9(\tfrac{1}{2}) = \pounds 36. \qquad (11.37)$$

Thus the minimum cost is £36 – exactly the same as the maximum net revenue.

This result is perfectly general – the maximum revenue is always equal to the minimum cost. This symmetry between the problems has led to the first maximising problem being called the *primal* problem, and the minimising cost problem is called the *dual*. The symmetry may be seen to extend to all aspects of the formulation of the problem. The coefficients in the objective function of maximising revenue (the net revenue of pipes and sheets, 5 and 2 respectively) become the constraints in the dual. And correspondingly the constraints (resource availability) in the primal maximising problem become the coefficients in the objective function minimising cost in the dual. Constraints and co-efficients simply swop places. And on the left-hand side of the in-equalities we observe that a column of coefficients in the primal simply becomes a row in the dual. And the inequality sign changes direction.

Obviously it is possible to represent the problem geometrically but since there are three dimensions it is not so easy as in the case of the primal problem. It will be observed that there are two inequalities as constraints and three variables – compared with three inequalities and two variables in the primal problem. (We do not count the simple non-negativity constraints here.) In the primal problem – with more con-straints than variables – we found the solution was to under-employ at least one of the fixed resources, writing the shadow price as zero. In the dual – with more variables than constraints – these variables are shadow prices and we always fix at least one of the variables at zero. Indeed the symmetry is exact.

As we have phrased the problem, however, it pays the entrepreneur to leave one resource less than fully employed and to produce each output. But let us suppose that the net value of a sheet were 2 but that the net revenue of a pipe were 7 instead of 5. As we see in the presenta-tion of the primal problem in Figure 11.1 this will lead to a solution at the corner C – producing 7 pipes only. The total net revenue of the firm will then be £49.

Now let us examine the dual solution. We write it formally

$$\text{minimise} \quad C = 24p_1 + 21p_2 + 9p_3 \quad\quad (11.38)$$

$$\text{subject to} \quad 4p_1 + p_2 + p_3 \geqslant 2, \quad\quad (11.39)$$

$$p_1 + 3p_2 + p_3 \geqslant 7, \quad\quad (11.40)$$

$$p_1 \geqslant 0, \tag{11.41}$$

$$p_2 \geqslant 0, \tag{11.42}$$

$$p_3 \geqslant 0. \tag{11.43}$$

Now from the primal solution we see immediately that there are machines and store racks unemployed. So we write the shadow price of these two resources as zero, i.e. $p_1 = 0$ and $p_3 = 0$. Thus C is a minimum when $p_2 = \frac{7}{3}$. The reader can verify that this value of p_2 is the one that satisfies the condition that all net revenue is allocated to one fixed factor, and that, at the same time, the cost is minimised. It will be found that the minimum cost (=maximum revenue) is £49.

Now let us examine the constraints when the values $p_1 = 0$, $p_2 = \frac{7}{3}$ and $p_3 = 0$ are inserted. The first one – relating to the production of a sheet – becomes

$$4(0) + \tfrac{7}{3} + 0 \geqslant 2. \tag{11.44}$$

But clearly since $\frac{7}{3}$ is *greater* than 2, we may eliminate the equality sign. Now in terms of the economics, this means that the *allocated cost (on the left hand side) exceeds the net revenue.* i.e. $\frac{7}{3} > 2$. The costs of resources used up in producing sheets (when such resources are valued at their shadow prices) exceed the net revenue obtained. Obviously sheets should not be produced at all. And this is precisely the same result that we found in the solution of the primal (engineering) problem. The result has now, in the dual (accounting) solution, been translated into the language of costs and revenues.

The second constraint – which relates to the production of pipes – becomes

$$0 + 3(\tfrac{7}{3}) + 0 \geqslant 7 \tag{11.45}$$

There is here no question of *in*-equality; the two sides must be equal, i.e. $3(\frac{7}{3}) = 7$. This implies therefore that the allocated cost (left side) is just the same as the net revenue from a pipe. When the allocated cost is *just equal* to the net revenue, it is profitable to produce the particular product, in this case pipes.

This therefore gives a general rule:

if allocated cost exceeds net revenue, do not produce the product;
if allocated cost is just equal to net revenue, produce the product.

This seems to be a sensible accountant's rule, except that it does not seem consistent with the normal nomenclature of the accounting profession. The entrepreneur is doing as well as he can if he produces goods where allocated cost is just equal to net revenue, i.e. in accounting terms when he is earning zero net profit! His object is to avoid losses.†
In the normal concepts of accounting the 'profit' would be the return on the fixed resources of the firm; or perhaps, more typically, the return over the 'costs' of the fixed resources. But in the dual we have valued the fixed resources at shadow prices that fully reflect the profitability of such fixed assets to the firm – given that they are used in the most profitable way. So that, since shadow prices are used in the allocation of cost, the maximum accounting profits are absorbed into cost. The best that the entrepreneur can do is to make no losses – and he can only achieve that by pursuing an optimum production policy.

There is, however, a natural use of shadow prices in planning the expansion or contraction of the firm. The shadow price tells us the value of an additional unit of the fixed resource – measured in terms of of the additional revenue that the unit would earn. If fixed resources can be bought on the market and installed at some future date, it suggests that we have a simple test of the market cost of that resource against the shadow price. If the shadow price exceeds the market cost, then it is worth while buying more of the resource. For example if the cost of floor space on the market were less than £$\frac{7}{3}$ per hundred square feet, in the above example, then it would be worthwhile renting more floor space for some future production plan. Note, however, that it would not be worth while to acquire new machines or store racks, however cheap they were. Their shadow prices were zero – and we have machines and store racks to spare.

But if the entrepreneur pursued a policy of expanding his floor space, he would observe that such a policy would be profitable only for a certain increment in square feet. Suppose that he bought an additional 6 hundred square feet of floor space, and he is considering whether or not to buy more. If we refer to the figure, we will find that with a total of 27 hundred square feet (21 originally and 6 bought) the 'full-employment' floor space line will run from E on the pipe axis parallel to CD. But at E we have reached the limit of the capacity of the

† The dual accounting rule gives one a way of choosing rationally from a list of possible outputs.

store racks. Thus the expansion of floor space from 27 to 28 hundred square feet will not result in any increase in total net revenue; that is to say the shadow price of floor space falls to zero. It is necessary to expand both floor space and store racks together.

Thus the use of a comparison between shadow price and market cost for investment decisions must be treated with some care. It is a valid rule only for *small* changes – and what is meant by 'small' will vary from one example to another. In practice, however, it is easy to determine the range of applicability of the rule and to make consistent decisions on expansion. We can easily find when we run up against another capacity constraint.

Before ending this discussion of the dual, it is worth noting that our particular numerical example had 'too many' resource constraints and 'too few' products. We might just as well construct an example with 'too few' resource constraints and 'too many' products. Then the primal problem would have 'too many' variables, and we should be concerned with finding which of those variables should be given a value of zero. In other words we must concentrate production on a number of products that is *less* than the number available.† The golden rule is that *as many commodities are produced as there are binding resource constraints*. And the converse is also true: *as many resource constraints are binding as there are commodities produced*.

We can illustrate the consequences of the rule with the resource constraints of the primal, and the accounting requirement constraints of the dual.

Primal
  if resource used = resource available, then shadow price > 0;
  if resource used < resource available, then shadow price $= 0$

Dual
  if allocated cost = net revenue, then output (x) should > 0;
  if allocated cost > net revenue, then output (x) should $= 0$

$$(11.46)$$

---

† Note that in the last example when we took net revenue from a pipe to be 7, we found that it was profitable to produce no sheets. But this was a consequence of the net revenues which were assumed. For net revenues of 5 for pipes and 2 for sheets, for example, we found that both should be made. But when there are more commodities than constraints, the production plan must *always* exclude *at least* the excess number of commodities over resource constraints – whatever the net revenues are.

Such elegant and simple symmetry is very useful in application and interpretation.

Some Complications and Developments

One of the great advantages of the programming approach is that various *ad hoc* restrictions may be easily incorporated into the model. For example, let us suppose that in the above example, the firm had entered into contracts to supply one sheet per period. Furthermore suppose that the contract stipulated that the sheet be supplied at market price – and let us imagine that the net revenues were 7 for pipes and 2 for sheets.

Obviously if the contract were not in force, the entrepreneur would prefer to produce at point C in the Figure. But the contract constrains him to produce at least one sheet. Thus the contractual limitation is expressed by drawing a line vertically at 1 on the sheet axis. The feasible region must then lie on or to the East of this line. In the algebraic statement of the problem we simply write a 'contract constraint' as

$$x_1 \geqslant 1, \tag{11.47}$$

and all the other constraints appear as before. But one can see immediately that this constraint is going to be binding. Without it, we found that it was profitable to produce only pipes. This constraint tells us that we must produce at least one sheet, so it must be binding.

The solution is easy to find (but we leave it as an exercise for the reader) and it is $x_1 = 1$, $x_2 = 6\frac{2}{3}$. Now since the contractual constraint is binding we can find the non zero shadow price of the contract. The profits (or net revenues) without the contractual constraint would be 49 pounds, whereas with the contractual constraint imposed the profits are $48\frac{2}{3}$, so the revenue foregone due to this contractual obligation is therefore $\frac{1}{3}$. This therefore represents the shadow price of this restriction.† One may then examine whether the contract is worth this loss of revenue – would it not be better to break the contract? Obviously

† The reader may try to put the contract requirement formally in the primal model. It will be noted, however, that a contractual obligation is a sort of *negative resource*. It is, if effective, a net liability and reduces profits. Formally therefore it is best written as $-x \leqslant -1$, and this is then consistent with the other constraints.

it would if the cost of breaking it were less than $\frac{1}{3}$ pounds; otherwise it is best to put up with the existing obligation.†

In many practical cases restrictions take the form of specifying a maximum sales volume of a commodity. For example the entrepreneur may be convinced that, although he can sell pipes at 7 pounds each (net of variable costs), he can only sell 5 of them. No larger quantity could be unloaded on the market. This implies that in the primal problem we write another constraint

$$x_2 \leqslant 5 \tag{11.48}$$

This is of exactly the same form as the resource constraints, and therefore gives rise to no additional difficulties. Geometrically we draw a line horizontally at $x_2 = 5$, and we specify that the feasible region lies to the south of that line. It is easy to see that the following constraints are then binding:

$$x_1 + x_2 = 9 \quad \text{store racks} \tag{11.49}$$

$$x_2 = 5 \quad \text{sales limitation} \tag{11.50}$$

Thus the solutions are $x_2 = 5$ and $x_1 = 4$.

Now consider the dual statement of the problem. The cost function is the same as before except for an addition term p_4 which represents the shadow price of the sales limitation (the lack of sales resources). So we have

$$\text{minimise} \quad C = 24p_1 + 21p_2 + 9p_3 + 5p_4 \tag{11.51}$$

$$\text{subject to} \quad 4p_1 + p_2 + p_3 \qquad \geqslant 2 \quad \text{sheet} \tag{11.52}$$

$$p_1 + 3p_2 + p_3 + p_4 \geqslant 7 \quad \text{pipe} \tag{11.53}$$

and the usual non-negativity conditions.

And the solutions are $p_1 = 0, p_2 = 0, p_3 = 2$, and $p_4 = 5$. Thus the minimum costs are 43 pounds, and the reader will check that this is a correct solution by calculating the profit (net revenue) with the solution to the primal problem above.

† Note that strictly we should have talked about reducing the contractual obligation by a *small* amount, but one can see in the example that such distinctions do not matter. In principle, however, they do.

It will be observed that the shadow price of the sales constraint appears only in the pipe equation – for that is the only product for which the sales restraint exists. We can interpret p_4 precisely as the net revenue which would be gained by relaxing the sales constraint by one unit. (Strictly this should be interpreted as an infinitesimal change only.) We see that net revenue would be increased by 5 – the shadow price of the sales constraint. We can treat the shadow price again as the returns to be expected from investment in breaking down the sales barrier. Thus if the marginal cost of relaxing the sales constraint by one unit were less than 5 pounds, it would pay the firm to devote resources to sales promotion.

It will be observed however that if the sales restraint were increased to $x_2 \leqslant 6$, the optimum sales mix would be that at V. There would be three constraints intersecting at V. (This is an accidental result – but one that does occasionally crop up in actual computations.) Obviously if the sales constraint were further relaxed, however, the shadow price would change; and the reader may check that it would become 1.

We have seen that it is not at all difficult to add constraints to the basic programming model – provided they are expressed in linear form. But one might suppose that many problems have constraints which appear in non-linear form and it is worthwhile exploring very briefly how one may deal with non-linearities.

One preliminary but very important point concerns the character of the non-linearity. We must ensure that any non-linear relationship defines a set that is *convex*. Broadly speaking this means that the surface of the feasible region must have no dents in it when we look from a position in the North-East. Thus we see that the non-linear relationship NRC in Figure 11.2 still gives a set that is convex, for there are no dents. The relationship MXD however gives a feasible region that is clearly not convex because there is a dent at X; similarly the curve LFE gives a set that is not convex because it is just one big dent.† The importance of convexity arises from the fact that there is, with convexity, a guarantee that there is only one maximum (or if there are many values of x which give rise to the same profit they are adjacent.) With non-convexity, however, there is no such comfort. Although we may find a maximum profit over one range of output mixtures, we cannot be sure that the

† An important theorem is that the overlap (or intersection) of two convex figures is itself convex.

particular value we have found is the *maximum maximorum*. There may be another higher profit at another mixture of outputs.

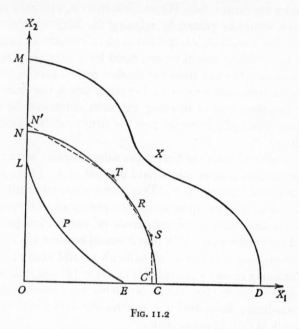

FIG. 11.2

Restricting the analysis to convex non-linear constraints, therefore, we can see that one obvious technique is to convert the problem into linear form by making piecewise linear approximations to the non-linear constraint. In principle we can get as close as we like to the curve *NRC* in Figure 11.2 by taking more and more linear approximations. In practice, however, it might be sufficient to take say three linear segments – as we have done in the broken lines in the figure. There will of course be a loss of accuracy by using approximations of this kind – but we can make the loss as small as we like provided we are willing to pay the cost of the increased computation involved.

Probably a more common form of non-linearity occurs in the objective function to be maximised (or minimised). For the especially important case when the objective function is a quadratic, special techniques have been developed. In principle these techniques apply the same criteria that are used in the linear approach – but naturally they are more complicated.

Another common form of question is to ask what will be the reaction of production arrangements as we vary the relative net revenues of the two products. When will the production programme shift and in what way will it move? This is the approach of *parametric programming*. We move one of the constants of the problem gradually and observe the results. The maximisation problem will then trace out the reactions of production to shifts in the relative prices.

Of course one is not restricted to varying only relative net revenues. Perhaps just as important in practice are the reactions to changes in the availability of fixed factors. It is easy to see how one can examine the effect of factor availability on output – provided it is changed one factor at a time. Another important *parametric problem* is that of tracing the effects of technical change and changes in efficiency. This takes the form of the coefficients changing gradually over time. Thus we might ask what are the consequences of gradual speeding up in the process of machining – so that sheets can be done more quickly. (Note that if all machining were improved at the same rate for all products, this would be the same as having more machines.) Again the result can be readily calculated by swinging out the slope of the machine limit line hinging it on A. Such a parametric approach is often useful for analysing the sensitivity of the solution to changes in the assumptions – or errors in the engineering specification. It is indeed a natural step from here to consider the problem where there are *random* variations in the resource availabilities or in the coefficients or in the net revenues. Of course one pays a price in terms of increased complexity for the increased degree of realism of the model. Whether that price is worth paying must be examined carefully in each individual case. As a rule it is best to keep the model simple until there is a compelling reason to complicate it. But the facts must decide.

We have cast the programming model in the form of the maximising profits of the firm that is subject to resource limitations. This is the most convenient – the most evocative – and perhaps the most common form in which the programming problem may be put. But there are a very large number of other uses. In fact it is difficult to imagine that there is any substantial body of economic thought to which programming cannot make a very large contribution. For programming essentially formalises the elementary problem of economics – making the most out of what little you have got.

Obviously one fruitful area of application of linear programming is in planning the national economy – especially where there is a strong centrally directed system. The objective function may well be (to maximise) real gross national product, and the constraints are set by the availability of labour, by the stock of equipment, of foreign currency, and so on. The programme will then determine the optimum distribution of resources, the product mix, and, through the dual solution, the shadow prices of resources.

One especially useful feature of this approach is that it gives us the shadow prices that represent the true economic value of resources – whatever their nominal price may be. These prices may be passed down to lower-echelon planning organisations – and they may be instructed to maximise their profits using these shadow prices as the units of value. In other words the programming approach provides a price system for *decentralisation* – for dispersing decision-making down to the 'establishment' level.

It is obvious that such a principle of decentralised decision-making with the aid of shadow prices is applicable not merely to the managed economy, but also to any large organisation. The dual provides a system of management accounting suitable for the devolution of decision-making and control into the separate plants or agencies or shops.

There are two major areas of programming left to be developed, which we might briefly discuss here. The first, on which much progress has been made recently, is called *dynamic programming*. With the model discussed above, one may observe that the situation is essentially static. True we did talk about expanding the resources but only in an *ad hoc* way. Consider now the more complex problem where we have the choice of either selling output or using it to expand the availability of resources for future outputs – such as using the pipes and sheets to make storage racks, machines, etc. Obviously this possibility enlarges the choices open enormously, for there is now the problem of optimising between one period and another.

The process of dynamic programming is to start at a certain point of time, and to maximise in that period. Then we go forward to the next period and maximise there and also revise the solution in the first period in the light of the second period information, so we proceed to the third period, and from our vantage point there we revise again not only the second period but also the first period yet again. And so the optimisation process is seen to involve larger and larger numbers as time goes on. The size of the problem grows quickly to enormous dimensions.† Even modern high speed computers find it hard work handling the problems to which practical applications lead. For these reasons dynamic programming is not nearly as popular for practical applications as ordinary linear programming.

Another area in which there has been even less progress is *integer programming*. One of the assumptions of linear programming is that the output and the technology generally is divisible. There are no lumps in linear programming. But in the real world there are lumps, discontinuities and so on. Some of them matter considerably – and clearly when they do the programming approach breaks down. Unfortunately there are no known neat ways of dealing with the optimisation problem when outputs are lumpy. We cannot apply ordinary marginal cost and marginal revenue concepts and one is forced to adopt *ad hoc* methods of looking for and testing an optimum. Probably this is the most serious shortcoming in the practical techniques of optimisation at the present time; but it is doubtful if a solution will be found in the very near future.

It is perhaps fortunate that programming was devised just as the high speed digital computer began a fantastically fast development. This increased enormously the practical applications of linear programming. The computing problem, except with the complicated variations, is now of no great importance as a barrier to the application of these techniques. Probably the imaginative formulation of problems in programming form is the most urgent need today. And in particular, one needs to appreciate the myriad uses to which one can put the information derived from programming. The great value of the programming approach as an integrative discipline – a technique that vividly shows the interrelationships between apparently different disciplines – has surely a great role to play in increasing understanding of processes and policies.

† It is interesting to observe that Pontriagin, a Russian mathematician, derived essentially the same solution – except that it was expressed in the functional form of differential equations.

Select Bibliography

TEXTBOOKS ON ECONOMETRIC THEORY AND METHODS

Christ, C. *Economic Models and Methods*, Wiley, 1966.

Goldberger, A. *Econometric Theory*, Wiley, 1964.

Johnstone, J. *Econometric Methods*, McGraw-Hill, 1963.

Klein, L. R. *A Textbook of Econometrics*, Row, Peterson, 1953.

Malinvaud, E. *Statistical Methods in Econometrics*, North Holland Publishing Company, 1966.

Theil, H. *Economic Forecasts and Policy*, North Holland Publishing Company, 1958.

Tintner, G. *Econometrics*, Wiley, 1952.

TEXTBOOKS ON THE THEORY OF STATISTICS

Kendall, M. G., and Stuart, A. *The Advanced Theory of Statistics*, 3 vols, Griffin, 1958, 1961.

Lindley, D. V. *Introduction to Probability and Statistics from a Bayesian Viewpoint*, 2 vols, Cambridge, 1965.

Mood, A., and Graybill, F. A. *Introduction to the Theory of Statistics*, McGraw-Hill, 1963.

CONSUMER EXPENDITURE AND BEHAVIOUR

Fisher, F. M. *A Priori Information and Time Series Analysis*, North Holland Publishing Company, 1963.
(A misleading title that disguises a good account of the demand for an intermediate good.)

Friedman, M. *A Theory of the Consumption Function*, National Bureau of Economic Research, Princeton, 1957.
(Undoubtedly the best book on the consumption function. It is also a masterly account of the problem of relating theory and data.)

Harberger, A. C. (ed.). *The Demand for Durable Goods*, Chicago, 1960.

Houthakker, H. S., and Prais, S. J. *The Analysis of Household Budgets*, Cambridge, 1955.
(This is probably the best account of the analysis of cross-section data on households.)

Schultz, H. *The Theory and Measurement of Demand*, Chicago, 1938.
(A pioneering American study.)

Stone, J. R. N. *The Measurement of Consumers' Expenditure and Behaviour in the United Kingdom, 1920–1938*, vols I and II, Cambridge, 1954–1967.
(This is the account of the results of a large study of market-demand functions in the United Kingdom.)

Farrell, M. J. 'The New Theories of Consumption', *Economic Journal 69*, pp. 678–96 (1959).
(A survey of consumption functions.)

Houthakker, H. S. 'New Evidence on Demand Elasticities', *Econometrica 33*, pp. 277–88.
(An international study.)

Modigliani, F. and Brumberg, R. 'Utility Analysis and the Consumption Function; An Interpretation of Cross-Section Data', in *Post-Keynesian Economics*, ed. K. K. Kurihara, Rutgers, 1954.
(The source of the 'life-cycle' hypothesis.)

Nerlove, Marc. *Distributed Lags and Demand Analysis*, Agriculture Handbook No. 131, U.S. Dept. of Agriculture, Washington, D.C.; G.P.O.

Shupack, M. B. 'The Predictive Accuracy of Empirical Demand Analysis', *Economic Journal 72*, pp. 550–75 (1962).

Stone, J. R. N. 'Linear Expenditure Systems and Demand Analysis; an Application to the Pattern of British Demand', *Economic Journal 64*, pp. 511–27 (1954).

—— 'Private Saving in Britain Past, Present and Future', *Manchester School 32* (1964).

—— and Rowe, D. A. 'The Durability of Consumers Durable Goods', *Econometrica 28*, pp. 405–16 (1960).

LINEAR PROGRAMMING

Allen, R. G. D. *Mathematical Economics*, 2nd ed., Macmillan, 1959.
(A very compact and neat account of the main theorems.)

Bellman, R. *Dynamic Programming*, Oxford, 1957.
(Mathematically difficult.)

Dorfman, R., Samuelson, P. A. and Solow, R. M. *Linear Programming and Economic Analysis*, McGraw-Hill, 1958.

Vajda, S. *Theory of Games and Linear Programming*, Methuen, 1956.
(A mathematical text on the main theorems.)

MODELS OF THE ECONOMY

Hart, P., Mills, G. and Whitaker, J. *Econometric Analysis for National Economic Planning*, Butterworths (1964).
(A conference of papers on planning.)

Klein, L. R., Ball, R. J., Hazelwood, A., and Vandome, P. *An Econometric Model of the U.K.*, Oxford, 1961.
(The first econometric model of the U.K.)

Leontief, W. *Input-Output Economics*, Oxford, 1966.
(Developments in input–output.)

MONEY

Commission on Money and Credit (United States). *Research Studies*, Prentice-Hall, 1963.
(Studies prepared for the Commission's Enquiry into the Monetary System.)

Friedman, Milton (ed.). *Studies in the Quantity Theory of Money*, Chicago, 1956.
(A series of quantitative studies of the classical theory of money. A new volume on this subject is soon to appear.)

—— and Schwartz, Anna. *A Monetary History of the United States*, National Bureau of Economic Research, Princeton, 1965.
(A quantitative monetary interpretation of history. A second volume is to include an analysis of trends and cycles.)

Allais, M. 'A Restatement of the Quantity Theory of Money', *American Economic Review 56* (1966).
(A sophisticated version of an old theory.)

Brown, A. J. 'Interest, Prices, and the Demand Schedule for Idle Money', *Oxford Econ. Pap. 2*, pp. 46–69 (1939).
(A pioneering paper in monetary econometrics.)

Friedman, Milton. 'The Demand for Money: Some Theoretical and Empirical Results', *Journal of Political Economy 67*, pp. 327–51 (1959).

—— and Schwartz, Anna. 'Money and Business Cycles', *Review of Econ. and Stats.*, Supplement (1963).

Kavanagh, N. J. and Walters, A. A. 'The Demand for Money in the U.K., 1877–1962; Some Preliminary Results', *Bulletin of the Oxford University Institute of Econ. and Stats.* (1965).

Latané, H. A. 'Income Velocity and Interest Rates – A Pragmatic Approach', *Review of Economics and Statistics XLII*, pp. 445–9 (1960).

Modigliani, F. and Sutch, R. 'Debt Management and the Term Structure of Interest Rates: An Empirical Analysis of Recent Experience', *Journal of Political Economy 75* (Supplement), pp. 567–95.

Teigen, R. L. 'Demand and Supply Functions for Money in the United States; Some Structural Estimates', *Econometrica 32*, pp. 476–509 (1964).

Telser, L. 'A Critique of Some Recent Empirical Research on the Explanation of the Term Structure of Interest Rates', *Journal of Political Economy 75* (Supplement), pp. 546–64 (1967).

PRODUCTION

Brown, Murray. *On the Theory and Measurement of Technical Change*, Cambridge, 1966.
(This study works empirically with many of the production functions discussed in Chapter 10).

Hildebrand, G. H., and Liu, T. C. *Manufacturing Production Functions in the United States 1957*, Cornell, 1965.
(This study is mainly concerned with inter-state cross-sections in the United States.)

Meyer, J. R., and Kuh, E. *The Investment Decision: An Empirical Study*, Harvard, 1957.

National Bureau of Economic Research. *Studies in Income and Wealth*, vol. 31, Princeton, 1967.
(A conference on production functions.)

Nerlove, Marc. *Estimation and Identification of Cobb-Douglas Production Functions*, North Holland Publishing Company, 1965.
(A useful account of the statistical problems of estimation.)

Salter, W. E. G. *Productivity and Technical Change*, Cambridge, 1960; 2nd ed., 1967.
(A pioneering study that nevertheless is easy to read.)

Alchian, Armen. 'Costs and Outputs', in *The Allocation of Economic Resources* by M. Abramoritz *et al.*, Stanford (1959).

—— 'Reliability of Progress Curves in Airframe Production', *Econometrica 31*, pp. 679–94 (1963).
(The classic paper on 'learning by doing'.)

Arrow, K. J. *et al.* 'Capital-Labor Substitution and Economic Efficiency', *Review of Econ. and Stats. 43*, pp. 225–45 (1961).

Eisner, R. 'A Distributed Lag Investment Function', *Econometrica 28*, pp. 1–29 (1960).

Hogan, W. P. 'Technical Progress and the Production Function', *Rev. of Econ. and Stats.* 40, pp. 407–11 (1958).
[A correction to Solow (1957).]

Marschack, J., and Andrews, W. H. 'Random Simultaneous Equations and the Theory of Production', *Econometrica 12*, pp. 143–205 (1944).

Phelps, Edmund and Charlotte. 'Factor Price Frontier Estimation of a "Vintage" Production Model of Post War U.S. Non-Farm Business Sector', *Rev. of Econ. and Stats. 48*, pp. 251–65 (1966).

Solow, R. W. 'Heterogeneous Capital and Smooth Production Functions: An Experimental Study', *Econometrica 31*, pp. 623–45 (1963).

—— 'Investment and Technical Progress', in *Mathematical Methods in the Social Sciences*, eds. K. Arrow, S. Karlin and P. Suppes, Stanford, 1959.

—— 'Technical Change and the Aggregate Production Function', *Review of Econ. and Stats. 39*, pp. 312–20 (1957).

Walters, A. A. 'Econometric Studies of Production and Cost Functions', *Encyclopaedia of the Social Sciences* (1968).

—— 'Production and Cost Functions; An Econometric Survey', *Econometrica 31*, pp. 1–66 (1963).

Index

Aggregate production function, 305–17
  aggregation, 305–8
  cross-section, 310
  time series studies, 314
Analysis of variance of residuals, 96–7
Assumptions, 14
  testing, 14
  validity of a theory, 15

Bayes Theorem, 58–61
  a priori or prior probabilities, 59
Bernoulli trials, 26

Cobb–Douglas, 319, 321–2, 331–2, 338
Concave function, 273
Confidence interval, 37
Constant elasticity of substitution production function, 282–8
  distribution parameter, 287
Consumer goods, 235
  durable household goods, 235
  non-durables, 236
Consumption function, 207, 208, 241
  permanent income hypothesis, 244
  life-cycle hypothesis, 244
Convex set, 273
  economies of scale, 275
Correlation coefficient, 95–7
  simple two-variable coefficient of, 97–8
  See also Partial correlation coefficient
Covariance, *see* Cross-product, 90
Cross-product, 90
  of x and e, 91–6
Cross-section studies, 327–9

Decentralisation, 368
Decision theory
  introduction, 50–3
  minimax principle, 64
Decision 'tree', 68–71
Degrees of freedom, 41

Demand function, 13, 14, 208–35
  log-log relation, 210
  aggregation to market demand, 220
Disturbance
  in simple linear regression equation, 86
  interpretation, 87–93
  distribution of, 87–8
  simpliste model, 213 f.
Dual, 359

Econometric models, 177
Econometrics: job of the econometrician, 21
Economics: normative, positive, 20
Endogenous variables, 178
Engel curve, 217–24
Entrepreneurship, 295–6
  economic efficiency, 296
  technical efficiency, 296
Equation systems, 177–98
  final form, 190
  impact multiplier, 192
  total multiplier, 192
  interim multiplier, 193
  triangular or recursive models, 196
Errors
  in simple regression equation, 84–6
  variance of, and x^2, 96–7
  See also Variance of residuals
Errors in variables
  two-variable case, 108–14
  grouping, 112–13
Estimation
  likelihood approach, 57–8
  the final form, 194
  of structural parameters, 195
Exogenous variables, 179
Extraneous estimators, 223

F distribution and rest, 49–50
Final form of equations, 190–4

Household budgets, 217–20
Hypothesis
    testing, 33
    alternative, 54
    rejecting a 'sharp' hypothesis, 53
    likelihood ratios, 56
    plausibility, 58

Identification, 163 f.
    'mongrel' equations, 168
    multicollinearity, 170
    bias, 173
    under- and over-identification, 185
Income
    elasticities from household budgets, 223
    measured, 250
Inference (statistical), 32

Keynes' *General Theory* (of aggregate consumption), 208, 242 f.

Least squares
    simple regression, 94–5
    multiple and partial regression, 120–31
    two-stage least squares, 187
    model for prediction, 188
Leontieff, 283
    production function, 283
Life-cycle hypothesis, 208
Likelihood, 50–7
    ratio, 56
    sampling error, 54
    specification error, 54
Linear expenditure models, 240
Linear programming, 341–71
    feasible set, 348
    objective function, 349
    binding constraints, 352
    shadow prices, 356
    primal problem, 359
    the dual, 359
    integer programming, 369

Maximum maximorum, 274, 365–6
Multicollinearity, 127–8
Multiple correlation coefficient, 129 ff.
    and residual variance, 129–30

analysis of variance, 131
analysis and interpretation, 154–8
Multiple regression, 120 ff.
    normal equations, 124
    coefficients, 124, 127
    See also Regression

Non-linearities
    two variables, 98–102
    logarithmic transform, 100
Normal distribution, 35

Partial correlation coefficient, 131 ff.
    relationship to R^2, 136–8
    sampling characteristics, 137–8
Permanent income, 244 f.
    formal development, 248
    measuring, 253–61
Predetermined variables, 180
Prediction, 216
Probability, 22 f.
    relative frequency definition, 22
    additive probabilities, 23
    Bernoulli trials, 26
    conditional probabilities, 27
    joint event probabilities, 27
    prior probabilities, 51
Production function, 270–337
    aggregate and micro-, 270
    as efficient set, 272
    Cobb–Douglas, 275
    economies of scale, 279
    elasticity of substitution, 282
    constant elasticity of substitution, 282 ff.
    conclusions, 337

Recursive systems, 196
Regression
    simple, 80–98
    and law of demand, 81–5
    coefficient of, by least squares, 91–5
    two regressions x on y and y on x, 105 ff.
    with fixed x's and with probabilistic x's, 107–8
    multiple and partial, 120–41
    sampling, 146 f.

Sampling
    distribution, 34
    problem of estimation, 36
    small samples, 38
    variance, 38
    large-sample theory, 43
Scatter diagram, 84
Shadow prices, 356
Significance: testing a hypothesis, 32–4
Specification error, 54, 197
Standard error: definition, 35
Structural equation systems, 181
    simple monetary model, 181

    flow diagram, 182
    reduced form equation, 183
Substitution between factors, 300
    ex post, 300
    ex ante, 300

t-distribution and test, 42
Time series, 257
    studies of production functions, 298
Two-stage least squares, 187–8

Variance of residuals, 94, 96–7
Vintage models
    embodied technical progress, 300